WORKSHOPS IN COMPUTING
Series edited by C. J. van Rijsbergen

Also in this series

continued on back page...

David Till (Ed.)

6th Refinement Workshop

Proceedings of the 6th Refinement
Workshop, organised by BCS-FACS,
London, 5–7 January 1994

Published in collaboration with the
British Computer Society

Springer-Verlag
London Berlin Heidelberg New York
Paris Tokyo Hong Kong
Barcelona Budapest

David Till, MA (Oxon), MSc
Department of Computer Science
City University, Northampton Square
London EC1V 0HB, UK

ISBN-13:978-3-540-19886-4   e-ISBN-13:978-1-4471-3240-0
DOI: 10.1007/978-1-4471-3240-0

British Library Cataloguing in Publication Data
Refinement Workshop : 5–7 January 1994 : London
   6th Refinement Workshop : Proceedings of the 6th Refinement Workshop,
   Organised by BCS-FACS. – (Workshops in Computing Series)
   I. Title II. Till, David III. Series
   005.1
ISBN-13:978-3-540-19886-4

Library of Congress Cataloging-in-Publication Data
A catalog record for this book is available from the Library of Congress

Typesetting: Camera ready by contributors

34/3830-543210 Printed on acid-free paper

Preface

The Sixth Refinement Workshop took place at City University in London from 5th to 7th January 1994. The present volume includes all of the papers which were submitted and accepted for presentation, together with two papers by invited speakers. The workshops in the series have generally occurred at one year intervals but in this last case a two year period had elapsed. These workshops have established themselves as an important event in the calendar for all those who are interested in progress in the underlying theory of refinement and in the take-up by industry of the methods supported by that theory.

One of the proposed themes of the sixth workshop was the reporting of successful adoption in industry of rigorous software development methods. The programme committee was perhaps slightly disappointed by the response from industry to the call in this respect. However, the recent period could be characterised as one of consolidation, when those companies which have made the decision that formal development methods are important to their business have been adopting them where appropriate and finding them to be worthwhile. On the other hand, the difficult economic climate which exists in most parts of the developed world is perhaps not the context within which companies still dubious about the benefits are going to opt for making major changes in their working practices.

As they have done for several previous workshops, Lloyd's Register provided financial support and their staff submitted papers to the workshop. Roger Shaw was also invited to expound his ideas about why many companies are unwilling to take the formal methods plunge, but in the event was not able to do so because of work pressures.

All of the invited speakers who were able to be present gave particularly interesting and stimulating presentations. David Garlan, whose work with Tektronix on reusable frameworks is now familiar as a cost-effective application of formal specification, explored the use of refinement in order to specify and re-use the connectors between system components. Jan Peleska, who stood in for Willem-Paul de Roever at very short notice, talked about the work which his company Deutsche System-Technik has been doing in collaboration with Willem-Paul and his group at the University of Kiel. He argued that the Ward and Mellor method, which has been widely adopted, has certain shortcomings which are made manifest when the attempt is made to provide a detailed semantics for the rather informal notation used. Steve Schuman and David Pitt gave a talk on object-oriented formal specification and behavioural refinement; they use a variant of the Z notation to express the state of a system and its behavioural properties in terms of transitions associated with events. No paper is included in the present volume for the talk: this work is based on results already presented in existing publications, and in a forthcoming article in the *Formal Aspects of Computing* journal (Springer-Verlag London Ltd). No doubt there will be future publications which further develop the ideas presented in the talk.

The submitted papers covered a broad range of issues in refinement. The first session comprised a group of papers reporting experience with the B-tool and the associated Abstract Machine method. Howard Haughton and Kevin Lano presented two papers in this group based on their work at Lloyd's Register; the first showed how ERA models with inheritance and specialisations can be expressed in the Abstract Machine notation and the second paper investigated the relationship between safety analysis and testing, suggesting that test cases may be selected by using substitutions establishing post-conditions for Abstract Machine expressions. Last in the group was a paper by Pierre Bieber and Nora Boulahia-Cuppens who used B to specify a protocol with various security aspects involving malicious agents.

Lindsay Groves next presented a paper looking at several language recognition algorithms, showing that they can be derived from a single abstract algorithm. Joakim von Wright described a prototype refinement tool based on a window inference system which supports a transformational style of reasoning in HOL. Mike Ainsworth and Peter Wallis discussed the amalgamation of partial specifications, a process which they call co-refinement. Raymond Nickson and Lindsay Groves described techniques which facilitate goal-directed refinement. Theodore Norvell addressed the problem of the correctness of code generators: he suggested that code generators may be derived from a statement of the relationship between source language programs and machine code programs where both are described in predicate logic. Xu Qiwen's paper investigates the laws of parallel programming in which processes communicate via shared variables; these laws are shown to form an algebraic framework for refinement and verification. Yves Ledru and Paul Collette presented an approach to the design of reactive systems, taking the environment as starting point for the development process. Kevin Lano addressed the problem of developing a semantic framework for object-oriented specification and refinement, mapping object-oriented Z into standard Z. Juan Bicarregui's paper looks closely at semantic models for 'external' clauses in VDM specifications, finding that there are some subtleties which have not been generally understood. In the final paper, Colin Fidge extends the usual rules for refinement of Z specifications into high-level language code by the addition of rules which ensure that specified real-time behaviour is preserved.

The organising committee consisted of Bernard Cohen, John Cooke, David Cooper, Tim Denvir, Jeremy Jacob (Chair and Tools Demonstrations Organiser), Kevin Lano, Roy McLean, Brian Monahan, Maurice

Naftalin, Mike Shields, Susan Stepney, David Till (Programme Chair and Local Organiser) and Peter Wallis.

The committee also wish to acknowledge the assistance of the following referees: Michael Ainsworth, Derek Andrews, Rosalind Barden, Mark Christian, Peter Fenelon, Jon Garnsworthy, Howard Haughton, Stephen Hughes, Walter Hussak, Kevin Lano, William Marsh, Peter Ryan, David Scholefield, Peter Sharbach and Roger Stone. All submitted papers were reviewed by members of the programme committee and the panel of referees before presentation; revised versions of papers were again reviewed before inclusion in the present proceedings.

March 1994   David Till
City University, London

Contents

Invited Papers

Using Refinement to Understand Architectural Connection

David Garlan

Department of Computer Science

5000 Forbes Avenue

Carnegie Mellon University

Pittsburgh, PA 15213

Abstract

The predominant use of refinement is to relate specifications of a system at two levels of abstraction. In this paper we describe a different application of refinement. We consider the problem of specifying reusable architectural connectors and the associated need to have formal rules for instantiating them for a specific system. We show that it is possible to use notations like CSP for these specifications and then to adapt the notion of process refinement to provide the rules for instantiation. We further show that these rules are sound with respect to deadlock freedom.

1 Introduction

The predominant use of refinement is to relate specifications of a system at two levels of abstraction. Typically an abstraction of a system is made more concrete in a lower-level specification that is closer to an implementation. In the extreme, the lower-level specification is some kind of machine-executable language.

For most systems of refinement a set of refinement rules provide the formal basis for deciding when one description is a legal refinement of another. The general idea behind all of these rules is that the lower-level description must have behavior that is consistent with the promised behavior of the more abstract description, but that it is free to make specific choices where the higher-level description has left that choice open.

While the use of refinement for developing correct implementations is certainly a good application of this general idea, it is not the only one. In this paper we illustrate a quite different application. We consider the problem of specifying reusable architectural connectors and the associated need to have formal rules for instantiating them in a specific system. As we will show, it is possible to use notations like CSP for these specifications and then to adapt the notion of process refinement to provide the rules for instantiation. We further show that the choice of refinement is not only intuitively appealing for this application, but also allows us to prove that certain important properties of the connector are maintained at the point of instantiation.

In the remainder of this paper we first outline the problem that motivates this work. Next we show how connector types can be defined as a collection of interacting protocols written in a language like CSP. Then we consider the problem of instantiating these connectors and show how process refinement

4

can be adapted as a solution. Finally, we show that this notion of refinement allows us to guarantee preservation of deadlock freedom in the presence of instantiation.

2 Architectural Specification

For large systems the overall system structure – or software architecture – becomes a critical design problem. Most systems of any size typically are presented in terms of a set of high-level interacting components. For example, a management information application may consist of a central database accessed by a set of applications which are accessed through a shared user interface.

The ubiquitous use of architectural concepts is highlighted by the typical informal documentation associated with system description. Usually a system is pictured as a boxes and lines diagram in which the boxes represent the main computational components and the lines represent interactions between those components. The prose that accompanies these figures uses phrases like "pipe and filter system", "client-server organization", "blackboard architecture", and "layered organization" to describe common idiomatic architectural patterns – or architectural styles [5].

For some domains architectural conventions have become standardized in a way that permits descriptions of architecture in terms of specific components and connectors. We are all familiar with the canonical architecture for a compiler. But other application-specific architectures (sometimes called "reference architectures") are becoming increasingly important to industry as a vehicle for design and code reuse, interoperability, standardization, and automated development support [8, 7, 4]. These systems gain their power by exploiting a set of design constraints and conventions that dictate such things as global system organization, and provide a common vocabulary of design elements (such as parsers and protocol layers).

While architectural description is crucial for large-scale software development, the relative informality of most architectural descriptions seriously limits their utility. It is often difficult to know precisely what is meant by terms such as "client-server". It is usually impossible to analyze the descriptions or to infer non-trivial properties from them. It is impossible to compare different architectural alternatives. It is hard to check that an implementation respects the constraints implied by an architectural description.

What is needed is a way to specify software architectures. Such a form of specification should allow a natural mapping of the informal notions into a more precise notation. In particular, it should be able to give meanings to boxes and lines diagrams and account for the idiomatic uses of architectural terms. It should also permit the designer to reuse general concepts from one architectural description to another. Further, it should allow one to check whether an architectural description is consistent, in the sense that the parts work well together.

It is important to note that this is not simply a problem of being able to specify a given system at a high level of abstraction. Rather, what is required is a building block approach to system specification. Concepts like "client-server" and "pipe connection" should become reusable specifications that can be incorporated into specific systems. This requirement is crucial to support the definition of architectural styles and reference architectures, which allow new products to be designed around a common vocabulary and set of conventions about system organization.

But the approach advocated here raises a number of fundamental questions: What does it mean to specify a reusable architectural building block? What does it mean to use (or "instantiate") one of these? What are the rules for checking that a use is consistent with its definition? What significant properties do these checks guarantee? In the following sections we provide partial answers to these questions.

3 The Wright Architectural Description Language

The approach that we will adopt is the following. We view the architecture of a system as a configuration of *components* and *connectors*. A component is the locus of computation, while a connector describes the interactions that can take place between a set of components. Components have a set of interaction points, or *ports* through which they interact with their environment. Connectors link the ports of two or more connectors. To specify a system we first define a set of component and connector *types*.[1] Second, we declare instances of these types and indicate how they are combined in a bipartite graph.

To make this concrete, we have developed the WRIGHT architectural description language for describing software architectures.[2] Figure 1 illustrates how a simple client-server system would be described in WRIGHT. In this system there are two component types: Client and Server. Here each components has a single port (although, in general a component might have many ports). Additionally with each component type we provide a component specification that specifies its function. (For the purposes of this paper, we will not concern ourselves with this specification).

In the figure we also declare a single connector type. A connector type is defined by a set of *roles* and a *glue* specification. The roles describe the expected local behavior of each of the interacting parties. In the above example, the client-server connector has a client role and a server role. As we will soon see, the client role might describe the client's behavior as a sequence of alternating requests for service and receipts of the results. The server role might describe the server's behavior as the alternate handling of requests and return of results. The glue specification describes how the activities of the client and server roles are coordinated. It would say that the activities must be sequenced in the order: client requests service, server handles request, server provides result, client gets result.

The figure also includes a declaration of a set of component and connector *instances*. These define the actual entities that will appear in the configuration. In the example, there is a single server (s), a single client (c), and a single C-S-connector instance (cs).

To provide a system definition, component and connector instances are combined by indicating which component ports are attached as (or instanti-

---

[1] Or better yet, import them from an existing library of architectural elements.

[2] The name refers to the architect Frank Lloyd Wright.

6

definition of style, external views, and relations among views. Each of these new products can be developed around a common vocabulary, and a set of expectations about system properties.

But all of this leverage and progress relies on the notion of architectural design. What does it mean to specify a module building block? What does it mean to use the "intersection" core of them? Suppose the external behavior that arises is compatible with detail alone? What might I implement that model that arises? In the following example, we provide partial answers to these questions.

    System SimpleExample
        Component Server
            port provide
                [provide protocol]
            spec *[Server specification]*
        Component Client
            port request
                [request protocol]
            spec *[Client specification]*
        Connector C-S-connector
            role client
                [client protocol]
            role server
                [server protocol]
            Glue *[glue protocol]*
    Instances
        s: Server
        c: Client
        cs: C-S-connector
    Attachments
        s.provide **as** cs.server;
        c.request **as** cs.client
    end SimpleExample.

Figure 1: A Simple Client-Server System

---

ate) which connector roles. In the example the client **request** and server **provide** ports are "attached as" the client and **server** roles respectively. This means that the connector **cs** coordinates the behavior of the ports c.**request** and s.**provide**. In a larger system, there might be other instances of C-S-connector that define interactions between other ports.

4 Specifying Connectors

The most interesting aspect of WRIGHT is its approach to specifying connectors. The roles of a connector describe the possible behaviors of each participant in the interaction, while the glue describes how these behaviors are combined to form a communication.

4.1 Notation

Our approach is to describe these behaviors as interacting protocols defined in a subset of CSP [6]. (In what follows, we will assume some familiarity with CSP.) The subset of CSP that we adopt is the use of events, and processes built out of primitives (e.g., STOP) and prefixing ($\rightarrow$), deterministic choice ($[\!]$), and non-deterministic choice ($\sqcap$). We also allow names to be associated with a (possibly recursive) process expression.

In addition to this standard CSP notation we adopt three notational conventions. First, we use the symbol $\sqrt{}$ to represent a successfully terminating process. This is the process that engages in the success event, $\sqrt{}$, and then stops. (In CSP, this process is called SKIP.) Formally, $\sqrt{} \stackrel{\text{def}}{=} \sqrt{} \rightarrow \text{STOP}$. Second, we allow the introduction of scoped names, as follows:

$$P = (\text{let } Q = expr1 \text{ in } R)$$

Third, as in CSP, we allow events and processes to be labeled. The event e labeled with label l is written $l.e$. The operator ":" allows us to label all of the events in a process, so that $l : P$ is the same process as P but with each of its events labeled. For our purposes we use the variant of this operator that does not label $\sqrt{}$. (The reason for this will become clear later.) We use the symbol Σ to represent the set of all unlabeled events.

The subset of CSP that we have chosen makes the process descriptions "finite-state". Later we explain our rationale for this decision. However, most of the discussion that follows would carry forward without modification if we used a more complete subset of CSP.

4.2 Connector Description

To describe a connector type we provide process descriptions for each of its roles and its glue. As a simple example, consider the client-server connector, introduced informally in Section 4.2. Ignoring transmission of data, this is how it might be written using the notation just outlined.

```
connector Pipe =
    role Writer = write→Writer ⊓ close→ √
    role Reader =
        let ExitOnly = close→ √
        in let DoRead = (read→Reader [] read-eof→ExitOnly)
        in DoRead ⊓ ExitOnly
    glue = let ReadOnly = Reader.read→ReadOnly
                        [] Reader.read-eof→Reader.close→ √
                        [] Reader.close→ √
           in let WriteOnly = Writer.write→WriteOnly [] Writer.close→ √
           in Writer.write→glue
               [] Reader.read→glue
               [] Writer.close→ReadOnly
               [] Reader.close→WriteOnly
```

Figure 2: A Pipe Connector

```
connectorService =
    role Client = request→ result → Client ⊓ √
    role Server = invoke→ return → Server [] √
    glue = Client.request→ Service.invoke→Service.return→
            Client.result→glue [] √
```

The Server role describes the communication behavior of the Server. It is defined as a process that repeatedly accepts an invocation and then returns; or it can terminate with success instead of being invoked. Because we use the alternative operator ([]) the choice of invoke or √ is determined by the environment of that role (which, as we will see, is the other roles and the glue).

The Client role describes the communication behavior of the user of the service. Similar to Server, it is a process that can call the service and then receive the result repeatedly, or terminate. However, because we use the decision operator (⊓) in this case, the choice of whether to call the service or to terminate is determined by the role process itself. Comparing the two roles, note that the two choice operators allow us to distinguish formally between situations in which a given role is *obliged* to provide some services — the case of Server — and the situation where it may take advantage of some services if it chooses — the case of Client).

The **glue** process coordinates the behavior of the two roles by indicating how the events of the roles work together. Here **glue** allows the Client role to decide whether to call or terminate and then sequences the remaining three events and their data.

As more substantive example, Figure 2 illustrates the definition of an infinite pipe connector type. The complexity of this definition arises from the need to account for the possibility that either role may decide to stop. If the writer stops, the reader must be prepared to accept an "end of file" marker.

4.3   Connector Semantics

Intuitively, the roles of a connector act as independent processes constrained only by the glue, which orchestrates the interactions between the roles. Formally, the meaning of a connector is the parallel composition of its role and glue processes, where we arrange things so that the alphabets of the roles do not intersect and the alphabet of the glue includes the union of the events of the roles.

Definition 4.1 The *meaning of a connector description* with roles R_1, R_2, ..., R_n, and glue *Glue* is the process:

$$Glue \parallel (\mathsf{R_1}{:}R_1 \parallel \mathsf{R_2}{:}R_2 \parallel \ldots \parallel \mathsf{R_n}{:}R_n)$$

where R_i is the (distinct) name of role R_i, and

$$\alpha\,Glue = \mathsf{R_1}{:}\Sigma \cup \mathsf{R_2}{:}\Sigma \cup \ldots \cup \mathsf{R_n}{:}\Sigma \cup \{\sqrt{}\}.$$

•

Here the glue's alphabet is the union of all possible events labeled by the respective role names (e.g., Client, Server), together with the $\sqrt{}$ event. This allows the glue to interact with each role. In contrast, (except for $\sqrt{}$) the role alphabets are disjoint and so each role can only interact with the glue. Because $\sqrt{}$ is not relabeled, all of the roles and glue can (and must) agree on $\sqrt{}$ for any of the processes to terminate successfully. Thus, successful termination of a connector is the joint responsibility of the all parties involved.

5   Connector Instantiation

Component ports are also specified by processes: The port process defines the expected behavior of the component at that point of interaction. For example, the **request** port of a client that makes a single request and then terminates successfully might look like:

component =
    port Request = request→ result → $\sqrt{}$
    other ports...

To use a connector to define a particular system we must create an instance of the connector and then "attach" it by associating component ports with the connector roles. (See Figure 1.) But what does this mean?

At first glance it might seem that there should be no problem to solve. If the port protocols are identical to the role protocols, then we can simply substitute the ports for the roles in the overall system description.

But, in general, we would not like to require that the port and role protocols be identical. As a simple example, note that the above port protocol required only one request for service while the role allows an infinite number. Similarly, we can well imagine a client-server connector that allows two kinds of services to be performed, but that a particular port only requires the use of one. As another example, a port that writes to a pipe may be designed to continue forever; in that case its protocol would not involve the *close* event.

Allowing that we would like to permit the role and port protocols to be different, we note that the port protocol defines the concrete interaction behavior of the component with its environment. Thus, when instantiated, the ports take the place of the roles in the actual system. It is reasonable, therefore, to define an instantiated connector as one in which all of its roles have been replaced by the ports of the components that it connects. Formally,

Definition 5.1 The meaning of attaching ports $P_1 \ldots P_n$ as roles $R_1 \ldots R_n$ of a connector with glue *Glue* is the process:

$$Glue \parallel (R_1 \colon P_1 \parallel R_2 \colon P_2 \parallel \ldots \parallel R_n \colon P_n)$$

●

But this now raises the key question: when is it legal to perform such an instantiation? We refer to this as the *port-role compatibility* problem.

As the examples above illustrate, it should be possible for roles not to exhibit all of the behavior allowed by a connector. On the other hand there are certain kinds of behavior that a port should not be allowed to exclude. For example, if a server must be initialized before a request is made, then the port had better include initialization as part of its promised behavior.

Evidently what is needed is a definition that allows the port to ignore optional (i.e., nondeterministic choices), while respecting the obligations of the connector (i.e., deterministic choices). But this is precisely the notion of refinement!

Unfortunately it is not possible to use the notion of CSP refinement directly. There are two reasons for this. The first reason is the technicality that CSP's $\sqsubseteq$ relation assumes that the alphabets of the compared processes are the same. We can handle this problem simply by augmenting the alphabets of the port and role processes so that they are identical. This is easily accomplished using the CSP operator for extending alphabets of processes: P_{+B} extends the alphabet of process P by the set B. (In this context, $P_{+B} = P \parallel STOP_B$). We extend the port's alphabet to that of the role, and vice versa.

The second, and more important, reason is that even if the port and role have the same alphabet it may be that the port process allows incompatible behavior, but that this behavior could never arise in the context of the connector to which it is attached. For example, suppose a component port has the property that it must be initialized before use, but that it will crash if it is initialized twice. If we put this in the context of a connector that *guarantees* that at most one initialization will occur, then the anomalous situation will not arise.

Thus to evaluate compatibility we need concern ourselves only with the behavior of the port *restricted to the contexts in which the role might find itself*. That is, to evaluate the suitability of a port to fill a given role, it is sufficient to consider the port's behavior over traces that are allowed by the role. Technically we can achieve this result by considering the new process formed by placing the port process in parallel with the deterministic process obtained from the role. For a role R, we denote this latter process $det(R)$. (For details, see [2].)

We are led to the following definition of compatibility (where "\" is set difference) :

Definition 5.2 P **compat** R ("P is compatible with R")
if $R_{+(\alpha P \backslash \alpha R)} \sqsubseteq P_{+(\alpha R \backslash \alpha P)} \parallel det(R)$ •

Under these definitions, we see that port $Request = \text{request} \rightarrow \text{result} \rightarrow \sqrt{}$ is compatible with role Client, but that it would not have been if the client had required an initialization event before a request.

6 Deadlock Freedom

An important goal in defining connector types is to be able to provide guarantees about the properties of their instances. If this were not possible there would be little benefit in having reusable connector types, since we would have to reestablish the properties of each connector instance whenever it is used.

One such property is deadlock-freedom. Intuitively, a deadlock-free connector is one in which the roles never get "stuck" in the middle of an interaction, each role expecting the others to take some action that can never happen. That is, if one of the connector's roles is prepared to make progress it should be possible for the connector as a whole to do so. On the other hand, we would like to allow the possibility that the connector as a whole can terminate successfully. For example, a client-server connector should allow the client to terminate the interaction, provided it does so at a point expected by the server. Similarly the pipe connector should allow termination when the writer closes the pipe.

In terms of our model of connectors, successful termination amounts to a joint transition (of all the roles and glue) to $\sqrt{}$, the process that announces success and then stops. (Recall that we have set up our renaming operator so that $\sqrt{}$ can be a shared event of all the roles and the glue). We can make this formal:

Definition 6.1 A connector C is *deadlock-free* if for all $(t, ref) \in failures(C)$ such that $ref = \alpha C$, then we have $tail(t) = \sqrt{}$. •

As argued above, such a property is only useful if it is preserved across connector instantiation. That is, we would like to be able to claim that an instance of a deadlock-free connector remains deadlock-free when instantiated by compatible ports.

Such a result would, of course, be trivially true if we used ports that were identical to the roles. But as we have argued above, ports and roles need not be identical. Less obvious, but equally true, is the fact that if ports are strict refinements of the roles then deadlock freedom is also preserved. This follows from the monotonic nature of process refinement, which requires the failures of a refinement to be a subset of the failures of the process it is refining. In other words, the refined process can't refuse to participate in an interaction if the role could not also have refused.

But we have deliberately chosen a weaker notion of refinement in order to provide greater opportunities for reuse of the connector. Because the port need only be considered a refinement when restricted to the traces of the role, it is possible that it may allow potentially deadlocking behavior, even though this behavior would never occur in the context of the role that it is playing.

Consequently, it is not immediately clear whether deadlock-freedom is preserved across compatible port substitutions. In fact, it is not. The problem arises if the glue permits behaviors outside the range of those defined by the roles of the connector. Suppose, for example, that the glue allows a behavior of the form "...$[]R1 : crash \rightarrow$ STOP" and that the event *crash* is not in the alphabet of role $R1$. Then the connector could be deadlock-free (in the sense defined above). Now consider a port that contains the same behavior (i.e.,...$[]R1 : crash \rightarrow$ STOP). It is possible for this port to be compatible with role $R1$. But the connector can deadlock if the port is substituted for the role in that connector.

To avoid this possibility we need to impose further restrictions on the glue. Specifically, we define a *conservative* connector to be one for which the glue traces are a subset of the possible interleavings of role traces.

Definition 6.2 A connector $C = Glue \parallel (R_1{:}r_1 \parallel R_2{:}r_2 \parallel \ldots \parallel R_n{:}r_n)$ is *conservative* if $traces(Glue) \subseteq traces(R_1{:}r_1 \parallel R_2{:}r_2 \parallel \ldots \parallel R_n{:}r_n)$

Armed with this definition we can now state the desired result:

Theorem 6.3 *If a connector* $C = Glue \parallel (R_1{:}R_1 \parallel R_2{:}R_2 \parallel \ldots \parallel R_n{:}R_n)$ *is conservative and deadlock-free, and if for* $i \in \{1..n\}$, P_i **compat** R_i, *then* $C' = Glue\parallel(R_1{:}P_1\parallel R_2{:}P_2\parallel \ldots \parallel R_n{:}P_n)$ *is deadlock-free.*

7 ' Conclusion and Future Prospects

In this paper we have illustrated how refinement can be applied to the problem of specifying software architectures. This work is motivated by the need for a practical formal basis on which software engineers can develop architectural designs using common vocabularies of components, connectors, and patterns of composition.

As a step in that direction we have focused on reusable specifications of architectural connectors. Given such specifications, refinement emerges as natural way to understand when it is legal to use a connector in a given context. We have also illustrated that pure refinement is not sufficiently flexible and provided a somewhat more permissive definition that permits reuse of connectors in a larger number of contexts. We further claimed that this definition is not too loose: it is still possible to guarantee preservation of properties across connector instantiation.

The specific notation used here was a subset of CSP, embedded in the Wright architectural description language. That subset was deliberately chosen to produce finite state processes. As a result, all of the major properties described in the paper (deadlock-freedom, conservatism, and compatibility) can be checked automatically by tools such as FDR [3]. In fact, we are incorporating FDR into an architectural design environment, and plan to use it routinely to check the properties of connectors and their instantiations.

However, the finite nature of the examples should not mislead the reader into thinking that the results apply only in the case of finite state processes. Indeed, all of the results carry over to full CSP. Of course, automated checking is no longer possible in that case. We also believe that the approach outlined in this paper extends beyond CSP itself. In principle, it should be possible to use alternative specification languages to define the protocols of connectors. For example, timed CSP could be used to express timing constraints on interactions to explain the behavior of such things as server timeouts. The notions of compatibility and conservatism would then have to be correspondingly augmented.

Acknowledgements

The results of this paper were developed jointly with Robert Allen. Several of the examples are adapted from other accounts of this work [1, 2]. The ideas have benefited substantially from comments by Steve Brookes, Daniel Jackson, Mary Shaw, and Jeannette Wing.

This research was sponsored by the National Science Foundation under Grant Number CCR-9357792, by the Wright Laboratory, Aeronautical Systems Center, Air Force Materiel Command, USAF, and the Advanced Research Projects Agency (ARPA) under grant number F33615-93-1-1330, and by Siemens Corporate Research. The views and conclusions contained in this document are those of the authors and should not be interpreted as representing the official policies, either expressed or implied, of Wright Laboratory, the U.S. Government, or Siemens Corporation.

References

[1] Allen, R. and Garlan, D. *Beyond Definition/Use: Architectural Interconnection.* in: **Proceedings of the ACM Interface Definition Language Workshop.** SIGPLAN Notices, Portland, OR, 1994.

[2] Allen, R. and Garlan, D. *Formal Connectors.* no. CMU-CS-192, Carnegie Mellon University, 1993. *In preparation.*

[3] **Failures Divergence Refinement: User Manual and Tutorial.** 1.2β. Formal Systems (Europe) Ltd., Oxford, England, 1992.

[4] Garlan, D. and Delisle, N. *Formal Specifications as Reusable Frameworks.* in: **VDM'90: VDM and Z – Formal Methods in Software Development.** Springer-Verlag, LNCS 428, Kiel, Germany, 1990, pp. 150–163.

[5] Garlan, D. and Shaw, M. *An Introduction to Software Architecture.* in: **Advances in Software Engineering and Knowledge Engineering, Volume I,** edited by V.Ambriola and G.Tortora. World Scientific Publishing Company, New Jersey, 1993.

[6] Hoare, C. **Communicating Sequential Processes.** Prentice Hall, 1985.

[7] **Open Systems Interconnection Handbook.** edited by G. R. McClain. Intertext Publications McGraw-Hill Book Company, New York, NY, 1991.

[8] Metalla, E. and Graham, M. H. *The Domain-Specific Software Architecture Program.* no. CMU/SEI-92-SR-9, Carnegie Mellon Software Engineering Institute, June 1992.

Formal Semantics for Ward & Mellor's Transformation Schemas

Carsta Petersohn, Willem-Paul de Roever

Christian–Albrechts–University at Kiel

Cornelis Huizing

Eindhoven University of Technology

Jan Peleska

DST Deutsche System-Technik GmbH

Abstract

A family of formal semantics is given for the Essential Model of the Transformation Schema of Ward & Mellor [WM85] using recent techniques developed for defining the semantics of Statecharts [Ha88] by Pnueli and Huizing. The models developed closely resemble those used for synchronous languages [Benveniste and Berry 92]. A number of ambiguities and inconsistencies in Ward & Mellor's original definition are resolved.

1 Introduction

1.1 Motivation and goal

Structured Analysis and Design methods (SM) aim at giving a specification of software which is independent of, and considerably more abstract and readable than, the code eventually produced. Their goal is to provide in this way a specification which:

a) exposes inconsistencies in the requirement document describing what a client 'thinks' she/he wants, as opposed to the finally debugged hopefully consistent requirement specification describing what she/he 'actually' wants, and

b) provides a consistent requirement specification and independent description of the task of the software to be written by the implementor.

Obviously, this process looses a lot of its potential value once the SM methods used contain in their definition bugs and inconsistencies themselves. This happens, e.g., in case of an executable specification language, when the execution of a specification does not faithfully represent the semantics of that specification as laid down in the document defining the method. This would endanger point a) above. As to point b), such inconsistencies might result in a specification of dubious value, since an implementor would not know exactly what to implement, when the meaning of the requirement specification is ambiguous or even inconsistent. Some industries realize this danger. Already some years ago the French company Alcatel/Alsthom invested a lot of energy in debugging the Statemate Tool [Ha90], which it planned to use for specification of the software for its 3rd-generation high-speed trains. Subsequently this tool was corrected by the company involved. This is an important step ahead! In the same spirit the present paper derives from a project by a local industry (DST) to make its specification method ([WM85]) automatically analyzable.

When looking at some of the Structured Analysis and Design Methods in use today (see [Davis 90] for an overview), a rather disappointing picture emerges in this respect. For example, the method of Ward and Mellor (W&M, described in [WM85]), claimed to be important for the structured representation of Real-Time systems and used by almost one sixth of all system specifiers in the USA according to [Wo], is sometimes ambiguous or inconsistent, and does not provide any characterization of real-time behaviour with enough rigour to express or deduce specific timing properties.

Yet W&M's method contains at least sufficient indications for us to try to *reconstruct* its intended meaning. We show that with the formal methods developed for the definition and analysis of so-called *synchronous* languages (see [Benveniste and Berry 92] for an overview) a consistent and precise semantics can be reconstructed for the W&M method. Incompleteness in description and downright contradictions in claimed 'definitions' can be identified and removed, and the rather remote link with timing can be built upon to form a foundation for what is promised by the method which is at least consistent. This is the main purpose of the present paper, in which we give a precise semantics for the Essential Model of W&M's method (Sec.3). Since the rigour of the underlying definition of this semantics may prevent it from actually being read by the SM community, in this paper (Sec.2) we also present a list of the main flaws in W&M's definition of the semantics of transition diagrams and our suggestions to resolve them. Our goal is to awaken at least some of the members of this community, once they see how trivial and natural the examples are in which these flaws occur. Also a formal definition of W&M's semantics enables the development of a symbolic interpreter, which is of great importance for point a) above.

Some people regard W&M's method as already outdated and succeeded by Harel's Statecharts [Ha88]. This is only partially so. As is argued in [PHP93], on the basis of comparing the two methods, W&M's method is probably still the best there is when a lot of data-processing is required, in combination with mildly complicated control. In case of modelling really complex real-time embedded systems, which do not involve such an amount of data-processing, Statemate is regarded as superior [Wo]. Moreover W&M's method is the most widely spread CASE method of the SM family in industry, so it makes sense to try to improve it.

1.2 Main technique

The method of W&M uses Transformation Schemas (TS) to represent a system. These are based on dataflow diagrams, but can also represent the control aspect of a system. Therefore a TS consists of data and control components, which are both divided into transformations (centers of activities), stores and flows.

The basic flaws in the definition of the semantics of Transformation Schemas in the Essential Model of W&M's method are the following (also see Sec.2):

1. The method lacks a consistent description of <u>when</u> a transformation can start computing upon its input. E.g., one interpretation of Ward's definition may lead to an unnecessary loss of data.

2. The interpretation of composed flows (carrying elements of Cartesian products or unions of data types) is not sufficiently worked out. There are, according to the information given in [WM85], still different interpretations of composed flows possible, so that these imply different possibilities for the observable behaviour of a TS (as seen by the outside world).

3. The definition of the time dependent behaviour of TS is ambiguous. For the life-span of a data-item depends on the interpretation of a 'discrete point in time', but a clear definition is missing of what a 'discrete point in time' is.

We resolve these flaws technically in section 3 by defining a formal operational semantics for that part of TS whose interpretation causes the above mentioned flaws. To be more precise we define a family of formal semantics. The members are *recursive causal chain*, *weakly fair* and *full interleaving semantics*. All of these semantics are interleaving semantics defined by transition systems. Referring to [Pet92] for a non graphical syntax of TS and their specifications, these semantics consist of *macro steps*, describing the observable behaviour as seen by the outside world, which in their turn are made up out of (sequences of) *micro steps*, describing the internal processing steps of a TS which describe the execution of its transformations. Depending on the family of the particular member of semantics it is belonging to, an internal sequence of micro steps can be characterized by properties such as *maximal* or *recursive-causal-chain* (which are defined later).

The Essential Model is characterized by an abstract notion of time. Every transformation needs zero time to react on input and to produce an output ([WM85] p.94). The abstract notion of time involved here is such that micro steps take no time for their execution. However a macro step takes a positive amount of external time (as can be interpreted from Table III [Wa86] p.206). This division between micro and macro steps is characteristic for the semantics of synchronous languages, in which the following idealization is adopted: synchronous systems produce their output synchronously with their input (Berry's Synchrony Hypothesis [BG88]). Of course this hypothesis does not hold for our usual notion of time. It merely expresses that the time taken by a finite number of internal steps of the system should be negligible in comparison with the time between successive external stimuli.

The formal technique dealing with these two notions of step (due to Pnueli, Huizing, and others) had not been sufficiently formalized around 1985 for W&M to be able to realize its consequences for a worked out semantics. Our contribution is that we adapt these techniques to define a family of semantics for TS, especially to W&M's model. In [PHP93] the differences with the Statechart model for which these techniques were originally developed are indicated.

1.3 Discussion of the family of semantics

We define a *family* of semantics, because every application area imposes its own criteria for being satisfactorily modelled. In particular, it turns out that

Ward's semantics, represented by our recursive causal chain semantics, is not suitable for modelling fault tolerant systems, because the latter impose other observability criteria (here, that a failure is observed by the system at the very moment it occurs). In this case we find that fault tolerant systems require our weakly fair interleaving semantics.

Another criterion for the use of a semantics is modularity. By *modularity* we mean that the observable behaviour of a proper part of a Transformation Schema, when regarding its extended interface with the outside world, is not different from the internal interface inside the Transformation Schema. Now our objection to W&M's method is that it is not modular, and nor is the weakly fair interleaving semantics (required for fault tolerant systems), whereas the full interleaving semantics is modular.

This objection is a consequence of an assumption which Ward makes in his article [Wa86 p.203] with respect to a semantics of Transformation Schemas: 'The consequences of the arrival of a value on a flow from outside the schema are worked out before any other value from outside the schema is accepted,....' The semantics modelling this assumption are therefore also not modular (see section 2.5). However, our semantics does explain this phenomenon by introducing macro and micro steps (see section 3.4.2).

1.4 Future work

A similar investigation should be made for the method of [Hatley and Pirbhai 88], which is also still used by approximately one sixth of the American SM users [Wo]. As next stages, we intend to integrate another real-time model as also described in [Wa86], to give a similar formalization of W&M's implementation model, described in vol. 3 of [WM85], and investigate its link (in terms of possible notions of refinement) with our formalization of the essential model in the present paper. Apart from the flaws mentioned in chapter 1.2 one might object that the method lacks any yardstick for determining correctness of data refinement, or even flow refinement. Building a symbolic interpreter for W&M's method, based on the formal semantics defined in this paper, is planned in cooperation with a local industry.

2 W&M's method and examples of unsolved ambiguities

In this section we discuss briefly some of the ambiguities in the interpretation of Transformation Schemas as defined in [WM85] and [Wa86]. (See [Pet92] for details.)

2.1 A short introduction to Transformation Schemas

Transformation Schemas (TS) consist of data and control components. We give here just a short introduction to their main constituent parts, called 'transformation','flow' and 'store'; these may be labeled by identifiers. We restrict ourselves in these pages to that part of W&M which is formally characterized in the present paper. For example, we do not assume that all flows are time–discrete, i.e., that they are not continuous.

Example 1 (TS with data-triggered transformation)

Transformation Schema :

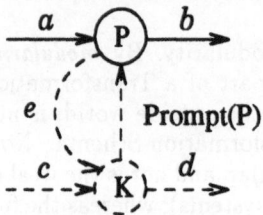

In the above, Transformation Schema P is a data transformation and K is a control transformation. The data flow a is an input flow and the data flow b is an output flow of transformation P. Flows which start from 'nowhere' (as flow a) and flows which end in 'nowhere' (as flow b) are connected to the outside world of the Transformation Schema. The flows c, d, e and $Prompt(P)$ are control flows. Data flows carry values and control flows carry events, except for the control flow named $Prompt(P)$ (which is a special notation of ours). An event is a special value which just indicates that something has happened. The control flow $Prompt(P)$ can carry the events 'ENABLE(P)' and 'DISABLE(P)'. These control flows are called *Prompts*. Their meaning is explained below.

If there is no value on the output flows b, e and the transformation P is not stopped by the control transformation K, then the transformation P computes an output along b or e as soon as an input arrives along a. Such behaviour is called *data–triggered*. The flow e is called *data condition* and represents the possibility that control signals can be fed back from a data transformation to a control transformation. The control transformation K stops the data transformation P by sending a value 'DISABLE(P)' to P along the flow $Prompt(P)$. If P is stopped, it can not compute outputs and throws arriving inputs away. The control transformation K starts P up again by sending a value 'ENABLE(P)'. When a transformation has no Prompt as an input flow, the transformation is never stopped. □

Example 2 (TS with explicit triggered transformation)

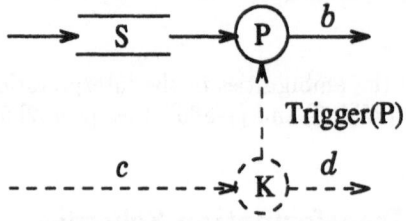

In the above TS a is a data store. A data store can be seen as a global variable. Its value can be read or written. The data transformation P gets its input information just from the data store. Therefore the transformation is not data-triggered. The control flow $TRIGGER(P)$ is called *Trigger* and has a special meaning. The work of the data transformation P is started by an event on 'TRIGGER(P)'. □

For every transformation of a Transformation Schema there must exist a *specification*. A control transformation is specified by a finite state automaton called State-Transition-Diagram (STD) (see example 3). For specifying a data transformation, W&M suggest a number of possibilities ([WM85 pp.81–91]). In the examples 3, 4 and 5 we specify both data and control transformations by State-Transition-Diagrams. In our formal semantic, we sketch in chapter 3, data transformations are specified by a relation which also takes values of data stores into account.

The behaviour of a data transformation could possibly display nondeterminism when there is more than one input data flow (see [Wa86] p.200). Therefore W&M restrict data transformations to one data input flow. However, for control transformations more than one input flow is allowed, because these can by their very definition react on only one input flow at a time (since the resulting non determinism is handled by the controlling automaton).

The meaning of a *composed* flow z in the drawing below makes it possible to combine values from flows x and y produced by different transformations Q and R into a pair used for a calculation by P (see chapter 2.3):

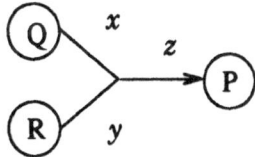

Composed flows are specified in a data-dictionary. They can carry values whose type is a Cartesian product or a union. In the above example the data-dictionary entry for the composed flow z with the type of Cartesian product of x and y is $z = x + y$ and with the type of the union of x and y is $z = [x|y]$.

In this paper we use composed control flows, which are an extension of [Wa86] and not explicitly mentioned in [WM86]. We introduce them by defining them to have the same dynamic behaviour as dataflows with the same specification. The use of control components especially composed control flows in the examples 3 and 4 makes the examples smaller than using data components, but the behaviour of transformations and composed flows we want to discuss is the same for both control and data components.

2.2   Behaviour of a transformation

According to [WM85] p.97 it is impossible for a transformation to output a new value along an output flow as long as some old output value (due to a previous computation) has not been 'cleared' from that flow. As a consequence, W&M's model implies that flows have a buffering capacity of 1. On the other hand [Wa86] p.200 states that as soon as an input arrives it will be processed. A model which meets both requirements may lead to a loss of output data of the transformation. Therefore we list below all possible alternatives we can think of for defining the behaviour of a transformation and discuss which one is best.

1.   a) The input is thrown away, if there is still an old value on an output flow. (This option seems to be implied in the implementational model of [Wa86 p.208]).

b) The output is calculated, but its placement on output flows is restricted to flows which are not occupied by old values.

c) Old outputs are overwritten by new ones.

2. An arrived input value of a transformation is processed only after consideration of the output flows;

a) The calculation is only started, when the resulting output values appear on flows which are free.

b) The transformation waits with the computation until all output flows are free.

Options 1) a) – c) lead to an arbitrary loss of data and are therefore useless for modelling data–processing systems. An example follows. Option 2a) requires foreknowledge and is therefore rejected. This leaves us option 2b) since we do not want arbitrary loss of data.

Example 3 (arbitrary loss of data)
The following figure is a Transformation Schema:

For the composed flow z there exists a data-dictionary entry $z = x + y$. A value on the composed flow z consists of a pair of values, the first one of which originates from x, and the second one from y. In this example we just use the following assumption about how z behaves. This behaviour is due to W&M and not in dispute. (For more information, see the discussion in 2.3). A value is put on flow z if flow x and y carry a value. If e.g. flow x carries a value but not flow y then the value on flow x is stored.

For transformation P_1 there exists a specification which, due to our restriction, is a finite state automaton called State-Transition-Diagram (STD). Its graphical representations is given below (observe that states are represented by rectangles, because the usual notation for them, circles, is already used in transformations for 'centres of activities'):

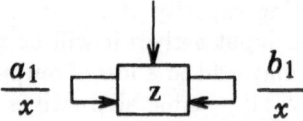

Now assume flows a_1, b_1 all have values put on them (by the outside world). With option 1 of the definition of the possible behaviour of a transformation given above a value may be arbitrarily lost. The critical internal processing steps for option 1 are the following. Assume P_1 starts processing the value on

a_1. The meaning of the label $a_1 \backslash x$ in the STD for P_1 is that occurrence of a value along flow a_1 immediately generates (in a micro step) a value along x. So a value along x is generated. Because flow y carries no value the value of x is regarded as being stored, waiting for a value on y. Now with option 1 transformation P_1 can take the value from b_1 away. Depending on which option from 1) a) – c) is taken, the input from b_1, the old output, or the new output along x, is lost for further computation of the TS above. With option 2 transformation P_1 is not able to take the value on flow b_2 away.

If the above TS is part of a bigger TS then the above described differences can also result in different output to the outside world. □

2.3 Composed flow

A lot of overhead in the notation of W&M is due to the occurrence of composed flows. Yet, neither in [WM85] nor in [Wa86] is the dynamic behaviour of composed flows precisely characterized. As a result a number of basic questions regarding such flows are unresolved.

We discuss as an example a flow z composed of flows x and y, where z carries information for the x and y flows and is specified with $z = x + y$. Assume flows z, x and y below are previously without value and now a value (represented by a token) on flow z arrives due to a calculation of transformation P. The two possible options of the resulting effects on flows x and y which we discuss are represented graphically in figure A and B. The described properties are illustrated in example 4.

A.

As we see in example 4 below, in the option shown in figure A above, flows z, x and y model a buffer of capacity 2 (for values of type z).

B.

As we see in example 4 with the option shown in figure B above, flows z, x and y together model a buffer of capacity 1 for the values of z, which only becomes empty once both tokens on flow x and y have been 'cleared' by transformations Q and R.

22

Example 4 (different macro steps)

We assume transformations to behave like option 2 from chapter 2.2. With this assumption, the TS and its specification shown below are used to show that option A and B of the behaviour of a composed flow z with $z = x + y$ can result in different output seen from the outside world. We represent this observable behaviour in our semantics as a macro step which is a maximal sequence of micro steps. Micro-steps are represented below with arrows as $\rightarrow_{a_1}^{\{z\}}$. Assume the following TS and specification:

<u>Transformation Schema :</u>   <u>Specification :</u>

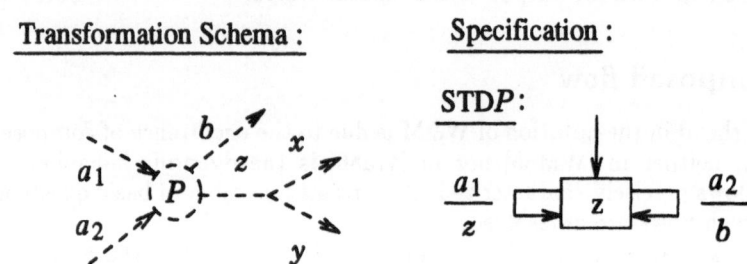

With option A, the TS reacts on inputs from flows a_1 and a_2 as represented graphically below:

<u>Internal sequence of processing steps :</u>

The value on flow z is immediately put on flows x and y. With option A, flow z carries no value any longer. The flow has a capacity of 2, because a new value can be placed on flow z. Therefore after outputting a value along z, P can immediately start operating upon a new input value and produce an output along flow b, while the tokens along x and y are still there.

With option B, the TS reacts to inputs from flows a_1 and a_2 as represented by:

Internal sequence of processing steps :

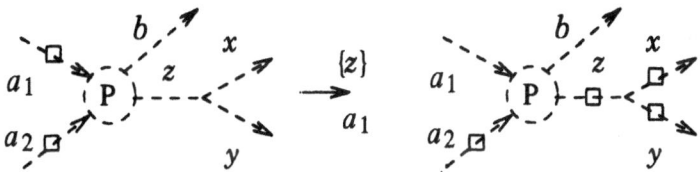

With option B, the value on flow z persists as long as a value on flow x or y exists, the flow has just a capacity of 1. Therefore Transformation P does not produce an output on flow b.

Because flow b is directed to the outside world the difference between the above described options can be seen from the outside world   □

We choose in our semantics the option shown in figure B on grounds of simplicity, and because of considerations of refinement. For consider the TS drawn below:

Transformation Schema :

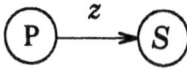

and assume we now refine S by:

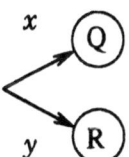

Then we would like to make the behaviour of P independent of this refinement. As seen above, this is not so in figure A, since then this process of refinement results in a buffer with bigger capacity than that of z alone (the capacity of z is 1, as stipulated in [WM85 p.46]).

The examples of figure A and B can be made more complex by assuming that there are still old values along either x or/and y left, i.e. by combining the ambiguity mentioned in subsection 2.2 with the present one. For discussion of this point we refer to [Pt92].

2.4   Life–span of values on flows

Conversely one can consider the case when a composite value z obtains its values from its component flows x and y. If there is a value on flow x but no value on flow y it is meaningful to store the value on flow x waiting for a value on flow y. But what happens if, e.g., flows y and z are connected with the outside world and no value along y ever appears as in the example TS below?

Transformation Schema :

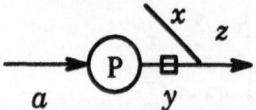

Neither [WM85] nor [Wa86] mention this case. Our solution to this problem is: Once the 'internal time–span' of one macro step, which is a maximal sequence of internal processing steps, is over, all values left on such 'blocked' internal flows of the TS are taken away.

2.5 Lack of modularity: an example

In this section we give an example which shows why our semantics for Transformation Schemas is not modular. This is due to the fact that we have to model the following assumption: 'The consequences of the arrival of a value on a flow from outside the schema are worked out before any other value from outside the schema is accepted,...', [Wa86 p.203].

Example 5 (different interfaces)

1. We assume a Transformation Schema T_1 having flows b and e as part of the interface with the outside world. The Transformation Schema T_1 and its specification is shown below:

Transformation Schema :

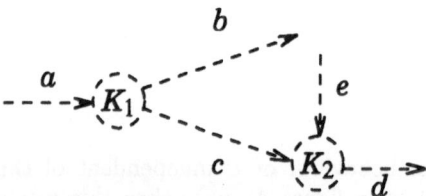

Specifications :

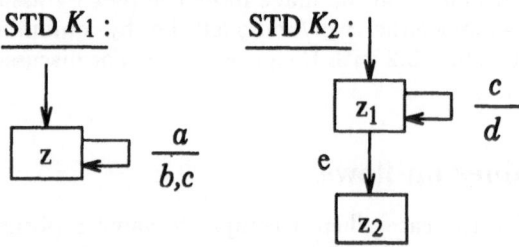

The only possible output to the outside world upon a value on flow a from the outside world are values on flows b and d. Upon an input on flow a a state change of transformation K_1 is caused, which results in a concurrent output on flow b and c. Then the transformation K_2, being in state z_1, reacts with an output on flow d.

2. Next we assume a Transformation Schema T_2 composed of the Transformation Schema T_1 and a control transformation K_3, so that the flows b and e are no longer part of the interface with the outside world. The Transformation Schema T_2 and the specification of the control transformation K_3 are shown below:

Transformation Schema :

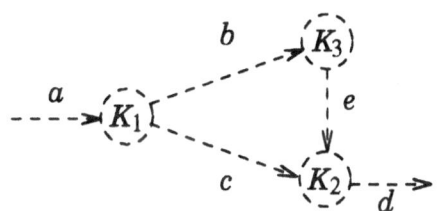

Specification :

STD K_3 :

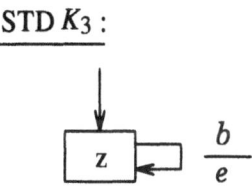

A possible result upon an input on flow a from the outside world is that there is no output on flow d to the outside world. In the Transformation Schema T_2 a value on flow b forces transformation K_3 to output a value on flow e. This value can cause a state change of transformation K_2 from z_1 to z_2 before the value along flow c is taken into account. When transformation K_2 reacts on the value on flow c, no state change nor any output on flow d takes place, because K_2 is in state z_2.

□

Example 5 shows, that the external interface between a Transformation Schema (such as T_1 in case 1) and the outside world is quite different from the internal interface between 'proper' parts of a Transformation Schema (such as T_1 and K_3 in case 2). In case 1, a value on flow b, which is part of the interface to the outside world, can not influence the reaction from T_1 on an input on flow a. But in case 2, a value on flow b, which is part of the (internal) interface between T_1 and K_3, does influence that reaction.

3   Sketch of a family of formal semantics

In this section we sketch a family of formal operational semantics of TS referring to a non-graphical syntax of TS. (In [Pet92] a more complete definition of the semantics is given). One member of this family closely reflects Ward's original ideas described in [Wa86]. All members of this family of semantics for TS consist of *macro steps* describing the observable behaviour of a TS as seen by the outside world. A macro step is made up of a sequence of internal processing steps called *micro steps*. Each member of our family of formal semantics is characterized by restrictions on the sequence of internal micro steps and restrictions on the macro steps. The internal sequence represents the reaction of a TS on information sent along flows by the outside world, and the macro step represents the abstract view of this sequence as presented to the outside world.

3.1 Micro step

A micro step represents an internal processing step of a data or control transformation belonging to a Transformation Schema T. It is defined formally as a labeled transition

$$(T, fl, \sigma) \rightarrow_{in}^{out} (T, fl', \sigma')$$

in the style of Plotkin [Pl83]. Here the flow *in* carries the value that causes the internal processing step that is represented by the micro step and the quantity *out* consists of flows getting new values as a result of the processing step. The tuple (T, fl, σ) is called a micro configuration and is defined as follows:

- T stands for a syntactic representation of a TS.

- fl denotes a state of the flows of T. It is a function mapping the names of flows of T to the 'values' they are carrying, where the symbol '$\perp$' represents a formal value indicating that the flow does not carry a computable value.

- σ denotes the state of the transformations of T, which maps, e.g., a name from a control transformation of T to the set $\{DISABLE\} \cup Z_A$, where Z_A is the set of states of the finite state automaton associated with the control transformation and DISABLE expresses that the transformation has stopped.

A micro configuration (T, fl, σ) induces micro configuration (T^*, fl^*, σ^*) for every transformation diagram T^* contained in T, where fl^* and σ^* denote corresponding restrictions of fl and σ to, respectively, the flows and transformations of T^*.

The micro step itself is defined inductively over the non-graphical syntactic structure of a TS. Therefore the formal definition of a micro step consists of two axioms, one for data transformations and one for control transformations, and a micro rule to describe a processing step of the whole TS using these axioms.

3.1.1 Axiom for control transformations

In the following we present the axiom for control transformations. A control transformation is represented syntactically by $Ktra(A, I, O)$, where A is the identifier of the transformation and I, O denote the sets of its input and output flows.

With every control transformation a finite state automaton is associated which is represented non-graphically by a tuple $M_A = (Z_A, Cond_A, Act_A, \delta_A, z_A, Anf_A)$ where

- Z_A is a set of states,

- $Cond_A$ and Act_A, respectively, denote the input and output alphabets,

- $z_A \in Z_A$ indicates the initial state,

- $Anf_A \in \mathcal{P}(Act_A)$ indicates the output of the automaton when it is initialized, and

- $\delta_A \subseteq ((Z_A \times \text{Cond}_A) \times (Z_A \times \mathcal{P}(\text{Act}_A)))$ determines the change of state and the output upon an input and the actual state.

An automaton M_A has great similarities with a Mealy–automaton (as defined in [Ho88], p.44). M_A differs from a Mealy-automaton in that the relation δ_A of M_A combines the relation of a Mealy-automaton that describes the change of states with a relation that describes the output action following an input in a certain state. Furthermore, Mealy-Automata can not output when they are initialized.

Example 6 (Specification of a control transformation)
We now give an example of a control transformation A which is specified by the state-transition-diagram STD A and also by the equivalent automaton M_A:

Control Transformation : STD A :

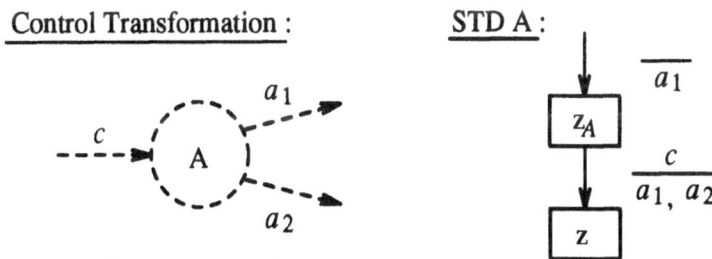

$$M_A = (\{z_A, z\}, \{c\}, \{a_1, a_2\}, \{((z_A, c),(z,\{a_1, a_2\}))\}, z_A, \{a_1\}).$$

Axiom 1
Assume fl, fl' are states of the set of flows $I \cup O$, σ and σ' are states of the control transformation (fl, σ representing the states before and fl' σ' after the processing of A), $in \in I$ (the value along in causes the processing) and $out \subseteq O$ (the flows of out carry the output), so that the following conditions hold:

1. The input flow in is not a Prompt and the following holds:

   (a) The precondition for the processing of the transformation is met:

   $$fl(f) \begin{cases} \neq \bot & , \text{if } f = in \\ = \bot & , \text{if } f \in O \end{cases}$$

   (b) The result of the processing of the transformation is:

   $$(fl', \sigma') = \begin{cases} (fl[\bot/in, 1/out], \sigma'), \\ \qquad \text{if } ((\sigma(A), in), (\sigma'(A), out)) \in \delta_A \\ (fl[\bot/in], \sigma) \wedge out = \emptyset, \text{otherwise.} \end{cases}$$

2. The input flow in is a Prompt, and the following holds:

   (a) The precondition for the processing of the transformation is met:

   $$fl(f) \begin{cases} \neq \bot & , \text{if } f = in \\ = \bot & , \text{if } f \in O \end{cases}$$

(b) The result of the processing of the transformation is:

$$\sigma'(A) = \begin{cases} \sigma(A) & \text{, if } fl(in) = \text{ENABLE} \wedge \sigma(A) \in Z_A, \\ \text{DISABLE} & \text{, if } fl(in) = \text{DISABLE} \end{cases}$$

Then also $fl' = fl[\perp/in]$ and $out = \emptyset$ holds.

$$\sigma'(A) = z_A, \text{if} fl(in) = \text{ENABLE} \wedge \sigma(A) = \text{DISABLE}.$$

Then also $fl' = fl[\perp/in]$ and $out = \text{Anf}_A$ holds.

The axiom is now defined as follows:

$$\boxed{(\text{KTra}(A, I, O), fl, \sigma) \to_{in}^{out} (\text{KTra}(A, I, O), fl', \sigma')}$$

$\square$

Here $fl' = fl[w/z]$ is an abbreviation of $fl'(x) = \begin{cases} w, & \text{if } x = z \text{ or } x \in z, \\ fl(x), & \text{otherwise,} \end{cases}$

where w is an arbitrary value or $\perp$.

3.1.2 Axiom for data transformations

In the following we present the axiom for data transformations. A data transformation is represented syntactically by $\text{Dtra}(A, I, O, Sp)$, where Sp denotes all stores, which can be written or read by the data transformation.

With every data transformation relation f_A a state is associated. The relation f_A specifies the relation between input and output data. The state of a data transformation is a tuple (dt, ds), where $dt(A)$ can be either ENABLE or DISABLE and $ds(A)$ maps every store of Sp to its value.

Axiom 2
Assume fl, fl' are states of the set of flows $I \cup O$, $\sigma = (dt, ds)$ and $\sigma' = (dt', ds')$ are states of the data transformation $in \in I$ and $out \subseteq O$, so that the following conditions hold:

1. The input flow in is a data flow or a Trigger and the following holds:

   (a) The precondition for the processing of the transformation is met:

   $$fl(f) \begin{cases} \neq \perp & \text{, if } f = in, \\ = \perp & \text{, if } f \in O. \end{cases}$$

   (b) The result of the processing of the transformation is:

   $((fl, ds), (fl', ds')) \in f_A$ and $out = \{o \mid fl(o) = \perp \wedge fl'(o) \neq \perp\}$,

   if $dt(A) = \text{ENABLE}$,

   $(fl', ds') = (fl[\perp/in], ds)$ and $out = \emptyset$,

   if $dt(A) = \text{DISABLE}$,

   and $dt' = dt$.

2. The input flow in is a Prompt, and the following holds:

(a) The precondition is met:

$$fl(in) \in \{ \text{ENABLE, DISABLE} \}.$$

(b) The result is:

$$dt'(A) = fl(in), (fl', ds') = fl[\perp/in], ds) \text{ and } out = \emptyset.$$

The axiom is now defined as follows :

$$\boxed{(\text{DTra}(A, I, O, Sp), fl, \sigma) \rightarrow_{in}^{out} (\text{DTra}(A, I, O, Sp), fl', \sigma')}$$

□

In the following we describe how the whole TS behaves if a transformation performs a processing step.

3.1.3 Composed flow

If a transformation R makes a processing step, it changes the values of its input and output flows. As shown in chapter 2.3, putting a value on a flow might result in the appearance of values on other flows because of flow (de)composition. Therefore we must also model changes of values along flows which are connected to input or output flows of R but are not input or output flows of R themselves. In the formal semantics this is characterized as follows.

Example 7 (behaviour of a composed flow)
The result of putting a value on an output flow z composed of two flows z_1 and z_2 is shown below graphically:

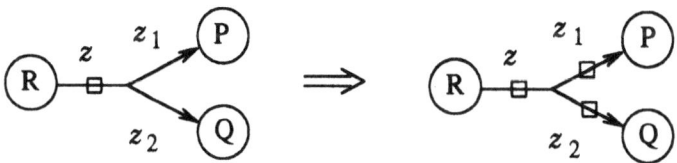

The flow carries structured values composed of values carried along flows z_1 and z_2. Since we restrict in this paper the data types of structured values carried by composed flows to the cartesian product, the data type of z is specified by the equation $z =_T z_1 \times z_2$. We assume that selectors $z.z_1$ and $z.z_2$ ([Jo86 p.119]) map the value carried by flow z to the values which can be carried by flow z_1, respectively, z_2.

To define a formula describing the result of an output along flow z, as shown graphically above, assume O_k is the set of output flows of R and fl_k, fl_k' are states of the input and output flows of transformation R (before and after the processing of R). Assume also fl, fl' are states of the set $\mathcal{F}$ of flows of the whole TS (before and after the processing of R). Now this formula is:

$$(\forall_{z \in O_k} : fl'(z) = fl_k'(z)) \wedge$$
$$(\forall_{z, z_1, \dots, z_n \in \mathcal{F}} : (fl(z) = \perp \wedge fl'(z) \neq \perp \wedge (z =_T z_1 \times \dots \times z_n))$$
$$\Rightarrow \forall_{i \in \{1, \dots, n\}} : fl'(z_i) = z.z_i(fl'(z)))$$

This formula describes the case that component flows are composed by a product. In the way this example is described by a formula also all other cases can be described. The complete formula is called RESULT(fl, fl', fl_k'), and is used below in the micro rule for parallel composition. We present this formula in Appendix A.

3.1.4 Parallel composition

A Transformation Schema is a network of $n \in \mathbf{N}$ components T_k, $k \in \{1, ..., n\}$, each one of which has I_k as its set of input flows, and O_k as its set of output flows. In this part we restrict these components to control transformations. (Data transformations are handled in the same way). The TS is represented non graphically by $T = (T_1 \parallel ... \parallel T_n)$. Consequently, a micro configuration $((T_1 \parallel ... \parallel T_n), fl, \sigma)$ induces by convention micro configurations (T_i, fl_i, σ_i) for the components T_i of $T_1 \parallel ... \parallel T_n$, for $i \in \{1, ..., n\}$. In the following we sketch the micro rule defining how the whole TS behaves if a transformation does a processing step.

Micro rule 3
Define $\mathcal{F}$ as the set of flows of T. Assume fl is the state of $\mathcal{F}$ which meets $\forall_{x \in (I_k \cup O_k)} : fl(x) = fl_k(x)$ and fl' is a state of $\mathcal{F}$, for which the formula RESULT(fl, fl', fl'_k) given above holds, which determines how the states fl, fl', fl'_k depend on each other, taking the semantics of a composed flow into account.

Then micro rule 2 for the parallel composition of TS is defined as follows, $n \geq 2, k \in \{1, ..., n\}$:

$$
\frac{
\begin{array}{c}
((T_k, fl_k, \sigma_k) \rightarrow_{in}^{out} (T_k, fl'_k, \sigma'_k)) \\
\mathrm{RESULT}(fl, fl', fl'_k) \\
\forall_{i \in \{1,...,n\} \setminus \{k\}} : \sigma_i = \sigma'_i
\end{array}
}{
((T_1 \parallel ... \parallel T_n), fl, \sigma) \rightarrow_{in}^{out} ((T_1 \parallel ... \parallel T_n), fl', \sigma')
}
$$

$\square$

Thus, we adopt an interleaving semantics.

3.2 Internal sequence of micro steps

Internal sequences of micro steps represent the way the input from the outside world is processed by a TS. Members of our family of semantics can be characterized by properties of the internal sequence of micro steps as *maximal* or *recursive-causal-chain*. These properties are closely related to statements made in [Wa86].

3.2.1 Maximal

One statement describing the internal processing of a TS in [Wa86] is as follows: 'the consequences of the arrival of a value on a flow from outside the schema are worked out before any other value from outside the schema is accepted, and the execution of simultaneously arriving values on flows from outside the schema is sequential but in indeterminate order.'

In terms of our formal semantics this statement is represented by the restriction that every internal sequence of micro steps must be maximal.

Definition 3.1 (maximal)
An internal sequence of micro steps is maximal if all possible micro steps due to one particular input from the outside world are part of the internal sequence.

□

If a maximal sequence is finite and consists of $n - 1 \in \mathbf{N}$ micro steps, we write

$$(T, fl_1, \sigma_1) \rightarrow_{in_1}^{out_1} \ldots \rightarrow_{in_{n-1}}^{out_{n-1}} (T, fl_n, \sigma_n) \not\rightarrow.$$

If a maximal sequence is infinite, we write

$$(T, fl_1, \sigma_1) \uparrow_{in_1}.$$

3.2.2   Recursive-causal-chain

Another statement concerning the further internal processing of input in [Wa86] is: 'in case of simultaneous placement of a number of tokens, the execution rules specify carrying out the interactions sequentially but in an arbitrary order.' ... 'each branch of the interaction is carried out till its conclusion before returning to the next one. If subbranches are encountered during an interaction, another arbitrary sequencing decision is made and the procedure is applied recursively.'

In terms of our formal semantics this statement is modelled by the restriction that the internal sequence of micro steps must be a recursive-causal-chain. It consists of a sequence of causal chains. A causal chain is a sequence of micro steps following each other as a result of causal dependency. In a micro step $(T, fl_i, \sigma_i) \rightarrow_{in}^{out} (T, fl_{i+1}, \sigma_{i+1})$, $i \in \mathbf{N}$ the output on out causally depends on the input on in. As a consequence of a discrete output on out, another transition might be triggered, etc.

Definition 3.2 (causal chain(m,n))
For an internal sequence the predicate $causal\ chain(m, n)$, $m, n \in \mathbf{N}, m \leq n$ holds, if it is a sequence

$$(T, fl_m, \sigma_m) \rightarrow_{in_m}^{out_m} (T, fl_{m+1}, \sigma_{m+1}) \rightarrow_{in_{m+1}}^{out_{m+1}} \ldots \rightarrow_{in_{n-1}}^{out_{n-1}} (T, fl_n, \sigma_n)$$

of micro steps, where $n = m + 1$ or

for all $i \in \{m + 1, \ldots, n - 1\}$ $fl_{i-1}(in_i) = \bot \wedge fl_i(in_i) \neq \bot$ holds,

and no micro step $(T, fl_n, \sigma_n) \rightarrow_{in_n}^{out_n} (T, fl_{n+1}, \sigma_{n+1})$ exists with

$$fl_n(in_n) = \bot \wedge fl_{n+1}(in_n) \neq \bot.$$

□

In a micro step more than one output value can be produced. The consumption of these values is non deterministic and in sequential order. An output value can cause a causal chain. If such is the case, the steps in this chain are taken *before* another output value of the micro step is consumed.

To characterize the first input flow in_k leading to a new causal chain, we define the predicate $con(i, k, x)$, $i, k \in \{1, ..., n\}$, $x \in \mathcal{F}$ below. It holds for a sequence of micro steps if the value on flow x produced in the i-th micro step has not been consumed till the k-th step and now can be consumed in the k-th step.

Definition 3.3 ($con(i, k, x)$)

$$con(i, k, x) =_{Def} (i = 1 \ \vee \ fl_i(x) = \bot) \ \wedge \ (\forall_{j \in \{i+1, ..., k\}} : fl_j(x) \neq \bot)$$
$$\wedge \ (\exists_{fl_x \in \mathrm{FL}(\mathcal{F}), \sigma_x \in \Sigma, out_x \subseteq \mathcal{F}} : (T, fl_k, \sigma_k) \rightarrow_x^{out_x} (T, fl_x, \sigma_x))$$

□

A value on flow in_k is consumed in a new corresponding causal chain when, recursively, all more recently produced values on flows for which consumption was possible have been consumed by corresponding causal chains. That is to say, this condition imposes a lastly-produced-first-consumed discipline upon the generation of new causal chains. This is expressed by $start \ new(in_k, k)$, where in_k is an input flow for the k-th micro step in the internal sequence:

Definition 3.4 (start new(in_k, k))

$$start \ new(in_k, k) =_{Def} \quad \exists_{i \in \{1, ..., k\}} : (\ con(i, k, in_k) \ \wedge$$
$$\neg \exists_{j \in \{i+1, ..., k\}} \exists_{x \in \mathcal{F}} : con(j, k, x))$$

□

Assume an internal sequence of micro steps of length $n \in \mathbf{N}$ or $n = \infty$, where the micro configurations are numbered from 1 to n. Now the predicate recursive-causal-chain(n) can be defined as follows.

Definition 3.5 (recursive-causal-chain(n))

$$recursive\text{-}causal\text{-}chain(n) =_{Def}$$
$$(n = 1 \wedge maximal) \vee$$
$$\exists_{m \in \{1, ..., n-1\}, m_1, ..., m_m \in \{1, ..., n\}} \forall_{i \in \{1, ..., m\}} : m_i \leq m_{i+1} \ \wedge$$
$$(\exists_{x \in \mathcal{F}} : start \ new(x, m_i)) \ \wedge \ causal \ chain(m_i, m_{i+1})$$

□

3.3 Macro step

A macro step represents a reaction on an input sent by the outside world of a Transformation Schema $T(I, O)$, where I is the set of flows of the TS coming from the outside world and O the set of flows of the TS directed towards the outside world. Correspondingly, a macro configuration (T, fl, σ) is defined similarly as a micro configuration, except that fl is a mapping of just $I \cup O$ (and not of all the flows of T) to the values carried on these flows. The macro step itself is defined as a labeled transition between macro configurations, which is derived from an internal sequence of micro steps. This is defined formally by the following macro rules. Depending on the different properties which the internal sequences of micro steps should satisfy, different macro rules and a *family of semantics* for TS are defined.

3.3.1 Recursive causal chain semantics

This semantics most closely reflects Ward's original ideas described in [Wa86], which are mentioned in section 3.2.1 and 3.2.2. Each internal sequence of micro steps must be maximal and must be a recursive causal chain. After each internal sequence of micro steps all values left on flows which could not be consumed are cleared before a new internal sequence of micro steps starts. Formally this is represented by:

Macro rule 4

Let $\mathcal{F}$ be the set of flows of T. Assume

- $(T, fl_1, \sigma_1) \rightarrow_{out_1}^{in_1} \cdots \rightarrow_{out_{n-1}}^{in_{n-1}} (T, fl_n, \sigma_n)$ with $n \in \mathbf{N}$ is an internal sequence of micro-steps of T, where

    - maximal and recursive-causal-chain($\{1, \ldots, n-1\}$) holds,
    - fl_1 satisfies $\forall_{z \in \mathcal{F} \backslash (I \cup O)} : fl_1(z) = \bot$,

- $in, out \subseteq (I \cup O)$, where $in = \{ x \in (I \cup O) \mid fl_{in}(x) \neq \bot \}$ and $out = O \cap \bigcup_{i=1}^{n} \{out_i\}$,

- fl_{in} is a state of $(I \cup O)$ which meets $\forall_{x \in (I \cup O)} : fl_{in}(x) = fl_1(x)$,

- fl_{out} is a state of $(I \cup O)$, which meets $\forall_{x \in (I \cup O)} : fl_{out}(x) = fl_n(x)$.

The macro rule 4.1 is defined as follows:

$$\frac{(T, fl_1, \sigma_1) \rightarrow_{in_1}^{out_1} \cdots \rightarrow_{in_{n-1}}^{out_{n-1}} (T, fl_n, \sigma_n) \nrightarrow}{(T, fl_{in}, \sigma_1) \Rightarrow_{in}^{out} (T, fl_{out}, \sigma_n)}$$

Assume $(T, fl_1, \sigma_1) \uparrow_{in_1}$ is an infinite internal sequence of micro steps, where recursive-causal-chain($\mathbf{N}$) holds, $in \subset (I \cup O)$ and fl_{in} is a state of $I \cup O$ as defined above, then the macro rule 4.2 is defined as follows:

$$\frac{(T, fl_1, \sigma_1) \uparrow_{in_1}}{(T, fl_{in}, \sigma_1) \uparrow_{in}}$$

$\square$

3.3.2 Weakly fair interleaving semantics

This semantics does not reflect Ward's statement mentioned in section 3.2.2, but the statement mentioned in 3.2.1. It has the same initialization and termination rules as the recursive causal chain semantics, but drops the recursive-causal-chain condition by allowing *any* possible transition to be taken for each micro step. The name given to this semantics is motivated by the fact that non-diverging specifications automatically possess a weak fairness property. This will be discussed in another article [PHP93].

3.3.3 Full interleaving semantics

This semantics drops the input restrictions by allowing new inputs from the environment to be placed and processed at each micro step. Every internal sequence of micro steps has a length of one. As a result no observable difference between macro and micro steps remains, and therefore macro steps are identified with micro steps. As a consequence there is no situation, where values placed on flows are cleared because they are left over after an internal sequence of micro steps.

3.4 Discussion of the family of semantics

Our family of semantics is not complete because one can easily think of more semantics fitting into the above framework. Therefore it is important to reflect upon the use of each semantics. One aspect is the *application area* of 'real-world' systems. Another aspect depends on more mathematical properties such as *modularity*. Modularity as described in 1.3 is important for expanding a TS, where parts of the old environment become part of a new bigger TS.

3.4.1 Application area

Our opinion is that every member of our family of semantics has its own application area in the 'real-world'. In [PHP93] an example from the field of fault-tolerant systems serves as a 'benchmark problem' to investigate the practical applicability of the above defined semantics. As a solution the best semantics for this purpose is the weakly fair interleaving semantics. With the recursive causal chain semantics it is not possible to model the system, whereas with the full interleaving semantics this is possible, but with an inappropiate level of abstraction.

3.4.2 Modularity

The full interleaving semantics models the extended interface of a proper part of a TS with the outside world in the same way as the internal interface inside the TS.

Both semantics, the recursive causal chain semantics and the weakly fair interleaving semantics are not modular because they are maximal. This is shown informally in example 5, which we now formalize.

Example 8 (different interfaces)
A Transformation Schema T is presented non-graphically by $T(I, O)$ in the view of the outside world. Symbol I stands for the set of all input flows and symbol O for the set of all output flows of T. A Transformation Schema is presented internally by the parallel composition (expressed by '$\|$') of the non-graphical presentation of its constituent transformations. Below we give a formal presentation of Transformation Schemas T_1 and T_2 of example 5:

$$T_1(\{a, e\}, \{b, d\}) = (\text{Ktra}(K_1, \{a\}, \{b, c\}) \| \text{Ktra}(K_2, \{c, e\}, \{d\}))$$

$$T_2(\{a\}, \{d\}) = T_1(\{a, e\}, \{b, d\}) \| \text{KTra}(K_3, \{b\}, \{e\})$$

The associated specifications are:

$$M_{K_1} = (\{z\}, \{a\}, \{b, c\}, \{((z, a), (z, \{b, c\}))\}, z, \emptyset),$$

$$M_{K_2} = (\{z_1, z_2\}, \{c, e\}, \{d\}, \{((z_1, c), (z_1, \{d\})), ((z_1, e), (z_2, \emptyset))\}, z_1, \emptyset) \text{and}$$

$$M_{K_3} = (\{z\}, \{b\}, \{e\}, \{((z, b), (z, \{e\}))\}, z, \emptyset).$$

1. The only possible macro step of T_1 upon an input on flow a is (case 1 of exp. 5):

$$(\sigma, fl_i) \Rightarrow_a^{\{b, d\}} (\sigma, fl_o), \text{ where}$$

$\sigma \in \Sigma$, $\sigma(K_1) = z$ and $\sigma(K_2) = z_1$, as well as $fl_i, fl_o \in FL(\{a, b, d, e\})$, where the following conditions hold:

$$fl_i(f) = \begin{cases} 1 & \text{, if } f = a, \\ \bot & \text{, otherwise,} \end{cases} \text{ and } fl_o(f) = \begin{cases} 1 & \text{, if } f \in \{b, d\}, \\ \bot & \text{, otherwise.} \end{cases}$$

This is the only macro step that occurs, because there exists only one maximal sequence of micro steps upon an input on flow a, as shown below:

$$(\sigma, fl_1) \rightarrow_a^{\{b, c\}} (\sigma, fl_2) \rightarrow_c^d (\sigma, fl_3) \text{ , where}$$

for all $i \in \{1, 2, 3\}$, $fl_i \in FL(\{a, b, c, d, e\})$ such that the following conditions hold:

$$fl_1(f) = \begin{cases} 1 & \text{, if } f = a \\ \bot & \text{, otherwise} \end{cases} \quad , fl_2(f) = \begin{cases} 1 & \text{, if } f \in \{b, c\} \\ \bot & \text{, otherwise} \end{cases}$$

as well as

$$fl_3(f) = \begin{cases} 1 & \text{, if } f \in \{b, d\}, \\ \bot & \text{, otherwise.} \end{cases}$$

2. A possible macro step of T_2 upon an input on flow a is (case 2 of exp. 5):

$$(fl_i, \sigma) \Rightarrow_a^{\emptyset} (fl_o, \sigma[z_2/K_2]), \text{where}$$

$\sigma \in \Sigma$, $\sigma(K_1) = z$, $\sigma(K_3) = z$ and $\sigma(K_2) = z_1$, as well as $fl_i, fl_o \in FL(\{a, d\})$ such that the following conditions hold:

$$fl_i(f) = \begin{cases} 1 & \text{, if } f = a \\ \bot & \text{, otherwise} \end{cases} \text{ and } fl_o(f) = \bot \text{ for all} f \in \{a, b, c, d, e\}.$$

A possible maximal sequence of micro steps upon an input on flow a is:

$$(fl_1, \sigma) \to_a^{\{b,c\}} (fl_2, \sigma) \to_b^e (fl'_3, \sigma) \to_e (fl'_4, \sigma[z_2/K_2]) \to^c (fl'_5, \sigma[z_2/K_2])$$

where for $i \in \{1, 2\}$, fl_i are defined above in point 1, and, for $i \in \{3, 4, 5\}$, $fl_i' \in FL(\{a, b, c, d, e\})$ s.t. the following conditions hold:

$$fl'_3(f) = \begin{cases} 1 & \text{, if } f \in \{c, e\} \\ \bot & \text{, otherwise} \end{cases} \quad , fl'_4(f) = \begin{cases} 1 & \text{, if } f = c \\ \bot & \text{, otherwise} \end{cases}$$

as well as

$$fl'_5(f) = \bot \text{ for all } f \in \{a, b, c, d, e\}.$$

$\square$

Appendix: Formula RESULT(fl, fl', fl'_k)

As promised earlier, we give here the complete formula RESULT(fl, fl'_k, fl'). This formula models the dependency of a state of the set of all flows of a transformation schema fl ($\in FL(\mathcal{F})$) before and fl' ($\in FL(\mathcal{F})$) after a processing step of a transformation R with the knowledge of the state of the flows of R after the processing step $fl_k'(FL(I_k \cup O_k))$.

On one hand, taking away a value of an input flow by R can result in the change of other flows conected to the input flow. On the other hand, placing produced values on output flows can also result in the change of other flows connected to the output flows. These two changes are modeled by two formulas $Outfl(fl, fl'_k, fl')$ and $Infl(fl, fl'_k, fl')$ which are defined below.

Both formulas consist of four cases depending on different kind of flows and their specifications. For their definition we introduce two formulas $komp^+(z_n, z, \ldots, z_{n-1})$ and $komp^|(z_n, z, \ldots, z_{n-1})$. The first holds, if and only if a data dictionary entry $z =_T z + \ldots + z_{n-1}$ or a similar one with a permutation of $z, \ldots, z_{n-1}$ exists. The second holds if and only if a datadictionary entry $z =_T [z | \ldots | z_{n-1}]$ or a similar one with a permutation of $z, \ldots, z_{n-1}$ exists. Not only are flows determined by their components but also by their direction. The formulas $together(z, z_1, \ldots, z_n)$ and $break(z, z_1, \ldots, z_n)$ are used to distinguish the different kinds of directions of flows. Examples can be seen in the pictures of case 1,3 respectively 2,4 of the illustration of both formulas below.

The set of possible values on a flow z is called W_z. Now we define the formulas $Outfl(fl, fl'_k, fl')$ and $Infl(fl, fl'_k, fl')$ and illustrate them with pictures, as we sketched in example 7 above.

Definition 3.6 (Formula Outfl)
For $fl, fl' \in FL(\mathcal{F})$ and $fl'_k \in FL(I_k \cup O_k)$ let $Outfl(fl, fl'_k, fl')$ be the formula

$$(\forall_{z \in O_k} : fl'(z) = fl'_k(z)) \wedge$$

$$(\forall_{z, z_1, \ldots, z_n \in \mathcal{F}} : (fl(z) = \bot \wedge fl'(z) \neq \bot) \Rightarrow ($$

1. $((z =_T z_1 + \ldots + z_n \wedge \text{break}(z, z_1, \ldots, z_n))$
   $\Rightarrow \forall_{i \in \{1,\ldots,n\}} : fl'(z_i) = z.z_i(fl'(z))$
   $)$

2. $\wedge ((\text{komp}^+(z_n, z, \ldots, z_{n-1}) \wedge \text{together}(z_n, z, \ldots, z_{n-1}) \wedge$
   $\forall_{i \in \{1,\ldots,n-1\}} : fl(z_i) \neq \bot)$
   $\Rightarrow (z_n.z(fl'(z_n)) = fl'(z) \wedge$
   $\forall_{i \in \{1,\ldots,n-1\}} : z_n.z_i(fl'(z_n)) = fl(z_i))$
   $)$

3. $\wedge ((z =_T [z_1| \ldots |z_n] \wedge \text{break}(z, z_1, \ldots, z_n))$
   $\Rightarrow (\exists_{i \in \{1,\ldots,n\}} : (fl'(z_i) = fl'(z) \wedge$
   $\forall_{j \in \{1,\ldots,n\} \setminus \{i\}} : fl'(z_j) = \bot))$
   $)$

4. $\wedge ((\text{komp}^|(z_n, z, \ldots, z_{n-1}) \wedge \text{together}(z_n, z, \ldots, z_{n-1}))$
   $\Rightarrow (fl'(z_n) = fl'(z) \wedge \forall_{i \in \{1,\ldots,n-1\}} : fl'(z_i) \in W_{z_i})$
   $)$

$)) \square$

The graphical illustration of the four cases are the following examples.

1. $z = z_1 + z_2$

2. $z_2 = z + z_1$

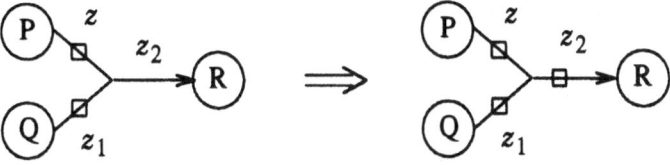

3. $z = [z_1|z_2]$

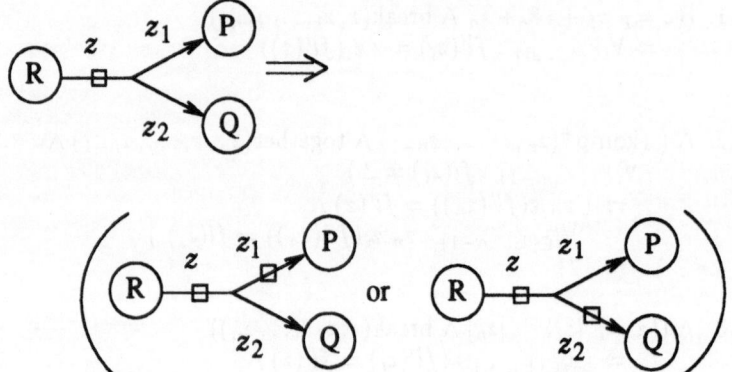

4. $z_2 = [z|z_1]$

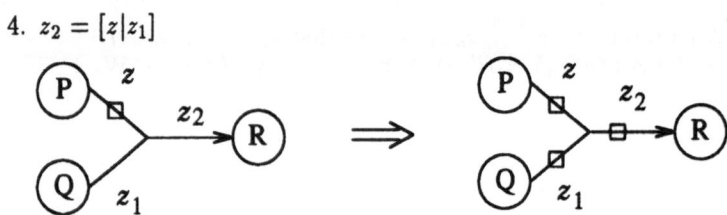

Definition 3.7 (Formula Infl)

For $fl, fl' \in \mathrm{FL}(\mathcal{F})$ and $fl'_k \in \mathrm{FL}(I_k \cup O_k)$ let $\mathrm{Infl}(fl, fl'_k, fl')$ be the formula

$(\forall_{z \in I_k} : fl'(z) = fl'_k(z)) \wedge$

$(\forall_{z, z_1, \dots, z_n \in \mathcal{F}} : (fl(z) \neq \bot \wedge fl'(z) = \bot) \Rightarrow ($

    1. $((z =_T z_1 + \dots + z_n \wedge \mathrm{together}(z, z_1, \dots, z_n))$
           $\Rightarrow \forall_{i \in \{1, \dots, n\}} : fl'(z_i) = \bot$
      $)$

    2. $\wedge\ ((\mathrm{komp}^+(z_n, z, \dots, z_{n-1}) \wedge \mathrm{break}(z_n, z, \dots, z_{n-1}) \wedge$
           $\forall_{i \in \{1, \dots, n-1\}} : fl'(z_i) = \bot)$
           $\Rightarrow fl(z_n) = \bot$
      $)$

    3. $\wedge\ ((z =_T [z_1| \dots |z_n] \wedge \mathrm{together}(z, z_1, \dots, z_n))$
           $\Rightarrow \forall_{i \in \{1, \dots, n\}} : fl'(z_i) = \bot$
      $)$

    4. $\wedge\ ((\mathrm{komp}^|(z_n, z, \dots, z_{n-1}) \wedge \mathrm{break}(z_n, z, \dots, z_{n-1}))$
           $\Rightarrow fl'(z_n) = \bot$
      $)$

$))\ \square$

Case 1, 2 and 4 are illustrated below and are similar to the *Outfl* formula.
Case 3 with $z = [z_1 | z_2]$ is represented graphically as case 1.

1. $z = z_1 + z_2$

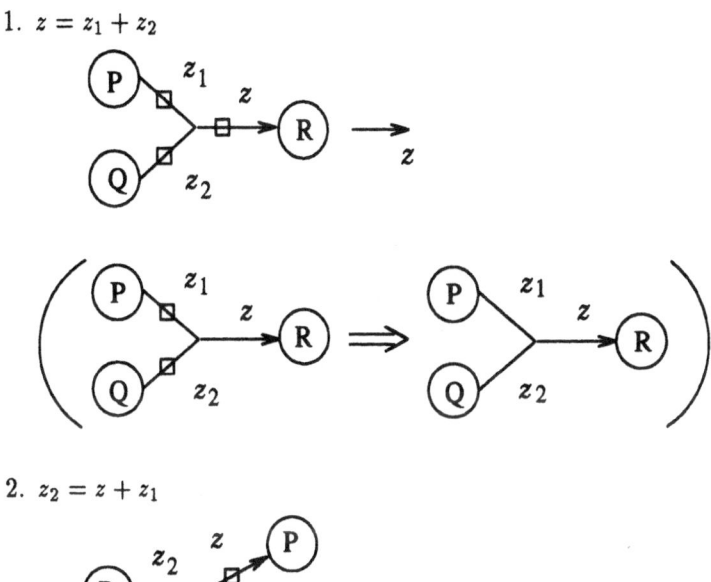

2. $z_2 = z + z_1$

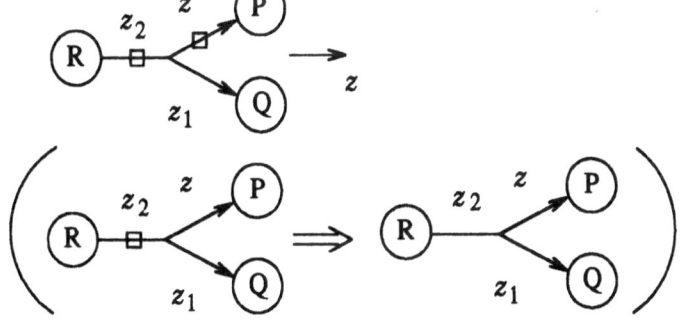

4. $z_2 = [z|z_1]$

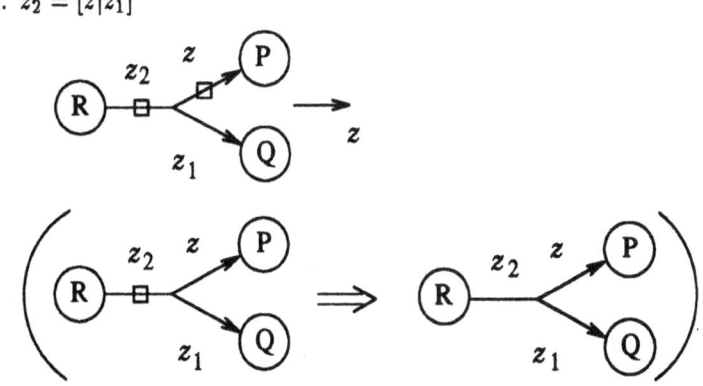

Both formulas $Infl(fl, fl_k{}', fl')$ and $Outfl(fl, fl_k{}', fl')$ determines changes from the old state fl to the new state fl' of the set of all flows $\mathcal{F}$. But the values of a flow x which is not connected with an input or output flow of transformation R is not determined by these formulas. Therefore a state fl'' could exist which models a change of the value of the flow x, (e.g. $fl'(x) \neq fl(x)$

holds), which is not caused by the processing step of R and is therefore arbitrary. To exclude this phenomenon the formula $Definite(fl, fl_k, fl')$ is defined as follows.

Definition 3.8 (Formula Definite)
For $fl, fl' \in FL(\mathcal{F})$ and $fl_k' \in FL(I_k \cup O_k)$ let $Definite(fl, fl_k', fl')$ be the formula

$$\neg \exists_{fl'' \in FL(\mathcal{F})} \exists_{x \in \mathcal{F}} : \mathrm{Infl}(fl, fl_k', fl'') \wedge \mathrm{Outfl}(fl, fl_k', fl'') \wedge$$
$$fl''(x) = fl(x) \wedge fl''(x) \neq fl'(x)$$

The formula $RESULT(fl, fl_k', fl')$ is now defined with the above defined formulas.

Definition 3.9 (Formula RESULT)
For $fl, fl' \in FL(\mathcal{F})$ and $fl_k' \in FL(I_k \cup O_k)$ let $RESULT(fl, fl_k', fl')$ be the formula

$$\mathrm{Infl}(fl, fl_k', fl') \wedge \mathrm{Outfl}(fl, fl_k', fl') \wedge \mathrm{Definite}(fl, fl_k', fl')$$

References

[BCH85] J.-L. Bergerand, P. Caspi, and N. Halbwachs. *Outline of a real-time data flow language.* In *Proceedings IEEE Real-Time Systems Symposium,* 1985.

[Benveniste and Berry 92] A. Benveniste and G. Berry *The Synchronous Approach to Reactive and Real-Time Systems,* in IEEE-Proceedings *"Another Look at Real-Time Programming",* 1992.

[BG88] G. Berry and G. Gonthier. *The esterel synchronous programming language: Design, semantics, implementation.* Technical report, Ecole Nationale Supérieur des Mines de Paris, 1988.

[Davis 90] Alan M. Davis *Software Requirements: analysis and specification,* Prentice-Hall, 1990.

[Ha88] D. Harel *On visual formalisms.* Communications of the ACM, 31:514–530, 1988.

[Ha90] D. Harel, H. Lachover, A. Naamad, A. Pnueli, M. Politi, R. Sherman, A. Shtull-Trauring, and M. Trakhtenbrot. *Statemate: A working environment for the development of complex reactive systems.* IEEE Transactions on Software Engineering, 16(4):403–414, April 1990.

[HG89] C. Huizing and R. Gerth. *On the semantics of reactive systems.* Technical report, Eindhoven University of Technology, 1989.

[Hatley and Pirbhai 88] Derek J. Hatley and Imtiaz A. Pirbhai *Strategies for Real-Time System Specification,* Dorset House Publ. Co., 1988.

[HGdR88] C. Huizing, R. Gerth, and W.-P. de Roever. *Modelling statecharts behaviour in a fully abstract way*. In *Proc. 13th CAAP*, LNCS 299, pages 271–294, 1988.

[HPPSS87] D. Harel, A. Pnueli, J. Pruzan-Schmidt, and R. Sherman. *On the formal semantics of Statecharts*. In *Proceedings Symposium on Logic in Computer Science*, pages 54–64, 1987.

[Ho88] Hopcroft, J.E. *Einführung in die Automatentheorie, Formale Sprachen und Komplexitätstheorie*. Addison-Wesley (Deutschland) GmbH (1988).

[Huizing and Gerth 92] C. Huizing and R.T. Gerth *Semantics of Reactive Systems in Abstract Time*, in *"Real-Time: Theory in Practice"*, proceedings of a REX workshop, June 1991, Mook, edited by J.W. de Bakker, W.-P. de Roever, G. Rozenberg, LNCS 600, Springer Verlag, Berlin, Heidelberg, 1992.

[Jo86] Cliff B. Jones *Systematic Software Development Using VDM*. Prentice-Hall International series in computer science (1986).

[Peleska] Jan Peleska. *Design and Verification of Fault Tolerant Systems using CSP*, Distributed Computing, 1991.

[PHP93] C. Petersohn, C. Hiuzing, J. Peleska. *Comparison of Ward&Mellor's TRANSFORMATION SCHEMA with STATECHARTS.*, Technical report, Christian-Albrechts-Universität Kiel, 1992. submitted.

[Place,Wood and Tudball 90] P.R.H. Place, W.G. Wood and M. Tudball, *Survey of Formal Specification Techniques for Reactive Systems*, Technical Report, Software Engineering Inst., CMU 1990.

[Pl83] Plotkin, G. *An operational semantics for CSP*. In *Proceedings of the IFIP Conference on the Formal Description of Programming Concepts II*, North Holland (1983) pp. 199-225.

[PS88] A. Pnueli and M. Shalev. *What is in a step*. Technical report, Department of Applied Mathematics and Computer Science, The Weizmann Institute of Science, Rehovot, Israel, 1988, Draft.

[Pt92] Carsta Petersohn *Modellierung reaktiver Systeme mit Transformationsschema und ein Vergleich mit Activity- und Statecharts*, Master's thesis, report, Christian–Albrechts–Universität zu Kiel, 1992.

[Wa86] Paul T. Ward, The Transformation Schema: *An Extension of the Data Flow Diagram to Represent Control and Timing*, IEEE TSE, Vol. SE-12, No. 2, pp. 198-210, Febr. 1986.

[WM85] Paul T. Ward and Stephen J. Mellor *Structured Development for Real-Time Systems* (3 vols), Yourdon Press Computing Series, Prentice-Hall, Englewood Cliffs, 1985.

[Wo] D.P. Wood and W.G. Wood *Comparative Evaluations of Specification Methods for Real-Time Systems*, draft, September 1989.

Submitted Papers

Improving the Process of System Specification and Refinement in B

K. Lano, H. Haughton

Lloyd's Register,
Croydon, UK

Abstract

This paper describes systematic approaches to the formalisation and refinement of domain and analysis models in the B Abstract Machine Notation (AMN). These are intended to improve the process of formalisation of requirements, and the feasibility of formal development from these formalised requirements.

Static and dynamic models are addressed, and a comparison of the effectiveness of two alternative approaches to formalisation is performed, based upon the proof requirements generated by these approaches. A strategy for refinement to code and reuse of existing developments in the context of the B methodology is also described. A number of case studies are used to illustrate the approach.

1 Introduction

We take the view that there are two significant barriers to the widespread adoption of fully formal development processes for high integrity systems:

- there are few methods for the integration of formal notations with current industrial software engineering practice (including modelling techniques such as state charts and ERA models);

- the practicality of proof, particularly refinement proofs, is still poor for existing formal methods and tools.

The benefits of using formal methods and structured methods together for high-integrity systems are becoming recognised by a number of groups, for example the work of Coleman at Hewlett-Packard [3], or of Hill at Rolls-Royce Associates [11]. The structured notations assist in the correct development of specifications (correct with respect to the user requirements), and the formal notations assist in the correct development of code (correct with respect to the specification). Both aspects are clearly essential for a safety-critical system. The IEC 65A 122 standard for safety-critical software also recommends the use of both structured and formal methods for software of the highest integrity level [21].

In this paper, we address in part each of these problems, and show how solutions to the first can suggest solutions to the second.

A substantial amount of work has been performed on the formalisation of structured method notations such as SSADM [4], and OMT [20] in formal specification languages. Some Z-based approaches are described in [17, 19, 6,

15]. Particularly in the security domain, significant software development and formal proof of systems have been performed using an integrated approach [7], in addition, software engineering methods such as FUSION [2], developed by Hewlett-Packard, are also adopting a combination of formal and diagrammatic notations (in this case, a VDM variant and OMT). Formal languages are used to add semantics to informal notations, and the informal notations are used to provide an easily comprehensible presentation of the formal specifications.

However there needs to be some means by which the quality of the formalisation and the strength of the link between the informal and formal models can be assessed. In this paper we provide systematic mapping techniques which can be used to correctly capture the standard meaning of data and dynamic models of the OMT notations in an initial formal specification. This mapping not only helps guide the correct development of code, but assists in the practicality of proof and the possibility of reuse of user theories for resolving the proof obligations which arise in development. OMT has been chosen because the meaning of its notations are relatively well-defined and unambiguous, and because its notations are consistent with standard notations used in software engineering.

In section 2 we introduce the B AMN language. In section 3 we describe the representation of data models, in sections 4 and 5 we describe two alternative representations of state models, and in section 6 the refinement and reuse of system specifications in order to quickly generate correct (although possibly inefficient) code.

2   Introduction to B

A brief introduction to the syntax of B Abstract Machines is given here. Full details of the language can be found in [1].

A general machine (without DEFINITIONS or ASSERTIONS) can be written in the form:

```
MACHINE  N(p)
CONSTRAINTS C
CONSTANTS k
PROPERTIES B
VARIABLES v
INVARIANT I
INITIALISATION T
OPERATIONS
    y  ←  op(x)  =
        PRE  P
        THEN
            S
        END
    . . . .
END
```

where declared SETS are combined with the constants k.

The machine N can be parameterised by a list of set-valued or scalar-valued parameters. The logical properties of these parameters are specified in the CONSTRAINTS of the machine. Optionally, constants, corresponding to axiomatic definitions in Z, can be declared in the CONSTANTS section. The definitions of these constants are given in the PROPERTIES section.

The variables of the machine are listed in the VARIABLES section. The constraints on the variables, including the typing of the variables, are specified in the INVARIANT of the machine. DEFINITIONS of mathematical abbreviations can be given in terms of the state variables and constants. The initialisation operation of the machine is specified in the INITIALISATION section of the machine. The methods or operations of the machine are listed in the OPERATIONS section. Input parameters are listed after the name of the operation in its definition, and output parameters are listed to the left of an arrow from the operation name.

3   Formalising Data Models

Entity relationship attribute (ERA) models provide an overview of the abstract entities in a system being specified, and support partitioning of a system into conceptually coherent subparts. They present candidates for modules and (in B terms) machines in the design of the system. From a user's viewpoint, they provide a simple description of the static properties of the system. The ERA notation we will adopt is that of Rumbaugh (OMT) object model diagrams [20].

Object models consist of named boxes for entities or object classes, in which all non-object valued attributes of the class are listed, together with their types. Relationships between entities are represented by lines. The number of participants in a relationship is indicated by means of circles or numeric annotations: a filled circle at the end of a line indicates that the adjacent entity may occur zero or more times in this relationship with one instance of the source entity. An unfilled circle indicates zero or one occurrences. A line with no circles indicates a 1:1 relationship.

Inheritance and specialisation can also be explicitly signalled on an object model diagram. An example of an object model, of a set of lines and boxes, is shown in Figure 1.

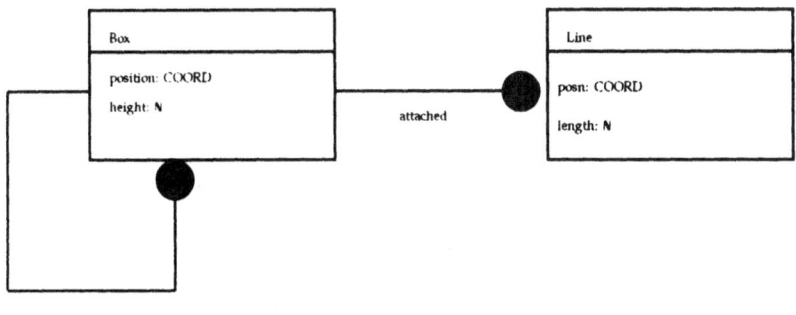

Figure 1: Object Model of Lines and Boxes

In this system, each box may be *connected* to many other boxes and may be *attached* to many lines.

Approximately, entity types in a OMT object model will be expressed as B machines, encapsulating the sets of possible and existing instances of the entity type, and a set of functions representing attributes of the type. Links between entity types are represented using the B inclusion mechanisms for machines.

The following process model can be used to map analysis models expressed in OMT object model notation into systems of B machines:

1. identify the *families* of entity types in the data model – that is, the sets of entity types which are subtypes of a given type T which has itself no supertypes;

2. identify the *access paths* which are needed by operations and attributes of the types within each family to types in other families;

3. on this basis, produce a directed acyclic graph, whose nodes are the families, and whose edges are inclusion relationships USES or SEES between the nodes;

4. define machines for each family, following the procedure outlined below, and include machines in other machines using the relationships identified in the previous step.

Note that step 3 may not always be possible. Cycles $A \to A$ are allowed in the graph, but cycles $A \to B$, $B \to A$ or longer cycles are not allowed (they would lead to cycles in the machine inclusion relations, which are not allowed). If such cycles are required in the system (rather than being a feature of the general domain), then the entities concerned must all be placed in a single abstract machine.

The simple case of an entity without subtypes (that is, of a family containing a single type) will be considered first. In step 4 in this case, each concept **Entity** with attributes or links **att1** : T1, **att2** : T2, ..., **attn** : Tn will have a corresponding machine *Entity.mch* of the form

```
MACHINE Entity
SETS
   ENTITY
VARIABLES
   entities,
   att1, att2, ..., attn
INVARIANT
   entities <: ENTITY &

   att1 : entities --> T1 &
   att2 : entities --> T2 &
   .....
   attn : entities --> Tn
   .....
END
```

This machine models a collection of **Entity** instances, rather than a single entity. If only one instance of the **Entity** was required, we would omit the declaration of *entities* and have instead a declaration of a machine *Entity*, together with variables *att1* : *T1*, *att2* : *T2*, etc.

The set *ENTITY* is the domain of object identities, and *entities* records the current set of **Entity** instances which are known to the system.

If there are relationships between entities in the object model, then some of the T1, ..., Tn will themselves involve other entities, say **Entity2**, **Entity3** .... In this case we must SEE or USE the associated machine:

```
MACHINE Entity
SEES Entity2, Entity3, ...
...
END
```

We use SEES if we only need to use the object identity sets *ENTITY2*, *ENTITY3*, etc, in the invariant of *Entity* (ie, to provide a range type for a link of **Entity**), and we use USES if we need to be more specific and use the set of existing entities *entities2*, etc, as range types in the invariant. If there is a 1-1 link for example, such a stronger typing constraint would be needed. We may also use a parameter to place a bound on the maximum number of instances of a given entity which we will allow:

```
MACHINE Entity(maxEntity)
CONSTRAINTS
   maxEntity >= 1
   ....
INVARIANT
   entities <: ENTITY &
   card(entities) <= maxEntity
   ...
END
```

If we have **Entity2** inheriting **Entity1**, then we need to place the constraint *entities2* ⊆ *entities1* in the invariant of the machine representing the supertype (most abstract entity).

```
MACHINE Entity1
SETS
    ENTITY1
VARIABLES
   entities1, entities2
INVARIANT
   entities1 <: ENTITY1 &

   entities2 <: entities1

   ...

END
```

Similarly with exclusive subtypes **Entity1** and **Entity2**, the constraint *entities1* ∩ *entities2* = ∅ is added to the invariant.

50

3.1 Example – Box/Line Specification

Using this approach, the Box/Line object model can be formalised as follows:

```
MACHINE Line(maxLine,COORD)
CONSTRAINTS
  maxLine > 0
SETS LINE
PROPERTIES card(LINE) = maxLine
VARIABLES
  lines, posn, length
INVARIANT
  lines <: LINE &
  posn : lines --> COORD &
  length : lines --> 1..1000 &
  card(lines) <= maxLine
INITIALISATION
  lines := {} || posn := {} || length := {}
OPERATIONS
    ll <-- create_line(pos,len) =
        PRE
          lines /= LINE &
          pos : COORD &
          len : 1..1000
        THEN
          ANY newl
          WHERE
            newl : LINE - lines
          THEN
            ll := newl ||
            posn(newl) := pos ||
            length(newl) := len ||
            lines := lines \/ {newl}
          END
        END ;

  change_pos(ll,pos) =
        PRE ll : lines &
            pos : COORD
        THEN
          posn(ll) := pos
        END
    ....

END´

MACHINE Box(maxBox,COORD)
USES Line
SETS BOX
VARIABLES
  boxes, position, height, attached, connected
```

```
INVARIANT
  boxes <: BOX &
  position : boxes --> COORD &
  height : boxes --> NAT &
  attached : boxes --> lines &
  connected : boxes --> boxes &
  card(boxes) <= maxBox
INITIALISATION
  boxes := {} || position := {} ||
  height := {} || attached := {} ||
  connected := {}
OPERATIONS
  /* operations updating or accessing
     attributes or links from Box */
END
```

The B abstract machine notation takes a particular approach to the specification of state transitions via operations and a state invariant. In contrast to the Z notation, for example, the explicit definition of a B AMN operation is expected to preserve the invariant of the machine. This requirement is formalised in a set of internal consistency proof obligations, which also involve checks that the formal model represented by a machine is non-contradictory or non-vacuous. One advantage of the B approach is that identity state transformations ($v' = v$ in Z) do not need to be explicitly written in operation definitions.

The proof obligations for the general machine given in Section 2 are:

$$
\begin{array}{ll}
(1) & \exists p.C \\
(2) & C \Rightarrow \exists k.B \\
(3) & B \wedge C \Rightarrow \exists v.I \\
(4) & B \wedge C \Rightarrow [T]I \\
(5) & B \wedge C \wedge I \wedge P \Rightarrow [S]I
\end{array}
$$

3.2 Refinement to Code

The specification approach described above allows the systematic refinement of specifications to code, using library machines for manipulating sets. These library machines are provided with one of the currently available B toolsets and allow the adaptation of existing C code to provide rapid implementation of new developments. This approach to reuse and rapid development is part of the B methodology, and it is expected that other toolkits for the language and method will also support the process described in this section.

The general process for implementing entity types is:

- attributes of a entity type are represented by fields of a record implemented by *Rename_fnc_obj(TYPEUNION, maxfld, maxEntity)*. *TYPEUNION* is the union of all attribute value types. Attribute names are replaced with integers in 1 .. *maxfld*;

- sets representing entity types are implemented by the domain *Rename_fnctok* of the record-valued function implementing the attributes of this entity type;

- operations to add and delete elements of the entity type are implemented via *Rename_CRE_FNC_OBJ* and *Rename_KIL_FNC_OBJ*;

- operations to obtain the value of a given attribute for an entity instance and to set this value are implemented via *Rename_VAL_FNC_OBJ* and *Rename_STO_FNC_OBJ* respectively;

- operations to test the fullness of the entity type set are implemented via *Rename_FUL_FNC_OBJ*.

A (minimal) example is given by the following implementation of the *Line* machine above.

```
IMPLEMENTATION   Line_1
REFINES Line
CONSTANTS
  posindx,
  lenindx
PROPERTIES
  LINE = Lines_FNCOBJ &
  posindx = 1 &
  lenindx = 2
SEES
  Bool_TYPE
IMPORTS
  Lines_fnc_obj(((1..1000)\/COORD),2,maxLine)
INVARIANT
  lines = Lines_fnctok &
  !ll.(ll : lines    =>
             posn(ll) = Lines_fncstruct(ll)(posindx)) &
  !ll.(ll : lines    =>
             length(ll) = Lines_fncstruct(ll)(lenindx))
OPERATIONS

  ll <-- create_line(pos,len)   =
                 VAR newline
                 IN
                   newline <-- Lines_CRE_FNC_OBJ;
                   Lines_STO_FNC_OBJ(newline,posindx,pos);
                   Lines_STO_FNC_OBJ(newline,lenindx,len);
                   ll := newline
                 END   ;

  change_pos(ll,pos)   =
                 BEGIN
                   Lines_STO_FNC_OBJ(ll,posindx,pos)
                 END
  ....

END
```

It is possible to use the decomposition of the specification on the basis of entity types in the object model at the implementation level as well. Specifically, if we have a decomposition clause INCLUDES A in the machine B at the specification level, then in the implementation B_1 of B, we can IMPORT A, and use its state in the invariants of B_1 and its operations in the operations of B_1 in a way parallel to the use of A by B at the specification level. Because any sets and constants of A will be visible *twice* in B_1 (once via the IMPORTS clause, and once via the INCLUDES/REFINES path), we must first factor out these items into a new machine C, which is seen by each of A, B_1 and B.

4 Formalising Dynamic Models

4.1 Process Model for Formalisation

Dynamic models for systems are often expressed in the form of *state charts*, which define a set of states that an object can be in, and a set of transitions between states. Typical notations are those of Harel [8] and Moore [16]. Transitions can depend upon the state of other instances of the type whose dynamic model is expressed in the chart, and can involve requests for transitions in other state models.

One technique that can be used for formal modelling of such systems is to create a machine encapsulating a set of instances of each object type, and the sets of instances of this object type that are in a given state. This representation regards such states as defining a 'transitory subtype' of the object type whose instances can be in these states. Transitions from one state to another are modelled by B AMN operations, with suitable preconditions and cases to express the different situations that can arise. One advantage of this scheme is that modularisation of the specification follows the structure of the problem domain, making it easier to trace the location of required changes to a system as a result of changes in the domain. Synchronisation between subsystems is expressed by means of operations which call operations from subsystem machines using the 'multiple generalised substitution' operator ||. The semantics of this operator is similar to that of ∧ in Z operation schemas: it specifies that the state transitions defined by its operands should both be performed, but does not specify any procedural order by which these transitions can be achieved. Naturally, the sets of variables updated by the two operands should be disjoint.

The associated process model extends that for transforming static data models into machines described in section 3. Steps of recognition of families of entity types and the creation of associated machines are still performed. However, each entity type E may now have an associated dynamic behaviour description given by a state model. For each state S in this model, a new 'transitory subtype' S of E is considered to exist, and an associated variable *ss* is added to the machine representing the family of types to which the entity type E belongs.

Each transition between states in this model becomes an operation in the associated machine. Activities within states also become operations of the associated machine. Synchronisation between instances of entities from different families is expressed using || combination of transitions from the individual machines, in a machine which includes all the 'sibling' machines in the development. At this level, or at the level of systems which use the set of machines, any required ordering of operations can be imposed (such as that an activity performed in a state is executed immediately after an instance arrives in that state).

The general steps are therefore:

- create machine *Entity.mch* for each entity type family **Entity** in the data model, and a variable *states* $\subseteq$ *entities* for each state in the chart for **Entity**;

- create operations of *Entity.mch* for each transition and activity;

- express synchronisation between subsystems by means of operations which call operations from subsystem machines using the 'multiple generalised substitution' operator ||.

In more detail:

- **states become sets of instances;**

- state sets are disjoint;

- state sets make up the entire set of entities;

- **attributes and links become functions;**

- the domain of an attribute may be a proper subset of the instance set of the entity (it may only make sense in certain states of the entity);

- **initial states become creation operations;**

- the creation operation of the *Entity.mch* specification initialises an instance to have the initial state (to be in the variable representing the set of instances in the initial state);

- **transitions between states become operations moving an instance from one state set to another;**

- transition preconditions become operation preconditions;

- transition preconditions depending on the state of other instances of **Entity** can be expressed;

- **activities in a state become operations that do not change the state** (and which are preconditioned by membership of the state of which they are activities).

This process will be illustrated by an extended example of a simple lift control system.

4.2 Example – A Lift System

This system is a simple control mechanism for an (unspecified) set of lifts and floors. The entities of the system are *Lift*, *Door*, *Button*. We also envisage the possibility that *Floor* may be regarded as an entity type, rather than a primitive unstructured type (since it may possess an attribute giving the floor number in addition to any special characteristic of the floor). A lift may have a *current floor* (the one it is on, if it is not moving or not in a decomissioned state), and it may have a *destination floor* (the floor it is moving to or has been requested to move to). These are *not* total attributes, since they only make sense for certain lift *states*. Floors and lift buttons are in 1-1 correspondence, as are lifts and doors. However, we would usually navigate from a lift to its associated door and from a button to its associated floor, since lifts and buttons will be the initiators or sources of actions which involve these associated objects.

The static data model of the system is therefore as shown in Figure 2, using OMT notation.

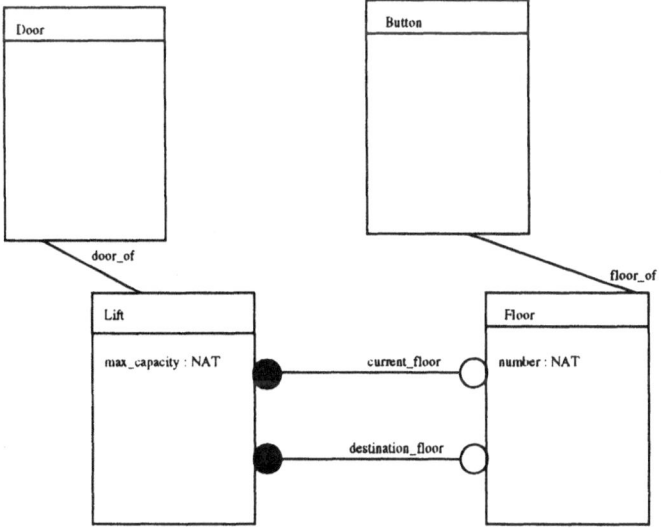

Figure 2: Static Data Model of Lift System

The notation expresses that for every instance of the *Lift* entity type, there is one or zero instances of the *Floor* entity type associated via the relation *current_floor*, and for every instance of the *Floor* entity type, there are many (zero or more) instances of the *Lift* entity type associated via the relation *current_floor*.

The state model notation of OMT [20] uses Harel state model diagrams [8] to express the dynamics of a system. A simple example, including the use of synchronisation between subsystems using communication from one state model to another, is given in Figures 3 and 4 to specify the dynamic behaviour of lifts and buttons.

Although lifts will usually be physically associated with a particular floor, we do not want to consider that each floor comprises a different state for a lift – since such a set of states would then be different in each particular lift configuration. Instead, we choose to consider only three essentially distinct states.

Button

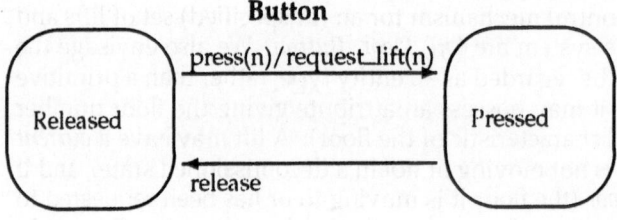

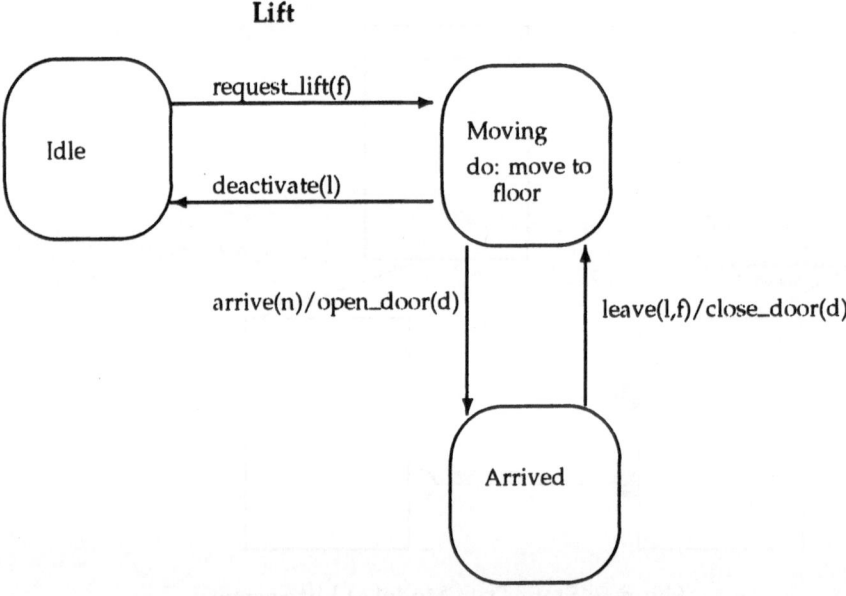

Figure 3: State models for Lift and Button

The state model for doors is shown in Figure 4.

Note that the preconditions for transitions between states may be quite complex, and can refer to the set of existing instances of the class concerned (and to those sets of instances in a given state).

As an example the precondition

$$destination\_floor^{-1}(\{ff\}) = \emptyset$$

of the *request_lift(ff)* event expresses the condition

$$\neg \exists ll.(ll \in moving\_lifts \wedge destination\_floor(ll) = ff)$$

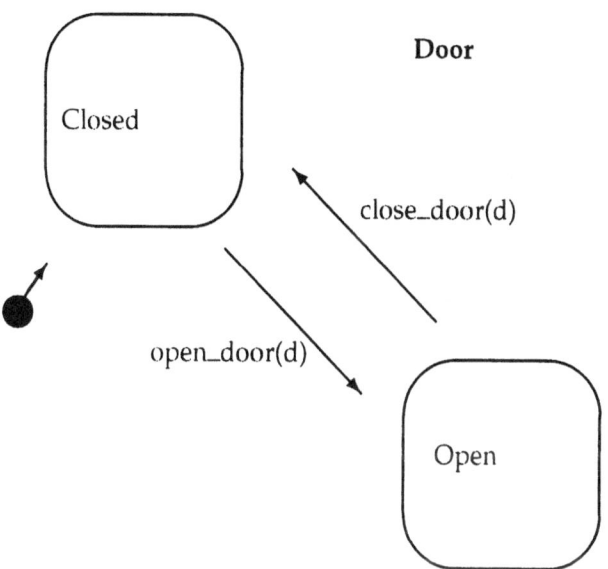

Figure 4: State model for Door

That is, no other lift is currently heading for the floor *ff* whose button issued the request.

Each machine representing a dynamically modifiable set of instances of an entity type will possess both a set representing the set of all *possible* instances of the object class type, and a variable which is the subset of this set representing the existing instances of the type. The set may be defined internally to the machine in the SETS clause, in order to be instantiated in an implementation of the machine. Alternatively, in the case that the machine will be included in other machines, with the set of possible instances being shared between several machines, or instantiated to a specific value, it must be defined as a parameter of the machine. In this case we wish to make the lift system entirely configurable by an external user, and so we choose to make the sets of possible instances of a type suitable parameters of the machines representing the types.

4.3 From Analysis to Specification

4.3.1 Floors

The static data model leads to the definition of four outline machines. The simplest is the machine representing floors (we omit the number representing the number of the floor):

```
MACHINE
   Floor(FLOOR)
CONSTANTS
   ground_floor
PROPERTIES
```

```
   ground_floor : FLOOR
END
```

This machine encapsulates the set of possible floors, and a special floor (which is not used in the present specification, but is provided with a view to reuse of the system in more sophisticated specifications, such as a system where the 'default' destination floor is the ground floor). Because this is a static entity type (new members are not dynamically added or deleted) we only have a given set *FLOOR* and not a set of existing entities *floors* ⊆ *FLOOR*.

There are no proof obligations for internal consistency of this machine.

4.3.2 Doors

The machine representing doors encapsulates three sets:

- *doors* – representing the instances of the door entity;

- *open_doors* – representing the instances of doors in the 'Open' state;

- *closed_doors* – representing the instances of doors in the 'Closed' state.

There are no other variables of the machine since doors have no actual attributes.

We must impose the condition that the sets of open and closed doors are disjoint and make up the whole of the set of doors – this is the same condition that is normally expected for disjoint subtypes of an entity type.

The outline specification is therefore:

```
MACHINE
   Door(DOOR)
VARIABLES
   doors, open_doors, closed_doors
INVARIANT
   doors <: DOOR &
   open_doors <: doors &
   closed_doors <: doors &

   open_doors \/ closed_doors = doors &
   open_doors /\ closed_doors = {}
INITIALISATION
   doors, open_doors, closed_doors := {}, {}, {}
OPERATIONS

   dd <-- create_door =
      PRE
         doors /= DOOR
      THEN
         ANY oo
         WHERE
             oo : DOOR - doors
         THEN
             dd := oo ||
```

```
              doors := doors \/ {oo} ||
              closed_doors := closed_doors \/ {oo}
         END
      END;

  add_door(dd) =
      PRE dd : DOOR - doors
      THEN
        doors := doors \/ {dd} ||
        closed_doors := closed_doors \/ {dd}
      END;

  open_door(dd) =
        PRE
           dd : doors
        THEN
           open_doors := open_doors \/ {dd} ||
           closed_doors := closed_doors - {dd}
        END;

  close_door(dd) =
        PRE
           dd : doors
        THEN
           closed_doors := closed_doors \/ {dd} ||
           open_doors := open_doors - {dd}
        END

END
```

The initial state of a door is *Closed*, which is expressed in the *create_door* operation.

There are 23 proof obligations for internal consistency, of which 21 are resolved automatically using the Alpha release of the B Toolkit produced by BP Ltd. The remainder are proved by the user asserting suitable proof rules which they believe are valid.

4.3.3 *Buttons*

The treatment of this is similar to the **Door** entity. It has the inclusion relations:

```
MACHINE
   Button(BUTTON)
SEES Floor
   ....
END
```

SEES is used as the inclusion mechanism since the *Floor* machine has no variables, and therefore SEES is equivalent to USES.

4.3.4 *Lifts*

Similarly, for the **Lift** entity type:

```
MACHINE
  Lift(LIFT)
SEES Floor
USES Door
VARIABLES
    lifts, moving_lifts, arrived_lifts,
    idle_lifts,
    current_floor, destination_floor, door_of
INVARIANT
    lifts <: LIFT &
    arrived_lifts <: lifts &
    moving_lifts <: lifts &
    idle_lifts <: lifts &

    arrived_lifts /\ moving_lifts = {} &
    idle_lifts /\ arrived_lifts = {} &
    idle_lifts /\ moving_lifts = {} &

    arrived_lifts \/ idle_lifts \/
          moving_lifts = lifts &

    current_floor : arrived_lifts --> FLOOR &
    destination_floor : moving_lifts --> FLOOR &
    door_of : lifts >--> doors

INITIALISATION
    lifts, arrived_lifts,
    idle_lifts, moving_lifts, current_floor,
    destination_floor, door_of   :=
                      {}, {}, {}, {}, {}, {}, {}

OPERATIONS
    add_lift(ll,dd) =
        PRE ll : LIFT &
            ll /: lifts &
            dd : doors &
            dd /: ran(door_of)
        THEN
          idle_lifts := idle_lifts \/ {ll} ||
          lifts := lifts \/ {ll} ||
          door_of(ll) := dd
        END;

    request_lift(ff) =
        PRE ff : FLOOR &
            (idle_lifts /= {}  or
             destination_floor~[{ff}] /= {})
```

```
                /*" #(kk).(kk:moving_lifts |·
                     destination_floor(kk) = ff) ) "*/

        THEN
          IF destination_floor~[{ff}] /= {}
                    /*" #(ll).(ll:moving_lifts |
                         destination_floor(ll) = ff) "*/
            THEN
              skip   /* there is already a lift
                         serving that floor */
            ELSE
              ANY ll
              WHERE ll : idle_lifts
              THEN
                idle_lifts := idle_lifts - {ll} ||
                moving_lifts := moving_lifts \/ {ll} ||
                destination_floor(ll) := ff
              END
          END
        END;

arrive(ll,ff) =
    PRE ff : FLOOR &
        ll : moving_lifts &
        destination_floor(ll) = ff
    THEN
      moving_lifts := moving_lifts - {ll} ||
      destination_floor :=
        destination_floor - {ll |-> ff} ||
      arrived_lifts := arrived_lifts \/ {ll} ||
      current_floor(ll) := ff
    END;

leave(ll,ff) =
    PRE ll : arrived_lifts &
        ff : FLOOR &
        ff /= current_floor(ll)
    THEN
      arrived_lifts := arrived_lifts - {ll} ||
      moving_lifts := moving_lifts \/ {ll} ||
      current_floor := {ll} <<| current_floor  ||
      destination_floor(ll) := ff
    END;

deactivate(ll) =
    PRE ll : moving_lifts
    THEN
      moving_lifts := moving_lifts - {ll} ||
      destination_floor := {ll} <<| destination_floor ||
```

```
                idle_lifts := idle_lifts \/ {ll}
            END
END
```

The attribute

  door_of : *lifts* ↣ *doors*

is recorded as a total injection from lifts to doors. That is, different lifts must
have different doors, but it is possible for doors to exist without an associated
lift, contrary to the static data model. The problem with directly expressing
the original one-to-one correspondence is that pairs of lifts and doors would
need to be created together, together with a record of their association via
door_of. Thus the sets of entity instances for these two types would need to be
defined as variables in the same machine (since at the abstract machine level,
we are not allowed to use sequential composition to compose operations from
INCLUDED machines).

4.3.5 Lift System

Synchronisation between subsystem components is performed by multiple
generalised substitutions of actions of individual components in a machine
which includes each component. We could therefore define:

```
MACHINE
   LiftSystem(BUTTON,LIFT,DOOR,FLOOR)
INCLUDES
   Button(BUTTON),
   Floor(FLOOR),
   Lift(LIFT),
   Door(DOOR)
PROMOTES
   release, create_door
OPERATIONS

   add_lift_and_door(ll,dd) =
         PRE ll : LIFT &
             dd :  doors &
             ll /: lifts &
             dd /: ran(door_of)
         THEN
           close_door(dd) ||
           add_lift(ll,dd)
         END;

   add_button_and_floor(nn,ff) =
         PRE
             nn : BUTTON &
             nn /: buttons &
             ff : FLOOR &
             ff /: ran(floor_of)
```

```
          THEN
            add_button(nn,ff)
          END;

  press_and_request_lift(bb) =
          PRE
            bb : buttons   /* and there is a lift to request */
            &
            (idle_lifts /= {}  or
                destination_floor~[{floor_of(bb)}] /= {})
          THEN
            press(bb) ||
            request_lift(floor_of(bb))
          END;

  arrive_and_open_door(ll,ff) =
          PRE
            ll : moving_lifts &
            ff : FLOOR &
            destination_floor(ll) = ff
          THEN
            arrive(ll,ff) ||
            open_door(door_of(ll))
          END ;

   leave_and_close_door(ll,ff) =
          PRE
            ll : arrived_lifts &
            ff : FLOOR &
            ff /= current_floor(ll)
          THEN
            leave(ll,ff) ||
            close_door(door_of(ll))
          END;

   deactivate_and_close_door(ll) =
          PRE ll : moving_lifts
          THEN
            close_door(door_of(ll)) ||
            deactivate(ll)
          END
```

END

In this composed system, each operation which combines operations from included machines must reproduce each precondition of every operation of which it is composed.

There are 7 proof obligations for internal consistency, of which 6 are proved automatically. Note that there are so few obligations since many obligations concerning operations used in the top-level specification of the system have been resolved at lower levels: this is a direct benefit of specification compartmentalisation.

4.4 Applications of Formalisation

The formalisation of the semantics of state charts which has been performed by the above translation can assist in establishing safety properties of the systems specified by these charts.

For example, if we were required to show that a lift can never be moving with its doors open, then we could formalise this assertion as the additional invariant clause of *LiftSystem*:

$$\forall ll.(ll \in moving\_lifts \Rightarrow \\ door\_of(ll) \in closed\_doors)$$

An attempt to establish this will identify that this can be proved, provided that

$$\forall ll.(ll \in idle\_lifts \Rightarrow \\ door\_of(ll) \in closed\_doors)$$

In refinements of the specification, these properties would also be required to hold in the refined state, so that the implemented code would satisfy this safety property.

5 Alternative State Representation

It is clear that the above approach becomes infeasible once the number of states of an entity to be handled climbs above 8 - 10. As an alternative, we have the following process:

- Create machine *Entity.mch* for each entity type family **Entity** in the data model, and a status variable $status_i\_flag : entities \rightarrow STATUS\_SET_i$ for the ith state chart factor for **Entity**, where $STATUS\_SET_i$ is the set of state representatives for the states in the ith factor;

- create operations of *Entity.mch* for each transition and activity in each state chart. Transitions which occur in more than one state chart require that two or more of the $status_i\_flag$ variables are simultaneously updated;

- synchronisation between subsystems is expressed as in the previous approach.

The overall process is thus quite similar to the previous approach, however:

- **states become sets of instances** defined by the inverse images of elements of the $STATUS\_SET_i$ sets under the $status_i\_flag$ functions;

- these state sets are therefore disjoint and exhaustive of *entities*;

- the creation operation of *Entity.mch* initialises each $status_i\_flag$ to the initial state of each state chart factor;

- transitions between states become operations updating the $status_i\_flag$ variables of the affected factors.

If each factor is itself complex, we may attempt to separate out the definition of different factors into different machines. DEFINITIONS may be used to define the state sets as the inverse images of certain $STATUS\_SET_i$ sets under the $status_i\_flag$ functions.

5.1 Comparison

The state function approach has the following advantages over the set based approach:

- fewer variables are used in the machines representing entity types;

- in general, fewer proof obligations are generated.

Conversely, it has the following disadvantages:

- statements regarding membership of a state become less clear, or require the use of DEFINITIONS to define the state sets from the state functions. Definitions are not transmitted from one machine to another by inclusion constructs such as INCLUDES, so must be duplicated in each machine in which they are needed;

- the proof obligations are generally more complex and more difficult to resolve automatically or manually.

A comparative study of the two approaches was carried out on the lift system. Figure 5 gives (1) the number of generated proof obligations for both the state function based and the set based approaches, (2) the number of proof obligations remaining after autoproof, and (3) the number of proof obligations remaining after 30 minutes of interactive proof effort for each development.

Machine	Generated POB's	Non-Autoproved	Non-Interproved
Lift (set)	49	12	8
Lift (function)	23	14	12
Door (set)	23	2	0
Door (function)	9	0	0
Button (set)	26	4	0
Button (function)	12	0	0
LiftSystem (set)	7	1	0
LiftSystem (function)	7	1	1

Figure 5: Comparative Proof Difficulty for Set and Function Approaches

6 Implementation and Reuse in B

A key component of the B methodology is the provision of techniques for reusing existing B developments at a high level of abstraction. This mechanism is implemented via the IMPORTS and REFINES constructs, and IMPLEMEN-TATIONS.

The general configuration of a B development from abstract specifications to concrete specifications and (almost) implementable code is shown in Figure 6. The abstract specification *A.mch* is refined to an implementation *A.imp*, and new requirements, formalised in an abstract specification *B.mch*, can either use or reuse the development *A* by importing the abstract specification *A.mch* into the implementation *B.imp* of *B.mch*. Code of a development is reused, but only indirectly via the (hopefully more concise and comprehensible) abstract specification of the development.

A.mch can be a machine which brings together a set of existing 'sibling' machines via EXTENDS or INCLUDES. Moreover, this pattern can be repeated for successive layers of implementation of one system upon another – a paradigm that is familiar from general software and systems engineering.

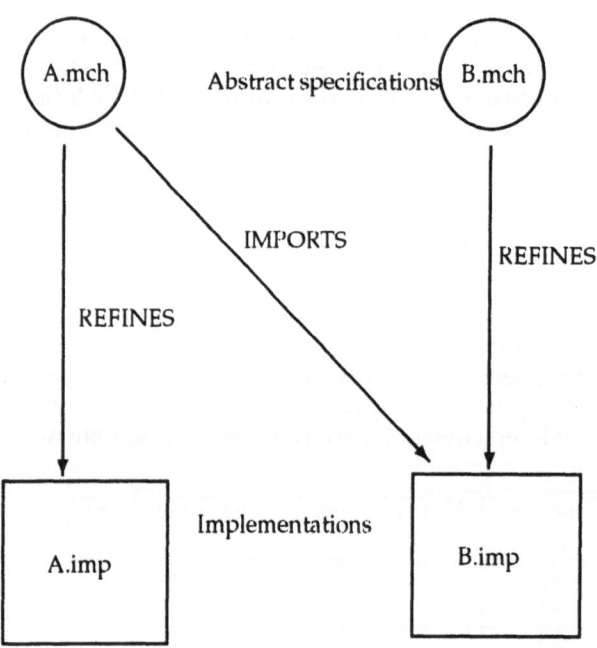

Figure 6: Use of REFINES / IMPORTS

The structural decompositions of systems that we have proposed in this paper, on the basis of domain models, can be carried out for both implementation and specification structures of the B AMN development. Implementation decomposition has also been found to be of considerable benefit in reducing the number of proof obligations associated with the refinement of a specification to code.

In one simple example, of a specification of a sequence of floating point numbers (represented as pairs of a mantissa and exponent), the 'monolithic' implementation approach produced a single implementation with 295 proof obligations, of which 100 were automatically resolved. In contrast, a decomposition approach based upon recognition of the entities within the system produced two separate developments, with 51 and 60 proof obligations respectively, of which 17 and 38 were automatically resolved [14].

7 Conclusions

We have introduced a number of techniques for the construction and refinement of B AMN specifications from requirements, and for the further refinement of these specifications to code. The significance of such systematic procedures are that they provide the possibility of precisely tracing the expression of specific requirements in a specification, and hence enhance the assessment of the correctness of the development and the mutual integrity of its products. This traceability is also of importance if a change to the system is needed as a result of changing requirements.

We have also examined the practicality of proof with respect to alternative formalisation approaches. It has been found that a systematic specification style assists in the reuse of proof rules and methods from one development to another, since the same general style of obligations arise in different specifications.

Acknowledgement

The research conducted in this paper was partially funded by the DTI under IEATP project IED4/1/2182 "B User Trials". The authors wish to thank the Committee at Lloyd's Register for permission to submit this paper for publication. The views expressed in the paper are the opinions of the authors and are not necessarily the views of Lloyd's Register.

References

[1] J.-R. Abrial, **Assigning Programs to Meaning**, Prentice Hall 1994, to appear.

[2] D. Coleman, F. Hayes, S. Bear, *Introducing Objectcharts or How to Use Statecharts in Object-Oriented Design*, IEEE Transactions on Software Engineering, Vol. 18, No. 1, January 1992.

[3] D. Coleman, F. Hayes, *Coherent Models for Object-Oriented Analysis*, Proceedings OOPSLA '91, 1991.

[4] M. Eva, *SSADM Version 4: A User's Guide*, McGraw Hill International Series in Software Engineering, 1992.

[5] A. Evans, *Position Paper*, Formal Specification and Object Orientation Workshop, Logica London, November 1992.

[6] R. France, *Semantically Extended Data Flow Diagrams: A Formal Specification Tool*, IEEE Transactions on Software Engineering, Vol. 18, No. 4, April 1992.

[7] C. Draper, *Practical Experiences of Z and SSADM*, Z User Meeting 1992.

[8] D. Harel, *Statecharts: A visual formalism for complex systems*, Science of Computer Programming 8 (1987), 231 - 274.

[9] J. Hares, **SSADM for the Advanced Practitioner**, Wiley, 1990.

[10] H. Haughton, *The B Method Manual*, BUT Project Document BUT/LLOYDS/HPH/8/V4, Lloyd's Register, June 1992.

[11] J. V. Hill, **Microprocessor Based Protection Systems**, Elsevier 1991.

[12] K. Lano, *Method Case Study: Invoice System*, BUT Project Document BUT/LLOYDS/KL/14/V1, 1992.

[13] K. Lano K., H. Haughton, A. C. Lee, *The B Methodology: A Practical Introduction*, BUT Project Document BUT/LLOYDS/KL/40/V1, March 1993.

[14] K. Lano, *B User Trials Code Generation Course*, BUT Project Document BUT/LLOYDS/KL/79/V1, October 1993.

[15] S. M. Merad, *Adding Formalism to Object-oriented analysis*, KBSL Conference on Requirements and Design Analysis for Object-Oriented Environments, 1992.

[16] E. F. Moore, *Gedanken-experiments on Sequential Machines*, in Automata Studies, Princetown University Press, Princetown N.J., 1956.

[17] F. Polack, M. Whiston, *Formal Methods and System Analysis*, Proceedings of Methods Integration Conference, Springer-Verlag 1992.

[18] D. R. Pyle, M. Josephs, *Enriching a Structured Method with Z*, Oxford University Programming Research Group, 1991.

[19] D. R. Pyle, M. Josephs, *Entity-Relationship Models Expressed in Z: A Synthesis of Structured and Formal Methods*, Oxford University Programming Research Group, 1991.

[20] J. Rumbaugh, M. Blaha, W. Premerlani, F. Eddy, W. Lorensen, **Object-Oriented Modelling and Design**, Englewood Cliffs, NJ, Prentice Hall Ltd., 1991.

[21] IEC/TC65A(Secretariat)123, *Functional Safety of Electrical/Electronic/Programmable Electronic Systems: Generic Aspects. Part 1 : General Requirements*, International Electrotechnical Commission, 1992.

Testing and Safety Analysis of AM (Abstract Machine) Specifications

H.P.Haughton

Lloyds Register of Shipping, 29 Wellesley Rd

Croydon, CRO 2AJ

K.Lano

Lloyds Register of Shipping, 29 Wellesley Rd

Croydon, CRO 2AJ

Abstract

The purpose of this paper is to describe how testing and safety analysis of Abstract Machine Specifications can be undertaken in a formal manner. It is also shown that safety properties are preserved under refinement.

1 Testing the Correctness and Safety of AM specifications

In this section we describe how AM's can be tested manually for correctness, and how such techniques can be modified to reflect safety aspects.

1.1 Testing for Correctness

Testing can be viewed as the process of ascertaining whether some facet exhibits a pre-specified behaviour. In this respect, more often than not, testing amounts to showing that a specification (program) responds correctly, i.e. that it contains no operational errors, for the modules tested. In the sequel, we will show that specifications are correct by showing that some property is satisfied by the specification. More formally we determine whether some post-condition is satisfied by a substitution.

The Abstract Machine Notation (AMN) is based on concepts such as information hiding, [3] and multiple generalised substitutions [1]. Below is a summary of the axioms for the various generalised (in AMN) substitutions in establishing a post-condition:

(1) $[P|S]R \equiv P \wedge [S]R$

(2) $[S[]T]R \equiv [S]R \wedge [T]R$

(3) $[P ==> S]R \equiv P \Rightarrow [S]R$

(4) $[if\ P\ then\ S]R \equiv P \Rightarrow [S]R \wedge \neg P \Rightarrow R$

(5) $[if\ P\ then\ S\ else\ T]R \equiv P \Rightarrow [S]R \wedge \neg P \Rightarrow [T]R$

(6) $[select\ P\ then\ S\ when\ Q\ then\ T\ ...\ when\ R\ then\ U\ end]Z \equiv$
     $[P ==> S\ []\ Q ==> T\ []\ ...\ R ==> U]Z$

(7) $[any\ z\ where\ P\ then\ S]R \equiv [@z.(P ==>S)]R \equiv \forall z.(P \Rightarrow [S]R)$

(8) $[skip]R \equiv R$

(9) [@z.S]R ≡ ∀z.[S]R (z\R)

(10) [x:∈E] R≡ ∀x'.(x'∈E => [x:=x']R)

(11) [x:P]R ≡ ∀x.(P => R)

(12) [T]Q ∧

∀d.(Q => V ∈ N) ∧

∀d.(Q ∧ G => [S]Q) ∧

∀d.(Q ∧ G => [n:=V][S](V<n)) ∧

∀d.(Q ∧ ¬G => R)

=>

[T;while G do S invariant Q variant V end]R

where [P|S] is syntactic sugar for PRE P THEN S.

The above substitutions constitute the majority of such substitutions available in AMN. Number (1) denotes an operation within which there is a precondition P and some expression S. Number (2) denotes the case of a nondeterministic choice between two substitutions. Number (3) denotes an operation which is guarded by a predicate P and S denotes the expression following the guard. Numbers (4) and (5) denote conditionals. Number (6) denotes a generalised conditional. Number (7) denotes an unbounded typed choice expression. Number (8) denotes skip. Numbers (9),(10),(11) are all specialisations of (7). Number (12) denotes a while loop.

If we look at the axiom for **any** we see that this can be 'reduced' by using some of the other axioms:

[@z.(P ==> S)]R

≡

∀z.[P => S]R

≡

∀z.(P => [S]R)

We can view the above reduction as a form of rewriting, where we are attempting to rewrite a substitution to an irreducible (normal) form. This type of rewritting will play a significant part in future discussions. Consider the following specification:

MACHINE
  spec

VARIABLES

  xx,yy

INVARIANT

  xx:NAT &
  yy:NAT

INITIALISATION

  xx:=0||
  yy:=0

OPERATIONS

```
op1 =
  BEGIN
    ANY vv WHERE
         vv:NAT
    THEN
      xx:=xx+vv
    END
  END;

op2(aa)=
  PRE
    aa:NAT
  THEN
    ANY oo WHERE
      oo:NAT
    THEN
      yy:=yy+oo
    END
       ||
    xx:=xx+aa
  END
END
```

In the above AM, there are two variables xx,yy. These variables are initially assigned values of 0. There are two operations op1,op2. The operation op1 non-deterministically increases the value of the variable xx. The operation op2 deterministically increases the value of xx however non-deterministically increases the value of yy. The || construct together with the ANY ... and xx.. denote a multiple generalised substitution. The effect of which is to constrain the left and right hand expressions to cases where they have no read/write variables in common.

If we conjecture that, at a particular instance of time, the operation op2 causes a certain condition to be true, e.g. yy>10 we have:

```
[PRE bb:NAT THEN ANY oo WHERE oo:NAT THEN
  yy:=yy+oo END || xx:=xx+bb END](yy>10)
    ≡
bb:NAT ∧ [ANY oo WHERE oo:NAT THEN
       yy:=yy+oo END || xx:=xx+bb](yy>10)
  ≡
bb:NAT ∧ [ANY oo WHERE oo:NAT THEN yy:=yy+oo END][xx:=xx+bb](yy>10)
  ≡
bb:NAT ∧ ∀oo.(oo:NAT => [yy:=yy+oo](yy>10))
  ≡
bb:NAT ∧ oo:NAT => yy+oo>10
```

If we knew what the current values of bb,oo,yy were, then we could determine the validity of the last statement. Note the process adopted in the above rewrites: apply an applicable axiom to the most outer substitution and apply such axioms until we are left with some statement construct involving only simple assignment substitutions.

What we have demonstrated above, is a process of determining the correctness of an operation by showing that its substitutions satisfy a certain post-condition. In the sequel we describe how we can automate the process of testing via test case selection.

2 Test case Selection for AMN

The process we adopt in selecting test cases, is as follows:

1. for each operation we determine the set of variables that are updated;

2. for each such variable above, we introduce a 'copy' of it via an **any** substitution of an operation. The term copy here means a variable having the same type as some other;

3. for any variable (identified in (1) above) on the RHS of a substitution, we replace this variable with its copy.

Consider for example the following:

```
MACHINE
  M1
VARIABLES
  v1,v2,v3
INVARIANT
  v1:seq(NAT) &
  v2:FIN(NAT) &
  v3:NAT
INITIALISATION

    v1:=<>||
    v2:={}||
    v3:=0

OPERATIONS

  op1(aa)=
    PRE
      aa:NAT
    THEN
      CHOICE
        v1:=v1^<aa>
      OR
        v2:=v2 \/ {aa}
      OR
        v3:=v3+aa
      END
    END
END
```

if we analyse the above operation then we derive the following operation:

```
op11(aa)=
   PRE
    aa:NAT
   THEN
      ANY vv1,vv2,vv3  WHERE
        vv1:seq(NAT) & vv2:FIN(NAT) & vv3:NAT
      THEN
         CHOICE
            v1:=vv1^<aa>
         OR
            v2:=vv2 \/ {aa}
         OR
            v3:=vv3+aa
         END
      END
   END
```

we can use this derived operation in a new AM as shown below:

```
MACHINE
   M2
VARIABLES
  v1,v2,v3
INVARIANT
  v1:seq(NAT) &
  v2:FIN(NAT) &
  v3:NAT
INITIALISATION

  v1:=<> ||
  v2:={} ||
  v3:=0

OPERATIONS

   op11(aa)=
     PRE
      aa:NAT
     THEN
        ANY vv1,vv2,vv3  WHERE
          vv1:seq(NAT) & vv2:FIN(NAT) & vv3:NAT
        THEN
           CHOICE
              v1:=vv1^<aa>
           OR
              v2:=vv2 \/ {aa}
           OR
              v3:=vv3+aa
           END
```

74

```
        END
      END
END
```

with this machine, it is now possible to 'test' the operation **op1** by the selection of test cases (given by the **ANY** clause).

3   Safety Analysis

Safety analysis (see Leveson [2]) is related to testing in that it can be viewed as determining the correctness of some facet. In addition to this however, safety analysis attempts to identify were possible faults can occur and the means by which these faults occur. Thus one way of viewing safety analysis is to identify the means by which a fault can occur. Typically this involves constructing a tree type representation, where the top node denotes the conjectured fault and subsequent (lower) nodes denote causes for the fault. This process is continued until the bottom nodes of the tree are irreducible.

In the sequel, we show how this tree type of analysis can be achieved via the use of weakest pre-condition calculation. We will use the notation $safety_R$ to denote analysis of specifications with respect to safety for a post-condition R. In other words $safety_R$ denotes a predicate describing a fault:

3.1   simple assignment

a fault $safety_R$ is conjectured for an assignment:

$[x:=v] safety_R \equiv safety_R[x/v]$

i.e. the replacement of all free occurrences of **x** in $safety_R$ by **v**.

3.2   multiple generalised substitution

a fault $safety_R$ is conjectured for an MGS:

$[x,y:=E,F] safety_R \equiv [x||y] safety_R \equiv [a:=E][b:=F][x:=a][y:=b] safety_R$

where **a** and **b** are two distinct fresh variables. These substitutions describe the effect of non-interference of read/write variables.

3.3   guarded substitution

a fault $safety_R$ is conjectured for a guarded substitution:

$[P ==> Q] safety_R \equiv P \wedge [Q] safety_R$

i.e. it must be the case that the guard evaluates to true and that the substitution establishes the fault.

3.4   conditional substitution 1

a fault $safety_R$ is conjectured for a conditional substitution:

[if P then S] $safety_R \equiv P \wedge [S]safety_R \vee \neg P \wedge safety_R$

i.e. it must be the case that either the guard is true and the substitution
establishes the fault, or that the guard is not true and that resultingly the fault
is established.

3.5   conditional substitution 2

a fault $safety_R$ is conjectured for a conditional substitution:

[if P then S else T] $safety_R \equiv P \wedge [S]safety_R \vee \neg P \wedge [T]safety_R$

i.e. it must be the case that the guard is true and the substitution S establishes
the fault, or that the guard is false and the substitution T establishes the fault.
    Consider the following example: a fault $safety_R$ occurs in:

```
if C1 then if C2 then S1 else S2 end
  else
      if C3 then S3 else S4 end
end
```

this corresponds to the following fault tree:

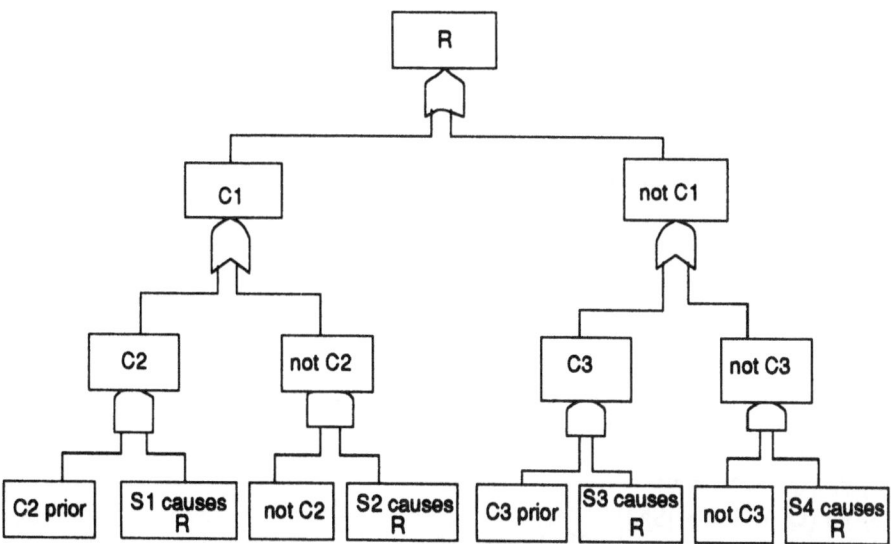

Figure 1: Fault Tree for conditional example

3.6   generalised conditionals

a fault $safety_R$ is conjectured for the generalised conditional **select**:

[select P then S when Q then T... when R then U end]$safety_R \equiv$
[P ==> S [] Q ==> T [] ... [] R ==> U]$safety_R$

i.e. it must be the case that either guard in the resulting choice of expressions must be true and that the substitution associated with the guard establishes the fault.

3.7   bounded choice substitution

a fault $safety_R$ is conjectured for a bounded choice substitution:

[S[]T[]...[]K]$safety_R \equiv$ [S]$safety_R \lor$ [T]$safety_R \lor ... \lor$ [K]$safety_R$

i.e. it must be the case that a substitution of the resulting choice expression establishes the fault.

3.8   unbounded choice substitution

a fault $safety_R$ is conjectured for an unbounded choice substitution:

[any v where P then S]$safety_R \equiv$ [@z.(P $\land$ S)]$safety_R \equiv \forall z.$[P $\land$ S]$safety_R$
$\equiv \forall z.$(P $\land$ [S]$safety_R$)

i.e. for any value of v chosen, it must be the case that the guard holds and the substitution S establishes the fault.

3.9   while loop

a fault $safety_R$ is conjectured for a loop:
a fault tree for loops looks as follows:

The axioms for safety of loops are:

(1) [T]$safety_R$
(2) $\forall d.(\neg G \land safety_R)$

these are for the most left side of the tree and:

(3) [T]Q
(4) $\forall d.(Q => V \in \mathbf{N})$
(5) $\forall d.(Q \land G => $[S]Q)
(6) $\forall d.(Q \land G => $[n:=V][S](V<n))
(7) $\forall d.(Q \land \neg G \land safety_R)$

for the right most side of the tree, where the interpretation of (3)..(6) are the same as for the testing case.

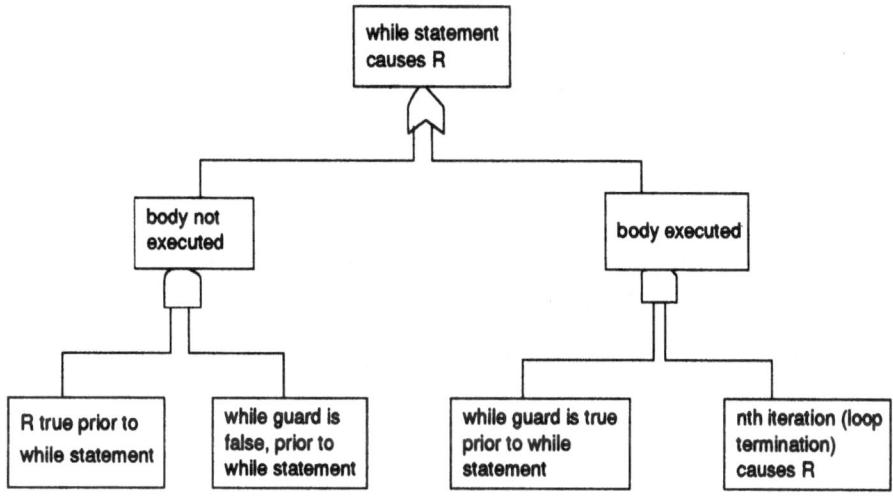

Figure 2: Fault Tree for a while loop

3.10   Refinement and Safety

A question we would like to ask ourselves is: does refinement preserve safety? The following formalisation of data refinement, if provable, is sufficient to show that a refinement preserves safety properties:

$$\forall P.([op][glue]P=>[op']P)$$

where op and op' are operations of the refined and refining machines respectively. The **glue** substitution denotes the multiple generalised substitution of the glueing invariant of a refinement and P denotes the safety property. As an example consider the following:

```
MACHINE                           REFINEMENT
   Maxset                            Maxsetref
VARIABLES                         REFINES
   yy                                Maxset
INVARIANT                         VARIABLES
 yy:FIN(NAT1)                        zz
INITIALISATION                    INVARIANT
   yy:={}                            zz = max(yy \/ {0})
OPERATIONS                        INITIALISATION
                                     zz:=0
   enter(nn)=                     OPERATIONS
     PRE
       nn:NAT                        enter(nn)=
     THEN                              PRE
       yy:=yy\/{nn}                      nn:NAT
     END;                             THEN
                                        zz:=max({zz,nn})
   mm<--maximum=                     END;
```

```
    PRE                                      mm<--maximum=
       yy/={}                                   PRE
    THEN                                            zz/=0
       mm:=max(yy)                              THEN
    END                                            mm:=zz
END                                            END
```

Assume that we chose a safety property of `mm = max(yy)` to be satisfied by `maximum` for P in the above refinement obligation for machine `Maxset`. Resulting from the change of variable for the refinement, P for Maxsetref will be in terms of mm and zz. Due to the glueing invariant, we can deduce that this P should be `mm=zz`. The following is an application of the refinement obligation to the maximum operation:

$\forall$ P.([op][glue]P => [op']P)

≡

([maximum][z:=max(yy $\cup$ {0})](mm=zz) =>
          [maximum'](mm=zz))

≡

yy/={} & [mm:=max(yy)][zz:=max(yy $\cup$ {0})](mm=zz) =>
               zz/=0 & [mm:=zz](mm=zz)

≡

yy/={} & max(yy)=max(yy $\cup$ {0}) =>
          zz/=0 & zz=zz

≡

yy/={} & TRUE => zz/=0 & TRUE

≡

yy/={} => zz/=0

≡

TRUE

Thus we have shown that the above refinement preserves safety properties. In a more general setting, a major benefit of this safety preserving facet, is that we need not 're-prove' already proven safety properties of refined machines. Thus, if we can show that the successive refinements of a machine are provably correct, then having shown that various safety properties are satisfied at the specification level, we can be assured that these properties are also provable for any of these refinements.

4   Conclusions

We have shown how test case selection of specifications can be achieved, within the AMN framework. The benefit of this is that we can animate our resulting specification in order to simulate a test suite, under which our original specification is the target. Additionally we have shown that there is a relationship between testing and safety analysis. The result of this is a formalisation of a weakest pre-condition semantics for the various substitutions of AM's. As a consequence we have found that refinement of AM's preserves safety properties.

References

[1] Abrial J. -R., *A Refinement Case Study (Using the Abstract Machine Notation)*, 4th Refinement Workshop, Workshops in Computing, Springer Verlag, 1991.

[2] Leveson N.G, Harver P.R., *Analyzing Software Safety*, Trans. on Software Eng. SE-9(5),IEEE (September 1983)

[3] Parnas D., *A technique for software module specification. CACM 15, 330-336*

Formal Development of Authentication Protocols*

Pierre Bieber, Nora Boulahia-Cuppens

ONERA-CERT

Toulouse, France

Abstract

In this paper, we apply the B method to the formal development of authentication protocols. Our approach consists in first providing a very abstract specification of authentication, and then refining progressively this specification in order to obtain an authentication protocol. During the refinement process we consider various ways to use encrypted messages and to distribute encryption keys that we relate with several existing protocols.

1 Introduction

Authentication protocol verification methods, as the work in [BAN90], have generally adopted a bottom-up approach. They first consider an already existing protocol, and then they build an abstract description of this protocol. This description is developed because it is more suitable than the existing protocol for the verification of security properties. Unfortunately, these methods failed to provide a mathematical counterpart of the link between the abstract description and the concrete protocol. This led to controversies on the value of the proofs that were performed on the abstract description, see [Nes90, Syv91]. We think that a formally defined theory of refinement could be used in order to provide such a mathematical counterpart.

In this paper, we propose to formally develop authentication protocols. We would like to show that it is possible to follow a top-down approach rather than the bottom-up approach currently used for the study of this kind of protocols. Our approach consists in first providing a very abstract specification of authentication, and then refining progressively this specification in order to obtain an authentication protocol. For that purpose we use an existing formal software development method called B [Abr91, Abr92]. This method contains a specification language that is state-oriented and that shares some notations with Z [Spi89]. We also use B-Toolkit [Abr92], a tool that supports every aspects of this method, in order to build and verify the various specifications and refinements found in this paper.

In the first section of the paper, we describe the basic concepts of security protocols. We also introduce the B-method and illustrate it with a model of a

---

*This work was supported by the Commission of the European Community, Contract Number S2011.The content of this paper does not reflect the views or legislation of the European Communities.

communication channel. Secondly, we propose an abstract model of authentication protocols and refine it. In this section, we show how to implement authenticated communication in the presence of malicious agents by using already distributed cryptographic keys. In the third section, we propose an abstract model of key distribution and refine it. In this last section, we show how to distribute keys on the channel in a secure fashion.

2 Services of Security Protocols

2.1 Communication with Malicious Agents

Authentication protocols are supposed to work in the presence of malicious agents that disrupt communication. Let's consider a step of a protocol corresponding to the following exchange of message:

$$A \longrightarrow B : m$$

This means that A sends to B message m and this message is received by B. We consider three basic malicious actions that could be performed by X a malicious agent :

- *Listening* (or eavesdropping) : A sends m to B, X and B receives message m.

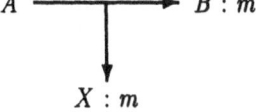

- *Blocking*: A sends m to B, X receives message m but B does not receive it.

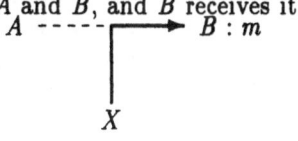

- *Masquerading* (or forging): X sends message m to B on the communication link devoted to A and B, and B receives it.

We can see from the definitions of these actions that in the presence of malicious agents:

- Whenever an agent sends a message it does know who will receive it.

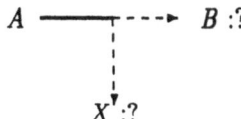

- Whenever an agent receives a message it does not know who has sent it.

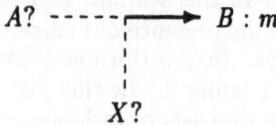

$$A? ----- \longrightarrow B : m$$

$$X?$$

When adding to a communication channel malicious agents the uncertainty about actual sender and receiver identities is increased. The goal of communication security properties is mainly to reduce this uncertainty. There are four communication security properties that appear as services of secure protocols in the ISO framework ([ISO87]):

- Data confidentiality and proof (or non-repudiation) of reception are concerned with the identity of agents that receive messages. In the context of a communication channel, data confidentiality is enforced if the agents that actually receive a message were authorized to receive it. And, proof of reception is achieved if every received message that an agent should receive is actually received by this agent.

- Data origin authentication and proof (or non-repudiation) of origin are concerned with the identity of the agents that sent the messages. In the context of a communication channel, data origin authentication is achieved if agents only send messages they are authorized to send. And, proof of origin is enforced if every sent message that an agent should send was actually sent by this agent.

2.2 Using the B-method: A Model of a Communication Channel

In the following, the mathematical model (or specification) of a communication channel is given in terms of a B abstract machine called *channel*. An abstract machine is divided in two parts:

- **Static description:** this part contains a declaration of mathematical objects used to model the state. These objects are the basic sets, constants, and the variables. There are two logical statements one corresponding to properties to be verified by the constants, and the other is an invariant that constrains the values of the variables.

- **Dynamic description:** this part contains a description of the initialisation of the machine and a description of the operations on the state variables.

2.2.1 Statics of a Communication Channel

The *channel* machine uses several sets.

SETS

   MSG, is the set of all messages.

CONSTANTS

ENV , is the set of messages that can be communicated.
CLEAR_MSG , is the set of clear-text messages.
AGENT , is the set of communicating agents identifiers.

Messages that can be communicated and clear-text messages belong to *MSG*. And we suppose that agent identifiers are clear-text messages.

PROPERTIES

$ENV \subseteq MSG \wedge$
$CLEAR\_MSG \subseteq MSG \wedge$
$AGENT \subseteq CLEAR\_MSG$

There are five variables in machine *channel*.

VARIABLES

channel , models all the communication links between pairs of agents.
rcvd_by , relates a message with agents that received it.
rcvd_from , relates a message with agents that are supposed to have sent it.
sent_by, relates a message with agents that have sent it.
sent_to, relates a message with agents that are intended to receive it.

The invariant contains properties that relate the variables with the sets we have just defined. We consider that *channel* is a relation from the set *ENV* to the set *AGENT* × *AGENT*, and *rcvd_by*, *rcvd_from*, *sent_to* and *sent_by* are relations from *ENV* to *AGENT*. In B, see [Abr92] the notations for sets, relations, functions are similar to that of Z [Spi89], so we do not explain them in great detail.

The invariant also contains properties that formally state the services offered by the channel. We consider two properties:

- *Every sent or received message has a destination and an origin.*

The formal statement corresponding to this property is that the set of messages sent by any agent $(\text{dom}(sent\_by))$ is equal to the set of messages sent to any agent $(\text{dom}(sent\_to))$ and the set of messages received by any agent $(\text{dom}(rcvd\_by))$ is equal to the set of messages received from any agent $(\text{dom}(rcvd\_from))$.

- *Every sent message is in transit on the channel or already received.*

This property is modelled by the equality of the set of sent messages $(\text{dom}(sent\_by))$ with the union of the set of messages in transit $(\text{dom}(channel))$ and the set of received messages $(\text{dom}(rcvd\_by))$.

INVARIANT

$channel \in ENV \leftrightarrow AGENT \times AGENT \wedge$
$rcvd\_by \in ENV \leftrightarrow AGENT \wedge$
$rcvd\_from \in ENV \leftrightarrow AGENT \wedge$
$sent\_by \in ENV \leftrightarrow AGENT \wedge$
$sent\_to \in ENV \leftrightarrow AGENT \wedge$
$\text{dom}(rcvd\_by) = \text{dom}(rcvd\_from) \wedge$
$\text{dom}(sent\_by) = \text{dom}(sent\_to) \wedge$
$\text{dom}(sent\_by) = \text{dom}(channel) \cup \text{dom}(rcvd\_from)$

Notice that according to the second property it is not certain that the identity of the actual sender is equal to the identity of the supposed sender. Hence, if we assume that the supposed sender is the authorized sender, data origin authentication is not enforced. And it is not certain that the identity of the actual receiver is equal to the identity of the intended receiver. Hence, if we assume that the intended receiver is the authorized receiver, data confidentiality is not enforced.

2.2.2 Dynamics of a Communication Channel

In this part of the abstract machine we describe how the channel may evolve. This is done by means of operations that change the value of the variables. In the B-method, the formal counterpart of operations is a generalisation of the notion of substitution of first-order logic, noted $[v := E]$ P, where P is a predicate, v a variable and E is an expression (a set-theoretic term). This construct denotes the formula obtained after replacing every free occurrence of variable v in P by E.

In the various machines and refinements of this paper we only use the following generalized substitutions:

- $x, y := E, F$ (or $x := E \| y := F$) :
  Multiple (or parallel) substitution that substitutes simultaneously several distinct variables x and y by two set-theoretic terms E and F. It can be defined, as follows:

  $$[x, y := E, F]P \Leftrightarrow [a := E][b := F][x := a][y := b]P$$

  where a and b are variables that are different from each other, different from variables x and y, and they are not free in P.

- PRE P THEN S END :
  The preconditioned substitution such that substitution S is applied only if P is true. It can be defined, as follows:

  $$[\text{PRE } P \text{ THEN } S \text{ END}]R \Leftrightarrow P \wedge [S]R$$

- ANY x WHERE P THEN S END :
  The non-deterministic substitution, that applies substitution S with any value of x that verifies P. It can be defined, as follows:

  $$[\text{ANY } x \text{ WHERE } P \text{ THEN } S \text{ END}]R \Leftrightarrow (\forall x.(P \Rightarrow [S]R))$$

- $x : P$:
  The non-deterministic substitution that applies any substition to x that establishes P. It can be defined, as follows, where y is distrinct from x and not free in P:

  $$[x : P]R \Leftrightarrow [\text{ANY } y \text{ WHERE } P \text{ THEN } x := y \text{ END}]R$$

The dynamic part of machine *channel* contains a substitution that establishes the initial state. Initially no message was transmitted, hence we use a parallel substitution that sets all the variables to the empty set.

INITIALISATION
$channel, \ rcvd\_by, \ rcvd\_from, \ sent\_by, \ sent\_to \ := \ \varnothing, \ \varnothing, \ \varnothing, \ \varnothing, \ \varnothing$

Machine *channel* contains five operations corresponding to honest sending, honest receiving of messages, and to the three malicious actions.

Operation $send(aa, bb, env)$ corresponds to agent aa sending to agent bb message env. We use a preconditioned substitution where the precondition is that aa and bb are two agents and env is a message then, simultaneously, it is recorded that env was sent by aa to bb and this message is put on the communication link devoted to aa and bb.

OPERATIONS
$send(aa, \ bb, \ env) \ \ \widehat{=}$
    PRE
        $env \in ENV \ \ \wedge$
        $aa \in AGENT \ \ \wedge$
        $bb \in AGENT$
    THEN
        $sent\_by := \{ env \mapsto aa \} \cup sent\_by \ \ ||$
        $sent\_to := \{ env \mapsto bb \} \cup sent\_to \ \ ||$
        $channel := \{ env \mapsto (aa \mapsto bb) \} \cup channel$
    END ;

Operation $receive(aa, bb, env)$ corresponds to agent bb receiving message env from agent aa. If aa and bb are two agents and env is a message that is on the communication link devoted to aa and bb then it is recorded that this message was received by bb from aa and this pair is removed from this communication link.

$receive(aa, \ bb, \ env) \ \ \widehat{=}$
    PRE
        $aa \in AGENT \ \wedge$
        $bb \in AGENT \ \wedge$
        $env \in ENV \ \wedge$
        $env \mapsto (aa \mapsto bb) \in channel$
    THEN
        $rcvd\_by := \{ env \mapsto bb \} \cup rcvd\_by \ \ ||$
        $rcvd\_from := \{ env \mapsto aa \} \cup rcvd\_from \ \ ||$
        $channel := channel - \{ env \mapsto (aa \mapsto bb) \}$
    END

Operation $listen(aa, bb, xx, env)$ corresponds to agent xx listening message env on the communication link devoted to agents aa and bb. It is similar to $receive(aa, bb, env)$ but it is recorded that this pair was received by malicious agent xx instead of bb and the message is not removed from the communication link.

$listen(aa, bb, xx, env) \;\; \widehat{=}$

PRE

   $aa \in AGENT \;\wedge$

   $bb \in AGENT \;\wedge$

   $xx \in AGENT \;\wedge$

   $env \in ENV \;\wedge$

   $env \mapsto (aa \mapsto bb) \in channel$

THEN

   $rcvd\_by := \{env \mapsto xx\} \cup rcvd\_by \;||$

   $rcvd\_from := \{env \mapsto aa\} \cup rcvd\_from$

END ;

Operation $block(aa, bb, xx, env)$ is similar to $listen$ but message env is removed from the communication link devoted to agents aa and bb.

$block(aa, bb, xx, env) \;\; \widehat{=}$

PRE

   $aa \in AGENT \;\wedge$

   $bb \in AGENT \;\wedge$

   $xx \in AGENT \;\wedge$

   $env \in ENV \;\wedge$

   $env \mapsto (aa \mapsto bb) \in channel$

THEN

   $rcvd\_by := \{env \mapsto xx\} \cup rcvd\_by \;||$

   $rcvd\_from := \{env \mapsto aa\} \cup rcvd\_from \;||$

   $channel := channel - \{env \mapsto (aa \mapsto bb)\}$

END ;

Operation $masquerade(aa, bb, xx, env)$ corresponds to agent xx sending message env on the communication link devoted to agents aa and bb. It is similar to $send(aa, bb, env)$ but it is recorded that env was sent by xx instead of aa.

$masquerade(aa, bb, xx, env) \;\; \widehat{=}$

PRE

   $aa \in AGENT \;\wedge$

   $bb \in AGENT \;\wedge$

   $xx \in AGENT \;\wedge$

   $env \in ENV$

THEN

   $sent\_by := \{env \mapsto xx\} \cup sent\_by \;||$

   $sent\_to := \{env \mapsto bb\} \cup sent\_to \;||$

   $channel := \{env \mapsto (aa \mapsto bb)\} \cup channel$

END

2.2.3 Verification of Machine channel

As we have specified the channel with a mathematical notation, we can formally prove its consistency. This is done by proving that the invariant holds in every state reached by the machine. We first have to prove that the initialization establishes the invariant. We should prove that the formula obtained by applying the substitution $init$ corresponding to the initialization on the invariant I is true:

$[init]I$

Then, we have to show that the invariant is preserved by the operations. We should prove for each operation that if the invariant and *Pre_opn* the precondition of the operation hold then the formula obtained by applying the substitution *opn* corresponding to the operation on the invariant also holds:

$$I \wedge Pre\_opn \Rightarrow [opn]I$$

The formulas to be proven are called proof-obligations. The proof can be made easier by generating proof obligations for each conjunct of the invariant rather than for the whole invariant. The machine *channel* has been created with the help of Btoolkit. It has been syntactically analysed, type-checked and its proof obligations were generated with this tool. Then the proof obligations were discharged using B-toolkit interactive prover.

3 Formal Development of Authentication Protocols

In this section, we describe the formal development of authentication protocols. We first create a very abstract specification of any of these protocols. Then we build various refinements of this specification and relate them with well-known protocols.

3.1 An Abstract Model of Authentication Protocols

The machine *authentic* contains an abstract specification of any authentication protocol. It is based on the formal statement of the authentication property. This statement, as well as the statement of other security properties, is explained in more details in [BBCLvW93].

MACHINE
 authentic

In order to state formally authentication we need three variables:

VARIABLES
 actual_sender , relates a clear-text message with agents that actually sent it.
 authorized_sender , relates a received clear-text message with agents that are authorized to send it.
 in_transit, is the set of sent clear-text messages that were not yet received.

As we have seen in section 2, data origin authentication is enforced if agents only send messages they are authorized to send. Here, we consider that this property is achived if, for every message that is not in transit, the actual senders of this message are also authorized senders. The last conjunct of the invariant is the formal counterpart of this statement. *in_transit* ◁ *actual_sender* is a relation from *CLEAR_MSG* to *AGENT* that is equal to relation *actual_sender* where all the pairs $m \mapsto a$ such that m belongs to *in_transit* are removed.

INVARIANT

$$actual\_sender \in CLEAR\_MSG \leftrightarrow AGENT \land$$
$$authorized\_sender \in CLEAR\_MSG \leftrightarrow AGENT \land$$
$$in\_transit \subseteq CLEAR\_MSG \land$$
$$in\_transit \vartriangleleft actual\_sender \subseteq authorized\_sender$$

Initially no messages are transmitted, hence all the variables are equal to the empty set.

INITIALISATION

$$actual\_sender \ , \ authorized\_sender \ , \ in\_transit := \varnothing \ , \ \varnothing \ , \ \varnothing$$

Machine *authentic* has two operations, *authentic_send* and *authentic_receive*. Operation *authentic_send*(aa, bb, mm) corresponds to the authenticated transmission by agent aa to agent bb of clear-text message mm. If aa, bb and mm are correctly typed then this operation is any substitution that establishes the invariant of machine *authentic* (and, in particular, the authentication property).

OPERATIONS

$$authentic\_send \ (\ aa \ , \ bb \ , \ mm \ ) \ \ \widehat{=}$$

PRE

$$aa \in AGENT \land$$
$$bb \in AGENT \land$$
$$mm \in CLEAR\_MSG$$

THEN

$$actual\_sender, \ authorized\_sender, \ in\_transit : Inv\_authentic$$

END

Operation *authentic_receive*(aa, bb, mm) corresponds to agent bb receiving from aa in an authenticated fashion clear-text message mm. This operation is defined as *authentic_send*(aa, bb, mm). Due to the definition of its two operations, the consistency of machine *authentic* can be proved very easily.

3.2 Authentication with Envelopes

In this section we build a first refinement of the *authentic* machine that shows how to implement authenticated communication on a communication channel with malicious agents.

3.2.1 Envelopes

As we have seen in section 2, a communication channel with malicious agents is unable to achieve any of the basic security properties. In order to implement data origin authentication on this kind of communication channel we consider two disjoint sets of messages: clear-text messages and envelopes. Clear-text messages are messages that should be protected and should not be sent directly on the channel. Envelopes are messages that can be transmitted on the channel (i.e. they are members of *ENV*), they model protected messages. An envelope has three attributes: content, address and source.

CONSTANTS

content , relates an envelope with clear-text messages that the envelope contains and protects.

address , relates an envelope with agents that are authorized to open the envelope and use its content for communication.

source, relates an envelope with agents that are authorized to create the envelope.

PROPERTIES

$$ENV = MSG - CLEAR\_MSG \wedge$$
$$ENV \cap CLEAR\_MSG = \varnothing \wedge$$
$$content \in ENV \leftrightarrow CLEAR\_MSG \wedge$$
$$source \in ENV \leftrightarrow AGENT \wedge$$
$$address \in ENV \leftrightarrow AGENT$$

Envelopes provide protection for the enclosed clear-text messages against the malicious agents. If a malicious agent blocks or listens an envelope and this agent does not belong to the address of the envelope then it cannot open it, hence it does not receive the enclosed clear-text messages. Conversely, if a malicious agent sends an envelope masquerading as another agent and this malicious agent is not included in the source then it did not create the envelope, it just forwarded it. The actual sender of clear-text messages enclosed in the envelope belongs to the source of the envelope. Hence, in order to transmit in a secure fashion a clear-text message it is sufficient to enclose this message into an envelope sealed with the identity of the creator in the source and the identity of the destination in the address.

3.2.2 Authentication with Sealed Envelopes

In order to transmit clear-text message m in an authenticated fashion for agents A and B, it is sufficient to send and receive m enclosed in an envelope which source is equal to $\{A, B\}$:

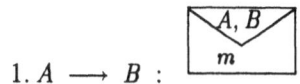

$$1. A \longrightarrow B :$$

In order to show formally this result we create a refinement *auth_env* of machine *authentic*. According to the B-method, the structure of a refinement is very similar to that of abstract machines. We explain how to build a refinement in this section and illustrate it with the *auth_env* refinement.

REFINEMENT

auth_env

REFINES

authentic

As an abstract machine, the refinement contains variables and an invariant that includes typing information about these new variables. Here, the refinement contains the variables and invariant of machine *channel* defined in section 2. But, the invariant also contains a change of variable that is given by a formula involving the variables of the machine being refined and of the refinement. This formula establishes the logical link between the abstract and the concrete variables.

90

We add to the invariant of machine *channel* the three equalities that relate variables of *authentic* and *auth_env*. The set of clear-text messages in transit is equal to the set of messages enclosed in envelopes that are transmitted on the communication links. Hence, *in_transit* is equal to the domain of the composition of *content*$^{-1}$ that relates clear-text message with all the envelopes it is enclosed in and *channel* that relates an envelope in transit with a communication link. The actual senders of a clear-text message are agents that actually sent an envelope containing it and that appear in the source of this envelope. Hence, *actual_sender* is equal to the composition of *content*$^{-1}$ and *sent_by* ∩ *source* that relates an envelope with agents that sent it and that belong to its source. The authorized senders of a received clear-text messages are the agents contained in the source of a received envelope enclosing this message. Hence, *authorized_sender* is equal to the composition of *content*$^{-1}$ with dom(*rcvd_from*) ◁ *source* that relates received envelopes (members of dom(*rcvd_from*)) with agents authorized to create them.

INVARIANT

$in\_transit = \mathrm{dom}(\ content\ ^{-1}\ ;\ channel\ ) \wedge$
$actual\_sender = content\ ^{-1}\ ;\ (sent\_by \cap source) \wedge$
$authorized\_sender = content\ ^{-1}\ ;\ (\mathrm{dom}(\ rcvd\_from\ ) \vartriangleleft source)$

The dynamic part of a refinement should contain definitions for the operations of the machine being refined as well as an initialisation of the new variables. Here, the initialisation is equal to that of machine *channel*. The modified definition of *authentic_send* states that *aa* may send to *bb* any envelope *env* that contains message *mm* and which source is {*aa*, *bb*}. The precondition of this operation is not modified. In the THEN part the non-deterministic substitution establishing the authentication property is replaced by a call to the *send*(*aa*, *bb*, *env*) operation of *channel* for any correct envelope *env*. The use of *send* in this operation may be regarded as an abbreviation, the complete definition of *authentic_send* could be obtained by expanding the definition of *send*. The definition of *authentic_receive* is very similar to that of *authentic_send*.

OPERATIONS

    authentic_send (aa , bb , mm) $\widehat{=}$

        PRE

            $aa \in AGENT \wedge$
            $bb \in AGENT \wedge$
            $mm \in CLEAR\_MSG$

        THEN

            ANY

                env

            WHERE

                $env \in ENV \wedge$
                $env \mapsto mm \in content \wedge$
                $source\ [\ \{\ env\ \}\ ] = \{\ aa\ ,\ bb\ \}$

            THEN

                send(aa,bb,env)

            END

        END ;

$authentic\_receive$ (aa , bb , mm) $\widehat{=}$
   PRE

     ...

   THEN
     ANY

        env

     WHERE

        $env \in ENV \land$
        $env \mapsto mm \in content \land$
        $source [\{ env \}] = \{ aa , bb \} \land$
        $env \mapsto (aa \mapsto bb) \in channel$

     THEN
        $receive(aa, bb, env)$

     END

   END ;

Furthermore, the refinement also contains definitions of the malicious operations. Operation *listen_attack* models a listen attack performed by agent *ee* on the communication link devoted to *aa* and *bb*.

$listen\_attack$ (aa , bb , ee) $\widehat{=}$
   PRE

     $aa \in AGENT \land$
     $bb \in AGENT \land$
     $ee \in AGENT$

   THEN
     ANY

        env

     WHERE

        $env \in ENV \land$
        $env \mapsto (aa \mapsto bb) \in channel$

     THEN
        $listen(aa, bb, ee, env)$

     END

   END

$block\_attack(aa, bb, ee)$ and $masquerade\_attack(aa, bb, ee)$ are defined in the same fashion than $listen\_attack(aa, bb, ee)$.

The correctness of a refinement may also be verified. According to [Abr92] this is done by proving, for each operation, that the new operation establishes that the old does not establish the negation of the invariant. We should prove, for each operation, that if the invariant $I_{abstract}$, $Pre\_opn_{abstract}$ the precondition of the abstract operation, and $I_{concrete}$ the invariant of the concrete machine hold then the formula obtained by applying the concrete substitution to the negation of the formula obtained by applying the abstract substitution on the negation of the concrete invariant also holds:

$I_{abstract} \land Pre\_opn_{abstract} \land I_{concrete} \Rightarrow [opn_{concrete}]\neg[opn_{abstract}]\neg I_{concrete}$

This refinement step was proved correct with the help of B-Toolkit.

Other refinements of *authentic* may be built. In particular, it should be possible to implement authenticated transmission on an ideal channel where no malicious agents is included. Such a refinement would only contain the two operations *authentic_send* and *authentic_receive*. As malicious agents cannot perform masquerade attacks, envelopes are no longer needed to protect the origin of clear-text messages. In this context open envelopes (i.e. envelopes that may be created and opened by any agent) may be transmitted. In this alternative refinement, we would replace $source[\{env\}] = \{aa, bb\}$ by $source[\{env\}] = AGENT$ in the definitions of *authentic_send* and *authentic_receive*. And the new change of variables would no longer contain reference to the source of the envelopes. The actual senders of a clear-text message are the actual senders of any envelope containing this message and the authorized senders are the agents that are expected to have sent the messages. This gives the new change of variables:

$$in\_transit = \text{dom}(\ content\ ^{-1}\ ;\ channel\ ) \wedge$$
$$actual\_sender = content\ ^{-1}\ ;\ sent\_by \wedge$$
$$authorized\_sender = content\ ^{-1}\ ;\ rcvd\_from$$

3.3 Authentication with Cryptographic Keys

In this section we build a new refinement that shows how authenticated communication may be implemented using cryptographic keys.

3.3.1 Basic Properties of Cryptographic Functions

Cryptographic functions is a fundamental technique used to enforce communication security. Agents use the two cryptographic functions, encryption and decryption, in order to compute messages that they exchange. Given a key k, encryption relates a message m with an enciphered message $\{m\}_k$. Given the decryption key k^{-1} corresponding to k, decryption relates $\{m\}_k$ with $\{\{m\}_k\}_{k^{-1}} = m$. We are interested by the two following properties of cryptographic functions:

- *Only agents knowing key k^{-1} can learn m from message $\{m\}_k$.*

- *Only agents knowing key k can create message $\{m\}_k$ from message m.*

We consider that envelopes may be implemented by encrypted messages. For that purpose, we associate each envelope with a key that is used to encrypt the content of the envelope.

CONSTANTS

key_comp , is a function that associates an envelope with the unique key used to seal this envelope.

key_inv , is a bijection that associates an encryption key with its corresponding decryption key.

key_authorize , relates keys with agents authorized to know them.

The *address* of an envelope is equal to the set of agents that are authorized to know the decryption key used to seal the envelope. Hence these agents can decrypt the encrypted message and learn the clear-text messages contained in it. The *source* of an envelope is equal to the set of agents that are authorized to know the encryption key used to seal the envelope. Hence these agents can encrypt the clear-text messages contained in the envelope.

PROPERTIES

$key\_comp \in ENV \rightarrow KEY \wedge$
$key\_inv \in KEY \twoheadrightarrow KEY \wedge$
$key\_authorize \in KEY \leftrightarrow AGENT \wedge$
$address = key\_comp \; ; \; key\_inv \; ; \; key\_authorize \wedge$
$source = key\_comp \; ; \; key\_authorize$

3.3.2 Authentication with Shared Keys

In the following, we will assume that we are using a symmetric cryptographic system where keys k and k^{-1} are equal. Hence, *key_inv* is equal to the identity relation on *KEY* and the source of an envelope is equal to its address. In this case, message $\{m\}_{k_{\{A,B\}}}$, where $k_{\{A,B\}}$ is a key shared by agents A and B, and m is a clear-text message is an implementation of an envelope that only contains message m and which source is $\{A, B\}$. Hence we can consider the protocol that is made of only one step, where A sends to B this message. A protocol of this kind appears under the name of one-way mutual authentication in the family of protocols proposed for standardization by ISO [ISO92]

$$1. \; A \longrightarrow B \; : \{m\}_{k_{\{A,B\}}}$$

We show that this protocol is a correct refinement of *authentic* by building *auth_key* that refines *auth_env*. This new refinement is purely algorithmic, it does not contain any new variable.

REFINEMENT

auth_key

REFINES

auth_env

We only change the definitions of *authentic_send* and *authentic_receive*. In the THEN part of operation *authentic_send* the *send* operation is called with any envelope and any key such that the envelope is sealed with the key and the only agents authorized to know the key are *aa* and *bb*. We perform a similar modification for the *authentic_receive* operation.

OPERATIONS

$authentic\_send \; (\; aa \; , \; bb \; , \; mm \;) \quad \widehat{=}$

    PRE

        ...

    THEN

        ANY

            $env \; , \; kk$

        WHERE

            $env \in ENV \wedge$

            $env \mapsto mm \in content \wedge$

$$kk \in KEY \wedge$$
$$env \mapsto kk \in key\_comp \wedge$$
$$key\_authorize\,[\,\{\,kk\,\}\,] = \{\,aa\,,\,\,bb\,\}$$
THEN
$$send(aa, bb, env)$$
END
END

Other refinements of *authentic* based on keys are possible. If we consider that assymetric cryptographic technique is used, agents may exchange message $\{m\}_{k_A{}^{-1}}$ where $k_A{}^{-1}$ is the private decryption key of A then every agent including B may know k_A and recognize that A is the creator of this message.

4 Formal Development of Key Distribution

In the previous refinement of *authentic* we considered that agents already shared keys. In this section, we study how these keys should be distributed. Again we create several refinements that we relate with existing protocols.

4.1 An Abstract Model of Key-distribution

We first build a refinement of *auth_key* that includes an operation devoted to the generation and distribution of keys. As the B method forbids to add new operation in a refinement, we suppose that the new operations were already existing in the refined machines and that there definition is the most non-deterministic substitution establishing the invariants of the refined machines.

REFINEMENT
  auth_dist
REFINES
  auth_key
VARIABLES
  used_key , is the set of already distributed keys.
  key_distribute , relates a distributed key with agents authorized
  to receive it.
  For every distributed key, the set of agents authorized to know the key is
  equal to the set of agents authorized to receive it.
INVARIANT
  $used\_key \subseteq KEY \wedge$
  $key\_distribute \in used\_key \leftrightarrow AGENT \wedge$
  $key\_distribute = \mathrm{dom}(\,key\_distribute\,) \lhd key\_authorize$
INITIALISATION
  $key\_distribute\,,\,used\_key := \varnothing\,,\,\varnothing$

Operation *distribute_key(aa, bb)* generates and distributes a key for agents *aa* and *bb*. It chooses any key that was never distributed and such that only *aa* and *bb* are authorized to know it. Then, it is recorded that *aa* and *bb* are authorized to receive this key and the key becomes a distributed key. Furthermore, we consider any substitution on communication variables that is consistent with the invariant of machine *channel*. This will allow to build refinements where keys are transmitted.

OPERATIONS

    distribute_key (*aa* , *bb*) $\hat{=}$

        PRE

            aa $\in$ *AGENT* $\wedge$

            bb $\in$ *AGENT*

        THEN

            ANY

                kk

            WHERE

                kk $\in$ *KEY* − *used_key* $\wedge$

                key_authorize [{ *kk* }] = { *aa* , *bb* }

            THEN

                key_distribute := *key_distribute* $\cup$ ({*kk* } $\times$ { *aa*,*bb*}) $\parallel$

                used_key := *used_key* $\cup$ { *kk* } $\parallel$

                rcvd_from,*rcvd_by*,*sent_to*,sent_by, channel : *Inv_channel*

            END

        END ;

In operations *authentic_send* and *authentic_receive* we replace *key_authorize* [{*kk*}] = {*aa*, *bb*} by *key_distribute*[{*kk*}] = {*aa*, *bb*}. Hence, when agents exchange messages in an authenticated fashion they use variable *key_distribute* in order to test the authorizations. This could be implemented by a trusted third party *AS* that would hold a database of authorizations and distribute the keys off-line.

4.2   On-line Key Distribution

We now propose that the trusted third party *AS* distributes the keys on the channel. It encloses the distributed key in two envelopes that should only be received by *aa* and *bb* and send them to *aa* and *bb*. Hence we study a protocol with a first step devoted to key distribution and a second step that is devoted to authenticated transmission.

1. $AS \longrightarrow A, B$:

2. $A \longrightarrow B$:

We build a refinement of *auth_dist* that contains two new operations devoted to the reception of the keys.

REFINEMENT

    auth_chan

REFINES

    auth_dist

VARIABLES

    $key\_receive\_r$, key reception authorizations according to B.

    $key\_receive\_s$, key reception authorizations according to A.

    For each key received by A, key reception authorizations according to A and to AS agree.

    For each key received by B, key reception authorizations according to B and to AS agree.

    $env\_distribute$, relates an envelope used to distribute the key with agents authorized to receive the key.

    The envelope should contain only one key.

INVARIANT

    $key\_receive\_r \in used\_key \leftrightarrow AGENT \land$

    $key\_receive\_s \in used\_key \leftrightarrow AGENT \land$

    $env\_distribute \in ENV \leftrightarrow AGENT \land$

    $key\_receive\_r = dom(\ key\_receive\_r\ ) \lhd key\_distribute \land$

    $key\_receive\_s = dom(\ key\_receive\_s\ ) \lhd key\_distribute \land$

    $KEY \lhd (content^{-1}\ ;\ env\_distribute) = key\_distribute \land$

    $dom(\ env\_distribute\ ) \lhd content \rhd KEY \in dom(\ env\_distribute\ ) \rightarrow KEY$

INITIALISATION

    $key\_receive\_s$, $key\_receive\_r$, $env\_distribute := \varnothing , \varnothing , \varnothing$

Operation $distribute\_key$ is modified in order to take into account the fact that two envelopes env_r and env_s are chosen such that they contain kk. Then, it is recorded that the content of these envelopes should be received by aa and bb, env_s is sent by AS to aa and env_r is sent by AS to bb.

OPERATIONS

    $distribute\_key\ (\ aa\ ,\ bb\ )\quad \widehat{=}$

        PRE

            ...

        THEN

            ANY

                env_r , env_s , kk

            WHERE

                $env\_r \in ENV \land$

                $env\_s \in ENV \land$

                $kk \in KEY - used\_key \land$

                $key\_authorize\ [\ \{\ kk\ \}\ ] = \{\ aa\ ,\ bb\ \} \land$

                $(content \rhd KEY)\ [\ \{\ env\_r\ \}\ ] = \{\ kk\ \} \land$

                $(content \rhd KEY)\ [\ \{\ env\_s\ \}\ ] = \{\ kk\ \}$

            THEN

                $key\_distribute := key\_distribute \cup (\ \{\ kk\ \} \times \{\ aa,\ bb\ \})\ \|$

                $used\_key := used\_key \cup \{\ kk\ \}\ \|$

                $env\_distribute := env\_distribute \cup (\{env\_r, env\_s\} \times \{aa, bb\})\ \|$

                $multiple\_send(\{env\_s \mapsto (AS \mapsto aa), env\_r \mapsto (AS \mapsto bb)\})$

            END

        END

To model the simultaneous sending by AS of the two envelopes we use the *multiple_send* operation that adds to *channel* the two pairs $env\_s \mapsto (AS \mapsto aa)$ and $env\_r \mapsto (AS \mapsto bb)$, and modifies adequately *sent_to* and *sent_by*. The use of *send(AS, aa, env_s)* ‖ *send(AS, bb, env_r)* would not be allowed by the B-method because simultaneous substitution should operate on distinct variables. Notice that in practice, see [BAN90, NS78], AS would send both envelopes to aa and, upon receiving env_s and env_r, aa would forward env_r to bb. If we want to model this behavior we would have to introduce a new operation *forward_key*.

Operation *receive_key_s*(aa, bb) corresponds to aa receiving from AS an envelope that contains a key to be shared with bb and aa stores this information locally.

$receive\_key\_s$ (aa , bb) $\hat{=}$

    PRE

        $aa \in AGENT \wedge$

        $bb \in AGENT$

    THEN

        ANY

            env , kk

        WHERE

            $env \in ENV \wedge$

            $kk \in used\_key \wedge$

            $env \mapsto kk \in content \wedge$

            $env\_distribute$ [{ env }] = { aa , bb } $\wedge$

            $env \mapsto$ ($AS \mapsto aa$) $\in channel$

        THEN

            $key\_receive\_s := key\_receive\_s \cup$ { $kk \mapsto aa$ } $\cup$ { $kk \mapsto bb$ } ‖

            $receive(AS, aa, env)$

        END

    END

Operation *receive_key_r*(aa, bb) that corresponds to bb receiving a key to be shared with aa is identical to *receive_key_s* with permutation of aa and bb, and bb stores the authorization in *key_receive_s* . In *authentic_send*, we replace *key_distribute* by *key_distribute_s*. And in *authentic_receive*, we replace *key_distribute* by *key_distribute_r*. Hence, now agents test their local view of authorizations when they exchange messages. The only variable that aa and bb test that is not modified by them is *env_distribute*. In practice see [BAN90, ISO92], agents would not test such a variable. They would instead test if the message was sent by AS and if it contains a key.

4.3 Secure Key-Distribution with Cryptographic Keys

Keys may be distributed securely using keys that are already shared by AS and the agents. If we follow the technique used in protocols as Otway-Rees or Yahalom protocols (see [BAN90]) then AS could use the key $k_{\{AS,A\}}$ that it shares with A in order to encrypt the distributed key, as well as the identity of the agent with whom the key is to be shared. AS can send a similar message to B with key $k_{\{AS,B\}}$. And then A and B may use key k to encrypt message m.

1. $AS \longrightarrow A : \{k, B\}_{k_{\{AS,A\}}}$
2. $AS \longrightarrow B : \{k, A\}_{k_{\{AS,B\}}}$
3. $A \longrightarrow B : \{m\}_k$

We build a refinement of $auth\_chan$ that does not contain any new variable. It replaces variable $env\_distribute$ by a constraint on sent envelopes.

REFINEMENT

    $auth\_sim\_env$

REFINES

    $auth\_chan$

In this particular key distribution protocol, the envelopes that contain keys to be shared by agent aa and bb model encrypted messages of the form $\{k, B\}_{k_{\{AS,A\}}}$ or $\{k, A\}_{k_{\{AS,B\}}}$. The source of these messages is $\{AS, A\}$ or $\{AS, B\}$, and the agent identifier they enclose is A or B. Hence envelopes used to distribute a key to be shared by A and B were sent (they belong to $\mathrm{dom}(sent\_by)$) and AS belongs to their source (they belong to $\mathrm{dom}(source \triangleright AS)$) and the union of their source without AS and the agent identifiers they contain (their image by relation $(source \triangleright \{AS\}) \cup (content \triangleright AGENT)$) is equal to $\{A, B\}$.

INVARIANT

    $env\_distribute =$
    $(\mathrm{dom}(\ sent\_by\ ) \cap \mathrm{dom}(\ source \triangleright \{\ AS\ \}\ ))$
    $\lhd ((\ source \triangleright \{\ AS\ \}\ ) \cup (\ content \triangleright AGENT\ ))$

In this refinement the definition of $distribute\_key$ is slightly modified in order to take into account encrypted messages.

OPERATIONS

    $distribute\_key\ (\ aa\ ,\ bb\ )\quad \widehat{=}$

        PRE

          ...

        THEN

            ANY

                $env\_r\ ,\ env\_s\ ,\ kk\ ,\ k\_a\ ,\ k\_b$

            WHERE

                $... \wedge$
                $k\_a \in KEY \wedge$
                $k\_b \in KEY \wedge$
                $key\_authorize\ [\ \{\ k\_a\ \}\ ] = \{\ AS\ ,\ aa\ \} \wedge$
                $key\_authorize\ [\ \{\ k\_b\ \}\ ] = \{\ AS\ ,\ bb\ \} \wedge$
                $env\_s \mapsto k\_a \in key\_comp \wedge$
                $env\_r \mapsto k\_b \in key\_comp \wedge$
                $(content \triangleright AGENT)\ [\ \{\ env\_r\ \}\ ] = \{\ bb\ \} \wedge$
                $(content \triangleright AGENT)\ [\ \{\ env\_s\ \}\ ] = \{\ aa\ \}$

            THEN   ...

            END

    END

In operation *receive_key_s* testing the membership to *env_distribute* is replaced by testing that the envelope is encrypted with a key shared with AS and that the envelope contains only one key and one agent. A similar modification is applied to *receive_key_r*

$receive\_key\_s$ (aa , bb) $\ \widehat{=}$

    PRE

        ...

    THEN

        ANY

            env , kk , k_a

        WHERE

            $env \in ENV \ \wedge$

            $kk \in used\_key \ \wedge$

            $k\_a \in KEY \ \wedge$

            $key\_authorize \ [\ \{ \ k\_a \ \} \ ] = \{ \ AS \ , \ aa \ \} \ \wedge$

            $(\ content \ \triangleright \ KEY) \ [\ \{ \ env \ \} \ ] = \{ \ kk \ \} \ \wedge$

            $(\ content \ \triangleright \ AGENT) \ [\ \{ \ env \ \} \ ] = \{ \ bb \ \} \ \wedge$

            $env \mapsto k\_a \in key\_comp \ \wedge$

            $env \mapsto (\ AS \mapsto aa \ ) \in channel$

        THEN   ...

        END

    END

In order to prove the correctness of this refinement we found out that we needed to constrain the messages that agents could send by using operations *authentic_send* or *masquerade*. We had to include that the sent envelope should already be sent or its source should not contain AS. Formally:

    $env \in dom(\ sent\_by \ ) \cup dom(\ source \ \triangleright \ \{ \ AS \ \} \ )$

Otherwise AS could send using operation *authentic_send* an envelope containing the distributed key to an agent that is not authorized to know this key. This would falsify the conjunct of the invariant stating that key reception authorizations according to the agents and AS agree. The added assumption is enforced in systems where AS never sends other envelopes than the one containing the distributed key, and where malicious agent cannot create envelopes containing in its source AS.

Other techniques using cryptographic keys to protect key-distribution exist. In particular, in the well-known Needham-Schroeder protocol [NS78], AS includes in the envelope that it sends to A a subenvelope containing the key that should be forwarded to B:

    1. $AS \ \longrightarrow \ A \ : \{k, B, \{k, A\}_{k_{(AS,B)}}\}_{k_{(AS,A)}}$

    2. $A \ \longrightarrow \ B \ : \{k, A\}_{k_{(AS,B)}}$

    3. $B \ \longrightarrow \ A \ : \{m\}_k$

5   Conclusion

Thanks to the formal development we have performed we can establish a taxonomy of authentication protocols. The classes correspond to the implementation choices that were made during the refinement process. For authentication, the main choices are the kind of malicious agents to be considered and the kind of cryptographic functions to be used. Then for key-distribution, off-line or on-line distribution, and the structure of the envelopes used are important. The following tree, relating authentication protocol specification with its refinements summarizes this taxonomy.

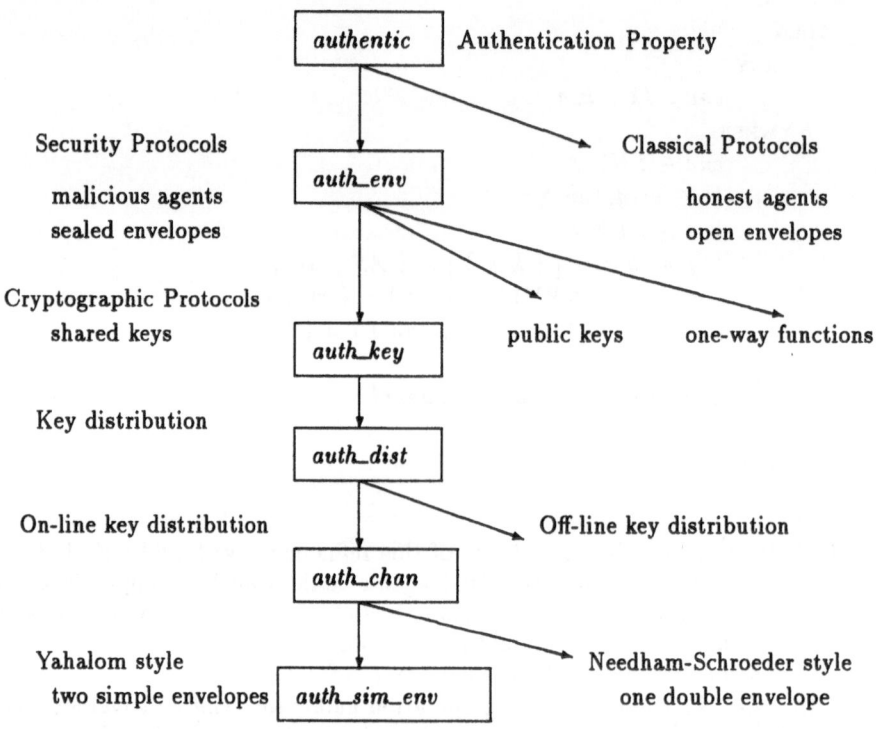

In this paper we omitted another important point in the development of authentication that are techniques for session management. These techniques are used in order to avoid or detect the replay of old messages by malicious a-gents. An abstract definition could be provided, it would be based on a variable that relates envelopes with session identifiers. There are several techniques to implement this relation with global or local clocks, time-stamps or nonces.

In this paper we have proposed a method for the development of security protocols that is based on a refinement technique that was designed for the p-reservation of functional correctness. It is well known since [Jac89] that security properties stated in terms of information flows are not preserved by refinement. These properties rely on the non-determinism of the system in order to hide information from malicious agents. Hence as refinement involves a reduction of the non-determinism of the system, such properties may not be preserved by a refinement step. In the case of confidentiality new forms of refinement were proposed [GCS91, O'H91]. We think that our results are not contradictory with these works because the security properties we are dealing with are less elaborated than information-flow properties. In our context, agents may only learn the content of a message by receiving, listening or blocking it. We do not consider that an agent can perform deductions in order to increase its knowledge. Hence we think that refinement should preserve this kind of security properties. A formal justification of this claim is a topic of further work.

Acknowledgement

We would like to thank Jean-Raymond Abrial, Erich van Wickeren and Thomas Lehmann for helpful discussions.

References

[Abr91]   J.R. Abrial. The B-method for large software specification, design and coding (abstract). In Prehn Toetenel, editor, *VDM'91*, volume 2. Springer-Verlag, 1991.

[Abr92]   J.R. Abrial. *Introducing B-Technologies*. B-core, 1992.

[BAN90]   M. Burrows, M. Abadi, and R. Needham. A logic of authentication. *ACM Transactions on Computer Systems*, 8(1):18 – 36, February 1990.

[BBCLvW93] P. Bieber, N. Boulahia-Cuppens, T. Lehmann, and E. van Wickeren. Abstract machines for communication security. In *Proc. of IEEE Workshop on Foundations of Computer Security VI*, 1993.

[GCS91]   J. Graham-Cumming and J. W. Sanders. On the Refinement of Non-Interference. In *Proc. of the computer security foundations workshop*, Franconia, 1991.

[ISO87]   ISO. Information processing system, open systens interconnection reference model, part 2: Security architecture. ISO/TC 97, 1987.

[ISO92]   ISO. Working draft: Entity authentication mechanisms part2: Entity authentication mechanisms using symmetric techniques. ISO/IEC/JTC1/SC 27/WG2 N 167, 1992.

[Jac89]   J. Jacob. On the derivation of secure components. In *IEEE Symposium on Security and Privacy*, Oakland, 1989.

[Nes90]   D. Nessett. A critique of Burrows, Abadi and Needham Logic. *ACM operating systems review*, 24(2), 1990.

[NS78]   R.M. Needham and M.D. Schroeder. Using Encryption for Authentication in Large Networks of Computers. *Communications of the ACM*, 21(12):993 – 999, December 1978.

[O'H91]   C. O'Halloran. Refinement and Confidentiality. In *Proc. of the fifth refinement workshop*, London, 1991.

[Spi89]   J.M. Spivey. *The Z Notation. A Reference Manual*. Prentice-Hall, 1989.

[Syv91]   P. Syverson. The use of Logics in the Analysis of Cryptographic
            Protocols. In *IEEE Symposium on Security and Privacy*, Oak-
            land, 1991.

Deriving language recognition algorithms: A case study in combining program specialisation and data refinement

Lindsay Groves

Department of Computer Science
Victoria University of Wellington
Wellington, New Zealand
lindsay@comp.vuw.ac.nz

Abstract

We show how several language recognition algorithms can be derived from a single abstract algorithm. This is done using a strategy that involves doing the initial development with a generalised specification, and then specialising the specification, and the development to that point, when this is necessary to expedite later steps — in particular, to allow data refinements. This strategy makes it clear which steps depend on which parts of the specification; we believe it also reflects more accurately the way in which many algorithms are actually discovered. This approach also focusses our attention on finding a common abstraction from which several familiar algorithms can be derived, which increases our understanding of the relationships between these algorithms, and suggests directions for deriving other related algorithms.

1   Introduction

One of the major problems in software development is that of controlling complexity. In a large software system there are an enormous number of details to be attended to and numerous interactions between related parts, and hence between design decisions, to be considered. This problem is even more apparent when we attempt to derive software formally — though as Dijkstra points out, the complexity was always there; the use of formalism only makes it more evident. The most effective way known of addressing this problem is separation of concerns: breaking a problem into parts that can be addressed separately and then combined. This division can be either *vertical*, leading to a modular structure, or *horizontal*, leading to a system composed of several layers. In practice both approaches are used in concert, and in both cases we need some kind of strategy for determining how to make the necessary divisions.

One strategy for horizontal division of a system is the use of data abstraction. We initially ignore details of data representation and derive an abstract program which does not depend on any particular data representation; we then introduce the details of a particular data representation, and perhaps make various optimisations admitted by the chosen representation. This process has been studied extensively and has become a major part of modern software design methods. Facilities for supporting various forms of data abstraction have been incorporated in many modern programming languages. The use of data abstraction has been formalised as *data refinement* (e.g. [16], [17]).

An alternative and complementary approach is to begin by considering a *generalisation* of the problem, obtained by ignoring some of the requirements; in particular we can ignore some of the assumptions about the inputs. We can then develop software for the generalised problem, and later *specialise* it to address the omitted requirements. Making use of these additional assumptions often allows the software to be made more efficient — in particular it may allow data refinements that were not previously possible — and may make it feasible. A useful strategy for deciding what to omit is to retain for the initial specification those parts that are common to a family of related problems, so the issue becomes one of identifying a suitable family of problems and finding suitable abstractions with which to describe them.

The use of program specialisation in the context of program refinement has been described by Gravell [7], who shows that a number of different search algorithms and some arithmetic algorithms can be obtained by specialising a generic search algorithm. In this paper, we illustrate the use of program specialisation in tandem with data refinement to derive a family of language recognition algorithms. We begin by considering some simple language recognition problems and derive a recognition algorithm for a generalisation of these. We then specialise this algorithm to obtain algorithms for a number of specific classes of languages. The derivations are presented fairly informally, to emphasis to strategy being used; they can all be formalised in the refinement calculus [15]. As well as demonstrating the utility of these derivation techniques, this also shows some interesting relationships between the algorithms derived.

We begin by formulating the language recognition problem in a very general way (Section 2) and deriving a generic language recognition algorithm (Section 3). We then consider a number of restrictions on the language handled, and data refinements that they allow, to obtain concrete algorithms. Section 4 introduces the techniques of program specialisation and data refinement while discussing the trivial class of singleton languages. Sections 5 through 7 deal with more interesting classes of languages: finite languages, regular languages and a subclass of context-free languages. In Section 8 we present our conclusions. Throughout, we assume standard terminology and definitions from language theory (see, for example, [10] or [11]).

2 Defining the problem

We wish to derive a family of language recognition algorithms, by first deriving a generic recognition algorithm and then specialising it to obtain the various particular algorithms. The kinds of algorithms we wish to derive are those used in common language processing programs such as compilers. In particular, we include recognisers for regular and (some) context-free languages. It is also instructive to consider the simpler cases of finite languages and singleton languages.

The common theme of these language recognition problems is that we are given some alphabet A (i.e. a finite set of symbols), a string s over A and a description of a language L over $\mathcal{A}$, and we require to determine whether s is a sentence in L. The problems differ in the class of language to which L must belong; and the details of the resulting algorithms depend heavily on the class of language for their operation.

We will begin with a very general statement of the language recognition problem, ignoring the issue of what kind of language we are recognising. At this stage, we will just take a language to be a set of strings; restrictions to particular classes of languages will be considered later. Thus, our initial statement of the problem is simply: Given a string s and a language L, both over an alphabet $\mathcal{A}$, we wish to determine whether $s \in L$.

We can now formalise this as a specification statement [15]. A specification statement $w : [\, Pre \,, Post \,]$ will establish the postcondition $Post$ altering only variables in w, provided the precondition Pre is true initially. If we return the result as a boolean variable, r, we can express our specification as:

$$r : [\, s \in \mathcal{A}^* \ \wedge \ L \subseteq \mathcal{A}^* \,, r \equiv s \in L \,]$$

We will assume that string comparison is not a primitive operation, so we are not able to simply compare s with each string in L — in any case, L may not be finite. Instead, we will inspect one symbol of s at a time, and use that to successively narrow down the part of L in which s could occur. We will look at symbols in s from left to right, since that is the way that most of the algorithms we are interested in operate, though other choices are certainly possible. We could formalise these assumptions in terms of a definition of the target programming language in which the solution is to be expressed (e.g. by specifying the operations that can be applied to strings); we prefer, however, to simply use this as guidance in deriving the initial algorithm.

We will introduce one further assumption at this stage: We assume that s and every string in L is terminated with a special "sentinel" symbol (for which we will use \$) which cannot occur anywhere else in s or L. We will formalise this requirement by defining, for any alphabet $\mathcal{A}$, the set of \$-terminated strings to be $\Sigma_\mathcal{A}$. Formally[1]:

$$\Sigma_\mathcal{A} \;\hat{=}\; \{\, w \in \mathcal{A}^* \mid \forall i \in 1 .. \#w \bullet w[i] = \$ \;\equiv\; i = \#w \,\}$$

Our assumption can now be expressed as $s \in \Sigma_\mathcal{A} \ \wedge \ L \subseteq \Sigma_\mathcal{A}$.

The main reason for making this assumption is that it simplifies our reasoning later, since it avoids having to make a special case when s is a prefix of some string in L but is not itself a sentence in L (see Section 3.2). It is common in automata theory to assume that the input ends with some kind of end-of-input (or end-of-tape) marker, presumably for exactly the same reason — to avoid excessive special cases; our sentinel symbol plays exactly the same rôle. The addition of the sentinel symbol can be considered as a data refinement. In many systems, strings, files, etc. are implemented like this anyway. In other cases, we need to add the sentinel symbol when the actual end of input is seen — in which case we have an explicit data conversion performed "on-the-fly".

With this additional assumption, the specification is now:

---

[1] We index strings from 1 and write $\#s$ for the length of string s. We write $s[i .. j]$ for the substring of s beginning at index i and ending at index j, which is empty (λ) if $i > j$, and use $s[i ..]$ as an abbreviation for $s[i .. \#s]$. To simplify notation, we do not distinguish between a symbol and a string of length one, thus we treat $s[i .. i]$ the same as $s[i]$.

$$r : [s \in \Sigma_A \land L \subseteq \Sigma_A, r \equiv s \in L]$$

Since the preconditions $s \in \Sigma_A$ and $L \subseteq \Sigma_A$ remain invariant throughout, we will treat them as global invariants and not include them explicitly in subsequent specifications, loop invariants, etc[2].

3 Deriving a generic language recognition algorithm

We will now proceed to derive a generic language recognition algorithm to implement the above specification. As indicated above, we will look at symbols in s one at a time, from left to right. Our generic recognition algorithm will therefore need a loop which iterates through successive symbols of s.

We observe that each symbol of s that the algorithm looks at effectively reduces the part of L in which s could occur. Thus, we can view the algorithm as computing a sequence of sets $L_1, L_2, \cdots$, where L_k is the set of strings in L that have $s[1 .. k - 1]$ as a prefix. We note that $L_1 = L$ and $L_{k+1} \subseteq L_k$ for $k = 1, \cdots, \#s$. If $L_k = \{\}$ for any $k \in 1 .. \#s$, then $s \notin L$; and if $\$ \in L_k$ for any $k \in 1 .. \#s$, then $s \in L$.

Rather than computing $L_1, L_2, \cdots$ explicitly, we will construct our generic algorithm so that it computes the sets $C_1, C_2, \cdots$, where C_k is the set of all strings that when contatenated with $s[1 .. k - 1]$ give a string in L (and in L_k). Thus, $L_k = \{s[1 .. k - 1]\} \frown C_k$. We can think of the set C_k at each step as the *candidate completion set*: s is in L if and only if the remaining input ($s[k ..]$) is in C_k. Thus, we need to maintain the following relationship:

$$s \in L \equiv s[k ..] \in C_k$$

This relationship can be taken as the basis of a loop invariant; we only need to add a constraint on k. The invariant we will use is:

$$I \;\widehat{=}\; k \in 1 .. \#s \land s \in L \equiv s[k ..] \in C_k$$

We can express C_k more directly by introducing a new function Rem, such that $Rem(s, L)$ is the set of all strings that can be concatenated to the right of s to form a sentence in L; i.e.

$$Rem(s, L) \;\widehat{=}\; \{t \mid s \frown t \in L\}$$

We now see that $C_k = Rem(s[1 .. k - 1], L)$.

Note that, for any strings u and v, $Rem(u \frown v, L) = Rem(v, Rem(u, L))$. In particular, $C_{k+1} = Rem(s[1 .. k], L) = Rem(s[k], Rem(s[1 .. k - 1], L)) = Rem(s[k], C_k)$.

Finally, we observe that when $C_k \neq \{\}$, the loop invariant implies that $s[1 .. k - 1] \in Prefixes(L)$, where $Prefixes(L)$ is the set of all prefixes of strings in L; i.e.

$$Prefixes(L) \;\widehat{=}\; \{w \in A^* \mid \exists t \in A^* \bullet w \frown t \in L\}$$

---

[2]This can be formalised using local invariants, as described in [14].

3.1 Loop design

We can now proceed to design a loop using the loop invariant I given above
and the variant $n - k$, and using a single variable C to hold successive values of
C_k. We will not attempt to compute r directly in the loop. Instead, the loop
will manipulate C into a form from which we can easily compute the required
value for r.

There are four steps in constructing the loop:

Initialisation: We can easily establish I by establishing $k = 1 \wedge C = L$, since
$C_1 = L$.

Guard: It is not yet clear what the guard should be, so we will just write it
as G for now[3].

Progress: We can ensure that the loop makes progress (i.e. decreases the
variant) by increasing k. We have already assumed that we will look at
one symbol of s at a time, so we will increase k by 1.

Maintain I: Since $C_{k+1} = Rem(s[k], C_k)$, we can maintain I as k increases,
by setting C to $Rem(s[k], C)$.

The algorithm at this stage is:

$$
\begin{aligned}
&|[\ \textbf{var } k, C \ \bullet \\
&\quad k := 1 \ || \ C := L; \\
&\quad \textbf{do } G \ \rightarrow \\
&\qquad k := k + 1 \ || \ C := Rem(s[k], C) \\
&\quad \textbf{od}; \\
&\quad r : [I \wedge \neg G, r \equiv s \in L] \\
&]|
\end{aligned}
$$

This algorithm is written using a parallel composition operator[4] ($||$), defined
by:

$$ w_1 : [P_1, R_1] \ || \ w_2 : [P_2, R_2] \equiv w_1, w_2 : [P_1 \wedge P_2, R_1 \wedge R_2] $$

A parallel assignment $x_1 := e_1 \ || \ x_2 := e_2$ is equivalent to the usual multiple
assignment $x_1, x_2 := e_1, e_2$ when $x_1 \neq x_2$. When $x_1 = x_2$, it is equivalent to
$x_1 := e_1$ if $e_1 = e_2$, and is miraculous otherwise. We use parallel composition
in preference to multiple assignments, since it makes the location and effect
of replacements during data refinement more obvious, and simplifies data refinements where an assignment data refines to more complex code. A parallel
composition is introduced using the following refinement law[5]:

$$ \text{Introduce } || : \quad \frac{w_1 \cup w_2 \subseteq w, \ P \Rightarrow P_1 \wedge P_2, \ R_1 \wedge R_2 \Rightarrow R}{w : [P, R] \sqsubseteq w_1 : [P_1, R_1] \ || \ w_2 : [P_2, R_2]} $$

[3] We are treating G as a metavariable [18].
[4] This is a very strong form of parallelism that cannot in general be turned into a sequential
composition without adding extra variables.
[5] This law only covers the binary case; it can be extended to an n-ary composition in the
obvious way.

3.2 Terminating conditions

In order to determine a suitable formula for G, we consider the various conditions under which the loop might terminate. The loop must terminate if s is found to be in L: this can be detected when $s[k] = \$$ and $\$ \in C$. The loop should also terminate if s is found not to be in L: this can be detected when $s[k]$ is not the initial symbol of any string in C[6].

In order to express these conditions concisely, we introduce a function Hds such that, for any set of strings X, $Hds(X)$ is the set of intial symbols of strings in X; i.e.

$$Hds(X) \; \hat{=} \; \{ a \in \mathcal{A} \mid \exists w \bullet a \frown w \in X \}$$

Noting that $\$ \in C$ is equivalent to $\$ \in Hds(C)$, we now want the loop to terminate when either $s[k] = \$ \land \$ \in Hds(C)$ or $s[k] \notin Hds(C)$ is true. That is, we wish to find a guard G such that $\neg G$ is equivalent to $(s[k] = \$ \land \$ \in Hds(C)) \lor s[k] \notin Hds(C)$.

With a little formula manipulation, we arrive at[7]:

$$G \; \hat{=} \; s[k] \neq \$ \land s[k] \in Hds(C).$$

We can now calculate r from $I \land \neg G$, since when this holds, s is in L if and only if $s[k] = \$ \land \$ \in Hds(C)$ is true.

The complete abstract algorithm is now:

```
|[ var k, C •
    k := 1  ||  C := L;
    do s[k] ≠ $ ∧ s[k] ∈ Hds(C)  →
        k := k + 1  ||  C := Rem(s[k], C)
    od;
    r := s[k] = $ ∧ $ ∈ Hds(C)
]|
```

This algorithm is still not executable because it is expressed in terms of the set variables L and C, and the set operations Hds and Rem which cannot be implemented for arbitrary sets. In order to obtain an executable program, we will have to place some restriction on L, and then explore suitable representations for L and C, and corresponding implementations for Hds and Rem. Obviously we won't be able to turn this into a concrete algorithm for all Ls: If L is not decidable, we won't be able to complete the data refinement.

We will now consider various restrictions on L and representations for C that can then be used to obtain recognition algorithms for particular classes of languages. In each case we will need to use the additional assumptions about L in order to justify the data refinement used to represent C. All of the languages will be assumed to be non-empty, since this allows simpler data representations to be used.

---

[6] These conditions are significantly simplified by our assumption about sentinel symbols.

[7] An alternative guard is $\lambda \notin C \land C \neq \{\}$. The guard chosen makes subsequent data refinement easier, since it ensures that C is never empty so long as L is not empty.

4   Specialisation where L is a singleton

For our first specialisation, we will consider the simpest possible case, where L is a singleton, so the recognition algorithm problem (and algorithm) reduces to one of string comparison. This will allow us to present the techniques of specialisation and data refinement in a very simple context.

To specialise a program, we introduce additional assumptions about the inputs, and propagate these through the resulting derivation. This process is justified, since we can show that if $w:[P,\,R] \sqsubseteq w':[P',\,R']$ then, for any additional assumptions A, we have $w:[P \wedge A,\,R] \sqsubseteq w':[P' \wedge A,\,R']$.

When L is a singleton, the additional assumption is $\#L = 1$. Adding this assumption does not affect the generic algorithm we have derived, but does strengthen the loop invariant and various preconditions, allowing us to choose good representations for L and C. We now consider how such representations are to be introduced.

Data refinement involves replacing a program fragment involving certain variables (known as *abstract variables*) by an "equivalent" fragment using different variables (known as *concrete variables*). The required relationship between abstract, concrete and other program variables, is specified in terms of a given *coupling invariant* (or *abstraction invariant*). Our data refinement technique is similar to those of [3] and [6], in that encoding and decoding is done using explicit statements; it is also similar to the auxiliary variable technique [13], in that the encoding and decoding statements are not responsible for variable declarations. A notable feature of our approach is that we allow data refinement of global variables, not just locals. Data refining a global variable imposes an obligation on the surrounding environment to deliver/receive the variable in the data refined form. The surrounding environment may be data refined in the same way, or may require an explicit mapping between the representation it uses and that introduced by the data refinement. If the surrounding environment is a user, then the onus is placed on the user to input or read values in the data refined form. This approach is discussed in more detail in [8]; a similar approach is found in [4].

Since L contains a single string, we can represent L by a string variable, say t; so the coupling invariant will entail $L = \{t\}$. We can now represent C using t and k, since $s[1\,..\,k-1] \in Prefixes(L)$ gives us $s[1\,..\,k-1] = t[1\,..\,k-1]$. Thus, $C = Rem(s[1\,..\,k-1], \{t\}) = \{t[k\,..]\}$.

We can express this relationship between the abstract variables L and C and the concrete variables t and k in terms of the coupling invariant:

$$L = \{t\} \ \wedge \ C = \{t[k\,..]\} \ \wedge \ k \in 1\,..\,\#t$$

It is easy to see that this representation exists whenever L is a singleton; i.e. for any singleton L, values of t and k can be found that satisfy the above coupling invariant.

With this representation we can implement $Hds(C)$ by $\{t[k]\}$, so $x \in Hds(C)$ becomes $x = t[k]$, and $Rem(s[k], C)$ by $\{t[k+1\,..]\}$, so long as $s[k] = t[k]$, which will be guaranteed by the loop guard.

We can now data refine the generic algorithm using this data representation. The net effect of the data refinement is to delete the declaration of C (we already have a declaration for k, and t is assumed to be global), and replace statements and guards involving L and C by corresponding code involving t and k. The required replacements are determined as follows (where $\sqsubseteq$ indicates algorithmic refinement and $\preceq$ denotes data refinement with respect to the given coupling invariant):

$$
\begin{aligned}
C := L \quad &\equiv \quad C\!:\![\,C = L\,] \\
&\preceq \quad k\!:\![\,\{t[k\,..]\} = \{t\}\,] \\
&\qquad (t \text{ can't change, since } L = \{t\} \text{ must be preserved}) \\
&\equiv \quad k\!:\![\,t[k\,..] = t[1\,..]\,] \\
&\equiv \quad k\!:\![\,k = 1\,] \\
&\sqsubseteq \quad k := 1 \\[1em]
x \in Hds(C) \quad &\preceq \quad x \in \{t[k]\} \\
&\equiv \quad x = t[k] \\
&\qquad (\text{The coupling invariant ensures } k \in 1\,..\,\#t) \\[1em]
C := Rem(s[k], C) \quad &\equiv \quad C\!:\![\,C = Rem(s[k], C_0)\,] \\
&\preceq \quad k\!:\![\,\{t[k\,..]\} = Rem(s[k_0], \{t[k_0\,..]\})\,] \\
&\qquad (t \text{ can't change, since } L = \{t\} \text{ must be preserved}) \\
&\equiv \quad k\!:\![\,\{t[k\,..]\} = \{t[k_0 + 1\,..]\}\,] \\
&\qquad (\text{Since the loop guard gives } s[k_0] = t[k_0]) \\
&\equiv \quad k\!:\![\,t[k\,..] = t[k_0 + 1\,..]\,] \\
&\equiv \quad k\!:\![\,k = k_0 + 1\,] \\
&\sqsubseteq \quad k := k + 1
\end{aligned}
$$

The specification statements used here have an implicit precondition, which is the weakest precondition to allow the statement to be feasible. Thus, the specification statement $w:[R]$ is equivalent to $w:[\exists w \bullet R, R]$. This form of specification statement is especially useful in performing data refinement since we often need to turn assignments into specification statements in order to data refine them. In practice, we often need to appeal to a stronger precondition, e.g. to take account of a loop invariant or guard, as in the data refinement of $C := Rem(s[k], C)$ above. This can be formalised by using assertions to propagate the required conditions or using miracles [12].

The loop invariant becomes:

$$
\begin{aligned}
& 1 \leq k \leq \#s \;\wedge\; s \in \{t[1\,..]\} \;\equiv\; s[k\,..] \in \{t[k\,..]\} \\
\Longleftrightarrow \quad & 1 \leq k \leq \#s \;\wedge\; s = t[1\,..] \;\equiv\; s[k\,..] = t[k\,..] \\
\Longleftrightarrow \quad & 1 \leq k \leq \#s \;\wedge\; s[1\,..\,k-1] = t[1\,..\,k-1]
\end{aligned}
$$

The resulting algorithm after performing this data refinement is:

```
|[ var k •
     k := 1 || k := 1;
     do s[k] ≠ $ ∧ s[k] = t[k]  →
         k := k + 1 || k := k + 1
     od;
     r := s[k] = $ ∧ $ = t[k]
]|
```

Note that the parallel composition has allowed us to data refine the assignments to C without touching the parallel assignments to k; with multiple assignments, we would have to convert the whole multiple assignment into a single specification statement before performing the data refinement. In this case, the assignments introduced by the data refinement duplicate ones that are already performed by the algorithm. Using the property of parallel assignments mentioned earlier, this algorithm simplifies to:

$$
\begin{aligned}
&|[\ \textbf{var}\ k\ \bullet \\
&\quad k := 1; \\
&\quad \textbf{do}\ s[k] \neq \$\ \wedge\ s[k] = t[k]\ \longrightarrow \\
&\qquad k := k + 1 \\
&\quad \textbf{od}; \\
&\quad r := s[k] = \$\ \wedge\ t[k] = \$ \\
&]|
\end{aligned}
$$

This is an elegant way of writing a string comparison algorithm, which deals with the problem of two stopping conditions rather nicely. It is reassuring to see that specialising a generic algorithm in this trivial case leads to such a simple algorithm.

In this derivation, we have assumed that L is given in terms of the representation used here, i.e. as the string t. The surrounding environment may either be similarly data refined so that it represents L in this way, or if L is obtained in some other way (e.g. it might be a substring of some other string), may require an explicit conversion to get it in this form.

5 Specialisation where L is a finite set of strings

We will now consider specialising the generic algorithm in the case where L is a non-empty finite language, so the additional assumption is $L \neq \{\}\ \wedge\ \#L \in \mathbb{N}$ (where $\mathbb{N}$ denotes the natural numbers). In this case the problem reduces to a table look-up where L is the set of keys in the table and s as the search key. Since we are processing s one symbol at a time, we should represent the table in a way that allows Hds and Rem to be computed efficiently.

If we represented C as a list of strings, we would need some way of keeping track of the remaining candidates, by either deleting or marking the strings that are no longer candidates. This would be cumbersome and inefficient, since on each iteration we would need to compare $s[k]$ with the kth element of every remaining candidate. We can avoid this overhead by using a representation for C in which the set $Hds(C)$ is represented explicitly for every value that C may assume. We can do this by representing C using a *trie* table (see, for example, [1], p163*ff*).

Informally, a trie is a tree in which each edge is labelled with a symbol from $\mathcal{A}$ and the labels on the out-edges of any node are distinct. Each path in the tree represents a string obtained by concatenating all of the symbols on the edges in the path. A trie represents the set of strings represented by all paths from the root to a leaf.

To describe this more formally, we will assume the following operators on trees:

$Root(T)$	The node at the root of tree T.
$Nodes(T)$	The set of all nodes of tree T.
$IsLeaf(p)$	True iff p is a leaf, where $p \in Nodes(T)$.
$OutLabels(p)$	The set of symbols labelling out-edges of p, where $p \in Nodes(T)$.
$Succ(a, p)$	The node at the other end of the out-edge of node p, labelled a, where $p \in Nodes(T)$, p is not a leaf and $a \in OutLabels(p)$.

We define a function Str such that, if p and q are nodes in T and there is a path from p to q, then $Str(p, q)$ is the string obtained by concatenating all of the symbols on the edges in that path; i.e.

$$Str(p, q) \cong \left\{ \begin{array}{ll} \lambda, & \text{if } p = q \\ a \frown t, & \text{if } Str(Succ(p, a), q) = t \end{array} \right.$$

We now define a function $Strings$ so that, for any node p, $Strings(p)$ is the set of all strings on paths from p to a leaf; i.e.

$$Strings(p) \cong \{ w \mid \exists q \in Nodes(T) \bullet IsLeaf(q) \wedge Str(p, q) = w \}$$

Thus, $Strings(Root(T))$ is the set of strings represented by a trie T.

We will represent L using a trie T, such that $Strings(Root(T)) = L$. There will be one leaf in the trie corresponding to each sentence in L. Our assumption about sentinels implies that each leaf has \$ as its in-edge label, and \$ doesn't occur on any other edges.

We observe that for each $w \in Prefixes(L)$, there is a unique node p in T such that $Str(Root(T), p) = w$ and $Strings(p) = Rem(w, L)$. Thus, we can represent C by a node in T. We also observe that if $Strings(p) = C$, then $Hds(C) = Outlabels(p)$ and $Rem(a, C) = Strings(Succ(a, p))$ for all $a \in Hds(C)$.

Thus, we can represent L by $Root(T)$, and C by a node in T, indicated by a variable p. The coupling invariant is now:

$$L = Strings(Root(T)) \wedge p \in Nodes(T) \wedge C = Strings(p)$$

It is easy to see that this representation exists whenever L is finite and non-empty[8]. If L is finite, $Prefixes(L)$ is finite, and so is T. Since T is finite, we can implement it and the required operations in any of the standard ways.

We can now data refine the generic algorithm using this data representation, by making the following replacements:

$$\begin{array}{rl} C := L & \equiv \quad C:[C = L] \\ & \preceq \quad p:[Strings(p) = Strings(Root(T))] \\ & \sqsubseteq \quad p:[p = Root(T)] \\ & \sqsubseteq \quad p := Root(T) \end{array}$$

---

[8] If we had allowed L to be empty, we would also need to allow T to be an empty tree, in which case $Root(T)$ would not exist, so some more complex representation would be required.

$$x \in Hds(C) \quad \preceq \quad x \in OutLabels(p)$$

$$
\begin{aligned}
C := Rem(s[k], C) \quad &\equiv \quad C:[\,C = Rem(s[k], C_0)\,] \\
&\preceq \quad p:[\,Strings(p) = Rem(s[k], Strings(p_0))\,] \\
&\equiv \quad p:[\,Strings(p) = Strings(Succ(s[k], p_0))\,] \\
&\quad\quad (\text{Since the loop guard gives } s[k] \in OutLabels(p_0)) \\
&\sqsubseteq \quad p:[\,p = Succ(s[k], p_0)\,] \\
&\sqsubseteq \quad p := Succ(s[k], p)
\end{aligned}
$$

The loop invariant becomes:

$$
\begin{aligned}
&\quad 1 \leq k \leq n \,\wedge\, s \in Strings(Root(T)) \equiv s[k\,..] \in Strings(p) \\
\Longleftrightarrow\ &\quad 1 \leq k \leq n \,\wedge\, s[1\,..\,k-1] = Str(Root(T), p)
\end{aligned}
$$

The resulting algorithm is:

```
|[ var k, p •
   k := 1 || p := Root(T);
   do s[k] ≠ $ ∧ s[k] ∈ OutLabels(p) →
      k := k + 1 || p := Succ(s[k], p)
   od;
   r := s[k] = $ ∧ $ ∈ OutLabels(p)
]|
```

This algorithm is simply a trie look-up, much as we would find in a data structures text book (e.g. [5], p217) — though it is simpler than most!

The refinement of $C := L$ assumes that we have T already available. We may either assume that L is initially given in this form or construct T from some other representation of L. If L is given, say as a list of strings, the precomputation required to construct the trie is an explicit data mapping from the external representation of L to the representation used here.

6 Specialisation where L is a regular language

Now consider the case where L is a non-empty regular language, described by a regular expression E. Thus, we specialise the initial specification and derivation, with the additional assumption $L \neq \{\} \,\wedge\, L = Lang(E)$, where $Lang(E)$ is the language denoted by the regular expression E. We will assume that the syntax and semantics of regular expressions are defined in the standard way (see, for example, [10] or [11]).

Once again, we want to represent C in a way that allows the Hds and Rem functions to be computed efficiently. Let's again try to represent C in such a way that $Hds(C)$ is represented explicitly using a tree, as we did for finite languages. Unfortunately, since L may be infinite, the resulting tree may be infinite, so we can't store it explicitly. Fortunately, however, we can construct a finite directed graph which contains the same information. We will use the same operations on graphs that we used on trees in Section 5.

Let T be the (possibly infinite) tree constructed as in Section 5. We construct a graph G corresponding to T as follows:

- Nodes in G correspond to equivalence classes of nodes in T; if $Strings(p) = Strings(q)$ for two nodes $p, q \in Nodes(T)$, then p and q map onto the same node in G.

- The root of G corresponds to the equivalence class containing the root of T.

- There is an a-edge from node p to node q in G if and only if there is an a-edge from a node in the equivalence class corresponding to p to a node in the equivalence class corresponding to q in T.

Note that this construction preserves the property that the labels on the out-edges of any node are distinct.

As with a trie, each path represents a string and the graph represents the set of strings represented by all paths from the root to a leaf. In fact, this graph will have exactly one leaf node, since $Strings(p) = \{\lambda\}$ for every leaf p in T. Our assumption about sentinels implies that all edges into this leaf node are labelled with \$, and these are the only edges labelled \$.

Since there may now be more than one path between two nodes, we define a new function STR such that for any nodes p and q in G, $STR(p, q)$ is the *set* of *all* strings on *any* path from p to q; i.e. $STR(p, q)$ is the *smallest* set such that:

(i) if $p = q$, then $\lambda \in STR(p, q)$, and

(ii) if $a \in OutLabels(p)$, then $\{a\} \frown STR(Succ(p, a), q) \subseteq STR(p, q)$.

Note that when G is acyclic, $STR(p, q) = \{Str(p, q)\}$ if there is a path from p to q, and $\{\}$ otherwise.

We again define $Strings$ so that, for any node p, $Strings(p)$ is the set of all strings on paths from p to a leaf; i.e.

$$Strings(p) \cong \{\, w \mid \exists q \in Nodes(G) \bullet IsLeaf(q) \land w \in STR(p, q) \,\}$$

Thus, $Strings(Root(G))$ is the set of strings represented by a graph G.

We will represent L using a graph G, such that $Strings(Root(G)) = L$. Observe that for each $w \in Prefixes(L)$, there is a unique node p in G such that $w \in Str(Root(T), p)$ and $Strings(p) = Rem(w, L)$. Thus, we can represent C by a node in G. We also observe that if $Strings(p) = C$, then $Hds(C) = OutLabels(p)$ and $Rem(a, C) = Strings(Succ(a, p))$ for all $a \in Hds(C)$.

Thus, we can represent L by $Root(G)$, and C by a node in G, indicated by a variable p. The coupling invariant is now:

$$L = Strings(Root(G)) \land p \in Nodes(G) \land C = Strings(p)$$

The loop invariant becomes:

$$1 \leq k \leq n \land s \in Strings(Root(G)) \equiv s[k\,..] \in Strings(p)$$
$$\iff 1 \leq k \leq n \land s[1\,..\,k-1] \in STR(Root(G), p)$$

The structure we have just described is, of course, a deterministic finite acceptor: Nodes correspond to states, edges correspond to transitions, the root is the start state, and the leaf node is the single accepting state.

This representation exists whenever L is regular. Because L is regular, the resulting graph has a finite number of nodes. This is a direct consequence of the Myhill-Nerode Theorem (see, for example, [10] or [11]). Since the graph is finite, we can implement it and the required operations in any of the standard ways.

The algorithm resulting from this data refinement is essentially the same as that for finite languages — the only difference is that the data structure may now contain cycles and it uses operations on graphs rather than on trees. This difference affects the loop invariant and the reasoning required to justify the data refinement, but does not affect the resulting code.

It is interesting to see how the DFA has emerged as a way of representing L to provide an efficient computation of Hds and Rem, with no a priori idea of state: States emerge by precomputing candidate completion sets. The similarity with the algorithm for finite languages highlights the fact that a trie is just a DFA whose graph is a tree. Applying the techniques of this section to a finite language would give us a directed acyclic graph rather than a tree.

Once again, in initialising C, we have assumed that the required data structure (in this case G) is available. Again, this might be provided, or might be obtained by a precomputation performing an explicit data mapping, e.g. from a regular expression or regular grammar describing L to the required DFA.

7 Specialisation where L is a Context Free Language

Suppose that L is a non-empty Context Free Language, described by a grammar G. As usual, G is a 4-tuple (V_N, V_T, S, P) giving nonterminals, terminals, start symbol and productions (see, for example, [10] or [11]); since $L \subseteq \mathcal{A}^*$, we can assume $V_T = \mathcal{A}$. We specialise the initial specification with the additional assumption $L \neq \{\} \wedge L = Lang(G)$, where $Lang(G)$ is the language defined by G. Knowing that not all context free languages can be recognised deterministically, we should expect to make some further assumptions about L. Rather than making such assumptions now, we will investigate one way of representing C when L is context free, and then consider the class of languages for which it can be used.

Again, consider how we might represent C. As in the regular case, constructing a tree to represent $Hds(C)$ leads (in general) to an infinite tree. This time, however, we can't collapse the tree into a finite graph. Thus, the representation of C requires more information about the form of acceptable completions. One approach is to encode the set of possible completions using a string of terminal and/or nonterminal symbols.

For any string $\sigma \in V^+$, where $V = V_N \cup V_T$, we define $Strings(\sigma)$ to be the set of all terminal strings that can be produced from σ. We can define $Strings(\sigma)$ in terms of the usual "produces" relation ($\Rightarrow_G^*$):

$$Strings(\sigma) \mathrel{\widehat{=}} \{\, w \in V_T^+ \mid \sigma \Rightarrow_G^* w \,\}$$

Alternatively, we can define $Strings(\sigma)$ recursively:

$$Strings(\sigma) \mathrel{\widehat{=}} \begin{cases} \{\sigma\} & \text{if } \sigma \in V_T^+ \\ \bigcup_{\sigma' \in \Sigma(\sigma)} Strings(\sigma') & \text{otherwise} \end{cases}$$

where $\Sigma(\sigma)$ is the set of strings (over V^+) that can be obtained by replacing one nonterminal symbol (N) in σ by the right hand side (α) of a rule in P with N as its left hand side; i.e.

$$\Sigma(\sigma) = \{\, \sigma' \mid \exists N \in V_N, \alpha, \phi, \psi \in V^* \bullet$$
$$\sigma = \phi N \psi \,\wedge\, \sigma' = \phi \alpha \psi \,\wedge\, N \to \alpha \in P \,\}$$

Clearly, L can be represented by the start symbol S; we will endeavour to also represent C by some string σ over V. Thus, the coupling invariant will be:

$$L = Strings(S) \,\wedge\, \sigma \in V^+ \,\wedge\, C = Strings(\sigma)$$

The loop invariant becomes:

$$1 \le k \le n \,\wedge\, s \in Strings(S) \;\equiv\; s[k \mathinner{\ldotp\ldotp}] \in Strings(\sigma)$$
$$\Longleftrightarrow\quad 1 \le k \le n \,\wedge\, S \Rightarrow_G^* s[1 \mathinner{\ldotp\ldotp} k - 1] \frown \sigma$$

The last conjunct says that $s[1 \mathinner{\ldotp\ldotp} k - 1] \frown \sigma$ is a *sentential form*.

With this representation, we can compute $Hds(C)$ using the function $First$ defined, for any non-empty string $\gamma \in V^+$ as follows:

$$First(\gamma) \;\hat{=}\; \begin{cases} \{\gamma[1]\} & \text{if } \gamma[1] \in V_T \\ \bigcup_{\gamma' \in \Gamma(\gamma[1])} First(\gamma') & \text{if } \gamma[1] \in V_N \end{cases}$$

where, for any nonterminal N, $\Gamma(N)$ is the set of right hand sides of rules in P that have N as their left hand side; i.e.

$$\Gamma(N) \;\hat{=}\; \{\, \alpha \mid N \to \alpha \in P \,\}$$

This definition of $First$ does not accommodate rules with empty right hand sides; thus we have an additional assumption about G, that the right hand sides of all rules in P are non-empty (i.e. G has no λ-productions)[9].

Now we have $Hds(C) = First(\sigma)$, which we can simplify to $First(\sigma[1])$. Computing $Rem(s[k], C)$ is not so simple; we will address it shortly.

We can now data refine the generic algorithm using this data representation, as follows:

$$
\begin{aligned}
C := L \;\;&\equiv\;\; C:[C = L] \\
&\preceq\;\; \sigma:[Strings(\sigma) = Strings(S)] \\
&\sqsubseteq\;\; \sigma:[\sigma = S] \\
&\sqsubseteq\;\; \sigma := S \\[2ex]
x \in Hds(C) \;\;&\preceq\;\; x \in First(\sigma[1]) \\[2ex]
C := Rem(s[k], C) \;\;&\equiv\;\; C:[C = Rem(s[k], C_0)] \\
&\preceq\;\; \sigma:[Strings(\sigma) = Rem(s[k], Strings(\sigma_0))] \quad (i)
\end{aligned}
$$

---

[9] It is straightforward to relax this restriction — we just need a slightly more complex definition for $First$ — but we prefer to avoid the additional complexity here.

Rather than compute $Rem(s[k], Strings(\sigma))$ directly, we will manipulate σ into a form which simplifies the computation: the required form is that the first symbol in σ is a terminal symbol. In modifying σ, we may reduce $Strings(\sigma)$, so long as we still have $s[k] \in Hds(C)$, i.e. $s[k] \in First(\sigma)$, which comes from the loop guard. Thus, we refine (i) as follows:

$$(i) \quad \sqsubseteq \quad \sigma: \left[s[k] \in First(\sigma) \; , \; \begin{array}{c} s[k] \in First(\sigma) \; \wedge \\ Strings(\sigma) \subseteq \\ Strings(\sigma_0) \; \wedge \\ \sigma[1] \in V_T \end{array} \right] ; \quad (ii)$$

$$\sigma: \left[\begin{array}{c} s[k] \in First(\sigma) \; \wedge \\ Strings(\sigma) \subseteq \\ Strings(\sigma_0) \; \wedge \\ \sigma[1] \in V_T \end{array} \; , \; \begin{array}{c} Strings(\sigma) = \\ Rem(s[k], Strings(\sigma_0)) \end{array} \right] \quad (iii)$$

If $\sigma[1]$ is not a terminal symbol $(\sigma[1] \notin V_T)$, it must be a nonterminal $(\sigma[1] \in V_N)$. We will manipulate σ into a form where $\sigma[1]$ is a terminal symbol by successively replacing $\sigma[1]$ by the right-hand side of some rule defining $\sigma[1]$.

$$(ii) \quad \sqsubseteq \quad \begin{array}{l} \mathbf{do} \; \sigma[1] \in V_N \; \rightarrow \\ \quad \alpha: [\sigma[1] \; \rightarrow \; \alpha \in P]; \\ \quad \sigma := \alpha \frown \sigma[2..] \\ \mathbf{od}; \end{array} \quad (iv)$$

The loop invariant is $Strings(\sigma) \subseteq Strings(\sigma_0) \; \wedge \; s[k] \in First(\sigma)$, where σ_0 is the value of σ at the beginning of the loop. The variant is the length of the longest derivation of a string beginning with $s[k]$ from σ. We must now show that this variant is reduced by the loop body, and find a way to implement (iv) deterministically.

In order to implement (iv) deterministically, we must be able to determine which rule to select, for a given $s[k]$ and $\sigma[1]$. This will be the case precisely when G is an LL(1) grammar. We thus add a further assumption: that L is an LL(1) language and G is an LL(1) grammar. We will implement (iv) using a new function $RightRule$ such that, for any terminal symbol a and nonterminal symbol N, such that $a \in First(N)$, $RightRule(a, N)$ is the right-hand side of the first rule to be used in producing a terminal string starting with a from N; i.e.

$$RightRule(a, N) = \alpha \; \equiv \; N \; \rightarrow \; \alpha \in P \; \wedge \; a \in First(\alpha)$$

This value is unique for an LL(1) grammar, since by definition, whenever $N \rightarrow \alpha_1 \in P$ and $N \rightarrow \alpha_2 \in P$, where $\alpha_1 \neq \alpha_2$, $First(\alpha_1) \cap First(\alpha_2) = \{\}$.
Thus, we have:

$$(iv) \quad \sqsubseteq \quad \alpha := RightRule(s[k], \sigma[1])$$

Assuming that G is an LL(1) grammar ensures that $RightRule(s[k], \sigma[1])$ is well defined when $s[k] \in First(\sigma)$, which is part of the (inner) loop invariant. This assumption also ensures that the variant is reduced, and thus that the loop terminates.

It now remains to implement (iii), which is easy. When $\sigma[1] \in V_T$, $First(\sigma) = \{\sigma[1]\}$. But we also have $s[k] \in First(\sigma)$, so we have we must have $s[k] = \sigma[1]$. Thus, we have:

(iii) $\sqsubseteq$ $\sigma := \sigma[2..]$

The resulting algorithm after performing this data refinement is:

$$
\begin{aligned}
&|[\text{ var } k, \sigma \bullet \\
&\quad k := 1 \;\|\; \sigma := S; \\
&\quad \text{do } s[k] \neq \$ \wedge s[k] \in First(\sigma[1]) \;\rightarrow \\
&\quad\quad \text{do } \sigma[1] \in V_N \;\rightarrow \\
&\quad\quad\quad \alpha := RightRule(s[k], \sigma[1]); \\
&\quad\quad\quad \sigma := \alpha \frown \sigma[2..] \\
&\quad\quad \text{od}; \\
&\quad\quad \sigma := \sigma[2..]; \\
&\quad\quad k := k + 1 \\
&\quad \text{od}; \\
&\quad r := s[k] = \$ \wedge \$ \in First(\sigma[1]) \\
&]|
\end{aligned}
$$

The algorithm we have arrived at is a table-driven LL(1) parser or "predictive" parser, in which σ acts as a stack: The operation $\sigma := \alpha \frown \sigma[2..]$ pushes the symbols in α onto the top of the stack, while $\sigma := \sigma[2..]$ pops the stack. It remains to choose suitable implementations for $First$ and $RightRule$, most likely as tables, and for the stack; but these details need not concern us here.

The main difference between this algorithm and the usual predictive parsing algorithm is the presence of the inner loop. This is required because of the loop invariant and variant we used, which requires k to be increased by one on each iteration. The usual predictive parsing algorithm (e.g. [2], p187) uses a single loop which, on each iteration, either increases k and pops the stack (after checking that the symbol at the top of the stack is $s[k]$) or replaces a nonterminal at the top of the stack. Our version, however, makes the operation of the algorithm clearer and the proof of termination easier: for each input symbol we successively reduce the nonterminal at the top of the stack until we get that terminal at the top, then remove it. Another difference is that the usual version doesn't need to test for $s[k] \in First(\sigma[1])$; if s is not a sentence, it will detect this either when the top of stack is a terminal not equal to $s[k]$ or when $RightRule(s[k], \sigma[1])$ is undefined. We could obtain the standard algorithm by using a different variant for the main loop (though this would destroy the symmetry with our other derivations), or by transforming the above version to combine the two loops.

Again, we have assumed that the language is given in the required form, which in this case means that the tables $First$ and $RightRule$ are already available. Constructing these tables will normally be done as a by-product of data refining the surrounding envoironment; they may be input in the required from or computed from the grammar.

8 Conclusions

We have illustrated the use of data refinement and program specialisation in deriving a family of language recognition algorithms. This development provides derivations for these algorithms which we believe to be more intelligible that would have otherwise been obtained using program refinement. Considerable care was taken over the loop structure in the abstract algorithm, and the final form was not settled until after a couple of specialisations had been worked through, which helped to identify the important concepts in the abstract algorithm. The resulting algorithm then led to elegant loop structures in all the concrete algorithms derived.

The development also highlights some common aspects of these algorithms. In particular, it provides a uniform explanation of use of tries, DFAs and stacks, respectively, in terms of representing the set of candidate completions at each stage. This, in turn, suggests ways in which other related algorithms could be derived. Using an approach more like that in Section 7, we could build a recogniser for regular languages by representing C as a regular expression, and defining suitable functions on regular expressions to implement Hds and Rem; alternatively, we could further specialise the representation used in Section 7 for the case where the grammar is regular — in which case the grammar tables end up being isomorphic to the graph operations of the DFA. If we had chosen a different representation for C in Section 7, we could have obtained an algorithm for some other class of context free languages; for example, it should be just as easy to obtain an LR(1) parser — giving a very different derivation from the one given in [9]. By using a somewhat more elaborate data structure (i.e. one carrying several alternative parses in parallel) we should be able to obtain Earley's algorithm.

The same approach can be applied to obtain a number of other related algorithms, where the language is defined in different ways. We can obtain a recogniser for a language defined by simple patterns consisting of symbols and symbol variables, by adding a binding table to the representation used in Section 4. If we let L be the set of all substrings of a string t, this approach should lead us to the Knuth-Morris-Pratt string searching algorithm.

References

[1] Alfred V. Aho, John E. Hopcroft and Jeffrey D. Ullman. *Data Structures and Algorithms*. Addison-Wesley, 1983.

[2] Alfred V. Aho, Ravi Sethi and Jeffrey D. Ullman. *Compilers: Principles, Techniques, and Tools*. Addison-Wesley, 1986.

[3] R. J. R. Back. *Data Refinement in the Refinement Calculus*. Technical Report Series A, No. 68, Inst. för Informationsbehandling, Åbo Akademi, Turku, Finland, 1988.

[4] Lucy Chubb. *A Data Refinement Model of Interfaces*. University of New South Wales, School of Computer Science and Engineering Report No. 9204, August, 1992.

[5] Rick Decker. *Data Structures*. Prentice-Hall, 1989.

[6] P. H. B. Gardiner and C. C. Morgan. "Data refinement of predicate transformers". *Theoretical Computer Science* **87** (1991), pp143–162.

[7] A. Gravell. "Specialising Abstract Programs". *Proc. 4th Refinement Workshop*, J. M. Morris & R. C. Shaw (Eds), Springer-Verlag, 1991, pp34–50.

[8] Lindsay Groves. "Deriving Sorting Algorithms using Data Refinement". *Proc. 16th Australian Computer Science Conference*, 1993, pp523–534.

[9] Wim H. Hesselink. "LR-parsing derived". Science of Computer Programming **19** (1992), pp171–196.

[10] John E. Hopcroft and Jeffrey D. Ullman. *Introduction to Automata Theory, Languages and Computation*. Addison-Wesley, 1979.

[11] John C. Martin. *Introduction to Languages and the Theory of Compuation*. McGraw-Hill, 1991.

[12] C. C. Morgan. "Data refinement using miracles". *Inf. Proc. Lett.* **26**, 5 (Jan. 1988), pp243–246.

[13] Carroll Morgan. "Auxiliary variables in data refinement". *Information Processing Letters* **29** (1988), pp293–296. Also in [16], pp79–85.

[14] Carroll Morgan. "Types and invariants in the refinement calculus". *Mathematics of Program Construction*, J. L. A. van de Snepscheut (Ed.), Lecture Notes in Computer Science, Vol. 375, Springer-Verlag, 1989.

[15] Carroll Morgan. *Programming from Specifications*. Prentice-Hall, 1990.

[16] Carroll Morgan, Ken Robinson and Paul Gardiner. *On the Refinement Calculus*, Technical Monograph PRG-70, Oxfrod University, 1988.

[17] J. M. Morris. "Laws of data refinement". *Acta Informatica* **26** (1989), pp287–308.

[18] Raymond G. Nickson and Lindsay J. Groves. "Metavariables and Conditional Refinements in the Refinement Calculus". *Proc. 6th BCS Refinement Workshop*, 1994.

Program Refinement by Theorem Prover

J. von Wright

Åbo Akademi University

Turku, Finland

Abstract

We describe a prototype tool for developing programs by stepwise refinement in a weakest precondition framework, based on the HOL theorem proving system. Our work is based on a mechanisation of the refinement calculus, which is a theory of correctness preserving program transformations. We also use a tool for window inference that is part of the HOL system. Our tool permits subcomponents of a program to be refined separately, and the tool keeps track of the overall effects of each individual refinement. In particular, we show how specifications can be refined into code and how data refinements (i.e., replacing an abstract data structure with one that is more concrete) can be handled. All refinements are proved as theorems in the HOL logic, so our system is in fact a secure environment for program development.

1 Introduction

Stepwise refinement is a methodology for developing programs from high-level program specifications into efficient implementations. In this approach to program development, the development of a program includes the proof of its correctness. This can be compared with program *verification*, where the program is first developed, using informal methods, and then checked for desired correctness properties. The *refinement calculus* [5, 27] is a formalisation of the stepwise refinement approach, based on the weakest precondition calculus of Dijkstra [15]. The refinement calculus is a calculus of program transformations that preserve total correctness. If C and C' are commands (program fragments), then the refinement $C \leq C'$ holds if and only if C' satisfies every total correctness assertion that C satisfies.

The refinement relation is reflexive and transitive. Furthermore, the ordinary control structures of sequential programming (sequential composition, conditional composition and iteration) are monotonic with respect to the refinement relation. This means that if the refinement $C \leq C'$ holds, then we can replace C by C' in any program context (so C' implements C).

A refinement step $C \leq C'$ is often proved by appealing to a high-level refinement rule. Particularly important are rules which encode useful program development principles. One such principle is data refinement (sometimes called data reification), where a data structure is replaced by another one in such a way that total correctness of the program is preserved. Data refinement has been extensively studied [6, 18, 28] and it is a central program development principle, e.g., in the VDM method [25]. Rules for data refinement make it possible to develop programs from specifications in just a small number of major refinement steps.

In recent years, there has been a growing interest in using mechanised formal systems (theorem provers) in the design of software. Most of this work has been directed at verification where the correctness of an already developed program is checked. Examples of this can be found in [19], using the Boyer-Moore prover, in [17], using the Larch theorem prover (LP), and in [1], using the Nuprl system. The HOL theorem prover, which has previously been used mostly for hardware verification [20], has more recently also been used for program verification. Various programming notations have been semantically embedded in the HOL logic. Examples include a simple while-language [21], CSP [13], UNITY [3] and guarded command languages [2, 10].

To our knowledge, there have been very few attempts to construct tools that support program refinement, based on theorem proving. There are a few examples of *refinement editors*, which support program refinement in the same style as we consider in this paper [30, 22]. However, these tools generally work on two independent levels. A verification condition generator produces formulas that must be checked for validity, in order for a given refinement to hold. These formulas are then checked using a separate system, e.g., by manual inspection or using a theorem prover. The advantage of using a single theorem prover all the way is obvious: we can handle all aspects of the refinement process within a single system. However, there have been doubts as to whether a useful tool could be based on a theorem proving approach [22].

This paper presents a *window refinement tool*: a simple prototype secure environment for program development by stepwise refinement, built on the HOL theorem prover. In this system, programs are terms of the HOL logic, and each refinement step in the development of a program is proved correct in HOL. The system makes use of a *window inference tool* for HOL, developed by Jim Grundy [23]. The window inference tool supports a transformational style of reasoning with the HOL theorem prover, based on the ideas presented by Robinson and Staples [29]. Grundy has also shown how his tool can be used for program refinement in a style where programs are predicates [23].

We show how the window inference tool can be used to refine programs in a weakest precondition framework. In particular, we are interested in data refinement, since that is a very powerful method for developing not only sequential, but also parallel and reactive programs [7, 8]. Data refinement is harder to handle in a refinement tool than ordinary algorithmic refinement, since data refinement generally speaking has to be done on a large program chunk all at once. However, we show how the method of data refinement with *abstraction commands* that we have put forward in [9, 31] permits our tool to do data refinement separately for each subcomponent, without compromising the strict safety that the theorem prover gives.

We have previously shown how a programming notation with a weakest precondition semantics can be embedded in the HOL prover and shown how one can reason about refinement (including data refinement) within this mechanised theory [10, 32]. This paper goes far beyond that: we show that it is actually possible to build a *tool* for refinement on top of the HOL system.

Overview of the paper

The rest of the paper is organised as follows. In Section 2 we give a brief overview of the HOL system and the window inference built on top of HOL. Section 3 describes a mechanised refinement theory. We show how a command notation with a weakest precondition semantics is embedded in the HOL logic. In fact, the semantics *is* the command notation: we define program constructs (e.g., *skip*) to be names for the corresponding predicate transformers. We show how the refinement relation is defined and how rules of program refinement can be proved as theorems of the HOL logic. In Section 4 we show how the window inference tool can be used for refining programs in our command notation. The user can enter a program text (a command) and then perform refinement steps on the subcomponents of this program, while the window inference systems keeps track of the overall effect of these separate refinements. We consider data refinement in Section 5, showing how the window inference tool permits subcomponents of a program to be data-refined separately. In Section 6, we develop a small program from a specification in three major steps, and in Section 7 we finish off with some conclusions and directions for future work.

The paper has four appendices. Appendix A lists the basic definitions used to mechanise the theory of refinement in HOL. In Appendix B, we list a number of theorems of the mechanised refinement theory that are referred to in the paper. Appendix C contains rules (theorems) of data refinement and Appendix D describes some commands that are used to handle the window refinement tool.

Notation

We use standard symbols for logical connectives and quantifiers. The scope of binders and quantifiers extends as far to the right as possible. We usually write function application without parentheses, and for higher-order functions application associates to the left. Thus $f\ x$ is the same as $f(x)$ and $f\ x\ y$ is the same as $(f\ x)y$.

Theorems that have actually been proved using HOL are indicated by a leading turnstile symbol $\vdash$. Names of theorems are written in sans-serif font. When we show what the user types into the HOL system, we use teletype font.

2 The HOL system and window inference

In this section we give a brief introduction to the HOL system and the window inference system. More detailed descriptions can be found, e.g., in [20, 23].

2.1 The HOL system

The HOL system is an interactive theorem-proving environment for higher-order logic. Its logic is an extension of Church's Simple Type Theory [14], with type variables. Essentially, it extends typed first-order logic by permitting lambda expressions that denote functions. It also permits higher-order functions and quantification over arbitrary types.

All HOL-terms must have a well-defined type. Atomic types are, e.g., *bool* (the booleans T and F) and *num* (the natural numbers). Compound types can be constructed using the pairing operator $\times$ and the function space operator $\rightarrow$. HOL also permits polymorphic types, through the use of type variables. Type variables always begin with an asterisk $*$.

The user accesses HOL through an ML interface. By evaluating ML expressions, the user can create new theories, access existing theories, make definitions and prove theorems.

An important feature of the HOL system is the amount of existing infrastructure for defining concepts and for proving theorems. Theorems can be proved by forward proof, applying inference rules (ML functions) to terms and existing theorems. The HOL system also supports goal-directed proof: the user sets up a goal and then proves it using goal-reducing functions called tactics. Elaborate tactics can be programmed in the ML language. There are a number of libraries in the HOL system. In these libraries, the user can find theorems about different data structures proved and ready to use, e.g., theorems about natural numbers, lists, trees, sets etc.

2.2   Window inference in HOL

In window reasoning, the user transforms an expression so that a reflexive and transitive relation R is preserved. The user is permitted to restrict attention to a subexpression of the original expression, provided that the subexpression occurs in a context which is monotonic with respect to the relation R. A transformation of the subexpression is at the same time a transformation of the whole expression.

To be more specific, we assume that $E[\ldots t \ldots]$ is an expression where t occurs as a subexpression. Our starting point is the *window*

$$R \star E[\ldots t \ldots]$$

The *focus* of the window is the expression $E[\ldots t \ldots]$ and the relation that we want to preserve is R. When the HOL window inference library has been loaded into the HOL system, this window can be set up by typing

```
#RBEGIN_STACK 'name' "(R)(E[...t...])";;
```

The first argument is the name of the window stack we start working with and the second argument is a term containing the relation and the initial focus (in HOL interaction, # is the system prompt, terms are written inside double quotes and ;; is the input terminator symbol).

The theorem associated with this window (the *window theorem*) is

$$\vdash \ E[\ldots t \ldots] \ R \ E[\ldots t \ldots]$$

which holds because R is reflexive.

Now we can *open a subwindow* on the subterm t by selecting it. In the plain window inference system, we do this by giving a path to the subterm (according to a specific syntax which we describe later):

```
#OPEN_WIN[...];;
```

In a more elaborate version of the window inference system, we can use a mouse to click on the subterm that we want to open a subwindow on. The result is the following window:

$$R \star t$$

with the corresponding window theorem (again by reflexivity)

$$\vdash\ t\ R\ t$$

Let us assume that we have some way of establishing that $t'\ R\ t$ holds (how this is done is not important, it can be by rewriting, by doing beta-conversions, by matching with pre-proved theorems etc). When this is done, the new window theorem is

$$\vdash\ t'\ R\ t$$

(the system uses the transitivity of R to draw this conclusion). Now we close the subwindow by typing

```
#CLOSE_WIN();;
```

At this point, the window inference system uses a collection of *window closing rules* that permit the following inference to be drawn:

$$\frac{\vdash\ t'\ R\ t}{\vdash\ E[\ldots t'\ldots]\ R\ E[\ldots t\ldots]}$$

Essentially, closing rules show that contexts are monotonic with respect to the relation R. The result of closing is the new window

$$R \star E[\ldots t'\ldots]$$

and the window theorem is the result we wanted in the first place:

$$\vdash\ E[\ldots t'\ldots]\ R\ E[\ldots t\ldots]$$

We can now store this theorem in a theory file. Finally, the stack is deleted by typing

```
#END_STACK 'name';;
```

2.3   Entering relations and closing rules

The window inference system can always be used for reasoning about boolean implication $\Rightarrow$ and also about equality for arbitrary types. For example, there is a rule for opening a subwindow on a right hand conjunct:

$$\Rightarrow \star A \wedge \boxed{B}$$

(we use a box to highlight the subexpression that we are going to focus on next). When we open a subwindow like this, the new window will have A as an *assumption*:

$$! \, A$$
$$\Rightarrow \star B$$

Assumptions are printed above the current window, with a leading exclamation mark. This means that we can use A as if it was a theorem when we transform B.

The user can easily add a new relation R into the system. Assume that R_REFL and R_TRANS are the names of the reflexivity and transitivity theorems for the relation R. We then type

```
#add_relation(R_REFL,R_TRANS);;
```

Furthermore, we must add window closing rules for the relation. Assume that op is a binary operator on the type underlying R. Furthermore assume that FST_op is the name of the following inference rule:

$$\frac{\vdash x' \; R \; x}{\vdash (op \; x' \; y) \; R \; (op \; x \; y)}$$

(an inference rule is implemented as a function in the metalanguage ML). We then type

```
#rstore_rule([RATOR;RAND],(\t. rator(rator t)="op"),FST_op,R,R);;
```

(in the ascii-syntax of the HOL-system, the backslash character stands for λ). This makes the system apply the rule FST_op whenever it closes a window that has been opened on the first operand of a term $op \; x \; y$. The first argument to rstore_rule is the path leading to the subterm. The path is given as a list: the RATOR (for 'operator') of the term $op \; x \; y$ is the term $op \; x$ and the RAND (for 'operand') of that is x. The second argument is a condition that checks that we have the binary operator op and the third argument is the name of the inference rule to be used when closing the window. The fourth and fifth arguments are the relations that are to be preserved in the subwindow and the parent window, respectively (these need not be the same; see Section 4.3).

3 A mechanised refinement calculus

The notion of refinement that we have represented in HOL is based on a weakest precondition semantics [15]. In such a semantics, the meaning of a command is a predicate transformer, i.e., a function from predicates to predicates.

3.1 States and predicates

A *state* is a tuple of values. When we consider states in general, we assume that they have polymorphic type $*u$ (standing for 'universal state'). In particular cases, this type will be instantiated to a product type with one component for each state component (program variable).

A *predicate* is a boolean function on states. We let $(*u)pred$ stand for the predicate type $*u \rightarrow bool$. We say that a predicate p *holds in the state* u if $p \; u = T$. For example, the predicate

$$\lambda(b, x, y). \neg b \wedge (x < y) \tag{1}$$

holds in the state $(F, 2, 3)$.

A predicate p is said to imply a predicate q if q holds whenever p holds. This gives us a partial order *implies* (or 'stronger than') on the predicates over a given state type.

$$\vdash\ p\ implies\ q\ =\ \forall u.\, p\ u \Rightarrow q\ u \qquad\qquad \text{[implies\_DEF]}$$

where u has generic type $*u$.

We also lift logical connectives from booleans to predicates. For example, *p and q* is the predicate which holds in a state u if and only if both p and q hold in u:

$$\vdash\ p\ and\ q\ =\ \lambda u.\, p\ u \wedge q\ u \qquad\qquad \text{[and\_DEF]}$$

We define the operators *not* and *or* similarly. The definitions can be found in Appendix A, where we have collected all those definitions of the mechanised refinement theory that are relevant to this paper. We also define the everywhere false predicate *false* and the everywhere true predicate *true* by lifting.

The predicates over a given state space form a *complete lattice*, which means that we can define general conjunction (greatest lower bound) and disjunction (least upper bound) operators (see Appendix A). We represent sets by characteristic functions, so in the expression *glb P*, the set P has type $(*u)pred \rightarrow bool$.

3.1.1 Substitution

Substitution in predicates is represented by a combination of function application and lambda abstraction. As an example, the substitution of 2 for x in the predicate (1) is represented as

$$\lambda(b, x, y).\, (\lambda(b, x, y).\, \neg b \wedge (x < y))(b, 2, y)$$

which by the HOL rule of beta conversion is equal to $\lambda(b, x, y).\, \neg b \wedge (2 < y)$. This corresponds exactly to the syntactic substitution of 2 for x in $\neg b \wedge (x < y)$.

3.1.2 A least fixpoint operator

For the semantics of iteration, we need least fixpoints of monotonic predicate transformers. We do not go into details here, we simply assume that *fix f* gives the least fixpoint of an arbitrary monotonic predicate transformer f. The definition of *fix* and the proofs of basic fixpoint properties are quite straightforward in HOL (see Appendix A). In particular, the following two theorems together show that *fix* really is the least fixpoint operator:

$$\vdash\ monotonic\ f\ \Rightarrow\ (f(fix\ f) = fix\ f) \qquad\qquad \text{[fix\_fp]}$$

$$\vdash\ (f\ p)\ implies\ p\ \Rightarrow\ (fix\ f)\ implies\ p \qquad\qquad \text{[fix\_least]}$$

The monotonicity operator *monotonic* is defined in Section 3.3

3.2 Commands

In weakest precondition semantics, the semantics of a command is given by associating a *predicate transformer* (i.e. a function that maps predicates to predicates) with the command. In this paper, we identify commands and their weakest precondition predicate transformers. This means that we work in a programming notation where commands are at the same time predicate transformers.

Commands have generic type $(*u')pred \rightarrow (*u)pred$, abbreviated $(*u, *u')cmd$. A command of this type can intuitively be interpreted as being executed in an initial state of type $*u$ and terminating in a final state of type $*u'$ (note that the state spaces need not be the same).

Our approach permits us to consider arbitrary predicate transformers as commands. However, we introduce some notation for those commands which we want to work with. This means that our *programming notation* is open; we can extend it by adding new constructs whenever we want to.

Each command construct is introduced by defining what predicate transformer it is. For example, we introduce sequential composition by defining the operator *seq* to have the following property:

$$\vdash (c_1 \; seq \; c_2)q \; = \; c_1(c_2 \; q) \qquad\qquad \text{[seq\_DEF]}$$

This is in exact correspondence to the ordinary definition of the weakest precondition semantics of sequential composition:

$$\mathrm{wp}(C_1; C_2, Q) \; = \; \mathrm{wp}(C_1, \mathrm{wp}(C_2, Q))$$

The list of commands that we consider at this point is the following:

assert g	assertion command
skip	skip command
assign e	state assignment command
nondass m	nondeterministic state assignment
$c_1 \; seq \; c_2$	sequential composition
cond g c_1 c_2	conditional composition
do g c	iteration

We define the command constructs to be predicate transformers, as follows. The assertion command *assert g* is an assertion about the state. If the predicate g (for 'guard') holds in the initial state, then it does nothing. Otherwise, it is nonterminating (i.e., it does not establish any postcondition, not even *true*).

$$\vdash assert \; g \; q \; = \; g \; and \; q \qquad\qquad \text{[assert\_DEF]}$$

The *skip* command is a 'no operation' command, i.e., it leaves the state unchanged.

$$\vdash skip \; q \; = \; q \qquad\qquad \text{[skip\_DEF]}$$

In the *assign* command, e is a state-state function. This represents a very general kind of assignment, in which we specify the function according to which the assignment is to be made.

$$\vdash assign \; e \; q \; = \; \lambda u . \, q \, (e \; u) \qquad\qquad \text{[assign\_DEF]}$$

As an example, consider the command

$assign$ $\lambda(b, x, y). (b, x + y, y)$

It corresponds to what is commonly written as $x := x + y$. Applying this command to the predicate $\lambda(b, x, y). x > y$ we get by a series of beta-reductions:

$(assign$ $\lambda(b, x, y). (b, x + y, y))(\lambda(b, x, y). x > y) = \lambda(b, x, y). x > 0$

which corresponds exactly to what is ordinarily written as

$\text{wp}(x := x + y, x > y) = x > 0$

The *nondass* command is a nondeterministic assignment, i.e., a command which nondeterministically chooses among a number of possible final states:

$\vdash$ $nondass$ m q $=$ $\lambda u. \forall u'. m$ u $u' \Rightarrow q$ u' [nondass_DEF]

A similar command was introduced in [4], as a way of expressing arbitrary input-output specifications. In the definition of *nondass*, m is a state-state-relation. Given an initial state u, the command makes a nondeterministic choice of final state u' such that m u u' holds. If there is no such final state, then the above definitions says that *nondass* m establishes any postcondition, even *false*. In this case we say that the nondeterministic assignment is *miraculous*, because it seemingly can make the predicate *false* hold. This kind of 'miracles' have been shown to be useful in program development [26]. They represent non-implementable commands, but they can be useful in intermediate steps of program development. Note that the the *assign* command is a (deterministic) special case of *nondass*.

As noted above, c_1 *seq* c_2 is the sequential composition of commands c_1 and c_2. The conditional *cond* g c_1 c_2 is an if-then-else command and *do* g c is iteration:

$\vdash$ *cond* g c_1 c_2 q $=$ $(g$ *and* $(c_1$ $q)) $ *or* $((not$ $g)$ *and* $(c_2$ $q))$ [cond_DEF]

$\vdash$ *do* g c q $=$ *fix* $(\lambda p. ((not$ $g)$ *and* $q)$ *or* $(g$ *and* $(c$ $p)))$ [do_DEF]

The definitions of *seq*, *cond* and *do* correspond exactly to traditional definitions of the weakest preconditions semantics for sequential composition, conditional and iteration [15, 16].

3.3 Characteristic properties of commands

As noted above, we permit arbitrary predicate transformers as commands. Traditionally, predicate transformers permitted as semantic functions for programs have been required to satisfy a number of criteria (often called 'healthiness conditions'). Four important such conditions are monotonicity, strictness, conjunctivity and termination.

$\vdash$ *monotonic* c $=$
      $\forall p$ $q. p$ *implies* $q \Rightarrow (c$ $p)$ *implies* $(c$ $q)$ [monotonic_DEF]

$\vdash$ *strict* c $=$ $(c$ *false* $=$ *false*)   [strict_DEF]

$$\vdash \quad conjunctive\ c \ = \ \forall P.\,(\exists p.\,P\ p)$$
$$\Rightarrow (c(glb\ P) = glb(\lambda q.\,\exists p.\,P\ p\ \wedge\ (q = c\ p)))\qquad \text{[conjunctive\_DEF]}$$

$$\vdash \quad terminating\ c \ = \ (c\ true = true)\qquad\qquad\qquad \text{[terminating\_DEF]}$$

Monotonicity is a basic assumption. Strict commands are nonmiraculous (they satisfies Dijkstra's 'Law of Excluded Miracle' [15]): Conjunctivity can be interpreted as saying that nondeterminism is resolved demonically.

All commands presented so far are monotonic and conjunctive. However, the *assert* and *do* commands may be nonterminating while the *nondass* command is not strict.

3.4 Blocks with local variables

The definition of a block with local variables is complicated by the fact that inside the block, the state space is extended with an additional component (which we add as a first component in the state tuple). The definition is the following, with the added component represented by the bound variable x:

$$\vdash \quad block\ p\ c\ q \ = \ \lambda u.\,\forall x.\,p(x, u) \Rightarrow c(\lambda(x', u').\,q\ u')(x, u)\qquad \text{[block\_DEF]}$$

In the command *block p c*, the added state component is given a value such that the predicate p (the *initialisation*) is established. After this, the body c is executed and finally the added component is removed from the state. Note that the name of the local variable does not show in the syntax of the block command. This is because variables are identified by their position in the state tuple rather than by name. If the initialisation predicate is *false*, then the block is miraculous.

Our definition of the block corresponds to the following traditional semantics:

$$\mathrm{wp}(\|[\ \mathbf{var}\ x.\ P;\ C\ ]\|, Q) \quad = \quad \forall x.\ P \Rightarrow C\,Q$$

3.5 The refinement relation

By lifting the *implies* order, we get a *refinement* order on commands:

$$\vdash \quad c'\ refines\ c \ = \ \forall q.\,(c\ q)\ implies\ (c'\ q)\qquad\qquad \text{[refines\_DEF]}$$

Usually, the refinement relation is written with the more refined command on the right hand side (e.g., *c ref c'*). However, we define the order in the reverse way to make it suit the window inference tool better.

Refinement can also be expressed in terms of total correctness. We say that a command c is *totally correct* with respect to precondition p and postcondition q, if c is guaranteed to establish q whenever it is executed in an initial state where p holds:

$$\vdash \quad correct\ p\ c\ q \ = \ p\ implies\ (c\ q)\qquad\qquad\qquad \text{[correct\_DEF]}$$

The refinement c' *refines* c then holds exactly when c' satisfies every total correctness specification satisfied by c. Thus c' *refines* c means that c' can be used as a replacement for c in any program (provided that context is monotonic with respect to the refinement relation).

Since we can write quite general specifications in our command notation, the refinement relation is useful in program development; if we want to show that a program c' satisfies a specification c, we show that the refinement c' *refines* c holds.

A large number of useful refinement rules can be proved directly from the definitions. A simple such rule is the following:

$$\vdash \ (skip\ seq\ c = c)\ \wedge\ (c\ seq\ skip = c) \qquad\qquad \text{[remove\_skip]}$$

Note that both conjuncts are equalities (i.e., mutual refinements). Equalities are useful because they can be used directly as rewrite rules by the HOL system.

Another example is the rule for implementing a nondeterministic assignment by a deterministic one:

$$\vdash \ (\forall u.\ m\ u\ (e\ u)) \Rightarrow (assign\ e)\ refines\ (nondass\ m) \quad \text{[nondass\_to\_assign]}$$

In Appendix B we list a number of refinement rules that are used in subsequent examples. Most of these can be proved directly from the command definitions and the definition of refinement. However, some rules for iteration require quite elaborate reasoning about fixpoints.

3.5.1 Using assertions in refinements

The *assert* command is used to indicate context information. Such information is often useful in program refinement. For example, given a sequential composition $(assert\ g)\ seq\ c$ we can make use of the fact that g holds when we refine c. An example of a rule that uses assertions is given in Section 5.5.

Rules for adding assertions in a program can be found in [5]. A simple example is the rule for using the guard in an iteration:

$$\vdash \ do\ g\ c\ =\ do\ g\ ((assert\ g)\ seq\ c) \qquad\qquad \text{[add\_assert\_do]}$$

3.6   Recursion

We have defined a recursive construct in our mechanised theory of refinement. The operator mu is defined to be the least fixpoint operator for monotonic functions on commands. We do not treat recursion in this paper, but we note that the following rule (which we have proved in HOL) can be used to refine a specification into a recursive program:

$$
\begin{aligned}
\vdash\quad &cmonotonic\ f \\
&\wedge\ (\forall x.\ ((assert\ \lambda u.\ t\ u = x)\ seq\ c) \\
&\qquad refines\ (f((assert\ \lambda u.\ t\ u < x)\ seq\ c)) \qquad \text{[cmd\_to\_mu]}\\
&\Rightarrow\ (mu\ f)\ refines\ c
\end{aligned}
$$

where *cmonotonic* f means that f is monotonic with respect to the *refines* relation (this monotonicity can be proved automatically for any function built using the command notation). Iteration can be shown to be a special case of recursion:

$$\vdash \ do\ g\ c\ =\ mu\ (\lambda x.\ cond\ g\ (c\ seq\ x)\ skip) \qquad\qquad \text{[do\_eq\_mu]}$$

4 Refinement as window inference

Since the *refines* relation is reflexive and transitive, it is well suited for window inference. Furthermore, the constructors (*seq, cond, do, block*) are monotonic in their subcommands with respect to the *refines* relation, so we can refine subcomponents of programs.

When we want to refine a specification (or program) *c*, we make it the initial focus for a window inference session. We then repeatedly focus on some subterm, do a refinement step and close the window, getting (automatically proved) theorems that say the new program refines the old one.

In this section, we show how this is done. We begin by considering a refinement on the top level and then move to refinement of subcomponents.

4.1 Top level refinement

A top level refinement is done simply by applying a refinement rule directly to the focus. As an example, we show how a nondeterministic assignment is made deterministic. Our nondeterministic assignment increases the value of the only state component (x) arbitrarily. We spell out this example in detail, in order to show how the user interacts with the window inference system. In subsequent examples, we will be less verbose.

The window stack is set up by typing

```
#RBEGIN_STACK 'EX1' "(refines)(nondass \x x'. x'>x)";;
```

to which the system replies by showing the initial window:

$$refines \star nondass \; \lambda x \; x'. x' > x$$

We now want to implement the nondeterministic assignment with a deterministic assignment which increments x by 1. The rule we want to use is **nondass_to_assign** (see Appendix B), with the assignment function e specialised to $\lambda x. x + 1$. We type

```
#C_MATCH_TRANSFORM_WIN (ISPEC "\x.x+1" nondass_to_assign);;
```

which matches the specialised theorem against the current focus and adds proof obligations as conjectures:

$$\times \; \forall u. (u + 1) > u$$
$$refines \star assign \; \lambda x. x + 1$$

Here the $\times$ symbol indicates a 'bad conjecture', i.e., a formula that has been used as an assumption even though it has not been proved. Now we can look at the window theorem (i.e., the theorem that has been proved) by typing

```
#WIN_THM();;
```

The theorem is

$$\vdash \; (assign \; \lambda x. x + 1) \; refines \; (nondass \; \lambda x \; x'. x' > x)$$

The dot to the left of the turnstile stands for the bad conjecture (undischarged proof obligation) which still has to be proved. In order to prove it, we first enter

```
#ESTABLISH (TOP_BAD());;
```

which sets up a new window with the first (and in this case only) bad conjecture as the focus:

$$\Rightarrow \star \, \forall u. \, (u+1) > u$$

Rewriting using some built-in theorems reduces the focus to T. We enter

```
#REWRITE_WIN[GSYM ADD1;GREATER;LESS_SUC_REFL];;
```

to get

$$\Rightarrow \star \, T$$

and after closing this window the bad conjecture has been turned into a lemma (indicated by an upside-down exclamation mark):

$$¡ \, \forall u. \, (u+1) > u$$
$$refines \star assign \; \lambda x. \, x+1$$

Now the desired theorem has been proved:

$$\vdash \; (assign \; \lambda x. \, x+1) \; refines \; (nondass \; \lambda x \; x'. \, x' > x)$$

If we want, we can store this theorem in the theory file.

4.2 Refining subcomponents

To be able to refine subcomponents we must supply window closing rules to the system. Considering our command notation, we need six different rules: one for each subcommand of the *seq* and *cond* commands, one for *do* and one for *block*.

Each rule is based on a theorem which expresses the monotonicity of the program construct with respect to the *refines* relation. For example, the theorem for sequential composition is

$$\vdash \quad monotonic \; c_1' \wedge (c_1' \; refines \; c_1) \wedge (c_2' \; refines \; c_2)$$
$$\Rightarrow (c_1' \; seq \; c_2') \; refines \; (c_1 \; seq \; c_2) \qquad \text{[seq\_mono\_ref]}$$

From this theorem it is straightforward to implement the two inference rules:

$$\frac{\vdash \; c_1' \; refines \; c_1}{\vdash \; (c_1' \; seq \; c_2) \; refines \; (c_1 \; seq \; c_2)}$$

and

$$\frac{\vdash \; monotonic \; c_1 \qquad \vdash \; c_2' \; refines \; c_2}{\vdash \; (c_1 \; seq \; c_2') \; refines \; (c_1 \; seq \; c_2)}$$

The monotonicity condition in the second rule is proved automatically by a small ML-program for any command in our notation, so it can always be discharged.

Similarly, we derive and add rules for conditional composition, iteration and blocks, based on the theorems cond_mono_ref, do_mono_ref and block_mono_ref (see Appendix B).

4.2.1 Example

We can now refine subcomponents of a program. To illustrate the idea, we consider the trivial example with initial window

$$refines \star (nondass \ \lambda x \ x'.x' > x) \ seq \ skip$$

Having set up this command to be refined, we open a subwindow on the non-deterministic assignment by typing

```
#OPEN_WIN[RATOR;RAND];;
```

(since we want the first operand of the binary operator *seq*) to get

$$refines \star nondass \ \lambda x \ x'. \ x' > x$$

We then proceed as in the example above, refining the nondeterministic assignment to the command *assign* $\lambda x. \ x + 1$. We then close the window and end up with

$$refines \star (assign \ \lambda x. \ x + 1) \ seq \ skip$$

The window theorem is then

$$\vdash \ ((assign \ \lambda x. \ x + 1) \ seq \ skip) \ refines \ ((nondass \ \lambda x \ x'. \ x' > x) \ seq \ skip)$$

This shows how we can do refinements to subcomponents of programs.

4.3 Mixing relations

The window inference system permits us to move between different relations. For example, we know that the initialisation of a block can be strengthened:

$$\vdash \ p' \ implies \ p \ \Rightarrow \ (block \ p' \ c) \ refines \ (block \ p \ c) \qquad \text{[block\_str\_init]}$$

Since *implies* is also a reflexive and transitive relation, we can add a closing rule that permits us to open a subwindow on the initialisation p of a block and to transform it into a new expression p' such that p' *implies* p holds.

Even when we are just using the *refines* relation, we are in a sense mixing different relations. This is because *refines* is polymorphic, and when we open a window inside a block we preserve one *refines* relation in the body of the block and another *refines* relation in the block as a whole.

5 Data refinement

Data refinement means replacing local variables in a program with new local variables of another type so that the new program refines the original program. Typically, the purpose of a data refinement is to replace variables that represent an abstract view of data (e.g., sets) with new variables that are more concrete, in the sense that they are more easily implemented (e.g., bit strings). Data refinement is generally proved by exhibiting an *abstraction relation* which shows how the abstract and concrete states are related.

In our framework, a data refinement is a refinement step of the following form:

$(block\ p'\ c')\ refines\ (block\ p\ c)$

In order to be useful for large programs, a method for data refinement must allow us to replace the subcomponents of the abstract body c separately. However, since the abstract and the concrete components do not work on the same state space, it seems that we can not find a data refinement relation, *drefines* say, that would be reflexive. Thus, the methods traditionally used for data refinement [24, 26, 6, 28] are not directly suitable for window inference.

However, we shall show how the method using *abstraction commands*, described in [9] can be adapted to work well together with window reasoning.

5.1 Abstraction commands

An abstraction command is a command which replaces the first component of the state by a component of another type and leaves the rest of the state unchanged. Abstraction commands have generic type $(*k \times *u, *a \times *u)\,cmd$ (a for 'abstract' and k for 'concrete').

The action of an abstraction command is coded in a relation r which shows how the abstract state (a, u) is related to the concrete state (k, u). The relation r has type $*a \times *k \times *u \to bool$

In particular, we make use of the *angelic abstraction command* for the relation r, defined as follows:

$$\vdash\ abst\ r\ q\ =\ \lambda(k, u).\,\exists a.\,r(a, k, u) \wedge q(a, u) \qquad \text{[abst\_DEF]}$$

Given an initial state (a, u), the command *abst r* makes an angelic choice between all the possible states (k, u) such that $r(a, k, u)$ holds. If no such state exists, then the abstraction command aborts.

The angelic abstraction command establishes a postcondition q if there exists at least one choice of final state that makes q hold. It is not conjunctive (in fact, it is disjunctive, i.e., it distributes over least upper bounds of predicates). For a more detailed discussion of disjunctivity and of how angelic choice can be interpreted, we refer to [12].

Dually to the abstraction command, we define a *representation command* for the relation r:

$$\vdash\ repr\ r\ q\ =\ \lambda(a, u).\,\forall k.\,r(a, k, u) \Rightarrow q(k, u) \qquad \text{[repr\_DEF]}$$

This is a conjunctive (i.e., demonic) command which replaces the abstract component a by the concrete component c, according to r. If this is not possible, then it is miraculous.

The relation between *abst r* and *repr r* is highlighted by the following theorem:

$$\vdash\quad \begin{aligned} &((repr\ r)\ seq\ (abst\ r))\ refines\ skip \\ \wedge\ &skip\ refines\ ((abst\ r)\ seq\ (repr\ r)) \end{aligned} \qquad \text{[abst\_repr]}$$

This means that abstraction and representation are a Galois connection (an adjoint pair). Intuitively, the representation command acts as a kind of inverted abstraction command. For a more detailed account of adjoint commands and their interpretation we refer to [9, 11].

5.2   Data refinement of blocks

The key to data refining blocks is the following theorem:

$$\vdash \quad (block\ (abst\ r\ p)\ ((abst\ r)\ seq\ c\ seq\ (repr\ r)) \\ refines\ (block\ p\ c)) \qquad \text{[block\_dref]}$$

If the original block body c works on the abstract state (a, u), then the refined block body,

$$(abst\ r)\ seq\ c\ seq\ (repr\ r)$$

works on the concrete state (k, u).

In the refined block, the initialisation predicate $abst\ r\ p$ is the predicate

$$\lambda(k, u).\ \exists a.\ r(a, k, u) \wedge p(a, u)$$

It can usually be rewritten into a more convenient initialisation, using the rule for strengthening block initialisations (rule block_str_init of Appendix B).

5.2.1   Alternative methods of data refinement

Traditionally, a program C has said to be data-refined by a program C' through abstraction relation R if the following condition holds for all predicates Q:

$$R \wedge wp(C, Q) \ \Rightarrow\ wp(C', \exists a.\ R \wedge Q)$$

In fact, rewriting shows that this condition in our framework can be formulated as

$$((abst\ r)\ seq\ c)\ refines\ (c'\ seq\ (abst\ r)) \qquad (2)$$

This condition can be used for a method of data refinement where the abstraction command is 'pushed through' a block, from left to right. Such a method is not well suited for window inference, though. Condition (2) can also easily be shown to be equivalent to the condition

$$((abst\ r)\ seq\ c\ seq\ (repr\ r))\ refines\ c' \qquad (3)$$

which is the one our method uses.

5.2.2   Simplifying notation

In order to make formulas more readable, we will from now on use the notation α for the abstraction command $abst\ r$ (if there is danger of confusion we index α with the name of the abstraction relation). For the representation command $repr\ r$, we similarly use the notation $\overline{\alpha}$. Furthermore, we write the seq operator as a semicolon (;). Thus we can write the rule block_dref as

$$\vdash \ (block\ (\alpha\ p)\ (\alpha;\ c;\ \overline{\alpha}))\ refines\ (block\ p\ c) \qquad \text{[block\_dref]}$$

5.3 Piecewise data refinement

The rule block_dref shows that we can do a data refinement of a block by replacing the body c with the new body α; c; $\overline{\alpha}$.

If c is a basic command (e.g., an assignment) then there may be some rule that can be directly applied to simplify the command α; c; $\overline{\alpha}$ (see Section 5.4). However, c will generally be composed of sequences, conditionals and iterations in addition to basic commands. In order to use the window inference principle for data refining these subcomponents, we must have a way of pushing the data refinement further into the structure of c.

We shall now see how this is done, by considering each constructor separately.

5.3.1 Sequential composition

If the block body is a sequential composition, then the following rule can be used (possibly repeatedly) to push the data refinement into the sequence:

$$\vdash \quad monotonic\ c_1$$
$$\Rightarrow ((\alpha;\ c_1;\ \overline{\alpha});\ (\alpha;\ c_2;\ \overline{\alpha}))\ refines\ (\alpha;\ (c_1;\ c_2);\ \overline{\alpha}) \qquad \text{[seq\_dref]}$$

This rule follows directly from theorem abst_repr and the associativity of sequential composition.

5.3.2 Conditional composition

It is also possible to push data refinement into a conditional composition. However, in this case there is a nontrivial proof obligation (verification condition):

$$\vdash \quad (\alpha(not\ g))\ implies\ (not(\alpha\ g))$$
$$\Rightarrow (cond\ (\alpha\ g)\ (\alpha;\ c_1;\ \overline{\alpha})\ (\alpha;\ c_2;\ \overline{\alpha})) \qquad \text{[cond\_dref]}$$
$$refines\ (\alpha;\ (cond\ g\ c_1\ c_2);\ \overline{\alpha})$$

The proof obligation can be rewritten in many different ways. A practically useful version is shown in Appendix C, rule cond_dref2. Essentially it says that under the abstraction relation r, the old and new guards must be equivalent.

5.3.3 Iteration

The rule for iteration is derived from the rule for conditional composition, using a number of facts about recursion and fixpoints that we do not need to consider here. The rule is

$$\vdash \quad monotonic\ c\ \wedge\ (\alpha(not\ g))\ implies\ (not(\alpha\ g))$$
$$\Rightarrow (do\ (\alpha\ g)\ (\alpha;\ c;\ \overline{\alpha}))\ refines\ (\alpha;\ (do\ g\ c);\ \overline{\alpha}) \qquad \text{[do\_dref]}$$

Using the rules seq_dref, cond_dref and do_dref we can push data refinement into the body of a block until we are left with only basic commands surrounded by $\overline{\alpha}$-α-pairs.

5.4 Data refinement of basic commands

Our main basic commands are the *skip* command and the two assignments. For the *skip* command, we have the simple rule

$$\vdash skip\ refines\ (\alpha;\ skip;\ \overline{\alpha}) \qquad\qquad \text{[skip\_dref]}$$

which follows immediately from **abst_repr**.

Before we consider the *assign* command we give a rule for the nondeterministic assignment:

$$
\begin{aligned}
\vdash\quad &(\forall a\ k\ k'\ u\ u'.\, r(a,c,u) \wedge n(k,u)(k',u') \\
&\quad \Rightarrow (\exists a'.\, r(a',k',u') \wedge m(a,u)(a',u'))) \qquad \text{[nondass\_dref]} \\
&\Rightarrow (nondass\ n)\ refines\ (\alpha;\ (nondass\ m);\ \overline{\alpha})
\end{aligned}
$$

The verification condition (antecedent) of this rule encodes the principle of *forward simulation*: given a pair of states satisfying the concrete next-state relation n and an initial abstract state such that r holds initially, we must be able to find a final state for *nondass m* such that r is established.

The rule nondass_dref can also be used to data-refine *assign* commands, in the following way. First, the assignment is rewritten as a nondeterministic assignment, using the rule **assign_eq_nondass** (Appendix B). Next, the nondeterministic assignment is data-refined using **nondass_dref**. If we do not want the result to be in the form of a nondeterministic assignment, we can refine it into an assignment, using the rule **nondass_to_assign**.

It is possible to give direct rules for assignments in some special cases. However, in this paper we are satisfied with the general strategy outlined above. Most rules for the *assign* command can be seen as instances of this strategy.

5.4.1 A note on backward simulation

The method of data refinement that is based on (2) covers not only ordinary (forward) simulation, but also a dual method of *backward simulation* (sometimes called upward simulation or or backward data refinement). This is the method we get when the abstraction command is conjunctive rather than disjunctive. However, backward data refinement does not seem to work well in window reasoning, since there is no analogy to (3) for the backward case.

5.5 Assertions in data refinement

Occurrences of the *assert* command can be treated in two different ways in a data refinement. The window refinement tool assumes that assertions will be used in the data refinement, so it does not treat a sequence of the form (*assert g*) *seq c* as a sequential composition but as a single command. Thus no $\overline{\alpha}$-α pair is added inside the sequence. If the second component is a nondeterministic assignment, we can use the following variant of the rule nondass_dref to perform the data refinement:

$$
\begin{aligned}
\vdash\quad &(\forall a\ c\ c'\ u\ u'.\, g(a,u) \wedge r(a,c,u) \wedge n(c,u)(c',u') \\
&\quad \Rightarrow (\exists a'.\, r(a',c',u') \wedge m(a,u)(a',u'))) \qquad \text{[nondass\_dref2]} \\
&\Rightarrow (nondass\ n)\ refines\ (\alpha;\ ((assert\ g);\ (nondass\ m));\ \overline{\alpha})
\end{aligned}
$$

In this rule, the assertion is used to add information that may make the verification condition easier to prove.

However, we may want to data-refine the assertion along with the rest of the program. This is done by focussing on the sequence $\alpha; ((assert\ g);\ c); \overline{\alpha}$ and typing

```
#ADD_REPR_ABST();;
```

to get it refined to

$$(\alpha; (assert\ g); \overline{\alpha}); (\alpha; c; \overline{\alpha})$$

Now we can focus on the left part and apply the following rule:

$$\vdash\ (assert\ (\alpha\ g))\ refines\ (\alpha; (assert\ g); \overline{\alpha}) \qquad \text{[assert\_dref]}$$

to get the assertion data-refined.

6 An example with data refinement

As an example, we derive a program that produces a number of distinct keys (natural numbers) and puts them in a list l (the list itself is not really important, the main idea is that N keys are 'produced' and 'consumed'). The example may be considered trivial, but it illustrates our method well. We start from a specification, expressed as a nondeterministic assignment. This specification is then implemented by a block with a loop, which uses a set-valued local variable. We do a data refinement to replace the local variable with one that ranges over the natural numbers and then finish off by making the program deterministic.

6.1 Initial specification

The initial window is the following:

$$refines \star nondass\ \lambda l\ l'. (LEN\ l' = N) \wedge (\forall j\ k.\ j < k < N \Rightarrow (EL\ j\ l' \neq EL\ k\ l'))$$

Here, N is a global constant (not a state component), LEN is the length operator for lists and $EL\ j\ l$ is the jth element of the list l. This command specifies that the list l should contain N distinct numbers.

6.2 Implementing the specification

In our first refinement step we use a command for implementing specifications (nondeterministic assignments) by loop blocks. The command NON-DASS_TO_LOOP_WIN applies the following theorem (essentially a version of the invariant-bound method for proving total correctness of loops):

$$\begin{aligned}
\vdash\quad &monotonic\ c\\
&\wedge\ (\lambda(x,u).\ p_0\ u \wedge q(x,u))\ implies\ inv\\
&\wedge\ ((not\ g)\ and\ inv)\ implies\ (\lambda(x,u).\ p\ u)\\
&\wedge\ (\forall x.\ correct\ (inv\ and\ g\ and\ (\lambda u.\ t\ u = x))\\
&\qquad\qquad c\\
&\qquad\qquad (inv\ and\ (\lambda u.\ t\ u < x)))\\
&\Rightarrow\ ((nondass\ \lambda u\ u'.\ p_0\ u'); (block\ q\ (do\ g\ c)))\\
&\qquad refines\ (nondass\ \lambda u\ u'.\ p\ u')
\end{aligned} \qquad \text{[nondass\_to\_loop]}$$

When applying NONDASS_TO_LOOP_WIN, the user supplies the following arguments:

p_0 the initialisation of the global variables in the new block
q the initialisation of the local variables in the new block
g the guard of the loop
c the body of the loop
inv the loop invariant
t the termination function of the loop

In our case, these are chosen so that the loop keeps track of all the keys distributed so far in a set-valued local variable a. On each iteration, a new key not in a is chosen. The new window is

$$refines \star (nondass \; \lambda l \; l'. \; l' = [\,]) \; seq$$
$$(block \; (\lambda(a, l). \; a = \{\})$$
$$(do \; (\lambda(a, l). \; LEN \; l < N)$$
$$(nondass \; \lambda(a, l)(a', l').$$
$$\exists m. (l' = CONS \; m \; l) \; \wedge \; \neg(m \; IN \; a) \; \wedge \; (a' = m \; INS \; a))))$$

where $[\,]$ is the empty list, $\{\}$ is the empty set (we use HOL's set library), IN is the set membership operator and INS is set insertion. In fact, this window has a number of bad conjectures (proof obligations) which will have to be proved. These obligations correspond to the conjuncts in the antecedent in the theorem nondass_to_loop (those conjuncts, that is, that were not proved automatically when the rule was applied). We do not show them here, as they would take up too much room (the printing of bad conjectures can be turned off with a switch).

These proof obligations can either be proved now or later. These proofs can either be carried out without the window inference tool (as indicated in Section 4.1), or we can use HOL's ordinary facilities for goal-directed proof. In the latter case, we first set up a new window with the first bad conjecture:

```
#ESTABLISH (TOP_BAD());;
```

and then start a goal-directed proof session by setting up the focus as our goal:

```
#goal (focus (TOP_WIN()));;
```

After the theorem has been proved, we rewrite the window with the theorem and close:

```
#REWRITE_WIN[top_thm()];;
#CLOSE_WIN();;
```

(the function call top_thm() returns the most recent theorem proved using the HOL goal stack).

6.3   Data refinement

We now move to the data refinement step. The idea is to give out increasing keys all the time. This way, we only need to keep track of the last key issued, so we can replace the set-valued local variable a with a new local variable k which ranges over the natural numbers. In fact, we only require that k be greater than the greatest member of a (this lets us avoid problems with the empty set). The abstraction relation is then

$$\lambda(a, k, u). (\forall n.\, n \ IN \ a \ \Rightarrow \ n < k)$$

We begin by opening a subwindow on the *block* command. Then we push data refinements into the current focus. This is done by calling the single rule DATAREF_WIN with the abstraction relation as argument. To make reading easier, we have replaced occurrence of

$$abst \, (\lambda(a, k, l). (\forall n.\, n \ IN \ a \ \Rightarrow \ n < k))$$

by α and similarly occurrences of

$$repr \, (\lambda(a, k, l). (\forall n.\, n \ IN \ a \ \Rightarrow \ n < k))$$

by $\overline{\alpha}$. The window is then the following, after the data refinement step:

$$refines \star block \boxed{(\alpha(\lambda(a, l).\, a = \{\}))}$$
$$(do \ (\alpha(\lambda(a, l).\, LEN \ l < N))$$
$$(\alpha; \ (nondass \ \lambda(a, l)(a', l').$$
$$\exists m. (l' = CONS \ m \ l) \ \wedge \ \neg(m \ IN \ a) \ \wedge$$
$$(a' = m \ INS \ a)); \overline{\alpha}))$$

This was the real data refinement. Now all that remains to do is to simplify and to prove all bad conjectures. We first simplify the initialisation of the block (highlighted above) by opening a subwindow on it:

$$implies \star \alpha(\lambda(a, l).\, a = \{\})$$

Rewriting using the definition of α and beta-reducing, we get

$$implies \star \lambda(k, u).\, \exists a. (\forall n.\, a \ n \Rightarrow n < k) \wedge (a = \{\})$$

A few simple transformations and we get the following simple result:

$$implies \star true$$

so when we close the window, we get

$$refines \star block \ true$$
$$(do \ \boxed{(\alpha(\lambda(a, l).\, LEN \ l < N))}$$
$$(\alpha; \ (nondass \ \lambda(a, l)(a', l').$$
$$\exists m. (l' = CONS \ m \ l) \ \wedge \ \neg(m \ IN \ a) \ \wedge$$
$$(a' = m \ INS \ a)); \overline{\alpha}))$$

We now open a subwindow on the guard of the iteration (highlighted above):

$$= \star \alpha(\lambda(a, l).\, LEN \ l < N)$$

Note that the window relation in this case is equality. This is because there is no window closing rule specifically for transforming the guard of an iteration. Since the guard does not refer to the local variable, we can easily reduce this window to

$$= \star\, \lambda(k, l).\, LEN\; l < N$$

We close the window and get

$$
\begin{aligned}
refines \star\; & block\; true \\
& (do\; (\lambda(k, l).\, LEN\; l < N) \\
& \quad (\alpha;\, (nondass\; \lambda(a, l)(a', l'). \\
& \qquad \exists m.\, (l' = CONS\; m\; l)\; \wedge\; \neg(m\; IN\; a)\; \wedge \\
& \qquad (a' = m\; INS\; a));\, \overline{\alpha}))
\end{aligned}
$$

Next we open a subwindow on the body of the loop. We can then use the rule of forward simulation nondass_dref, supplying the new next-state relation

$$\lambda(k, l)(k', l').\, k < k'\; \wedge\; (l' = CONS\; k\; l)$$

This adds one more proof obligation and when we close, we get

$$
\begin{aligned}
refines \star\; & block\; true \\
& (do\; (\lambda(k, l).\, LEN\; l < N) \\
& \quad (nondass\; \lambda(k, l)(k', l').\, k < k'\; \wedge\; (l' = CONS\; k\; l)))
\end{aligned}
$$

Closing up, we get to the top level to see our current program:

$$
\begin{aligned}
refines \star\; & (nondass\; l\, l'.\, l' = []); \\
& (block\; true \\
& \quad (do\; (\lambda(k, l).\, LEN\; l < N) \\
& \qquad (nondass\; \lambda(k, l)(k', l').\, k < k'\; \wedge\; (l' = CONS\; k\; l))))
\end{aligned}
$$

which is a correct refinement of the initial specification.

6.4 Final refinements

As final refinements, we make the nondeterministic assignments deterministic. We open a subwindow on the initialisation:

$$refines \star\; nondass\; \lambda l\; l'.\, l' = []$$

and transform it into an ordinary assignment:

$$refines \star\; assign\; \lambda l.\, []$$

After closing this window, we focus on the initialisation *true* of the block. We transform it to the deterministic initialisation $\lambda(k, l).\, k = 0$. This is permitted, since the relation *implies* is preserved here (*true* is the weakest of all predicates).

Finally we focus on the loop body:

$$refines \star\; nondass\; \lambda(k, l)(k', l').\, k < k'\; \wedge\; (l' = CONS\; k\; l)$$

As we did in a previous example, we can easily transform this into a deterministic assignment:

$$\textit{refines} \star \textit{assign } \lambda(k, l). (k + 1, \textit{CONS } k \; l)$$

Closing up once again, we get the final window:

$$\begin{aligned}
\textit{refines} \star (\textit{assign } &\lambda l. [\,]); \\
&(\textit{block } (\lambda(k, l). k = 0) \\
&\quad (\textit{do } (\lambda(k, l). \textit{LEN } l < N) \\
&\quad\quad (\textit{assign } \lambda(k, l). (k + 1, \textit{CONS } k \; l))))
\end{aligned}$$

and a theorem which states that this is a correct refinement of the original
specification. In a more traditional notation, our final program corresponds to
the program

$$\begin{aligned}
&l := [\,]; \\
&|[\; \mathbf{var} \; k; \; k := 0; \\
&\quad \mathbf{do} \; \textit{LEN } l < N \; \rightarrow \; k, l := k + 1, \textit{CONS } k \; l \; \mathbf{od} \\
&]|
\end{aligned}$$

7 Conclusions and future directions

We have described a tool for stepwise refinement of programs, based on the
HOL theorem proving system. Our approach is based on a command notation
with a weakest precondition semantics. It supports both ordinary algorithmic
refinement (e.g., transforming specifications into code) and data refinement.
The difficult problem of data refining program components separately [22] has
been solved by a method that involves abstraction-representation command
pairs.

The example we have given is small; it is mainly intended to convey the
basic ideas of our window refinement tool. However, preliminary experiments
indicate that it works well for larger examples also. One problem with our approach is that more realistic software will produce verification conditions that
the HOL system is not very good at proving. The HOL system has a number
of libraries for working with sets, lists etc., but the user may still find herself
spending unreasonable amounts of time proving insignificant verification conditions. One solution is simply to leave some verification conditions unproved.
They will then appear as assumptions (undischarged) in the window theorem.

Our tool differs from previously described refinement editors in that every
refinement step is checked to rock bottom, using the HOL theorem prover.
In this respect, it gives us a secure environment for program development by
stepwise refinement. In many applications, such security may be an overkill,
but we feel confident that there are situations where it is a great advantage if
specific critical software is developed using such a secure system.

Our tool is a prototype. It has no bells and whistles, but we believe we
have shown that the window inference idea is potentially very useful in program
refinement. A visual interface for the window inference tool has been developed,
which permits the user to select subterms by pointing and clicking, making the
interaction smoother. However, this interface is not very flexible, so it would

have to be customised to suit the approach to program refinement that we have taken.

Our tool can be used in a flexible way: the user can prove verification conditions immediately but one can also postpone proving them until one is certain that the chosen line of refinement is reasonable.

An obvious question is to what extent our ideas scale up. In one sense, the window inference idea is explicitly intended for handling large expressions: we can focus on subexpressions and transform them, while the system keeps track of what happens to the top-level expression. However, large programs mean extremely large terms, and even on a large computer, the HOL system may run into trouble. On the other hand, it should be possible to build larger programs out of modules that are developed separately. If each module can be developed using the window refinement tool, then we never need to consider extremely large program texts. We have experimented with *functional procedures*, i.e., program fragments that implement a specified function. Our results are encouraging, and we think this approach potentially can be used to develop quite sizable software in a totally secure environment.

Acknowledgements

I want to thank Jim Grundy for numerous discussions on window inference and for answering my many questions about the window inference tool. This research was partly funded by grants from the Science and Engineering Research Council of Great Britain, the Academy of Finland and the Foundation for the Åbo Akademi University of Turku, Finland.

References

[1] M. Aagard and M. Leeser. Verifying a logic synthesis tool in Nuprl. In *Proc. 4th Workshop on Computer-Aided Verification*, Montreal, Canada, June 1992. Springer-Verlag.

[2] S. Agerholm. Mechanizing program verification in HOL. DAIMI IR–111, Aarhus University, Apr. 1992.

[3] F. Andersen. *A Theorem Prover for UNITY in Higher Order Logic*. PhD thesis, Technical University of Denmark, Lyngby, Denmark, Mar. 1992.

[4] R.J.R. Back. *Correctness Preserving Program Refinements: Proof Theory and Applications*, volume 131 of *Mathematical Center Tracts*. Mathematical Centre, Amsterdam, 1980.

[5] R.J.R. Back. A calculus of refinements for program derivations. *Acta Informatica*, 25:593–624, 1988.

[6] R.J.R. Back. Changing data representation in the refinement calculus. In *21st Hawaii International Conference on System Sciences*, January 1989.

[7] R.J.R. Back. Refinement calculus, part II: Parallel and reactive programs. In *REX Workshop for Refinement of Distributed Systems*, volume 430 of

Lecture Notes in Computer Science, Nijmegen, The Netherlands, 1989. Springer–Verlag.

[8] R.J.R. Back and K. Sere. Superposition refinement of parallel algorithms. In K.R. Parker and G.A. Rose, editors, *Formal Description Techniques IV*, pages 475–493. Elsevier Science Publishers (North-Holland), 1992.

[9] R.J.R. Back and J. von Wright. Refinement calculus, part I: Sequential programs. In *REX Workshop for Refinement of Distributed Systems*, volume 430 of *Lecture Notes in Computer Science*, Nijmegen, The Netherlands, 1989. Springer–Verlag.

[10] R.J.R. Back and J. von Wright. Refinement concepts formalised in higher-order logic. *Formal Aspects of Computing*, 2:247–272, 1990.

[11] R.J.R. Back and J. von Wright. Statement inversion and strongest postcondition *Science of Computer Programming*, 20:223–251, 1993.

[12] R.J.R. Back and J. von Wright. Combining angels, demons and miracles in program specifications. *Theoretical Computer Science*, 100:365–383, 1992.

[13] A.J. Camilleri. Mechanizing CSP trace theory in higher order logic. *IEEE Transactions of Software Engineering*, 16(9):993–1004, 1990.

[14] A. Church. A formulation of the simple theory of types. *Journal of Symbolic Logic*, 5:56–68, 1940.

[15] E.W. Dijkstra. *A Discipline of Programming*. Prentice–Hall International, 1976.

[16] E.W. Dijkstra and A.J.M. van Gasteren. A simple fixpoint argument without the restriction to continuity. *Acta Informatica*, 23:1–7, 1986.

[17] U. Engberg, P. Groenning and L. Lamport. Mechanical verification of concurrent systems with TLA. In *Proc. 4th Workshop on Computer-Aided Verification*, Montreal, Canada, June 1992. Springer-Verlag.

[18] P.H. Gardiner and C.C. Morgan. Data refinement of predicate transformers. *Theoretical Computer Science*, 87(1):143–162, 1991.

[19] D. M. Goldschlag. Mechanizing UNITY. In M. Broy, editor, *TC2 Working Conference on Programming Concepts and Methods*, pages 374–401, Israel, 1990. IFIP.

[20] M.J.C. Gordon. HOL: A proof generating system for higher-order logic. In G. Birtwistle and P.A. Subrahmanyam (ed.), *VLSI Specification, Verification and Synthesis*. Kluwer Academic Publishers, 1988.

[21] M.J.C. Gordon. Mechanizing programming logics in higher-order logic. In G. Birtwistle and P.A. Subrahmanyam (ed.), *Current Trends in Hardware Verification and Theorem Proving*. Springer-Verlag, 1989.

[22] L. Groves and R. Nickson. A tactic driven refinement tool. In Jones et al, editor, *Proc. 5th Refinement Workshop*, London, Jan. 1992. Springer-Verlag.

[23] J. Grundy. A window inference tool for refinement. In Jones et al, editor, *Proc. 5th Refinement Workshop*, London, Jan. 1992. Springer–Verlag.

[24] C.A.R. Hoare. Proofs of correctness of data representation. *Acta Informatica*, 1(4):271–281, 1972.

[25] C.B. Jones. *Systematic Software Development Using VDM*. Prentice–Hall International, 1986.

[26] C.C. Morgan. Data refinement by miracles. *Information Processing Letters*, 26:243–246, January 1988.

[27] C.C. Morgan. *Programming from Specifications*. Prentice-Hall, 1990.

[28] J.M. Morris. Laws of data refinement. *Acta Informatica*, 26:287–308, 1989.

[29] P.J. Robinson and J. Staples. Formalising the hierarchical structure of practical mathematical reasoning. Techn. Rep. 138, Key Centre for Software Technology, University of Queensland, Australia, 1990.

[30] T. Vickers. An overview of a refinement editor. In *5th Australian Software Engineering Conference*, Sydney, May 1990.

[31] J. von Wright. The lattice of data refinement. Reports on computer science and mathematics 130, Åbo Akademi, 1992. To appear in *Acta Informatica*.

[32] J. von Wright, J. Hekanaho, P. Luostarinen and T. Långbacka. Mechanising some advanced refinement concepts. *Formal Methods in System Design*, 3:49–81, 1993.

A Definitions

This appendix lists a number of definition for the mechanised theory of refinement, in alphabetical order. We have divided up the definitions in two sections, one concerns predicates and the other one concerns commands.

Predicates

$$\vdash \; p \; and \; q \; = \; \lambda u. \, p \; u \; \wedge \; q \; u \qquad\qquad \text{[and\_DEF]}$$

$$\vdash \; false \; = \; \lambda u. \, F \qquad\qquad \text{[false\_DEF]}$$

$$\vdash \; fix \; f \; = \; glb(\lambda p. \, (f \; p) \; implies \; p) \qquad\qquad \text{[fix\_DEF]}$$

$$\vdash \; glb \; P \; = \; \lambda u. \forall p. \, P \; p \Rightarrow p \; u \qquad\qquad \text{[glb\_DEF]}$$

$$\vdash \; p \; implies \; q \; = \; \forall u. \, p \; u \; \Rightarrow \; q \; u \qquad\qquad \text{[implies\_DEF]}$$

$$\vdash \; lub \; P \; = \; \lambda u. \exists p. \, P \; p \wedge p \; u \qquad\qquad \text{[lub\_DEF]}$$

$$\vdash \; not \; q \; = \; \lambda u. \neg \; q \; u \qquad\qquad \text{[not\_DEF]}$$

$$\vdash \; p \; or \; q \; = \; \lambda u. \, p \; u \; \vee \; q \; u \qquad\qquad \text{[or\_DEF]}$$

$$\vdash \; true \; = \; \lambda u. \, T \qquad\qquad \text{[true\_DEF]}$$

Commands

$$\vdash\ abst\ r\ q\ =\ \lambda(k,u).\exists a.\,r(a,k,u) \wedge q(a,u) \qquad \text{[abst\_DEF]}$$

$$\vdash\ assert\ g\ q\ =\ g\ and\ q \qquad \text{[assert\_DEF]}$$

$$\vdash\ assign\ e\ q\ =\ \lambda u.\,q\,(e\ u) \qquad \text{[assign\_DEF]}$$

$$\vdash\ block\ p\ c\ q\ =\ \lambda u.\forall x.\,p(x,u) \Rightarrow c(\lambda(x',u').\,q\ u')(x,u) \qquad \text{[block\_DEF]}$$

$$\vdash\ cond\ g\ c_1\ c_2\ q\ =\ (g\ and\ (c_1\ q))\ or\ ((not\ g)\ and\ (c_2\ q)) \qquad \text{[cond\_DEF]}$$

$$\vdash\ conjunctive\ c\ =\ \forall P.\,(\exists p.\,P\ p) \\ \Rightarrow (c(glb\ P) = glb(\lambda q.\exists p.\,P\ p\ \wedge\ (q = c\ p))) \qquad \text{[conjunctive\_DEF]}$$

$$\vdash\ correct\ p\ c\ q\ =\ p\ implies\ (c\ q) \qquad \text{[correct\_DEF]}$$

$$\vdash\ do\ g\ c\ q\ =\ fix\ (\lambda p.\,((not\ g)\ and\ q)\ or\ (g\ and\ (c\ p))) \qquad \text{[do\_DEF]}$$

$$\vdash\ monotonic\ c\ =\ \forall p\ q.\,p\ implies\ q \Rightarrow (c\ p)implies(c\ q) \qquad \text{[monotonic\_DEF]}$$

$$\vdash\ nondass\ m\ q\ =\ \lambda u.\forall u'.\,m\ u\ u' \Rightarrow q\ u' \qquad \text{[nondass\_DEF]}$$

$$\vdash\ reprr\ r\ q\ =\ (\lambda(a,u).\forall k.\,r(a,k,u) \Rightarrow q(k,u)) \qquad \text{[repr\_DEF]}$$

$$\vdash\ (c_1\ seq\ c_2)q\ =\ c_1(c_2\ q) \qquad \text{[seq\_DEF]}$$

$$\vdash\ skip\ q\ =\ q \qquad \text{[skip\_DEF]}$$

$$\vdash\ strict\ c\ =\ (c\ false = false) \qquad \text{[strict\_DEF]}$$

$$\vdash\ terminating\ c\ =\ (c\ true = true) \qquad \text{[terminating\_DEF]}$$

B Theorems of the refinement theory

This appendix lists a number of theorems (including refinement rules) that we have proved in HOL, listed in alphabetical order.

$$\vdash\ ((repr\ r)\ seq\ (abst\ r))\ refines\ skip \\ \wedge\ skip\ refines\ ((abst\ r)\ seq\ (repr\ r)) \qquad \text{[abst\_repr]}$$

$$\vdash\ assign\ e\ =\ nondass\ \lambda u\ u'.\,u' = e\ u \qquad \text{[assign\_eq\_nondass]}$$

$$\vdash\ (c'\ refines\ c) \Rightarrow (block\ p\ c')\ refines\ (block\ p\ c) \qquad \text{[block\_mono\_ref]}$$

$$\vdash\ p'\ implies\ p \Rightarrow (block\ p'\ c)\ refines\ (block\ p\ c) \qquad \text{[block\_str\_init]}$$

$$\vdash \quad (c_1' \text{ refines } c_1) \land (c_2' \text{ refines } c_2)$$
$$\Rightarrow (cond \ g \ c_1' \ c_2') \text{ refines } (cond \ g \ c_1 \ c_2) \qquad \text{[cond\_mono\_ref]}$$

$$\vdash (c' \text{ refines } c) \Rightarrow (do \ g \ c') \text{ refines } (do \ g \ c) \qquad \text{[do\_mono\_ref]}$$

$$\vdash monotonic \ f \Rightarrow (f(\text{fix } f) = \text{fix } f) \qquad \text{[fix\_fp]}$$

$$\vdash (f \ p) \text{ implies } p \Rightarrow (\text{fix } f) \text{ implies } p \qquad \text{[fix\_least]}$$

$$\vdash (\forall u. \ m \ u \ (e \ u)) \Rightarrow (assign \ e) \text{ refines } (nondass \ m) \quad \text{[nondass\_to\_assign]}$$

$$\vdash (skip \ seq \ c = c) \land (c \ seq \ skip = c) \qquad \text{[remove\_left\_skip]}$$

$$\vdash \quad monotonic \ c_1' \land (c_1' \text{ refines } c_1) \land (c_2' \text{ refines } c_2)$$
$$\Rightarrow (c_1' \ seq \ c_2') \text{ refines } (c_1 \ seq \ c_2) \qquad \text{[seq\_mono\_ref]}$$

$$\vdash \quad monotonic \ c$$
$$\land (\lambda(x, u). \ p_0 \ u \land q(x, u)) \text{ implies } inv$$
$$\land ((not \ g) \ and \ inv) \text{ implies } (\lambda(x, u). \ p \ u)$$
$$\land (\forall x. \ correct \ (inv \ and \ (g \ and \ (\lambda u. t \ u = x)))$$
$$c \qquad \text{[nondass\_to\_loop]}$$
$$(inv \ and \ (\lambda u. (t \ u) < x)))$$
$$((nondass \ \lambda u \ u'. \ p_0 \ u') \ seq \ (block \ q \ (do \ g \ c)))$$
$$\text{refines } (nondass \ \lambda u \ u'. \ p \ u')$$

C   Rules of data refinement

This appendix lists a number of rules for data refinement that we have proved in HOL. In this listing, we use the abbreviation α for *abst r* and $\overline{\alpha}$ for *repr r*.

$$\vdash (assert \ (\alpha \ g)) \text{ refines } (\alpha; (assert \ g); \overline{\alpha}) \qquad \text{[assert\_dref]}$$

$$\vdash (block \ (\alpha \ p) \ (\alpha; \ c; \overline{\alpha}) \text{ refines } (block \ p \ c) \qquad \text{[block\_dref]}$$

$$\vdash \quad (\alpha(not \ g)) \text{ implies } (not(\alpha \ g))$$
$$\Rightarrow (cond \ (\alpha \ g) \ (\alpha; \ c_1; \overline{\alpha}) \ (\alpha; \ c_2; \overline{\alpha})) \qquad \text{[cond\_dref]}$$
$$\text{refines } (\alpha; (cond \ g \ c_1 \ c_2); \overline{\alpha})$$

$$\vdash \quad (\forall a \ a' \ k \ u. \ r(a, k, u) \land r(a', k, u) \land g(a', u) \Rightarrow g(a, u))$$
$$\Rightarrow (cond \ (\alpha \ g) \ (\alpha; \ c_1; \overline{\alpha}) \ (\alpha; \ c_2; \overline{\alpha})) \qquad \text{[cond\_dref2]}$$
$$\text{refines } (\alpha; (cond \ g \ c_1 \ c_2); \overline{\alpha})$$

$$\vdash \quad monotonic \ c \land (\alpha(not \ g)) \text{ implies } (not(\alpha \ g))$$
$$\Rightarrow (do \ (\alpha \ g) \ (\alpha; \ c; \overline{\alpha})) \text{ refines } (\alpha; (do \ g \ c); \overline{\alpha}) \qquad \text{[do\_dref]}$$

$$\vdash \quad (\forall a\ c\ c'\ u\ u'.\ r(a, c, u) \wedge n(c, u)(c', u')$$
$$\Rightarrow (\exists a'.\ r(a', c', u') \wedge m(a, u)(a', u')))$$
$$\Rightarrow (nondass\ n)\ refines\ (\alpha; (nondass\ m); \overline{\alpha}) \qquad \text{[nondass\_dref]}$$

$$\vdash \quad (\forall a\ c\ c'\ u\ u'.\ g(a, u) \wedge r(a, c, u) \wedge n(c, u)(c', u')$$
$$\Rightarrow (\exists a'.\ r(a', c', u') \wedge m(a, u)(a', u')))$$
$$\Rightarrow (nondass\ n)\ refines\ (\alpha; ((assert\ g); (nondass\ m)); \overline{\alpha}) \qquad \text{[nondass\_dref2]}$$

$$\vdash \quad monotonic\ c_1$$
$$\Rightarrow ((\alpha; c_1; \overline{\alpha}); (\alpha; c_2; \overline{\alpha}))\ refines\ (\alpha; (c_1; c_2); \overline{\alpha}) \qquad \text{[seq\_dref]}$$

$$\vdash \quad skip\ refines\ (\alpha; skip; \overline{\alpha}) \qquad \text{[skip\_dref]}$$

D   Commands for window refinement

This appendix describes some commands for handling the window refinement tool that are essential for this paper. We lists those commands that are part of the basic window inference tool first.

Window inference commands

add_relation(thm1,thm2)
Adds a relation to the database. **thm1** is the reflexivity theorem and **thm2** is the transitivity theorem for the relation added.

rstore_rule(path,cond,rule,rel1,rel2)
Stores a window closing rule in the database. **path** is the path to the focus at opening, **cond** is a condition of applicability for the rule and **rule** is the inference rule (ML program) applied when closing. **rel1** and **rel2** are the relations preserved in the subwindow and the parent window, respectively.

focus win
Returns the focus of the window **win**.

CLOSE_WIN()
Closes the current window (always matches exactly one **OPEN_WIN** command).

CONVERT_WIN conv
Converts the current window, using the conversion **conv**, e.g., beta-conversion.

END_STACK 'name'
Deletes the named stack.

ESTABLISH term
Sets up a new window, with the goal of proving **term** by reducing it to T under the relation $\Rightarrow$ (implication).

OPEN_WIN path
Opens a subwindow at the indicated location. **path** is a list containing the keywords **RATOR**, **RAND** and **BODY** (used when opening inside an abstraction).

RBEGIN_STACK name term
Set up a new stack with the given name and initial window.

REWRITE_WIN thms
Rewrite the current window using the theorems in the list **thms**.

UNDO()
Undo the last action that affected the window stack.

TOP_WIN()
Returns the current window.

WIN_THM()
Show the current window theorem.

Window refinement commands

ADD_REPR_ABST()
Transforms the current window (under *refines*) by adding a $\overline{\alpha}$-α pair into a sequential composition.

C_MATCH_TRANSFORM_WIN thm
If **thm** is a theorem of the form $\vdash t'\, R\, t$, then this command tries to match t to the current focus and transform it according to the theorem. If the theorem has assumptions, then these are added as 'bad' conjectures.

DATAREF_WIN r
A data refinement is performed on the current window and pairs of abstraction and representation commands are pushed into all program structures (except after assertions).

NONDASS_TO_LOOP_WIN p0 q g c inv t
A nondeterministic assignment is transformed into an initialised loop block, with the given initialisations, loop guard, loop body, invariant and termination function.

TOP_BAD()
Returns the first bad conjecture of the current window.

Co-Refinement

Mike Ainsworth   Peter JL Wallis

School of Mathematical Sciences, University of Bath,
Claverton Down, Bath BA2 7AY, United Kingdom
Email: ma,pjlw@uk.ac.bath.maths

Abstract

One way of tackling the problems of large-scale formal specification is to use a series of partial specifications. These *viewpoint* specifications have several advantages for the specification stage of a development, since their flexibility is highly suited to incremental specification and distributed working. However, in order to implement such a specification, we must find an *amalgamation* — a single specification which combines the properties of each of the viewpoint specifications. This process is related to refinement, and can be formalised in terms of a modified refinement relation, which we call *co-refinement*.

1 Introduction

An approach to the development of large specifications that has been used with some success is the *viewpoint* approach, in which different aspects (viewpoints) of a system are quite separately described and then combined to generate a description of the complete system. The process of combining several viewpoints into an integrated whole we call *(viewpoint) amalgamation*. Viewpoint techniques are relatively little used in current practice, but have been used in a number of projects in areas such as requirements capture (Kotonya & Sommerville, 1992), incremental software development (Feather, 1989) and database schema integration (Batini *et al.*, 1986).

The viewpoint approach to the specification of large software systems is intuitively appealing because it models the way that people habitually think and learn about complex systems. Therefore it seems to us that there is scope for much wider appreciation of viewpoint techniques than is currently the case. The aim of the work described here is to suggest a basis for a formal mathematical investigation of the process of viewpoint amalgamation and its properties.

1.1 Example

We start with a simple instance of viewpoint specification that serves as an example of the way we informally illustrate many of our ideas. Suppose that at a motor company we have two designers: Ray, who designs radios; and Eddie, who is responsible for the design of the car's electrical system. Suppose that each of them specifies a design for their part of a project. These individual designs are *viewpoints* — each gives a partial specification of the whole car.

If we give Ray a car, and show him that inside the car is a radio, then his viewpoint specification has been satisfied. However, installing the radio into the car may impose additional constraints arising from the other viewpoints, for instance, the radio may only work if the car's ignition is switched on. This suggests that one concern of a study of viewpoint amalgamation will be the different ways in which viewpoints may interact.

1.2   Amalgamation and Refinement

Amalgamation is the process of combining formal descriptions representing different viewpoints of a system into an integrated formal description reflecting all the viewpoints. Another way of representing this process is to take the viewpoints to represent the requirements of separate customers who can all be satisfied by supplying each of them with an instance of the amalgamated product. This alternative approach suggests connections between the process of viewpoint amalgamation and that of refinement, for refinement may be generally characterised as the process of adding information to a product in such a way that all previous customers for the product remain satisfied. This connection between amalgamation and refinement was first suggested by Lindsay Groves (Groves, 1992). The use of refinement in shared systems was also considered by Jeremy Jacob in (Jacob, 1989) using Hoare's CSP notation (Hoare, 1985).

Exploring the formal properties of refinement has provided a formal basis for results identifying valid and invalid refinements and proof obligations, and ultimately leads to the refinement calculus. The objective of the present work is to suggest a basis for a similar formal development of results and calculi relating to amalgamation. Specifically, we introduce a new relation called *co-refinement* that is closely related to refinement and may be formally related to it: the formal properties of co-refinement are developed from those of refinement. We then suggest that a formal model for the process of amalgamation can be developed that presents amalgamation as a series of co-refinement steps. Throughout this paper, our model of a viewpoint is a specification statement (Morgan, 1988). This simple model restricts viewpoints to stipulations affecting the precondition, postcondition and frame of the amalgamated product, making viewpoints easier to handle than in a fully general case where, for instance, we might have non-functional requirements to consider (Kotonya & Sommerville, 1992). Furthermore, this model has the great advantage that there is already a body of formal work on specification statements and refinement that we can draw on directly.

2   Preliminaries

This section covers necessary preliminaries by reviewing some relevant definitions and discussing some ways in which specification statements can be combined.

2.1   Specifications

In the refinement calculus (Morgan, 1990), a specification statement (Morgan, 1988) is written as

$$\overline{w}: [\, pre\, ,\, post\,]$$

where $\overline{w}$ is the set of variables which the specification may change, *pre* is the precondition of the operation and *post* is the postcondition of the operation. References to the initial value of a variable are denoted by subscripting the variable name with a zero.

This denotes an operation which, if it is executed in a state satisfying *pre*, will change the values of no variables other than those in $\overline{w}$ and terminate in a state satisfying *post*.

One problem in discussing the amalgamation of viewpoint specifications is that different viewpoints may refer to different sets of variables. Before we can discuss co-refinement, we need some terms to discuss variables.

Definition 2.1 (Frame) *(Morgan, 1990) The set of variables which a specification A may change is called its* frame, *we denote this by* frame A.

Definition 2.2 (Implicit Signature) *(Ward, 1993) The set of variables used in a specification A (precondition, postcondition and frame) is called its* implicit signature. *We denote this by* sig A.

We assume, without loss of generality, that if the same variable name occurs in two different viewpoints then they are references to the same variable. (Any accidental name clashes between viewpoints can be resolved by renaming the offending variables).

If we can produce a program which will satisfy a specification, then we say that the specification is *feasible*. An infeasible specification is called a *miracle*.

Definition 2.3 (Feasibility) *(Morgan, 1990) A specification $\overline{w}$: [pre , post] is feasible iff*

$$pre \Rightarrow (\exists \overline{w} \bullet post)$$

2.2 Refinement

The aim of the refinement calculus is to allow a specification to be turned into code through a series of correctness-preserving transformations. Such a transformation is known as a *refinement*.

Refinement can be defined in a number of different ways, (Morgan, 1990) defining it in terms of weakest preconditions. However, the definition used in this paper is based on that in (Morris, 1987), for the simple reason that it allows us to refer to the preconditions and postconditions of the viewpoints in a more explicit way than other equivalent definitions.

Definition 2.4 (Refinement) *(Morris, 1987) Given two specifications*

$$A = \overline{w}: [pre_A , post_A]$$
$$B = \overline{v}: [pre_B , post_B]$$

B is a refinement *of A iff*

$$(pre_A \Rightarrow pre_B) \wedge ((pre_A[\overline{w}\backslash\overline{w_0}] \wedge post_B) \Rightarrow post_A)$$

where $\overline{w_0}$ denotes the initial values of the variables in A[1].

We write this as $A \sqsubseteq B$.

Note: *The first conjunct in the above expression is referred to as* applicability, *the second conjunct is* correctness.

---

[1] This convention is used throughout.

2.3   Data Refinement

Data refinement is normally used to replace abstract datatypes in a specification (e.g. sets, bags) with more concrete datatypes (e.g. arrays). Following (Josephs, 1988; Morgan *et al.*, 1988), we consider an "abstract" operation $\overline{a}: [\mathit{pre}_A, \mathit{post}_A]$, a "concrete" operation $\overline{c}: [\mathit{pre}_C, \mathit{post}_C]$ and a relation CI describing how the abstract states are represented by the concrete states (known as the *coupling invariant*).

Definition 2.5 (Data Refinement) *(Josephs, 1988) For C to be a valid refinement of A the following two statements must be satisfied.*

Applicability $\mathit{pre}_A \wedge CI \Rightarrow \mathit{pre}_C$

Correctness $\mathit{pre}_A[\overline{a}\backslash\overline{a_0}] \wedge CI[\overline{a}\backslash\overline{a_0}][\overline{c}\backslash\overline{c_0}] \wedge \mathit{post}_C \Rightarrow \exists\, a \bullet \mathit{post}_A \wedge CI$

If I_A is an initialisation for a part of the abstract model space, and I_C is an initialisation for the equivalent part of the concrete model space, the following statement must also be satisfied.

Initialisation $(\exists\,\overline{c} \bullet I_C) \wedge (\forall\,\overline{c} \bullet (\exists\,\overline{a} \bullet I_C \Rightarrow I_A \wedge CI))$

We write this as $A \preceq_{CI} C$

Operation refinement can be regarded as a special case of data refinement, where the coupling invariant is simply *true*.

2.4   Combining Specifications

Nigel Ward (Ward, 1993) defines conjunction and disjunction in the refinement calculus. Those operators are equally useful for co-refinement, and we add an additional operator: *union*.

2.4.1   Conjunction

The conjunction of two specifications specifies an operation which if executed in a state satisfying both preconditions will terminate in a state satisfying both postconditions.

Definition 2.6 (Conjunction) *(Ward, 1993) The conjunction of two specification statements*

$\overline{w}: [\mathit{pre}_A, \mathit{post}_A]$
$\overline{v}: [\mathit{pre}_B, \mathit{post}_B]$

is another specification statement

$\overline{w}, \overline{v}: [\mathit{pre}_A \wedge \mathit{pre}_B, \mathit{post}_A \wedge \mathit{post}_B]$

We write this as $A \curlywedge B$.

2.4.2 Disjunction

The disjunction of two specifications specifies an operation which if executed in a state satisfying one of the preconditions will terminate in a state satisfying one of the postconditions (it may satisfy both, but this is not guaranteed).

Definition 2.7 (Disjunction) *(Ward, 1993) The* disjunction *of two specification statements*

$$\overline{w}: [\, pre_A \,,\ post_A \,]$$
$$\overline{v}: [\, pre_B \,,\ post_B \,]$$

is another specification statement

$$\overline{w}, \overline{v}: [\, pre_A \lor pre_B \,,\ (pre_A[\overline{w}\backslash\overline{w_0}] \land post_A) \lor (pre_B[\overline{v}\backslash\overline{v_0}] \land post_B)\,]$$

We write this as $A \curlyvee B$.

2.4.3 Union

The union operator is a hybrid of the above two. It can be thought of as a more deterministic form of disjunction, since when it is executed in a state satisfying both preconditions it guarantees satisfaction of both postconditions on termination, rather than (possibly) choosing between them.

Definition 2.8 (Union) *The* union *of two specification statements*

$$\overline{w}: [\, pre_A \,,\ post_A \,]$$
$$\overline{v}: [\, pre_B \,,\ post_B \,]$$

is another specification statement

$$\overline{w}, \overline{v}: \left[\, pre_A \lor pre_B \,,\ \begin{array}{l} (pre_A[\overline{w}\backslash\overline{w_0}] \land pre_B[\overline{v}\backslash\overline{v_0}] \land post_A \land post_B) \lor \\ (pre_A[\overline{w}\backslash\overline{w_0}] \land \neg\, pre_B[\overline{v}\backslash\overline{v_0}] \land post_A) \lor \\ (\neg\, pre_A[\overline{w}\backslash\overline{w_0}] \land pre_B[\overline{v}\backslash\overline{v_0}] \land post_B) \end{array} \right]$$

We write this as $A \uplus B$.[2]

Properties of Union

- $(A \curlywedge B) \sqsubseteq (A \uplus B)$.

- $(A \curlyvee B) \sqsubseteq (A \uplus B)$.

- If $A \sqsubseteq B$ then $A \uplus B \equiv B$.

- If the preconditions are equivalent, i.e. pre $A \equiv$ pre B, then $A \uplus B \equiv A \curlywedge B$.

- If the preconditions are disjoint, i.e. $\forall$sig A, sig $B \bullet$ pre $A \land$ pre $B =$ *false*, then $A \uplus B \equiv A \curlyvee B$.

---

[2] The small circle decorating our viewpoint operators being suggestive of an eye!

2.4.4 Example

Suppose we have two simple specification statements

$$A = y: [y = 1, y = 2]$$
$$B = z: [z = 2, z = 4]$$

These could be merged in the following ways:

$$A \curlywedge B = y, z: [y = 1 \wedge z = 2, y = 2 \wedge z = 4]$$
$$A \curlyvee B = y, z: [y = 1 \vee z = 2, (y_0 = 1 \wedge y = 2) \vee (z_0 = 2 \wedge z = 4)]$$
$$A \bowtie B = y, z: \left[y = 1 \vee z = 2, \begin{array}{l} (y_0 = 1 \wedge z_0 = 2 \wedge y = 2 \wedge z = 4) \vee \\ (y_0 = 1 \wedge z_0 \neq 2 \wedge y = 2) \vee \\ (y_0 \neq 1 \wedge z_0 = 2 \wedge z = 4) \end{array} \right]$$

3 Introduction to Co-Refinement

From the above example we can see that viewpoints may be combined in a number of different ways. We now give an initial definition of co-refinement and use it to define formally the relationship between viewpoints and their amalgamation.

3.1 Co-Refinement

When we amalgate viewpoint specifications, the amalgamation will often contain more variables than the individual viewpoints. Our aim for an amalgamation is a specification in which the variables of the amalgamation appear to be under the same constraints as they were in the individual viewpoints. This can be construed as saying that the amalgamation will appear to be a refinement of each viewpoint if we restrict our attention to the variables in that particular viewpoint.

3.1.1 Example

To return to our two simple specification statements:

$$A = y: [y = 1, y = 2]$$
$$B = z: [z = 2, z = 4]$$

The conjunction or disjunction of these statements will be a co-refinement of both A and B, in that, if we restrict our attention to the variables from one viewpoint, they will appear to be under the same constraints. However, the amalgamation will only behave like the original viewpoints under certain conditions.

$$A \curlywedge B = y, z: [y = 1 \wedge z = 2, y = 2 \wedge z = 4]$$
$$A \curlyvee B = y, z: [y = 1 \vee z = 2, (y_0 = 1 \wedge y = 2) \vee (z_0 = 2 \wedge z = 4)]$$

In the conjunction, the amalgamation will only behave like the original viewpoint for one specific value of the other variable. In the disjunction, the amalgamation will behave like the original viewpoint for all values of the other variable except one (if $y_0 = 1 \wedge z_0 = 2$ then the program's behaviour is non-deterministic). However, if we consider the union of the two specifications:

$$A \uplus B \;=\; y, z: \left[\; y = 1 \vee z = 2, \quad \begin{array}{l}(y_0 = 1 \wedge z_0 = 2 \wedge y = 2 \wedge z = 4)\; \vee \\ (y_0 = 1 \wedge z_0 \neq 2 \wedge y = 2)\; \vee \\ (y_0 \neq 1 \wedge z_0 = 2 \wedge z = 4)\end{array} \;\right]$$

in this case the amalgamation satisfies the original viewpoint irrespective of the value of the other variable.

Formally, we can give an initial definition of co-refinement as:

Definition 3.1 (Co-Refinement) *A specification B is a* co-refinement *of another specification A, iff*

$$\exists(\text{sig } B - \text{sig } A) \bullet (\text{pre } A \Rightarrow \text{pre } B) \wedge ((\text{pre } A[\overline{w} \backslash \overline{w_0}] \wedge \text{post } B) \Rightarrow \text{post } A)$$

We write this as $A \subseteq B$.

Co-refinement means that under some conditions B appears to be a refinement of A. To return to our initial example, co-refinement means that there is some setting of the ignition key such that the car radio will satisfy Ray's original specification. Since this type of co-refinement may impose additional constraints on a specification, we sometimes refer to it as *restrictive co-refinement*.

If an amalgamation refines a viewpoint irrespective of the values of the variables in the other viewpoints, then we call it a *non-restrictive co-refinement*.

Definition 3.2 (Non-Restrictive Co-Refinement) *A specification B is a* non-restrictive co-refinement *of another specification A, iff*

$$\forall(\text{sig } B - \text{sig } A) \bullet (\text{pre } A \Rightarrow \text{pre } B) \wedge ((\text{pre } A[\overline{w} \backslash \overline{w_0}] \wedge \text{post } B) \Rightarrow \text{post } A)$$

If B is a non-restrictive co-refinement of A, then whatever the values of the variables from other viewpoints, B will do everything A did. So in our example the car radio would work irrespective of the ignition key setting.

An amalgamation is simply a specification which co-refines all the viewpoints.

Definition 3.3 (Amalgamation) *B is an* amalgamation *of viewpoints $A_1, \ldots, A_n$ iff*

$$\bigwedge_{i=1}^{n} A_i \subseteq B$$

which we can write as

$$A_1, \ldots, A_n \subseteq B$$

In Section 4 we will show that both the above forms of co-refinement may be considered to be special cases of a more general form, which is defined in terms of data refinement.

The choice between restrictive co-refinement and non-restrictive co-refinement depends on a number of factors. In many cases, it may not be possible to form a non-restrictive co-refinement, and in some cases it may not be desirable to do so. To return to our example, we may explicitly want to restrict the radio's operation by means of the ignition key as a security measure.

3.1.2 Properties of Co-Refinement

Proofs of these results are mainly trivial.

- If sig B = sig A, then co-refinement is equivalent to normal refinement.

- If $A \sqsubseteq B$, then $A \underline{\sqsubseteq} B$.

- Co-refinement is reflexive, transitive and anti-symmetric.

- Co-refinement is not monotonic (in general), since we can add variables to the frame during co-refinement steps.

3.2 Co-Refinement and Specification Constructors

The definition of the co-refinement relationship gives us a way of stating the properties that are required of an amalgamation. However, in itself it does not tell us how to produce such an amalgamation.

In the refinement calculus, we have a set of transformation laws which are known to produce valid refinements. In a similar way, we can use the definition of co-refinement to produce a set of laws which are known to produce co-refinements. In particular, we can determine under what conditions each of the specification constructors will produce a co-refinement of its operands.

In the refinement calculus, we can change a specification by strengthening its postcondition or weakening its precondition, and in general, when we use the specification constructors to combine specifications, the resulting specification will not be a refinement of the original specifications because of their effect on pre- and postconditions. Although co-refinement is a weaker relation than refinement, the specification constructors will still only produce a valid co-refinement under certain conditions.

3.2.1 Conjunction

The conjunction of two specifications will, in general, have a stronger precondition than the individual viewpoints. The following lemma gives the condition required for the conjunction to be a valid co-refinement of both conjuncts.

Lemma 3.2.1 $A, B \underline{\sqsubseteq} (A \curlywedge B)$ *iff*

$$(\exists(\text{sig } B - \text{sig } A) \bullet \text{pre } A \Rightarrow \text{pre } A \wedge \text{pre } B) \wedge$$
$$(\exists(\text{sig } A - \text{sig } B) \bullet \text{pre } B \Rightarrow \text{pre } A \wedge \text{pre } B)$$

Proof *Follows from definitions of co-refinement and conjunction.*

If the preconditions of the viewpoints are equivalent, or if the viewpoints have no variables in common, then the conjunction will always be a co-refinement.

Corollary 3.2.2 *If* pre $A \equiv$ pre B, *then* $A, B \underline{\sqsubseteq} (A \curlywedge B)$. *This is a non-restrictive co-refinement.*

Proof *Follows directly from above lemma.*

Corollary 3.2.3 *If* sig A *and* sig B *are disjoint (i.e.* sig $A \cap$ sig $B = \varnothing$*), then*
$A, B \underline{\underline{\mathbb{C}}} \ (A \curlywedge B)$.

Proof *Follows directly from above lemma.*

3.2.2 Disjunction

The disjunction of two specifications will have a weaker precondition than the original viewpoints, but will also have a weaker postcondition. Consequently, for the disjunction to be a valid co-refinement of its operands, we have to show that the following condition on the postconditions holds.

Lemma 3.2.4 $A, B \underline{\underline{\mathbb{C}}} \ (A \curlyvee B)$ *iff*

$$(\exists(\text{sig } A - \text{sig } B) \bullet (\text{pre } B[\overline{v}\backslash\overline{v_0}] \wedge (\text{pre } A[\overline{w}\backslash\overline{w_0}] \wedge \text{post } A) \Rightarrow \text{post } B)) \wedge$$
$$(\exists(\text{sig } B - \text{sig } A) \bullet (\text{pre } A[\overline{w}\backslash\overline{w_0}] \wedge (\text{pre } B[\overline{v}\backslash\overline{v_0}] \wedge \text{post } B) \Rightarrow \text{post } A))$$

Proof *Follows from definitions of co-refinement and disjunction.*

As simple corollaries to the above result, we can show that if the preconditions of the viewpoints are disjoint (i.e. the disjunction is always deterministic), or if the postconditions are equivalent, then the disjunction is always a co-refinement.

Corollary 3.2.5 *If* pre A *and* pre B *are disjoint (i.e.* pre $A \wedge$ pre $B \equiv$ *false),
then* $A, B \underline{\underline{\mathbb{C}}} \ (A \curlyvee B)$. *This is a non-restrictive co-refinement.*

Proof *Follows directly from above lemma.*

Corollary 3.2.6 *If* post $A \equiv$ post B *then* $A, B \underline{\underline{\mathbb{C}}} \ (A \curlyvee B)$. *This is a non-restrictive co-refinement.*

Proof *Follows directly from above lemma.*

3.2.3 Union

The union operator combines the features of conjunction and disjunction, consequently it has the interesting property that it always forms a co-refinement of its operands.

Lemma 3.2.7 *For any specifications A and B,* $A, B \underline{\underline{\mathbb{C}}} \ (A \uplus B)$.

Proof *Follows directly from definitions.*

3.2.4 Refinement

The following result provides a useful way of thinking about modularisation and viewpoints. If one viewpoint has an abstract definition of some element, and another viewpoint contains a more concrete definition, then their amalgamation will incorporate the more concrete version.

Lemma 3.2.8 *If $A \sqsubseteq B$ then $A, B \underline{\underline{c}} B$.*

Proof *From the definition of co-refinement, we can show that*

$$(A \sqsubseteq B) \Rightarrow (A \underline{\underline{c}} B)$$

and since co-refinement is reflexive,

$$B \underline{\underline{c}} B$$

The result follows.

4 Co-Refinement and Data Refinement

In this section we will show how our existing co-refinement relation may be defined in terms of data refinement, and extend our ideas on co-refinement to include more general forms of the relation.

Variable Names

In previous sections we have assumed that where variable names are identical in different viewpoints they are references to the same variable. However, in the more general forms of co-refinement it is convenient for each variable to be uniquely named, and to use the coupling invariant to describe explicitly when variables are equivalent. The simplest way to accomplish this is to add a viewpoint reference to each variable name (usually a numeric suffix).

4.1 Example

Our viewpoints from the previous section could therefore be written using our new naming convention as:

$$A = y1: [y1 = 1, y1 = 2]$$
$$B = z1: [z1 = 2, z1 = 4]$$

And we could write their conjunction as:

$$A \curlywedge B = y2, z2: [y2 = 1 \wedge z2 = 2, y2 = 2 \wedge z2 = 4]$$

$(A \curlywedge B)$ is a restrictive co-refinement of A, since it only satisfies the co-refinement criteria of Def 3.1 when $z2_0 = 2$.

If we use distinct names for the variables, then we have to make the relationship between variables in the viewpoint and variables in the amalgamation explicit. This can be accomplished by using a coupling invariant. $(A \curlywedge B)$ can be considered to be a data refinement of A with the following coupling invariant:

$$CI \quad = \quad (y2 = y1) \wedge (z2_0 = 2)$$

4.2   Coupling Invariants

The coupling invariant in the above example contains two components, which we describe in general as:

An *eyepiece* which describes how viewpoint variables are represented in the amalgamation (e.g. $y2 = y1$).

The *restrictions* under which the amalgamation is a valid co-refinement (e.g. $z2_0 = 2$). For a non-restrictive co-refinement, this component would be absent.

It is often convenient to be able to split the coupling invariant into terms related to specific variables.

Definition 4.1 (Factoring) *Given a coupling invariant CI and a set of variables S, CI factored by S (written $CI \uparrow S$) is defined to be those terms from CI which involve variables in S.*

Conversely, we use $CI \downarrow S$ to denote those terms from CI which do not involve variables in S.

This notation allows us to give simple definitions for the eyepiece and restrictions.

Definition 4.2 (Eyepiece) *Given a coupling invariant CI between a viewpoint V and an amalgamation A, the eyepiece, $\mathcal{E}_V$, for that viewpoint is given by*

$$\mathcal{E}_V \quad = \quad CI \uparrow (\text{sig } V)$$

Definition 4.3 (Restrictions) *The restrictions, $\mathcal{R}_V$, for the viewpoint are given by*

$$\mathcal{R}_V \quad = \quad CI \downarrow (\text{sig } V)$$

4.3   Step-wise Co-Refinement

If we wish to use co-refinement in a step-wise manner, we must ensure that our relation has two crucial properties:

Transitivity If $P \sqsubseteq Q$ and $Q \sqsubseteq R$ then $P \sqsubseteq R$

Monotonicity If $P \sqsubseteq Q$ then $F(P) \sqsubseteq F(Q)$ for any function F.

Both the restrictive and non-restrictive forms of the co-refinement relation are transitive. However, co-refinement differs from conventional refinement in that it allows variables to be added to the frame of the specification, and this affects the monotonicity of the relation.

Lemma 4.3.1 (Transitivity) *Co-refinement is transitive.*

Proof *At each co-refinement step we may impose restrictions on the values of variables added to the frame (if we are creating a restrictive co-refinement). However, since we can only impose restrictions upon added variables, and not on variables present in the original specification, it follows that in a sequence of co-refinement steps, each variable may be subject to only one restriction imposed by the co-refinement process. Therefore, we can build a coupling invariant for the entire sequence of co-refinement steps by forming the conjunction of the coupling invariants for the individual steps without any possibility of the restrictions interfering with each other.*

Non-restrictive co-refinement does not impose any restrictions on the values of added variables, and thus is trivially transitive.

Lemma 4.3.2 (Monotonicity 1) *Non-restrictive co-refinement is monotonic. Restrictive co-refinement is not (necessarily) monotonic.*

Proof *Non-restrictive co-refinement is monotonic since it is independent of any variables added to the frame of the specification. Restrictive co-refinement however, depends on the values of the variables added to the frame, and thus could become invalid if subsequent changes impose new constraints on those variables in any surrounding program. Therefore, restrictive co-refinement is not monotonic.*

4.4 Conservative Extensions

When we want to perform a sequence of several amalgamations, we need to ensure that the coupling invariants used at each step are consistent and do not interfere with each other. One way of doing this is to require the coupling invariants used for a step to be a *conservative extension* of any preceding coupling invariants.

Definition 4.4 (Conservative Extension) *Given two functions f and g, g is a* conservative extension *of f if*

$$g(x) \ = \ f(x)$$

for any x in dom f.

If g and f are predicates describing coupling invariants, then g is a conservative extension of f if

$$g \ \Rightarrow \ f$$

4.5 Augmented Co-Refinement

Co-refinement as described so far in this paper does not have the monotonic replacement property because of the possibility of interference between viewpoints manifested by the restrictions. The operation of *augmented co-refinement* is now introduced: it is the same as existing co-refinement relation, with the exception that the coupling invariants (comprising eyepieces and restrictions) are taken into account at each stage.

Definition 4.5 (Augmented Specification) *An* augmented specification *is a specification together with a coupling invariant. I.e., an augmented specification is a tuple* $(S, \mathcal{E}, \mathcal{R})$ *where*

S *is a specification.*

$\mathcal{E}$ *is a predicate describing eyepieces.*

$\mathcal{R}$ *is a predicate describing restrictions.*

In *augmented co-refinement*, we carry the coupling invariants forward with each co-refinement step, accumulating them as we go.

Definition 4.6 (Augmented Co-Refinement) $(A, \mathcal{E}_A, \mathcal{R}_A) \tilde{\underline{\mathbb{C}}} (B, \mathcal{E}_B, \mathcal{R}_B)$ *iff.*

$$A \preceq_{(\mathcal{E}_{AB} \wedge \mathcal{R}_{AB})} B$$
$$\wedge \quad \mathcal{E}_B = \mathcal{E}_A \wedge \mathcal{E}_{AB}$$
$$\wedge \quad \mathcal{R}_B = \mathcal{R}_A \wedge \mathcal{R}_{AB}$$

where $\mathcal{E}_{AB}$ *and* $\mathcal{R}_{AB}$ *form the coupling invariant for this particular co-refinement.*

Lemma 4.5.1 *Augmented co-refinements form a sequence of conservative extensions.*

Proof *Follows from definitions.*

Lemma 4.5.2 (Monotonicity 2) *Augmented co-refinement is monotonic.*

Proof *Restrictive co-refinement is non-monotonic since we cannot be certain of the effects of the rest of the specification on the restrictions. In augmented co-refinement however, we carry the restrictions forward at each stage, thus ensuring consistency of the final amalgamation. Hence, augmented co-refinement is monotonic.*

5 Co-Refinement and Amalgamation

Now that the co-refinement relation has been introduced it remains to show how viewpoint amalgamation can be modelled in terms of it. We proceed in a similar way to discussions of refinement: refinement in general may be defined as a sequence of steps, each of which is either a data refinement or an operation refinement. Viewpoint amalgamation may be defined likewise as a sequence of separate co-refinement steps.

There is a minor problem here: the co-refinement operator as defined in Sections 3 and 4 is of the form

$$A_1, \ldots A_n \underline{\mathbb{C}} P$$

with a single product (viewpoint) on the RHS whereas, by analogy with the breakdown of the refinement process into steps, it is more fruitful to model amalgamation as a sequence of co-refinement steps, each of these co-refining a collection of viewpoints into another collection that satisfies the requirements of them all.

The previous definition of the co-refinement operator is therefore extended to allow the use of multiple viewpoints on the RHS: in terms of the union operator ⊎ of Section 2 the required definition for two pairs of viewpoints is

$$A, B \sqsubseteq C, D \mathrel{\widehat{=}} (A \sqsubseteq (C \uplus D)) \wedge (B \sqsubseteq (C \uplus D)).$$

Generalising this equation to arbitrary numbers of viewpoints we obtain the full definition of the co-refinement relation between arbitrary number of viewpoints as

$$A_1, \ldots A_n \sqsubseteq B_1, \ldots B_m \mathrel{\widehat{=}} \bigwedge_{i=1}^{n} (A_i \sqsubseteq (\uplus_{j=1}^{m} B_j)).$$

A simple yet pleasing consequence of this definition that a straightforward rearrangement of separate requirements between customers represented by a set of viewpoints becomes a trivial co-refinement: a customer requiring an FM radio and a metric speedometer, and another requiring an AM radio and an Imperial speedometer can obviously both be trivially satisifed if we have two products to offer, one comprising the two radios and the other comprising the two speedometers.

Having introduced co-refinements involving abitrary numbers of viewpoints, we may now define the *amalgamation* of viewpoints $A_1, \ldots, A_n$ to produce a single product P as a sequence of co-refinements:

$$A_1, \ldots, A_n \sqsubseteq \ldots \sqsubseteq P$$

However, as already explained, co-refinement does not satisfy the monotonic replacement property: to obtain this important property we must use *augmented co-refinement* instead, thus our model for viewpoint amalgamation is of the form:

$$\begin{matrix} A_1, \ldots, A_n \\ true, true \end{matrix} \; \widetilde{\sqsubseteq} \cdots \widetilde{\sqsubseteq} \; \begin{matrix} P \\ \mathcal{E}, \mathcal{R} \end{matrix}$$

By using our augmented co-refinement relation, the eyepieces and restrictions will be *true* for the initial viewpoints and will gradually accumulate through the amalgamation process. The eyepieces and restrictions that are attached to the final amalgamated product correspond to the *amalgamation trail* of the MFD Model (Wallis, 1992; Wallis, 1993) which enables the entire process to be reversed.

6 Conclusions

We have both modelled viewpoint amalgamation as a sequence of co-refinement steps, and related co-refinement formally to notions of refinement. This gives us a basis for a formal investigation of the operation of viewpoint amalgamation and its properties, which should lead to the formulation of laws and proof obligations for co-refinement. The work reported here takes a viewpoint as representable as one of Morgan's specification statements; the question of the extent to which it carries through unchanged for other types of viewpoint remains to be investigated.

This work forms part of a more substantial project aimed at producing a general model for the process of viewpoint amalgamation and using this to gain a better understanding of issues affecting both viewpoint amalgamation and modularisation. The development of the model itself is explained in (Wallis, 1992; Wallis, 1993) while its application to the development of Z specifications is discussed in (Ainsworth *et al.*, 1993; Ainsworth *et al.*, 1994). Our eventual aim is both to illuminate the many issues addressed by investigations of viewpoint techniques and modularity, and to suggest ways in which viewpoint techniques might be more widely used in practice. Viewpoints and modularity are intuitively appealing tools for handling complexity in formal descriptions: we plan to build on this intuitive appeal so that improved working practices may result.

Acknowledgements

We are grateful for useful discussions with Lindsay Groves, Tony Cruickshank, Steve Riddle and Jackie Ainsworth. Jeremy Jacob provided many useful comments on the draft version of this paper.

Mike Ainsworth is supported by a UK SERC research studentship.

References

Ainsworth, M, Cruickshank, AH, Groves, LJ, & Wallis, PJL. 1993 (18th–20th August). Formal Specification via Viewpoints. *Pages 218-237 of:* Hosking, J (ed), *Proc. 13th New Zealand Computer Conference.* New Zealand Computer Society, Auckland, New Zealand.

Ainsworth, M, Cruickshank, AH, Groves, LJ, & Wallis, PJL. 1994. Viewpoint Specification and Z. *Information and Software Technology*, **36**(1). (To appear).

Batini, C, Lenzerini, M, & Navathe, SB. 1986. A comparative analysis of methodologies for database schema integration. *ACM Computing Surveys*, **18**(4), 323–364.

Feather, MS. 1989. Constructing specifications by combining parallel elaborations. *IEEE Transactions on Software Engineering*, **15**(2), 198–208.

Groves, LJ. 1992. *Private communication.*

Hoare, CAR. 1985. *Communicating Sequential Processes.* International Series in Computer Science. Prentice-Hall.

Jacob, JL. 1989. Refinement of Shared Systems. *Pages 27-36 of:* McDermid, J (ed), *The Theory and Practice of Refinement: Approaches to the Formal Development of Large-Scale Software Systems.* Butterworths.

Josephs, MB. 1988. The Data Refinement Calculator for Z. *Information Processing Letters*, **27**, 29–33.

Kotonya, G, & Sommerville, I. 1992. Viewpoints for requirements definition. *Software Engineering Journal*, **7**(6), 375–387.

Morgan, C. 1988. The specification statement. *ACM TOPLAS*, **10**(3), 403–419. Reprinted in (Morgan *et al.*, 1988).

Morgan, C. 1990. *Programming from Specifications*. International Series in Computer Science. Prentice-Hall.

Morgan, C, Robinson, K, & Gardiner, P. 1988. *On the Refinement Calculus*. Technical Monograph PRG-70. Oxford University Computing Laboratory Programming Research Group.

Morris, JM. 1987. A Theoretical Basis for Stepwise Refinement and the Programming Calculus. *Science of Computer Programming*, **9**(3), 287–306.

Wallis, PJL. 1992. *A New Approach to Modular Formal Description*. Technical Report 92-57. University of Bath.

Wallis, PJL. 1993. *Modular Formal Description*. Submitted to Computer Journal.

Ward, N. 1993. Adding specification constructors to the refinement calculus. *Pages 652–670 of:* Woodcock, JCP, & Larsen, PG (eds), *FME'93: Industrial-Strength Formal Methods*. Odense, Denmark: Springer-Verlag, for Formal Methods Europe. Lecture Notes in Computer Science 670.

Metavariables and Conditional Refinements in the Refinement Calculus

Raymond G. Nickson

Software Verification Research Centre

University of Queensland

Brisbane, Australia

Lindsay J. Groves

Department of Computer Science

Victoria University of Wellington

Wellington, New Zealand

Abstract

We describe two techniques for the refinement calculus that facilitate goal-directed development. The techniques achieve this by allowing the deferring of decisions about the precise form of refinement steps, so high-level choices can be expressed as soon as those choices are appropriate. *Metavariables* are place-holders for components of partly developed programs that will be instantiated when they are suitably constrained by later refinements. The *conditional refinements* technique allows the development of alternative refinements of a specification, and the collection of those alternative refinements into a guarded command set.

We think that programmers developing programs using the refinement calculus make use of both of these techniques informally, but the written derivation does not usually reflect their use. We describe and illustrate a rigorous way to apply these techniques and record their use.

1 Introduction

The refinement calculus [1, 2, 3] provides a set of rules for deriving programs from formal specifications. Each rule defines a small step from specification to program; by building an appropriate sequence of rule applications, we can develop programs hand in hand with their proofs, with the confidence that the whole proof is correct arising from our belief in the validity of each rule. Specifications and executable code are written in a unified *wide-spectrum* language. Programs in this language are transformed by *refinement rules*, each of which is a schema describing how one program fragment (the *subject*) can be transformed to another (the *result*) providing some *applicability condition* holds. Rules generally contain *schema variables* that must be instantiated to provide a concrete refinement theorem that can be used in a development.

We have implemented a tool supporting the refinement calculus in which higher-level strategy is represented by *tactics* [4], which allow sequences of refinements to be packaged into logical units. One of our aims in doing this is to be able to emulate in the refinement calculus some of the *goal-directed* strategies discussed in Gries's textbook [5] on the formal development of programs from their specifications. The essence of the goal-directed approach is that derivation steps are motivated by the structure of the specification (in particular, the structure of the postcondition). A key aspect of this approach is that the general form of a command may often be suggested by a pattern in the specification, but the details must be calculated, perhaps much later in the development. The result is an overall development strategy that builds sequential compositions backwards and **if** and **do** commands inside out: in general, we postulate a command to address part of the postcondition, then calculate a precondition (often but not always the weakest precondition) for that command to establish our whole postcondition, and then produce preceding commands or surrounding guards to set up the required condition.

This strategy conflicts slightly with the top-down development that is a feature of the refinement calculus. The most obvious way to apply a rule is to instantiate all its schema variables, check its applicability condition and then calculate the result. We would like to apply a rule, leaving some of its variables unbound, then determine appropriate instantiations for those variables later in the development. For example, we might want to introduce a sequential composition in which the intermediate assertion is not known, and then develop the second component and calculate the appropriate intermediate assertion. Similarly, we might want to build an **if** or **do** command by developing the commands in the body and then generating guards to guarantee their preconditions; we may not even know how many guarded commands will be needed. This we normally do informally when performing refinements by hand, and only write down the details of the rule applications afterwards. We want to be able to support the application of rule schemas while deferring the fine details of the application, and to record the choice of schema when it is made. Most importantly, we must do this without compromising the soundness of the refinement method that arises from the rigorous application of fully instantiated rules and checking of applicability conditions.

Our *metavariables* technique supports this approach. A rule can be applied without instantiating all its schema variables; the result of this application itself contains metavariables. The applicability condition too may be only partly instantiated; in that case, it must be posted as a constraint on the later binding of the metavariables in it. A second technique, *conditional refinements*, is used in conjunction with metavariables to allow the development of **if** and **do** commands one guarded command at a time. The value of the techniques is that they allow a development where design decisions can be written down as soon as they are made, instead of waiting for the full details to be worked out. Using these techniques, we can develop a program in a more convenient way, avoiding some of the need to work out parts of the development on one side before recording them in the derivation.

Section 2 presents an example that shows the style of development we expect in the 'traditional' refinement calculus, and discusses the shortcomings exposed by that example. The same example is used in Sections 3 and 4 to illustrate the novel techniques. Section 3 describes metavariables and illustrates their use in several small examples. Section 4 describes how we use conditional refinements to develop naked guarded commands, and combine alternative conditional refinements to form guarded command sets. In Section 5 we present

---

Introduce Assignment $(\tilde{x}, \tilde{e})$

$$\frac{\tilde{x} \subseteq \tilde{w}}{pre \Rightarrow post[\tilde{x} := \tilde{e}]}$$

$$\tilde{w}:[\, pre \; / \; post \,] \quad \sqsubseteq \quad \tilde{x} := \tilde{e}$$

Figure 1: The **Introduce Assignment** refinement rule.

a larger example illustrating both techniques — the derivation of an algorithm for calculating the least common multiple.

2 Refinement

In this section, we describe the refinement calculus in a little more detail, and present the derivation of a simple program using refinement rules from [1] and [3], instantiating them fully before application. This serves to introduce the traditional style of development in the calculus, and shows how the goal-directed strategies we wish to use sometimes conflict with the disciplines of this style.

Specifications are written in the wide-spectrum language as *specification statements*. A specification statement $\tilde{w}:[\, pre \; / \; post \,]$ is a command that will establish the postcondition *post* by changing only variables in the frame $\tilde{w}$, providing the precondition *pre* holds initially. The wide-spectrum language allows arbitrary mixing of specification constructs with executable (*code*) constructs like **if** commands and assignments. To produce a finished, executable program, specification constructs must be implemented in code. The process of transforming specification to code proceeds by a sequence of applications of *refinement rules*, which are schemas of the general form

$$\frac{condition}{subject \; pattern \quad \sqsubseteq \quad result \; pattern}$$

Each such rule states that an occurrence of an instance of the subject pattern can be replaced by the corresponding instance of the result pattern providing the instantiated condition holds.

An example of a refinement rule appears in Figure 1. This rule is **Introduce Assignment** from [3]. The subject pattern $\tilde{w}:[\, pre \; / \; post \,]$ will match any specification statement, and the result pattern $\tilde{x} := \tilde{e}$ gives the form of the assignment command that the rule produces. The applicability condition constrains the rule to apply only when the variables $\tilde{x}$ changed by the assignment are all in the frame $\tilde{w}$ and the precondition implies that the substituted postcondition is true.

The schema variables in **Introduce Assignment** are $\tilde{w}$, *pre*, *post*, $\tilde{x}$ and $\tilde{e}$. Schema variables are subdivided into *subject variables* (occurring in the subject pattern) and *parameters* (listed in the heading of the rule)[1]. Subject variables

---

[1] Our implementation also has *body variables*, which are used to calculate results.

$$\tilde{w}:[\,pre \wedge (\textstyle\bigvee_i b_i) \;/\; post\,] \quad \sqsubseteq \quad \text{if } [\!]_i\, b_i \to \tilde{w}:[\,pre \wedge b_i \;/\; post\,] \text{ fi}$$

Figure 2: Morgan and Robinson's original **if** rule.

allow a rule to be applied to any of a collection of possible subjects. Parameters allow us to apply the same rule in the same circumstances and arrive at different results. In **Introduce Assignment**, the subject variables are $\tilde{w}$, *pre* and *post*, and the parameters are $\tilde{x}$ and $\tilde{e}$. Matching the subject against the subject pattern of the selected rule instantiates the subject variables. For the simple matching of abstract syntax we use with refinement rules, this instantiation is unique[2]. The parameters must normally be instantiated explicitly by the rule user when the rule is invoked: our implemented rules are annotated with procedural code to obtain instantiations for parameters.

We now present an example to illustrate this style of development. Consider the specification 'set z to the greater of the two integers x and y', formalized as follows:

$$\begin{aligned}
\big[\big[\quad & z = max(x,y) \mathrel{\widehat{=}} z \geq x \wedge z \geq y \wedge (z = x \vee z = y) \;\bullet \\
& z:[\,true \;/\; z = max(x,y)\,] \\
\big]\big]
\end{aligned}$$

Here the notation $z = max(x,y) \mathrel{\widehat{=}} z \geq x \wedge \cdots$ introduces a local definition of a two-place function max that can be used inside the block. The body of the definition block is a specification statement, which must be implemented by code that alters z to satisfy $z = max(x,y)$, under the trivial initial assumption *true*.

Our goal directed strategy says that when there is a disjunction in the postcondition, we should consider introducing an **if** command, with one branch for each disjunct. In this case there is an implicit disjunction (in the definition of max) with two disjuncts, so we will introduce an **if** with two branches, though it is not yet clear what the guards should be. We shall compare two versions of the law for introducing **if** (from [1] and [3]), and see how the choice affects the reasoning process required in this problem.

First, consider Morgan and Robinson's original rule for introducing an **if** command (Figure 2). This rule is unconditional and has no parameters; when we apply it to a subject there are no further decisions or proofs required. The obvious interpretation of this rule, however, is it will apply only when the subject is a specification statement whose precondition has the syntactic form $pre \wedge (b_1 \vee \cdots \vee b_n)$. In this case, to make the rule applicable, we must introduce the tautology $x \geq y \vee y \geq x$ into the precondition – in a refinement tool, we must then ensure that the tool does not immediately remove the tautology as a simplification! Thus, before applying the rule, we have to determine how many branches to use and what the guards will be, then manipulate the specification statement so that the disjunction of the guards is explicit in the precondition, which involves showing that one of the guards must be true when *pre* is true.

---

[2]More complex matching, such as associative-commutative matching, is done by our tool in other circumstances.

Introduce IF $(b_1, \ldots, b_n)$

$$pre \Rightarrow (\textstyle\bigvee_i b_i)$$

$\tilde{w}:[\,pre \;/\; post\,] \quad \sqsubseteq \quad \textbf{if } []_i \; b_i \;\rightarrow\; \tilde{w}:[\,pre \wedge b_i \;/\; post\,] \textbf{ fi}$

Figure 3: The **Introduce IF** refinement rule.

Introduce IF (two branch instance) (b_1, b_2)

$$pre \Rightarrow b_1 \vee b_2$$

$$\tilde{w}:[\,pre \;/\; post\,] \quad \sqsubseteq \quad \begin{array}{l} \textbf{if } \; b_1 \;\rightarrow\; \tilde{w}:[\,pre \wedge b_1 \;/\; post\,] \\ [] \;\; b_2 \;\rightarrow\; \tilde{w}:[\,pre \wedge b_2 \;/\; post\,] \\ \textbf{fi} \end{array}$$

Figure 4: The two-branch instance of **Introduce IF**.

Now consider the **if** rule from [3], shown in Figure 3. This rule can match any specification statement, and has the guards as parameters. The applicability condition requires that the precondition of the subject implies that at least one of the guards is true. To use this rule, we must determine how many branches are required and select the appropriate guards to provide as parameters to the rule. In our max example, the guards required are $x \geq y$ and $y \geq x$. The proof that one of the guards will be true is then associated directly with the rule application, rather than with an application of another rule that simply rewrites the precondition. This fits our desired goal-directed strategy much better than does Morgan and Robinson's original rule. Still, as we shall see, we might want to leave the choice of guards until later.

To introduce the **if** in our max example, we invoke the two-branch instance of **Introduce IF** shown in Figure 4. The subject pattern of that rule is $\tilde{w}:[\,pre \;/\; post\,]$; matching our subject specification statement against this binds $\tilde{w}$, pre and $post$ appropriately:

$$\begin{array}{lcl} \tilde{w} & \mapsto & z \\ pre & \mapsto & true \\ post & \mapsto & z = max(x, y) \end{array}$$

The parameters supplied for b_1 and b_2 are the guards $x \geq y$ and $y \geq x$. The instantiated applicability condition is $true \Rightarrow x \geq y \vee y \geq x$, whose validity is easily proved. The result of this rule application is the program:

$$\begin{array}{l} \textbf{if } \; x \geq y \;\rightarrow\; z:[\,x \geq y \;/\; z = max(x, y)\,] \\ [] \;\; y \geq x \;\rightarrow\; z:[\,y \geq x \;/\; z = max(x, y)\,] \\ \textbf{fi} \end{array}$$

Before applying the rule, we had to decide how many guarded commands were needed, and what the guards should be. In this case, we know we want a two-branch **if**, and have an idea what commands we want inside it, but would rather calculate the guards. In more complex examples, we might not know in advance how many guarded commands are needed.

The specifications in the branches can be satisfied by assignment commands, introduced with the rule **Introduce Assignment** (Figure 1). In the first branch, matching the subject pattern with the specification statement yields the bindings $\tilde{w} \mapsto \{z\}$, $pre \mapsto x \geq y$ and $post \mapsto z = max(x, y)$. The parameters of the rule are $\tilde{x}$ and $\tilde{e}$; we supply the values $\{z\}$ and $\{x\}$ for these, giving the assignment command $z := x$. The second branch behaves similarly; the bindings are $\tilde{x} \mapsto \{z\}$ and $\tilde{e} \mapsto \{y\}$ giving $z := y$. The subject variable and parameter bindings must also be applied to the applicability conditions of the rule, yielding the instances

$$\{z\} \subseteq \{z\}, \quad x \geq y \Rightarrow (z = max(x, y))[z := x] \quad \text{and}$$
$$\{z\} \subseteq \{z\}, \quad y \geq x \Rightarrow (z = max(x, y))[z := y]$$

These are easily discharged by performing the substitutions, expanding max and simplifying. The resulting program is

if $x \geq y \rightarrow z := x$
$[\!]$ $y \geq x \rightarrow z := y$
fi

3 Metavariables

We suggest that deferring the instantiation of parameters would allow us to develop programs in the goal-directed style, while still retaining the top-down refinement calculus approach. If we invoke a rule without first instantiating all of its parameters, the resulting program contains uninstantiated schema variables. It will be convenient to give these variables names distinct from the names of the parameters in the rule (in part so we can distinguish different applications of the same rule); we shall reserve the term *metavariables* for them, and use initial capital letters for their names. If the applicability condition of the partially instantiated rule contains metavariables, we shall not be able to discharge it immediately. We cannot discard the obligation, as the soundness of the refinement depends on it; instead, we post it as a *constraint* on the metavariables within it, which future instantiations of those metavariables must satisfy. Typically, later refinements of the program containing metavariables will add further constraints, and heuristics can be used to *solve* the set of constraints, suggesting suitable instantiations for the metavariables.

As long as every metavariable in a development is eventually instantiated in a way that satisfies all constraints, the soundness of the development is not compromised. To demonstrate this, the development can be presented as a strict sequence of applications of fully instantiated refinement rules: the motivation for the choice of parameters will be lost, but the proof obligation associated with each refinement will be explicit and can be checked. The use of metavariables and the posting and solving of constraints is recorded in the development, so the choice of a rule schema is associated with the specification that motivated it, and the details of metavariable (parameter) instantiations are associated with the stage in the derivation where the constraints were solved.

Split Specification (mid)

$$\tilde{w}:[\,pre\ /\ post\,] \quad \sqsubseteq \quad \tilde{w}:[\,pre\ /\ mid\,]\ ;\ \tilde{w}:[\,mid\ /\ post\,]$$

Figure 5: The Split Specification refinement rule.

Weakest Prespecification (s)

$$\frac{s \text{ changes only } \tilde{w}}{\tilde{w}:[\,pre\ /\ post\,] \quad \sqsubseteq \quad \tilde{w}:[\,pre\ /\ wp(s, post)\,]\ ;\ s}$$

Figure 6: The Weakest Prespecification refinement rule.

3.1 Metavariables and Sequential Composition

The rule that introduces sequential composition (;) is shown in Figure 5, in which the intermediate assertion is the parameter. An alternative is the rule **Weakest Prespecification** (Figure 6), described in [1]. This rule introduces an arbitrary command s (the parameter) as the second component of the composition, and allows the calculation of an appropriate intermediate assertion: this well supports the goal-directed development strategy, since the appropriate command s is often suggested by examining the input specification. **Weakest Prespecification** works well where s is an assignment (in which case it behaves just like *following assignment* [3]) or a sequential composition of assignments, but is usually inconvenient when s is an **if** or **do** command, because the formula for the weakest precondition can be quite complicated. In these cases, it is usually more convenient to construct the required command, then find an adequate precondition satisfying one of Dijkstra's basic theorems for the alternative and repetitive constructs [6, pp37–40]. But we can avoid directly appealing to such theorems, because we have designed our **Introduce IF** and **Introduce DO** rules to take them into account.

We propose to achieve the effect of **Weakest Prespecification** by using **Split Specification** (Figure 5), but deferring the instantiation of the *mid* parameter. The subject specification statement is matched to the subject pattern of **Split Specification**, instantiating $\tilde{w}$, *pre* and *post*. There is no applicability condition. The partially instantiated result pattern (with a metavariable *Int* as the intermediate assertion) replaces the subject in the program. Now we have a sequence of two specifications; the first has *Int* as its postcondition, and the second has *Int* as its precondition. By refining the second component $\tilde{w}:[\,Int\ /\ post\,]$ to some command s, we generate constraints on the metavariable whose cumulative effect is $Int \Rightarrow wp(s, post)$; solving these constraints instantiates *Int* so we can proceed with the refinement of the first component of the sequence. We have thus achieved a practical approximation of the effect of **Weakest Prespecification** without actually calculating a weakest precondition (the individual refinements will constrain *Int* to be no weaker than the weakest precondition), without explicitly checking that s changes only the variables $\tilde{w}$ (the refinements themselves will do that), and without necessarily knowing in advance exactly what command s we wanted.

If we use Split Specification with a metavariable as before, then refine the first component $\tilde{w}:[\,pre\ /\ Int\,]$ to some command s (perhaps less likely in a goal-directed system, since we do not know its postcondition), we get the effect of calculating an approximation to the strongest postcondition $sp(pre, s)$ (actually, it may not be the *strongest* postcondition, but it will be no stronger). By combining the single rule Split Specification with the metavariables technique, we have subsumed the two rules Weakest Prespecification and Strongest Postspecification. If the command s in either case is a simple assignment (introduced by Intro Assignment, Figure 1), we have subsumed Morgan's *following assignment* and a powerful version of *leading assignment*.

A simple example

Given the specification $x, y:[\,true\ /\ x = 1 \wedge y = 2\,]$, the goal directed strategy suggests attacking each conjunct in the postcondition in turn. Since the conjuncts have no variables in common, it seems likely that we shall need one command for each, so we first split the specification, leaving a metavariable Int as the intermediate assertion:

$$x, y:[\,true\ /\ x = 1 \wedge y = 2\,]$$

$\sqsubseteq$ Split Specification (Int)

$$x, y:[\,true\ /\ Int\,]\ ;\ x, y:[\,Int\ /\ x = 1 \wedge y = 2\,]$$

No refinement of the first component of the composition suggests itself, since we do not know the form of the postcondition. In the second component, the conjunct $y = 2$ in the postcondition suggests an assignment $y := 2$, so we try Introduce Assignment:

$$x, y:[\,Int\ /\ x = 1 \wedge y = 2\,]$$

$\sqsubseteq$ Introduce Assignment $(y, 2)$

$$y := 2$$

The proof obligation is $Int \Rightarrow (x = 1 \wedge y = 2)[y := 2]$. Simplifying the obligation yields $Int \Rightarrow x = 1$, but no further simplification can be performed without instantiating the metavariable Int. We record the simplified obligation as a constraint on the metavariable. In this case, we can immediately solve the constraint by binding Int to the value $x = 1$, resulting in the expected sequence $x, y:[\,true\ /\ x = 1\,]\ ;\ y := 2$, which is then refined in the traditional way to $x := 1\ ;\ y := 2$. In other circumstances we might leave the binding of the metavariable until later.

3.2   Metavariables and the Alternative Command

Gries gives the following strategy for developing an alternation [5, p174]:

> To invent a guarded command, find a command C whose execution will establish postcondition R in at least some cases; find a Boolean B satisfying $B \Rightarrow wp(C, R)$; and put them together to form $B \rightarrow C$. Continue to invent guarded commands until the precondition of the construct implies that at least one guard is true.

This strategy is based on a theorem [5, p135] which states that Q is an adequate (but not necessarily weakest) precondition for **if** $[]_i(b_i \rightarrow s_i)$ **fi** to establish the postcondition R if and only if $Q \Rightarrow \bigvee_i b_i$ and for each i from 1 to n, $Q \wedge b_i \Rightarrow wp(s_i, R)$. It is goal directed in the sense that it makes use of commands built to satisfy parts of the postcondition, and then sets up their preconditions (the guards) to ensure the satisfaction of the whole postcondition.

Consider again the max specification:

$$
[\![\quad z = max(x, y) \mathrel{\hat{=}} z \geq x \wedge z \geq y \wedge (z = x \vee z = y) \bullet
$$
$$
z:[\,true \;/\; z = max(x, y)\,]
$$
$$
]\!]
$$

Again, we want a two-branch **if**, but this time we want to calculate the guards based on refinements of the body. We invoke **Introduce IF**, leaving metavariables C and D for the guard parameters b_1 and b_2:

$$
z:[\,true \;/\; z = max(x, y)\,]
$$
$$
\sqsubseteq \quad \textbf{Introduce IF} \;\; (C, D)
$$
$$
\textbf{if } C \rightarrow z:[\,C \;/\; z = max(x, y)\,]
$$
$$
[\!]\; D \rightarrow z:[\,D \;/\; z = max(x, y)\,]
$$
$$
\textbf{fi}
$$

The **if** command was obtained by:

- matching the specification statement (subject) with the subject pattern $\tilde{w}:[\,pre \;/\; post\,]$, giving the bindings $\tilde{w} \mapsto \{z\}$, $pre \mapsto true$ and $Post \mapsto z = max(x, y)$;

- supplying metavariables C and D for the parameters b_1 and b_2; and

- substituting into the result pattern and simplifying.

The instantiated applicability condition is $true \Rightarrow (C \vee D)$, which is simplified to $C \vee D$. This contains metavariables, so it cannot be proved immediately. Instead, its proof is deferred until the metavariables become bound. That is, $C \vee D$ constrains the possible values of those metavariables; no later instantiations of (or constraints on) C and D will be accepted that conflict with this constraint.

Then we decide to introduce an assignment command inside each guarded command, suggested by the presence of the $variable = value$ disjuncts which are still implicit in the postcondition. In the first branch, we introduce $z := x$, and in the second $z := y$. Applying the corresponding subject variable and parameter bindings to the applicability conditions gives the respective instances

$$
\{z\} \subseteq \{z\}, \quad C \Rightarrow (z = max(x, y))[z := x] \quad \text{and}
$$
$$
\{z\} \subseteq \{z\}, \quad D \Rightarrow (z = max(x, y))[z := y]
$$

Performing the substitutions, expanding max and simplifying yields $C \Rightarrow x \geq y$ and $D \Rightarrow y \geq x$. These can be simplified no further, and since they contain metavariables, they are posted as constraints.

Now the constraint solver (whether human or machine) detects possible bindings for C and D that satisfy all constraints, and posts the tentative bindings $C \mapsto x \geq y$ and $D \mapsto y \geq x$. This solution is not unique (in particular, there are two other solutions where one of C and D is strengthened to a strict inequality), so we must be prepared to retract those bindings in the event that further inconsistent constraints appear later.

3.3 Sequential Composition and Alternation

We can modify the *max* example slightly to illustrate an extension of Gries's alternative command strategy. The extension allows us to calculate a sequence whose second component is an **if** command, and whose first component prepares the state so that the **if** does not abort. Such constructs arise frequently when using a goal-oriented approach, wherein we introduce commands to achieve part of the postcondition, and then calculate a precondition for those commands to achieve the whole postcondition. The calculated precondition serves as the postcondition of the first component of a sequence.

Consider the specification $v, z:[\,true \ / \ z = max(x,y) \wedge v = x + 1\,]$. It is fairly obvious in this case that we should consider satisfying $v = x + 1$ with an assignment that is independent of the *max* calculation; we can do it before or after the **if**, or even within each branch. For the sake of the example, let us imagine that it is not obvious. First, we anticipate the sequential composition as before; we can make this a general goal-directed strategy for introducing **if**, since in the case where the composition was not necessary, its first component will refine to **skip** and we can use the identity **skip**; $S \ = \ S$. A sequential composition is introduced with **Split Specification**, using a metavariable P as the *mid* parameter. There is no applicability condition, so no constraint is posted at this stage.

We cannot do more with the first component now, since the method is goal-directed (based on the form of the postcondition), and we do not yet know its postcondition. We can address the hidden disjunction of equalities in the postcondition of the second component; as before, we make the **if** guards metavariables C and D, and introduce assignments. The derivation looks like:

$$v, z:[\,true \ / \ z = max(x,y) \wedge v = x+1\,]$$

$\sqsubseteq$ **Split Specification** (P)

$\qquad v, z:[\,true \ / \ P\,]\,;$ *(i)*

$\qquad v, z:[\,P \ / \ z = max(x,y) \wedge v = x+1\,]$ *(ii)*

(ii) $\sqsubseteq$ **Introduce IF** (C, D)

$\qquad$ **if** $C \to v, z:[\,P \wedge C \ / \ z = max(x,y) \wedge v = x+1\,]$ *(iii)*

$\qquad$ $[\!]\ D \to v, z:[\,P \wedge D \ / \ z = max(x,y) \wedge v = x+1\,]$ *(iv)*

$\qquad$ **fi**

(iii) $\sqsubseteq$ **Introduce Assignment** (z, x)

$\qquad z := x$

(iv) $\sqsubseteq$ **Introduce Assignment** (z, y)

$\qquad z := y$

The constraints posted are:

$$P \Rightarrow C \vee D \qquad \qquad \text{from the } \mathbf{if} \text{ rule}$$
$$P \wedge C \Rightarrow x \geq y \wedge v = x + 1 \quad \text{from the first assignment}$$
$$P \wedge D \Rightarrow y \geq x \wedge v = x + 1 \quad \text{from the second assignment}$$

Once again, there is no single solution. A heuristic that we have found appropriate in such circumstances [7] is to treat the right-hand sides of the implications in the last two constraints as sets of conjuncts. Conjuncts in the intersection of the sets ($v = x + 1$ in this example) are associated with the common conjunct P on the left-hand side; the rest are associated with the other conjuncts C and D on the left-hand side. This suggests the bindings $P \mapsto v = x + 1$, $C \mapsto x \geq y$, $D \mapsto y \geq x$. These bindings satisfy all three constraints adequately, though once again the solution is not unique and we must be prepared to seek alternatives if later constraints demand it.

Instantiating P instantiates it everywhere, so the first component (i) of the sequential composition becomes $v, x:[true \ / \ v = x + 1]$, which can be satisfied by a single application of the assignment rule.

4 Conditional Refinements

Metavariables as described above allow us to support the strategy of building the commands inside an **if** or **do** before the guards. They do not give us the full strategy of Gries, in which the guarded commands are added one at a time until all cases are covered. For that, we propose to use *conditional refinements*.

The idea is to build guarded commands one at a time and then combine them into an **if** or **do** command once all the necessary cases have been covered. To do this, we need a semantics for guarded commands independent of the **if** or **do** that normally surrounds them; this is provided by an extension to the guarded commands language ([8, 9]) that treats the normal **if** command as being a composition using distinct operators: guarding ($\rightarrow$), demonically non-deterministic alternative composition ($[\![$), and **if** itself. Each of these operators has its own weakest preconditions semantics (**do** is defined in terms of **if** and recursion, as usual):

$$wp(b \rightarrow s, \psi) \quad \hat{=} \quad b \Rightarrow wp(s, \psi)$$
$$wp(s \, [\!] \, t, \psi) \quad \hat{=} \quad wp(s, \psi) \wedge wp(t, \psi)$$
$$wp(\mathbf{if} \ s \ \mathbf{fi}, \psi) \quad \hat{=} \quad wp(s, \psi) \wedge \neg wp(s, false).$$

Using these definitions, the meaning of a 'normal' **if** command

$$\mathbf{if} \ b_1 \rightarrow s_1 \ [\!] \cdots [\!] \ b_n \rightarrow s_n \ \mathbf{fi}$$

is the same as it is according to Dijkstra, providing the commands s_i are not miraculous.

We can then define refinement rules to introduce a naked guarded command, to combine commands into a nondeterministic composition, and to enclose a command in an **if** or **do**. Possible versions of these are shown in Figure 7. The last three of these rules differ from rules we have seen so far in this important way: some of their applicability conditions are themselves refinements. To

---

Introduce Naked Guarded Command (b)

$$\tilde{w}{:}[\,pre\ /\ post\,] \quad \sqsubseteq \quad b \to \tilde{w}{:}[\,pre \wedge b\ /\ post\,]$$

Introduce Demonic Nondeterminism $(t_1, \ldots, t_n)$

$$\frac{s \sqsubseteq t_1, \quad \ldots, \quad s \sqsubseteq t_n}{s \quad \sqsubseteq \quad t_1 \,[\!]\, \cdots \,[\!]\, t_n}$$

Introduce IF (t)

$$\frac{\begin{array}{c} s \sqsubseteq t \\ \neg wp(t, false)^3 \end{array}}{s \quad \sqsubseteq \quad \textbf{if } t \textbf{ fi}}$$

Introduce DO (var, inv, t)

$$\frac{\begin{array}{c} pre \Rightarrow inv \\ \tilde{w}{:}[\,inv \wedge var = var_0\ /\ inv \wedge var < var_0\,] \quad \sqsubseteq \quad t \\ inv \wedge wp(t, false) \Rightarrow post \end{array}}{\tilde{w}{:}[\,pre\ /\ post\,] \quad \sqsubseteq \quad \textbf{do } t \textbf{ od}}$$

Figure 7: The rules for introducing naked guarded commands, demonic nondeterminism, **if** and **do** constructs.

apply such a rule, we treat the refinement *lemmas* in the same way as we treat lemmas in deductive reasoning: they are proved independently of the development in which they are used (either before the step or after it). We attempt to prove lemmas before applying the rule, and post as constraints any lemmas that cannot be proven until metavariables within them are bound.

Sadly, the **if** and **do** constructors are not monotonic with respect to the refinement relation. That is, for programs S and T where $S \sqsubseteq T$, it does not necessarily follow that **if** S **fi** $\sqsubseteq$ **if** T **fi** and **do** S **od** $\sqsubseteq$ **do** T **od**. As a counter-example for either, take $S \mapsto (x \neq 0 \to x := 0)$ and $T \mapsto (false \to x := 0)$. The practical effect of this is to prevent us from doing further refinement (other than by equivalence) on the guarded commands once **Introduce IF** or **Introduce DO** has been used. This is acceptable if we are using the rules in Figure 7, since we choose t to be the desired code, prove its derivation (from s, in the case of **Introduce IF**, or from $\tilde{w}{:}[\,inv \wedge var = var_0\ /\ inv \wedge var < var_0\,]$ in the case of **Introduce DO**), and then apply **Introduce IF** or **Introduce DO** with

---

[3]Theodore Norvell has pointed out that this could be weakened to $wp(s, true) \Rightarrow \neg wp(t, false)$: in cases where s would fail to terminate, if t **fi** need not terminate either, so t need not be feasible. Similarly, $wp(s, true)$ could be added to the antecedent of the last applicability condition in **Introduce DO**.

the derivation of t satisfying the refinement lemma. We can make this more practically appealing using metavariables: we introduce the **if** or **do** with a metavariable for t, so the applicability conditions of the rule become constraints on t. We then address the refinement lemma (containing the metavariable), and instantiate the metavariable on the way.

4.1 The max Example

Let us address the max example using these rules. First, assume we have recognized the need for an **if** command, but have not analysed the number of branches needed or what their guards should be. We invoke **Introduce IF** with a metavariable T as parameter.

$$z:[\,true \;/\; z = max(x,y)\,]$$
$$\sqsubseteq \quad \textbf{Introduce IF} \;\; (T)$$
$$\textbf{if } T \textbf{ fi}$$

The partly instantiated applicability conditions are $z:[\,true \;/\; z = max(x,y)\,] \sqsubseteq T$ and $\neg wp(T, false)$. The first of these will be addressed immediately; the second is posted as a constraint on T.

We now wish to find a T satisfying both the refinement lemma and the constraint. The postcondition of the specification statement in the refinement lemma contains implicit disjuncts $z = x$ and $z = y$. Because of the first of these, we want to introduce the assignment $z := x$, as a guarded command. First, we first introduce a naked guarded command, with a metavariable as the guard:

$$z:[\,true \;/\; z = max(x,y)\,]$$
$$\sqsubseteq \quad \textbf{Introduce Naked Guarded Command} \;\; (C)$$
$$C \to z:[\,C \;/\; z = max(x,y)\,]$$

The rule has no applicability condition, so no constraint on C is posted. Upon refining the body to $z := x$, we obtain the constraint $C \Rightarrow x \geq y$ as before. Now, $C \to z := x$ is a candidate for T, but this cannot satisfy the constraint on T from **Introduce IF**, since $\neg wp(C \to z := x, false) = C$, and C is at least as strong as $x \geq y$. Instead, we put that refinement aside, and return to the original specification. We introduce a naked guarded command with a different metavariable D, and this time refine the body to $z := y$, generating the constraint $D \Rightarrow y \geq x$.

We have now produced two alternative refinements of the same specification, and each has generated its own conditions on the values of the metavariables. We can combine the alternative refinements with the rule **Introduce Demonic Nondeterminism**. We already have constraints that guarantee the necessary refinement lemmas, so the partially instantiated refinement rule

$$z:[\,true \;/\; z = max(x,y)\,] \sqsubseteq C \to z := x$$
$$z:[\,true \;/\; z = max(x,y)\,] \sqsubseteq D \to z := y$$
$$\rule{10cm}{0.4pt}$$
$$z:[\,true \;/\; z = max(x,y)\,] \quad \sqsubseteq \quad C \to z := x \;[\!]\; D \to z := y$$

needs no further proof, and no more constraints are generated.

Finally, we bind T from our application of **Introduce IF** to this alternation. The constraint is $\neg wp(C \rightarrow z := x \,[\!]\, D \rightarrow z := y, \, false)$, which reduces to $(C \vee D)$. We now have the same three constraints as in the earlier treatment of this example, and so can produce the same solution. If we could not find suitable bindings, we could prove further conditional refinements and add the resulting guarded commands to the demonic choice before binding T.

5   Example: Least Common Multiple

Dijkstra [6, p49] gives a simple, elegant modification of Euclid's greatest common divisor algorithm that additionally computes the least common multiple (and sets its proof as an exercise). Proving this four-line algorithm correct, and even getting an intuitive idea of how it works, demands a deep understanding of the factorization properties of the integers involved, and a great deal of insight. Here we present a development of a rather less elegant but more intuitive least common multiple algorithm that well illustrates the metavariables and conditional refinements techniques discussed above.

5.1   Specifying Least Common Multiple

The least common multiple $\mathsf{lcm}(x, y)$ of positive integers x and y is defined by

$$z = \mathsf{lcm}(x, y) \mathrel{\hat=} x \mid z \wedge y \mid z \wedge \neg(\exists z' < z \bullet x \mid z' \wedge y \mid z')$$

That is, $\mathsf{lcm}(x, y)$ is the smallest number that is evenly divisible by both x and y. The notation $a \mid b$ (read 'a divides b') is defined to be true when $a \in \mathbb{N}$, $b \in \mathbb{N}$ and $\exists c \in \mathbb{N} \bullet a = b \times c$. For convenience, we shall use conventional (real-valued) division $\frac{a}{b}$ in the development, which is well-defined wherever $b \neq 0$.

With these definitions in place, we can state the specification of our problem:

$$z:[\, x \geq 1 \wedge y \geq 1 \;/\; z = \mathsf{lcm}(x, y)\,]$$

In our refinement, we shall not expand the definition of lcm directly; rather, we appeal to several theorems about the distribution of $\times$ through lcm. The first unconditionally distributes a common factor through both arguments of lcm, while the others are conditional rules that distribute through one argument or the other. These theorems are easily proved from the definition of lcm.

×-distrib-lcm-both:	$\mathsf{lcm}(a \times b, a \times c) = a \times \mathsf{lcm}(b, c)$
×-distrib-lcm-left:	$\mathsf{lcm}(a \times b, c) = a \times \mathsf{lcm}(b, c)$ if $\gcd(a, c) = 1$
×-distrib-lcm-right:	$\mathsf{lcm}(b, a \times c) = a \times \mathsf{lcm}(b, c)$ if $\gcd(a, b) = 1$

5.2   Initial Refinement

We now plan our strategy for refining the specification. We want to enumerate the prime factors of x and y: the product of the bag maximum of the factors is the desired least common multiple[4]. To find the prime factors, we use local

---

[4]Bag maximum combines bags B and C such that the number of times any element appears in the maximum is the greater of the number of times it appears in B and C.

variables u and v, whose values are initially x and y, then divide factors from u and v as we find them and accumulate their product in the output z. We shall use a third new variable i to enumerate the potential factors. Rather than generating primes explicitly, we rely on the fact that the smallest prime factor of any number is smaller than any composite factor. This means that having divided out all factors i from u and v, we can simply increment i without concern as to whether the result is prime: if it is composite, it will certainly not be a factor since all primes smaller than it have already been tried.

We clearly need a loop. We use **Split Specification** with a metavariable *Int* as the intermediate assertion. The first component of the resulting composition will be refined to the initialization, the second to the loop itself.

$$z{:}[\,x \geq 1 \wedge y \geq 1 \;/\; z = \mathsf{lcm}(x,y)\,] \tag{i}$$

$(i)\quad \sqsubseteq \quad$ **Introduce Variable** $\;(u,v,i:\mathbb{N})$

$\qquad$⟦ **var** $u,v,i:\mathbb{N}$ •
$\qquad\quad u,v,i,z{:}[\,x \geq 1 \wedge y \geq 1 \;/\; z = \mathsf{lcm}(x,y)\,] \tag{ii}$
$\qquad$⟧

$(ii)\quad \sqsubseteq \quad$ **Split Specification** $\;(Int)$

$\qquad u,v,i,z{:}[\,x \geq 1 \wedge y \geq 1 \;/\; Int\,]\,; \tag{iii}$
$\qquad u,v,i,z{:}[\,Int \;/\; z = \mathsf{lcm}(x,y)\,] \tag{iv}$

5.3 Building the Loop

We want the loop invariant to establish the value of z as the product of the factors found so far. Since we are dividing the factors from u and v, some rearrangement suggests putting $z = \mathsf{lcm}(\frac{x}{u},\frac{y}{v})$ in the invariant. This will establish the postcondition when both u and v reach 1. The invariant must also ensure that all factors found have been correctly divided out of u and v: $u \mid x \wedge v \mid y \wedge (\forall j \in 2\mathinner{.\,.}i-1 \bullet j \nmid u \wedge j \nmid v)$ achieves this. Additionally, we shall maintain $u \geq 1 \wedge v \geq 1$, and we only want to try for potential factors greater than one, so $i \geq 2$. Putting this together gives the invariant:

$$\Omega: \begin{cases} z = \mathsf{lcm}(\frac{x}{u},\frac{y}{v}) \wedge u \mid x \wedge v \mid y \wedge \\ (\forall j \in 2\mathinner{.\,.}i-1 \bullet j \nmid u \wedge j \nmid v) \wedge \\ u \geq 1 \wedge v \geq 1 \wedge i \geq 2 \end{cases}$$

We also require a variant (Gries calls it a bound function) to establish termination; this should be a positive function that decreases as we progress towards termination. If we can decrease either u or v we must certainly eventually terminate, but this is too difficult to establish, since some values for i will not divide u or v evenly. Increasing i also makes some progress towards termination, since eventually we shall find an i that divides one or both of u and v. With this in mind, we postulate the variant $\tau : (u+v) \mathbin{\dot-} i$, where $a \mathbin{\dot-} b$ is $a-b$ if $a > b$ and zero otherwise. This variant is indeed strictly decreasing, since $(u+v) - i$ will only become negative at the very last stage of the loop, when $u = v = 1$.

We can now introduce the loop itself, supplying as parameters the invariant, variant and a metavariable S to become the command inside the **do**.

(iv) ⊑ **Introduce DO** (Ω, τ, S)

    do S **od** (v)

The proof obligations are:

$C1:$ $Int \Rightarrow \Omega$

$C2:$ $u, v, i, z{:}[\Omega \wedge \tau = \tau_0 \; / \; \Omega \wedge \tau < \tau_0] \; \sqsubseteq \; S$

$C3:$ $\Omega \wedge wp(S, false) \Rightarrow z = \mathsf{lcm}(x, y)$

We shall address constraint $C2$ by further refinements shortly, which will bind the metavariable S; this binding must satisfy $C3$.

$C1$ can most easily be satisfied by putting $Int \mapsto \Omega$. This fully instantiates the initialization specification (iii), which we now refine to an assignment:

(iii) ⊑ **Introduce Assignment** $([u, v, i, z], [x, y, 2, 1])$

        $u, v, i, z := x, y, 2, 1$

This step requires us to prove that the precondition (of (iii)) implies the substituted postcondition $\Omega[u, v, i, z := x, y, 2, 1]$:

$x \geq 1 \wedge y \geq 1 \Rightarrow$
    $1 = \mathsf{lcm}(\frac{x}{x}, \frac{y}{y}) \wedge x \mid x \wedge y \mid y \wedge$
    $(\forall j \in 2 .. 1 \bullet \cdots) \wedge x \geq 1 \wedge y \geq 1 \wedge 2 \leq 2$

The first conjunct of the consequent follows from the definition of lcm; the $\forall j$ conjunct is trivially true since $2 .. 1$ is an empty range; and the other conjuncts are trivial.

5.4   Building the Guarded Commands

We now focus on $C2$, refining $u, v, i, z{:}[\Omega \wedge \tau = \tau_0 \; / \; \Omega \wedge \tau < \tau_0]$ to a guarded command set S. We build guarded commands one at a time until their nondeterministic composition satisfies $C3$. We do not yet know how many branches S will have, nor what the guards will be. So, we start generating guarded commands using **Introduce Naked Guarded Command** with a metavariable as parameter. The appropriate refinements, then, are of the form

        $u, v, i, z{:}[\Omega \wedge \tau = \tau_0 \; / \; \Omega \wedge \tau < \tau_0]$ (vi)

⊑ $G_k \rightarrow S_k$

where each S_k is chosen to decrease the variant τ, while maintaining the invariant Ω under the assumption G_k.

We can reduce τ by decreasing either u or v, or by increasing i. Let us try each of these in turn. To decrease u, but maintain the invariant, we can divide

u by i and multiply z by the same thing, and similarly for v:

(vi) $\sqsubseteq$ **Introduce Naked Guarded Command** (G_1)

$$G_1 \rightarrow$$
$$u, v, i, z{:}[\, G_1 \wedge \Omega \wedge \tau = \tau_0 \; / \; \Omega \wedge \tau < \tau_0 \,] \qquad\qquad (vii)$$

(vii) $\sqsubseteq$ **Introduce Assignment** $([u, z], [\frac{u}{i}, z \times i])$

$$u, z := \frac{u}{i}, z \times i$$

and similarly,

(vi) $\sqsubseteq$ **Introduce Naked Guarded Command** (G_2),
Introduce Assignment $([v, z], [\frac{v}{i}, z \times i])$

$$G_2 \rightarrow v, z := \frac{v}{i}, z \times i$$

The applicability conditions of the **Introduce Assignment** steps here produce the constraints

$$G_1 \wedge \Omega \wedge \tau = \tau_0 \Rightarrow (\Omega \wedge \tau < \tau_0)[u, z := \tfrac{u}{i}, z \times i]$$

and

$$G_2 \wedge \Omega \wedge \tau = \tau_0 \Rightarrow (\Omega \wedge \tau < \tau_0)[v, z := \tfrac{v}{i}, z \times i].$$

Expanding the definitions of Ω and τ on the right-hand side of the first of these constraints yields

$$G_1 \wedge \Omega \wedge \tau = \tau_0 \Rightarrow \left(\begin{array}{l} z \times i = \mathsf{lcm}(x/\tfrac{u}{i}, \tfrac{y}{v}) \wedge \\ \tfrac{u}{i} \mid x \wedge v \mid y \wedge \\ (\forall j \in 2 .. i - 1 \bullet j \nmid \tfrac{u}{i} \wedge j \nmid v) \wedge \\ \tfrac{u}{i} \geq 1 \wedge v \geq 1 \wedge i \geq 2 \wedge \\ \tfrac{u}{i} + v \dotdiv i < \tau_0 \end{array} \right)$$

To simplify this, we recall that we defined divisibility so that $u \mid x \Rightarrow \frac{u}{i} \mid x$ only when $\frac{u}{i}$ is an integer; that is, when $i \mid u$. In this case, $x/\frac{u}{i}$ in the *lcm* conjunct on the right-hand side is an integer (so *lcm* is well-defined), and is equal to $\frac{x}{u} \times i$. Further, if $\frac{u}{i} < u$ then $\frac{u}{i} + v \dotdiv i \leq u + v \dotdiv i$, and is strictly less providing $u + v > i$. Also, the theorem ×-**distrib-lcm-left** applies to the rewritten *lcm* conjunct providing $\gcd(i, \frac{y}{v}) = 1$. Finally, $j \nmid u \Rightarrow j \nmid \frac{u}{i}$, which means that the $\forall j$ conjunct follows from the corresponding conjunct of Ω on the left-hand side. Thus we simplify further:

$$G_1 \wedge \Omega \Rightarrow v \mid y \wedge u \geq 1 \wedge i \geq 2 \wedge u + v > i \wedge i \mid u \wedge \gcd(i, \tfrac{y}{v}) = 1$$

The first three conjuncts of the consequent appear directly in Ω in the antecedent. If $i \mid u \wedge u \geq 1$ then $i \leq u$, so if $v \geq 1$ then certainly $u + v > i$. Multiplication distributes through (both sides of) gcd, so $\gcd(i, \frac{y}{v}) = 1$ if and only if $\gcd(v \times i, y) = v$, which in turn holds as long as $\gcd(v, y) = v \wedge i \nmid v$. The first conjunct of this is true since $v \mid y$. We finish with the constraint $G_1 \wedge \Omega \Rightarrow i \mid u \wedge i \nmid v$, which we solve by putting G_1 equal to the right-hand side. A similar line of reasoning is used to solve for G_2. Our first two refinement lemmas are then

(vi) $\sqsubseteq$ $i \mid u \wedge i \nmid v \rightarrow u, z := \tfrac{u}{i}, z \times i$ $\qquad\qquad$ (viii)

and

(vi) $\sqsubseteq$ $i \nmid u \wedge i \mid v \rightarrow v, z := \tfrac{v}{i}, z \times i$ $\qquad\qquad$ (ix)

Our third guarded command increases i:

$$(vi) \quad \sqsubseteq \quad G_3 \to i := i + 1 \tag{x}$$

To determine G_3, we need $G_3 \wedge \Omega \wedge \tau = \tau_0 \Rightarrow (\Omega \wedge \tau < \tau_0)[i := i + 1]$. Expanding Ω, substituting, simplifying and removing subsumed conjuncts on the right-hand side yields

$$G_3 \wedge \Omega \wedge \tau = \tau_0 \Rightarrow \left(\begin{array}{l} (\forall j \in 2 \mathinner{\ldotp\ldotp} i \bullet j \nmid u \wedge j \nmid v) \wedge \\ i \geq 1 \wedge \\ (u + v) \mathbin{\dot-} (i + 1) < u + v \mathbin{\dot-} i \end{array} \right)$$

The $\forall$ conjunct on the right-hand side requires $i \nmid u \wedge i \nmid v$ in addition to the one in Ω. We do not want to treat $\dot-$ as code, so we observe that $a \mathbin{\dot-} (b+1) < a \mathbin{\dot-} b$ providing $b < a$, and replace the last conjunct by $i < u+v$. The result suggests the binding $G_3 \mapsto i \nmid u \wedge i \nmid v \wedge i < u + v$.

To satisfy the $\Omega \wedge wp(S, \textit{false}) \Rightarrow \textit{Post}$ applicability condition of **Introduce DO**, we are going to need $\Omega \wedge \neg(\bigvee_k G_k) \Rightarrow z = \mathsf{lcm}(x, y)$. The three guards we have so far do not give this, and the calculation suggests we now need to handle the case where i divides both u and v.

$$(vi) \quad \sqsubseteq \quad G_4 \to u, v, z := \tfrac{u}{i}, \tfrac{v}{i}, z \times i \tag{xi}$$

Calculating the applicability conditions and simplifying as above (this time using **×-distrib-lcm-both**) yields the constraint $G_4 \wedge \Omega \Rightarrow i \mid u \wedge i \mid v$, which we solve once again by putting G_4 equal to the right-hand side.

5.5 Combining the Guarded Commands

Now we use **Introduce Demonic Nondeterminism** to combine the guarded commands $(viii) \ldots (xi)$. The obligations are the four refinement lemmas we just proved, and the result is $(vi) \sqsubseteq (viii) \,[\!]\, (ix) \,[\!]\, (x) \,[\!]\, (xi)$. If we bind S (from **Introduce DO**) to that alternation, we must show the binding satisfies our delayed constraints $C2$ and $C3$. $C2$ is exactly what we proved with **Introduce Demonic Nondeterminism**: $(vi) \sqsubseteq S$. $C3$ is $\Omega \wedge wp(S, \textit{false}) \Rightarrow z = \mathsf{lcm}(x, y)$:

$$
\begin{aligned}
& wp(S, \textit{false}) \\
= \ & \textstyle\bigwedge_k (G_k \Rightarrow wp(S_k, \textit{false})) \\
= \ & \textstyle\bigwedge_k (\neg G_k) \quad \text{[since each } S_k \text{ is code]} \\
= \ & i \nmid u \wedge i \nmid v \wedge u + v \leq i
\end{aligned}
$$

The conjunct $\forall j \in 2 \mathinner{\ldotp\ldotp} i - 1 \bullet j \nmid u \wedge j \nmid v$ from Ω means that the only possible factors of u and v are unity and numbers bigger than i. But i is bigger than either u or v, so that option is ruled out; u and v must both be one[5]. And $\Omega \wedge u = 1 \wedge v = 1$ gives $z = \mathsf{lcm}(x, y)$, as required. The completed, collected

---

[5] In fact, this shows that we could weaken the last conjunct of G_3 to $u \neq 1 \vee v \neq 1$ if we so chose.

program is then

$$
\begin{aligned}
&\lceil\!\lceil \quad \textbf{var}\ u, v, i : \mathbb{N} \bullet \\
&\qquad u, v, i, z := x, y, 2, 1\ ; \\
&\qquad \textbf{do}\quad i \mid u \wedge i \not| v \qquad\qquad\qquad \rightarrow \quad u, z := \tfrac{u}{i}, z \times i \\
&\qquad\qquad\ i \not| u \wedge i \mid v \qquad\qquad\qquad \rightarrow \quad v, z := \tfrac{v}{i}, z \times i \\
&\qquad\qquad\ i \not| u \wedge i \not| v \wedge i < u + v \ \rightarrow \quad i := i + 1 \\
&\qquad\qquad\ i \mid u \wedge i \mid v \qquad\qquad\qquad \rightarrow \quad u, v, z := \tfrac{u}{i}, \tfrac{v}{i}, z \times i \\
&\qquad \textbf{od} \\
&\rfloor\!\rfloor
\end{aligned}
$$

6 Conclusions

We have demonstrated two techniques that allow users of the refinement calculus to record developments in a more convenient way. We have also described how supporting these techniques in a tool gives its users the ability to develop programs in a more experimental fashion, by suggesting refinement schemes and having the tool assist with the calculation of appropriate instantiations of those schemes.

Our metavariables technique allows us to select a rule that seems likely to work in a particular situation, but defer specifying exactly what instance of the rule will be used. The applicability condition of the rule will partly constrain the available instantiations, and later refinements will constrain it further. The metavariables can then be instantiated (subject to the accumulated constraints) at any time we find convenient. We have found this technique useful in many of the derivations we have done by hand; for another example, see [10]. We hope to implement an extension to our refinement tool that represents metavariables with Prolog variables and collects the constraints on them using the co-routining mechanisms available in some versions of Prolog [11].

Clement [12] has used metavariables in the context of proof by natural deduction in the μral proof tool [13]. There, too, the benefit is avoiding the need to plan ahead so that steps can be done when they prove necessary, rather than needing to be anticipated. Clement's metavariables can represent predicate symbols (with arguments); our metavariables can stand for complete terms, formulas or commands only.

The conditional refinements technique allows guarded commands to be developed one at a time, hence deferring the decision of how many branches an **if** or **do** command should have. The semantics makes each guarded command alone a 'minor miracle' [14] that behaves magically if executed when its guard is false. Each individual guarded command is then an alternative valid refinement of the original specification. These alternatives can be combined using rules for introducing demonic choice, and feasibility and termination checks can be made by rules that introduce **if** and **do**. Our proposed implementation includes support for recording and combining alternative developments, but we must also weaken our definition of monotonicity and replace the refinement relation by one (actually a family) with respect to which the **if** and **do** constructors are monotonic.

Support for these techniques is useful in a practical tool, since it allows the tool's user to develop a program in a more convenient way, avoiding some of the need to work out parts of the development by hand before performing them with the tool. Supporting the user's thought processes brings us another benefit too: the sequence of operations can be represented more explicitly in the recorded derivation. If all relevant data are stored, we can provide a view of the completed derivation at any desired level, which may differ depending on the reader's aims. If the reader is interested only in obtaining a correct program, we can easily present that. If a demonstration of the correctness of the program is desired, we can present the derivation as a sequence of applications of (instantiated) refinement rules; the order of presentation may or may not be the order in which the rules were actually applied. When the derivation reader requires a more thorough understanding of the algorithm or of how it was actually developed, full details of the sequence of operations and the motivation for particular instantiations may be required.

The theme that unifies the two techniques described here is the benefit arising from deferring decisions about refinement details. There may be other techniques that users of the refinement calculus apply informally when exploring possible derivations. Identifying, categorizing and formalizing these techniques merits further investigation.

References

[1] Carroll C. Morgan and Ken Robinson. Specification statements and refinement. *IBM Journal of Research and Development*, 31(5):546–555, September 1987.

[2] R. J. R. Back. A calculus of refinements for program derivations. *Acta Informatica*, 25:593–624, 1988.

[3] Carroll Morgan. *Programming from Specifications*. Prentice Hall, 1990.

[4] Lindsay Groves, Raymond Nickson and Mark Utting. A tactic driven refinement tool. In Cliff B. Jones, Roger C. Shaw and Tim Denvir, editors, *Fifth Refinement Workshop*, Workshops in Computing, pages 272–297. BCS FACS, Springer-Verlag, 1992.

[5] David Gries. *The Science of Programming*. Springer-Verlag, 1981.

[6] E. W. Dijkstra. *A Discipline of Programming*. Academic Press, 1976.

[7] Lindsay J. Groves and Raymond G. Nickson. An intelligent editor for constructing correct programs. In *Proceedings of the Third New Zealand Conference on Expert Systems*. New Zealand Expert Systems Special Interest Group, 1988.

[8] Carroll Morgan. The specification statement. *ACM Transactions on Programming Languages and Systems*, 10(3):403–419, July 1988.

[9] Greg Nelson. A generalization of Dijkstra's calculus. *ACM Transactions on Programming Languages and Systems*, 11(4):517–561, October 1989.

[10] Lindsay Groves. Deriving language recognition algorithms: A case study

in combining program specialisation and data refinement. In David Till and Roger C. F. Shaw, editors, *Sixth Refinement Workshop*, Workshops in Computing. BCS FACS, Springer-Verlag, 1994.

[11] L. Naish. Negation and quantifiers in NU-Prolog. In *Proceedings of the Third International Conference on Logic Programming*, 1986.

[12] Tim Clement. Using metavariables in natural deduction proofs. In Cliff B. Jones, Roger C. Shaw and Tim Denvir, editors, *Fifth Refinement Workshop*, Workshops in Computing. BCS FACS, Springer-Verlag, 1992.

[13] C. B. Jones, K. D. Jones, P. A. Lindsay and R. Moore. *mural: A Formal Development Support System*. Springer-Verlag, 1991.

[14] Joseph M. Morris. A theoretical basis for stepwise refinement and the programming calculus. *Science of Computer Programming*, 9:287–306, 1987.

Machine Code Programs are Predicates Too

Theodore S. Norvell

norvell@cs.toronto.edu

norvell@comlab.ox.ac.uk

Abstract

I present an interpretation of machine language programs as boolean expressions. Source language programs may also be so interpreted. The correctness of a code generator can then be expressed as a simple relationship between boolean expressions. Code generators can then be calculated from their specification.

1 Introduction

A predicate divides its domain in two. In the specification of computational behaviour we wish to divide the set of all imaginable computations in two parts: acceptable computations and unacceptable computations. Predicates provide a convenient way of expressing this division.

In this paper we are interested in two kinds of computational behaviour: the behaviour specified by high level language programs in terms of source level variables, and the behaviour specified by machine language programs in terms of registers and memory. By using predicate logic as a common framework to describe both forms of behaviour we can relate them and write down the logical relationship that should exist between the input and output programs of a compiler. This relationship serves as a specification from which we can derive a code generator.

Except for the derivation of an example code generator, all proofs and derivations have been omitted. Where proofs are not straight forward, an outline is presented. Proofs of most of the theorems can be found in my thesis [Norvell 1993].

2 Motivation

The problem of compiler correctness is clearly an important one for computer reliability. The point of proving a high-level language program correct is diminished if that program is submitted to a compiler that is not correct. It can be expected that a great many source programs will be submitted to a single compiler. As the correct execution of all of them depends —potentially— on the compiler, proving the compiler can be highly worthwhile. Furthermore testing compilers is notoriously difficult, involving, as it does, either reasoning about the machine code output or testing the object program; the former is quite difficult and the latter is indirect and likely to fail to find all bugs.

Aside from this practical consideration, the problem is of interest to those interested in the formalization of reasoning about programs. It involves the interaction of two formal descriptions of language, one for the source language, and one for the target language.

Quite a lot of previous research has been done on proving compilers and on automatically producing compilers from formal descriptions of languages, for example, [McCarthy and Painter 1967, Morris 1973, Milne and Strachey 1974, Thatcher *et al.* 1980, Mosses 1980, Polak 1981, Manasse and Nelson 1984, Hoare 1990, Sampaio 1993]. This research has employed almost the gamut of approaches to formalizing reasoning about programs: operational, algebraic, denotational.

The research presented below uses yet another approach —the predicative. Reasoning about specification (including programs) represented by predicates has proved to be a very effective way to develop correct programs. The question is whether the predicative approach will yield a promising line of attack on compiler correctness.

In addition the compiler correctness problem serves as an interesting case study in the use of the predicative approach. This is another motivation.

As a first step towards compiler correctness, we will look at using predicates to model machine programs. Quite apart from its application to compiler correctness this aspect of the work has applications all its own. For example, the resulting description of the CPU architecture could be used as a departure point for developing a proved implementation of the CPU in hardware.

3 Notation

Among the numbers, we will be using mostly the integers, but sometimes the naturals and the extended naturals. The extended naturals are the naturals together with a single infinity value ∞ which is larger than all naturals.

The number operators $(+, -, =, -, <, \leq, >, \geq)$ have their usual meanings.

A *string* is a sequence of items. The length of a string s is written $\#s$. The string of length zero is written as nil. A string of length one is equal to its sole element. The catenation of two strings s and t is written $s; t$.

The boolean operators $(\equiv, \not\equiv, \Rightarrow, \Leftarrow, \wedge, \vee, \neg)$ also have the usual definitions. The expression $x \, \langle\!\langle b \rangle\!\rangle \, y$ for boolean b has value x when b is true and y when b is false.

Function application is written $f.x$. The function $\langle \lambda f \cdot \langle \lambda z \cdot y \, \langle\!\langle z = x \rangle\!\rangle \, f.z \rangle \rangle$ which mutates its functional argument is written $x \mapsto y$.

Other notations and terms will be introduced and explained as needed; but for future reference, the precedence of all the operators is shown in Table 1.

Variables will generally follow the following typing conventions. When they do, I will feel free to omit mention of their types.

i	instructions
s, t, u	strings of instructions
n	natural numbers *nat*
j, k, l	integers *int*
P, Q, R	specifications
C, D	conditions

$\# \quad \heartsuit \quad \clubsuit \quad \downarrow \quad \uparrow$	left associative
$+ \quad -$	left associative
$:= \quad \mapsto$	
$;$	associative
$@ \quad !$	
$\circ$	associative
$\langle\! b\! \rangle$	right associative
$= \quad \neq \quad < \quad \leq \quad > \quad \geq$	
$\neg$	
$\wedge \quad \vee$	lifting
$\equiv \quad \not\equiv \quad \Rightarrow \quad \Leftarrow$	lifting; $\Rightarrow$ is right associative; $\Leftarrow$ is left associative; $\equiv$ and $\not\equiv$ are associative
$\because \quad \because \quad \therefore$	

Table 1: Precedence of operators

S, T, U	source level specifications
V, W, X	machine level specifications
f, g, h	functions

4 Specifications

State spaces are sets of states. We will use two state spaces Σ and M representing the source and machine level states respectively.

We will be particularly interested in functions of type

$$(\Sigma \times \Sigma \times M \times M) \rightarrow bool$$

which will be called *specifications*. For convenience, specifications will be written as boolean expressions with the variables (σ and σ' of type Σ, and μ and μ' of type M) representing their four parameters respectively. Accordingly the substitution notation is used for applying or partially applying specifications. For example, P_x^σ is the application of P to x at parameter σ. As a special case $P_{\sigma';\mu'}^{\sigma;\mu}$ is notated by P'.

A specification is called *machine level* if its value does not depend on the value of the σ and σ' parameters; and is called *source level* if its value does not depend on the value of the μ and μ' variables.

The boolean operators and constants are lifted pointwise to specification operators and constants. Specifications may be compared with the operator

$$(P \cdot: Q) \quad \equiv \quad \langle \forall \sigma; \mu; \sigma'; \mu' \cdot P \Leftarrow Q \rangle$$

In words, $P \cdot: Q$ is written P *is refined by* Q. We write $P :\cdot Q$ for $Q \cdot: P$ and $P ::\cdot Q$ for $(P \cdot: Q) \wedge (P :\cdot Q)$, which is equality of specifications. We define the operator $\circ$ on specifications as

$$P \circ Q \quad ::\cdot \quad \langle \exists \sigma''; \mu'' \cdot P_{\sigma'';\mu''}^{\sigma';\mu'} \wedge Q_{\sigma'';\mu''}^{\sigma;\mu} \rangle$$

This has an identity $ok \; ·:\; \sigma';\mu' = \sigma;\mu$. We will also have occasion to use $ok_{M} \; ·:\; \mu' = \mu$ and $ok_{\Sigma} \; ·:\; \sigma' = \sigma$.

In this paper we are interested in *batch* computations at either the source or machine level. A batch computation consists of an initial and a final state. For source level specifications, σ represents the initial state and σ' the final state. For machine level specifications, μ represents the initial state and μ' the final state. The predicates in

$$(\Sigma \times \Sigma \times M \times M) \rightarrow bool$$

that we are calling 'specifications' represent specifications —in an informal sense— by selecting those computations which are acceptable. The comparison $P \; ·:\; Q$ thus means that Q accepts no computation that P does not accept, and thus clearly deserves reading 'P is refined by Q'. The least useful specification is **true**, and the entirely miraculous specification is **false**.

> **Remark** It should be clear from the above that —unlike the common convention in Z— specifications that allow infinite computations are represented by weak predicates rather than strong predicates.

5   Predicative semantics and source programs

A *predicative semantics* for a programming language (or a specification language) is an interpretation of the members of that language as predicates. This idea is illustrated with a source level language in this section and with a machine level language on the next.

5.1   Abstract syntax

Our example source language is the very simple one shown in Table 2, in which the syntactic variables are used as follows: S, T, and U range over statements; E, F, and G range over expressions; v ranges over source variables; c ranges over constants (**true**, **false**, 0, −1, 1, ...); *bop* ranges over binary operators (+, −, =, **and**, and **or**); *uop* ranges over unary operators (**not** and −); and *ty* ranges over type constants (**int**, and **bool**).

The state space Σ for this language is the cross product of the types of the source variables. We denote the projections of σ and σ' with the unprimed and primed names of the source variables. Thus for a source variable x we write x to represent its value in the initial state and x' to represent its value in the final state. Furthermore the substitution notation is extended so that —for example— S^{x}_{E} means $S^{\sigma}_{f.\sigma}$ where f is a function that leaves every component of a state alone, except for x which it sets to E.

> **Extra explanation** This sounds rather complex, but it just means that we can write a specification S that specifies the final value of x is to be 1 more than its initial value as $x' = x + 1$, and that the specification that says the final value of x is to be three can be written as either $x' = 3$ or, equivalently, S^{x}_{3}.

$$S \quad \rightarrow \quad \text{nil}$$
$$\mid \quad T; U$$
$$\mid \quad v := E$$
$$\mid \quad \text{if } E \text{ then } T \text{ else } U \text{ fi}$$
$$\mid \quad \text{while } E \text{ do } T \text{ od}$$
$$E \quad \rightarrow \quad v$$
$$\mid \quad c$$
$$\mid \quad F \text{ bop } G$$
$$\mid \quad uop \ F$$

Table 2: The abstract syntax of the source language.

nil	ok_Σ
$T; U$	$T \circ U$
$v := E$	$(ok_\Sigma)^v_E$
if E then T else U fi	$T \ (\!\!\mid E \mid\!\!\rangle \ U$
while E do T od	see text

Table 3: The semantics of the source language.

One global source variable is always t_σ of type $xnat$ representing time; t_σ represents the time at which a computation starts and t'_σ represents the time at which the computation ends —at least in an abstract sense. It is assumed there are no explicit references to t_σ in any program.

5.2 Semantics

We interpret each abstract syntax term as a specification according to table 3. For example if the global source variables are x, y, z, t_σ,

$$(x := 1; y := y + x) \quad \because \quad x' = 1 \wedge y' = y + 1 \wedge z' = z \wedge t'_\sigma = t_\sigma$$

while E **do** T **od** is defined using a method called the *weakest progressive pre-fixedpoint*. Define the function wh from specifications to specifications by

$$\text{wh}.U \quad \because \quad (T \circ (t_\sigma := t_\sigma + 1) \circ U) \ (\!\!\mid E \mid\!\!\rangle \ ok_\Sigma$$

Now we postulate that S, such that $S \because$ **while** E **do** T **od**, has the following three properties

$$t'_\sigma \geq t_\sigma \quad \because \quad S$$
$$\text{wh}.S \quad \because \quad S$$
$$\langle \forall U \cdot (t'_\sigma \geq t_\sigma \quad \because \quad U) \wedge (\text{wh}.U \quad \because \quad U) \Rightarrow (S \quad \because \quad U) \rangle \tag{1}$$

For example, it can be shown from this that **while true do** nil **od** $\because t'_\sigma = \infty$.

Further reading on predicative semantics may be found in [Hehner 1984], [Hehner 1993], [Hoare 1992], and [Norvell 1993].

Remark Although predicative semantics is used in this paper to represent specifications of batch computations, it should not be inferred that it is limited to batch computations. One of the strengths of the approach is its ability to handle interactive computations.

6 A machine language and its semantics

In this section I present the semantics of a simple machine language. It should be understood that this is to present a general method of defining machine languages. All the theorems of the paper which do not mention specific instructions hold true for any machine language that meets the conditions spelled out in Section 6.2.

The machine language semantics is presented in two parts: machine dependent and machine independent. The machine dependent part defines the structure of the machine level state space M, the instruction set, and axioms defining the semantics of individual instructions. The machine independent part consists of additional axioms that define how individual instructions act together. Theorems based on the machine independent axioms are reusable for all machine languages.

6.1 Machine dependent aspects

The example machine for this paper has a state space M of four components

- p : *int* The program counter.

- t_μ : *xnat* The time. The type *xnat* includes all natural numbers and a special ∞ value larger than all natural numbers.

- a : *int* The accumulator.

- m : *int* $\rightarrow$ *int* The memory.

Thus M is the product ($int \times xnat \times int \times (int \rightarrow int)$). The four projections of μ are written p, t_μ, a, and m; and the four projections of μ' as p', t'_μ, a', and m'.

Each instruction in the instruction set is a string of length one and is interpreted as a specification according to the axioms in Table 4. As a convenience, we write $x :=_M E$ for $(ok_M)^x_E$ with x any string of component names and E an equal length string of expressions. Note that only backward and self jumps are considered to take any time.

6.2 Assumptions about machine dependent aspects

We will make four assumptions about the machine dependent axioms. These serve as the interface between the machine independent axioms and the machine dependent ones. Each should be demonstrated about the machine dependent axioms in order to ensure the applicability of the rest of the theory.

Axioms   For any integer j,

$$\text{enter } j \quad \because \quad p; a :=_M p + 1; j$$
$$\text{load } j \quad \because \quad p; a :=_M p + 1; m.j$$
$$\text{add } j \quad \because \quad p; a :=_M p + 1; a + m.j$$
$$\text{store } j \quad \because \quad p; m :=_M p + 1; (j \mapsto a).m$$
$$\text{jump } j \quad \because \quad p; t_\mu :=_M p + j; (t_\mu + 1 \ \langle\!| j \leq 0 |\!\rangle \ t_\mu)$$
$$\text{zjump } j \quad \because \quad p; t_\mu :=_M p + (j \ \langle\!| a = 0 |\!\rangle \ 1); (t_\mu + 1 \ \langle\!| a = 0 \wedge j \leq 0 |\!\rangle \ t_\mu)$$

Table 4: Axioms for instructions

Assumption   M should possess a component p of a subtype of *int* and a component t_μ of type *xnat*.

Assumption   Machine Level. Each instruction i should be a machine level specification.

Assumption   Implementability. For all instructions i

$$\langle \forall \mu \cdot \langle \exists \mu' \cdot i \rangle \rangle$$

Assumption   Progress. For all instructions i

$$t'_\mu \geq t_\mu \quad \because \quad i$$

All theorems in the remainder of Section 6 depend only on these assumptions and machine independent axioms. None directly rely on any specifics of the example machine presented.

6.3   Machine independent aspects

The machine independent axioms define the operators '!' and '@', which both take a string of instructions and an integer and produce a specification.

6.3.1   The ! operator.

The specification $s\,!\,l$ specifies the acceptable behaviour of a computer loaded with instruction string s beginning at location l in the program memory over the execution of a single instruction. It is defined by the

Axioms

$$\text{nil} \,!\, l \quad \because \quad true$$
$$i \,!\, l \quad \because \quad (p = l) \Rightarrow i$$
$$s;t \,!\, l \quad \because \quad (s \,!\, l) \wedge (t \,!\, l + \#s)$$

The following theorems follow from these axioms and the assumptions.

Theorem   Noninterference.

$$(l \le p < l + \#s) \vee (s \,!\, l)$$

Theorem   Implementability.

$$\langle \forall \mu \cdot \langle \exists \mu' \cdot s \,!\, l \rangle \rangle$$

Theorem   Progress.

$$t'_\mu \ge t_\mu \quad \because \quad (l \le p < l + \#s) \wedge (s \,!\, l)$$

6.3.2   The @ operator.

The specification $s \,@\, l$ describes the acceptable behaviour of a computer loaded with string s beginning at location l over the time the instruction counter points to instructions in s.

Definition   For each s and each l we define the following function iter from specifications to specifications

$$\text{iter}.V \quad \because \quad (s \,!\, l \circ V) \; \langle l \le p < l + \#s \rangle \; ok_M$$

A specification is a *pre-fixedpoint of* iter just if

$$\text{iter}.V \quad : \quad V$$

A specification is a *fixedpoint of* iter just if

$$\text{iter}.V \quad \because \quad V$$

We define $s \,@\, l$ with the following axioms:

Axiom   Construction. $s \,@\, l$ is a pre-fixedpoint of iter.

$$\text{iter}.(s \,@\, l) \quad : \quad s \,@\, l$$

> **Axiom**   Progression. $s @ l$ is progressive.
>
> $$t'_\mu \geq t_\mu \;\;\because\; s @ l$$

> **Axiom**   Induction. $s @ l$ is as weak as any progressive pre-fixedpoint of iter.
>
> $$\langle \forall V \cdot (\text{iter}.V \;\;\because\;\; V) \wedge (t'_\mu \geq t_\mu \;\because\; V) \Rightarrow (s @ l \;\because\; V) \rangle$$

These axioms are consistent by virtue of the Knaster-Tarski theorem [Tarski 1955].

The weakest progressive pre-fixedpoint of iter is also a fixedpoint. Indeed it is the weakest progressive fixedpoint.

> **Theorem**   Fixedpoint. $s @ l$ is a fixedpoint
>
> $$\text{iter}.(s @ l) \;\;\because\;\; s @ l$$

> **Theorem**   Weakest progressive fixedpoint.
>
> $$\langle \forall V \cdot (\text{iter}.V \;\;\because\;\; V) \wedge (t'_\mu \geq t_\mu \;\because\; V) \Rightarrow (s @ l \;\because\; V) \rangle$$

The following two theorems give a slightly more operational perspective.

> **Theorem**   Okness.
>
> $$s @ l \equiv ok_M \;\;\because\;\; (p < l) \vee (p \geq l + \#s)$$

> **Theorem**   Single stepping.
>
> $$i \circ (s; i; t @ l) \equiv s; i; t @ l \;\;\because\;\; p = l + \#s$$

The specifications we get are reasonable in the sense of being implementable.

> **Theorem**   Implementability. $\langle \forall \mu \cdot \langle \exists \mu' \cdot s @ l \rangle \rangle$.

Proof sketch. If we can show there is one implementable and progressive pre-fixedpoint of iter, then by the induction axiom, $s @ l$ must also be implementable.

From the construction and progression axioms we know there is at least one progressive pre-fixedpoint, implementable or not, namely $s @ l$. Let R be some progressive pre-fixedpoint. Construct Q as

$$Q \;\;\because\;\; R \vee (\neg \langle \exists \mu' \cdot R \rangle \wedge t'_\mu = \infty)$$

It is trivial that Q is progressive and implementable and not hard to show it is a pre-fixedpoint. $\square$

As long as a computer is executing the code in a certain region of its program memory, the contents of the rest of the program memory may be disregarded.

This is a crucial separation of concerns. It will be particularly important when we are deriving code generators; it will mean that the object code can be constructed by the code generator bit by bit rather than all at one go.

We can capture the idea formally with the following theorem.

Theorem   Separation.

$$s; t; u @ l \quad \because \quad t @ l + \#s \circ s; t; u @ l$$

Proof sketch [Cook 1993]. Consider a graph in which nodes are states in $\Sigma \times M$ and there is an edge from μ to μ' just when $s \mathbin{!} l$. Then $s @ l$ is satisfied by μ and μ' just when either there is a finite path from μ to μ' on which μ' is the only state in which $\neg(l \leq p < l + \#s)$, or $t'_\mu = \infty$ and there is an infinite path from μ on which for all states $l \leq p < l + \#s$.

Suppose μ and μ' satisfy $s; t; u @ l$, there is a suitable path in the graph for $s; t; u @ l$, this path can be divided at the first node where $\neg(l + \#s \leq p < l + \#s + \#t)$ to get paths that show the right hand side is satisfied. Likewise if the right hand side is satisfied, that gives two paths that can be catenated to show the left hand side is satisfied. □

7   Coupling source and machine levels

In order to use a machine to simulate source level computations, we will need an example correspondence between source and machine states. This can be represented by a specification R dependent on only σ and μ.

An example of such a specification is given as follows. Let n be the number of components, aside from t_σ, comprising Σ, and let v_j, for $0 \leq j < n$, refer to component j. Define two one-one functions from integers

$$\textbf{abs}_{int} : int \rightarrow int$$
$$\textbf{abs}_{int}.i = i$$
$$\textbf{abs}_{bool} : int \rightarrow bool$$
$$\textbf{abs}_{bool}.0 = \textbf{false}$$
$$\textbf{abs}_{bool}.i = \textbf{true} \quad \text{for } i \neq 0$$

and a one-one function from $0, ..., n - 1$ to memory addresses

$$\textbf{addr} : 0, ..., n - 1 \rightarrow int$$

The R predicate is then

$$(t_\sigma = t_\mu) \wedge \langle \forall j : 0, ..., n - 1 \cdot v_j = \textbf{abs}.(m.(\textbf{addr}.j)) \rangle$$

8   Code generator specification

Consider the following "thought experiment". We wish to simulate the behaviour of a source program S starting in a state σ. We initialize a machine to a state μ that is related to σ by R and has $p = l$, and then run program $s @ l$. We check the final state μ' and consider all high-level states σ' that correspond to it. If they all could be reached by running S, we say that $s @ l$ has simulated S. If for all l and all initial states σ, the specification $s @ l$ must simulate the high level program S, then s is a suitable translation of S for the given representation relation R.

We can easily formalize the thought experiment as the following definition

---

Definition   We say that s *simulates* S, in notation sim.s.S, just if

$$\langle \forall l; \sigma; \mu \cdot R \wedge p = l \Rightarrow \langle \forall \mu' \cdot s @ l \Rightarrow \langle \forall \sigma' \cdot R' \Rightarrow S \rangle \rangle \rangle$$

In order to express this as refinement of either machine or source level specifications, we define two operators parameterized by R.

$$P{\downarrow}S \quad \because \quad \langle \forall \sigma; \sigma' \cdot R \wedge R' \wedge P \Rightarrow S \rangle$$
$$P{\uparrow}V \quad \because \quad \langle \exists \mu; \mu' \cdot R \wedge R' \wedge P \wedge V \rangle$$

When P is omitted, it defaults to **true**. Note that, for any P, $(P{\uparrow})$ and $(P{\downarrow})$ are functions related by the Galois property

$$(P{\downarrow}S \quad \because \quad V) \equiv (S \quad \because \quad P{\uparrow}V) \tag{2}$$

The definition of sim.s.S can be rewritten as any of

$$\langle \forall l \cdot (p = l){\downarrow}S \quad \because \quad s @ l \rangle \tag{3}$$
$$\langle \forall l \cdot S \quad \because \quad (p = l){\uparrow}(s @ l) \rangle$$
$${\downarrow}S \quad \because \quad s @ p$$

It is reasonable —on the grounds of the thought experiment— to insist on the following restrictions on R.

$$\langle \forall l \cdot \langle \forall \sigma \cdot \langle \exists \mu \cdot R \wedge p = l \rangle \rangle \rangle$$
$$\langle \forall \mu \cdot \langle \exists! \sigma \cdot R \rangle \rangle$$
$$t_\sigma = t_\mu \quad \because \quad R$$

It can easily be seen that the example R defined in Section 7 meets these three requirements.

9   Prelude to code generator derivation

In the next section I will sketch the derivation of a code generator using the example specifications of the machine language, source language, and representation relation described above. The goal is to derive a function C such that for all abstract syntax terms S

$$\text{sim}.(C.S).S$$

Before doing so we need a number of results relating some of the concepts defined above.

9.1 Nice strings

A little thought shows that $\text{sim}.t.T \wedge \text{sim}.u.U$ does not —as one might hope— imply $\text{sim}.(t;u).(T;U)$ The difficulty is that t need not leave the program counter pointing to the first instruction of u.

It is not possible to simply add the requirement that

$$p' = p + \#s \quad \because \quad s @ p$$

for all strings s generated by our code generator, because it is quite possible that $s @ p$ will loop forever. If a program is executed from a state from which it may take an infinite amount of time, it can not be expected to set the program counter to a particular value. This is a consequence of our choice of the *weakest* progressive prefixed point.

So we make the following definition

Definition   A string s is called *nice* just if

$$p' = p + \#s \quad \because \quad s @ p \wedge t'_\mu \neq \infty$$

We notate this as $\heartsuit s$.

Definition   A string s will be a *correct compilation* of an abstract syntax term S just if

$$\text{sim}.s.S$$
$$\heartsuit s$$

9.2 Useful facts

Because R defines a function onto the source state space, it has some useful manipulative properties.

Theorem (4) $\downarrow$ over $\circ$. For specifications P and Q

$$\downarrow(P \circ Q) \quad \because \quad \downarrow P \circ \downarrow Q$$

Theorem (5)   If P is a machine level condition,

$$\downarrow(Q \, \langle\!\langle P \rangle\!\rangle \, R) \quad \because \quad \downarrow Q \, \langle\!\langle P \rangle\!\rangle \, \downarrow R$$

Definition   A specification V is *explosive* just if

$$\langle \exists \mu' \cdot t'_\mu = \infty \wedge V \rangle \quad \because \quad \langle \forall \mu' \cdot t'_\mu = \infty \Rightarrow V \rangle$$

That is, just if for all initial states for which V does not specify termination, V does not specify anything stronger than progressiveness. The notation $\clubsuit V$ will be used to say that V is explosive.

> **Theorem**   Source explosiveness. For all abstract syntax terms S, we have $\clubsuit \downarrow S$.

Clearly, if $\heartsuit s$ and $\heartsuit t$, then $\heartsuit(s;t)$. Furthermore, $\heartsuit$nil so nice strings form a submonoid of the strings. But we can also see that if $s;t$ is started at its beginning and terminates then it will execute by first executing s and then t.

> **Theorem (6)**   Nice catenation. If
>
> - $\heartsuit s,\ \heartsuit t,\ \clubsuit V,\ \clubsuit W$,
>
> - $V \ \because\ s \ @\ p$
>
> - $W \ \because\ t \ @\ p$
>
> then $V \circ W \ \because\ s;t \ @\ p$.

> **Theorem (7)**   Storing.
>
> $$\downarrow((ok)^{v\,m}_{\textsf{abs}.a}) \ \because\ \textsf{store addr}.m \ @\ p$$

> **Theorem (8)**   Jumping. If
>
> - $\heartsuit s,\ \heartsuit t,\ \clubsuit V,\ \clubsuit W$,
>
> - $V \ \because\ s \ @\ p$
>
> - $W \ \because\ t \ @\ p$
>
> then
>
> $$V \ \langle a \neq 0 \rangle \ W \ \because\ u \ @\ p$$
>
> where $u = \textsf{zjump}\ (2 + \#s); s; \textsf{jump}\ (1 + \#t); t$

> **Notation**
>
> $$\textsf{mtick} \ \because\ a' = a \wedge m' = m \wedge t' = t + 1$$

> **Theorem (9)**   Looping. If
>
> - $\heartsuit s,\ \heartsuit t,\ \clubsuit V,\ \clubsuit W$,
>
> - $V \ \because\ s \ @\ p$
>
> - $W \ \because\ t \ @\ p$
>
> then $V \circ (W \circ \textsf{mtick} \circ u \ @\ l \ \langle a \neq 0 \rangle \ ok_{\textsf{M}}) \ \because\ u \ @\ l$ where $u = s; \textsf{zjump}\ (2 + \#t); t; \textsf{jump}\ (-1 - \#t - \#s)$

> **Theorem** (10)   The expression theorem. If f is a function from either the integers or the booleans to source level specifications, and E is an expression of the right type, then
>
> $$f.E \quad \because \quad (\text{abs}.a' = E \land ok_\Sigma) \circ f.(\text{abs}.a)$$

9.3 Expression correctness

We will say that a string e is a correct compilation of an expression E just if

$$\langle \forall l \cdot (p = l) \downarrow (\text{abs}.a' = E \land ok_\Sigma) \quad \because \quad e @ l \rangle$$
$$\heartsuit e$$

10 Code generator derivation

Throughout this section, we will assume as induction hypotheses that t is a correct compilation of T, u is a correct compilation of U, and e is a correct compilation of E.

The goal is to find a correct compilation of program S whatever its form.

10.1 The nil statement

We have $S = $ nil

$$
\begin{array}{ll}
\quad \downarrow ok_\Sigma & \quad \{ \downarrow ok_\Sigma \quad \because \quad ok_\mathrm{M} \} \\
\because \quad ok_\mathrm{M} & \\
\because \quad \text{nil} @ p &
\end{array}
$$

10.2 The sequential composition statement

We have $S = T; U$.

$$
\begin{array}{ll}
\quad \downarrow (T \circ U) & \{ \downarrow \text{ over } \circ \ (4) \} \\
\because \quad \downarrow T \circ \downarrow U & \{ \text{nice catenation (6), induction hypotheses} \} \\
\because \quad t; u @ p &
\end{array}
$$

So $\mathsf{C}.(S; T)$ can be $\mathsf{C}.S; \mathsf{C}.T$.

10.3 The assignment statement

We have $S = (v_m := E)$.

$$
\begin{array}{ll}
\quad \downarrow ((ok_\Sigma)_E^{v_m}) & \{ \text{the expression theorem (10)} \} \\
\because \quad \downarrow ((\text{abs}.a' = E \land ok_\Sigma) \circ (ok_\Sigma)_{\text{abs}.a}^{v_m}) & \{ \downarrow \text{ over } \circ \ (4) \} \\
\because \quad \downarrow (\text{abs}.a' = E \land ok_\Sigma) \circ \downarrow ((ok_\Sigma)_{\text{abs}.a}^{v_m}) & \\
\multicolumn{2}{l}{\{ \text{storing (7), nice catenation (6), induction hypotheses} \}} \\
\because \quad e; \text{store } addr.m &
\end{array}
$$

10.4   The if statement

We have $S = $ **if** E **then** T **else** U **fi**.

$$\downarrow(T \ \langle\!E\!\rangle \ U) \qquad \{\text{the expression theorem (10)}\}$$

$\cdot:\quad \downarrow((\text{abs}.a' = E \wedge ok_\Sigma) \circ (T \ \langle\!\text{abs}.a\!\rangle \ U)) \qquad \{\downarrow \text{ over } \circ \ (4)\}$

$\cdot:\quad \downarrow(\text{abs}.a' = E \wedge ok_\Sigma) \circ \downarrow(T \ \langle\!\text{abs}.a\!\rangle \ U) \qquad \{\downarrow \text{ over } \langle\!\rangle \ (5)\}$

$\cdot:\quad \downarrow(\text{abs}.a' = E \wedge ok_\Sigma) \circ (\downarrow T \ \langle\!\text{abs}.a\!\rangle \ \downarrow U)$

$\{\text{jumping (8); nice catenation (6), induction hypotheses}\}$

$\cdot:\quad e; \text{zjump } 2 + \#t; t; \text{jump } 1 + \#u; u @ p$

10.5   The while statement

We have $S = $ **while** E **do** T **od**.

Now (3) says we want an s such that

$$(p = l)\downarrow S \quad \cdot: \quad s @ l$$

From the laws about while loops, only one has S on the left-hand side of a '$\cdot:$': induction. But to use induction requires the S to be isolated.

$\{\text{Galois connection (2)}\}$

$\equiv \quad S \quad \cdot: \quad (p = l)\uparrow(s @ l)$

Let $U^{\cdot} = (p = l)\uparrow(s @ l)$ and apply (1).

$\Leftarrow \quad (t'_\sigma \geq t_\sigma \quad \cdot: \quad U) \wedge (\text{wh}.U \quad \cdot: \quad U)$

The first conjunct easily reduces to **true**. The derivation continues with the second conjunct:

$\{\text{definition wh and } U\}$

$\equiv \quad T \circ (t_\sigma :=_\Sigma t_\sigma + 1) \circ (p = l)\uparrow(s @ l) \ \langle\!E\!\rangle \ ok_\Sigma \quad \cdot: \quad (p = l)\uparrow(s @ l)$

$\{\text{Galois connection (2)}\}$

$\equiv \quad (p = l)\downarrow T \circ (t_\sigma :=_\Sigma t_\sigma + 1) \circ (p = l)\uparrow(s @ l) \ \langle\!E\!\rangle \ ok_\Sigma \quad \cdot: \quad s @ l$

The remainder of the derivation is fairly straight forward and works towards being able to apply the looping theorem (9) to finally get

$\Leftarrow \quad s = e; \text{zjump } 2 + \#t; t; \text{jump } - 1 - \#t - \#e$

10.6   Summary of the compiler

Assuming the existence of a correct code generator CE for expressions, the results of this section constitute a proof that the compiler

$$\text{C.nil} \ = \ \text{nil}$$
$$\text{C.}(T; U) \ = \ \text{C.}T; \text{C.}U$$
$$\text{C.}(v_m := E) \ = \ \text{CE.}E; \text{store addr.}m$$
$$\text{C.}(\textbf{if } E \textbf{ then } T \textbf{ else } U \textbf{ fi}) \ = \ \text{CE.}E; \text{zjump } 2 + \#\text{C.}T; \text{C.}T;$$
$$\text{jump } 1 + \#\text{C.}U; \text{C.}U$$
$$\text{C.}(\textbf{while } E \textbf{ do } T \textbf{ od}) \ = \ \text{CE.}E; \text{zjump } 2 + \#\text{C.}T; \text{C.}T;$$
$$\text{jump } - 1 - \#\text{C.}T - \#\text{CE.}E$$

is correct.

11 Conclusion

In the preceding I have outlined an approach to the predicative semantics of machine code and given a small example of its application to the specification and derivation of a simple compiler. Obviously, the compiler arrived at above could be written informally with much less effort. But, the simple compiler of the paper is only an example. The specification of the compiler is generic; it is valid for all source languages, machine languages, and representation relations, provided the semantics of the source language is given predicatively, and the machine language and representation relation meet the conditions mentioned in the paper. Similarly, most of the theorems used in the derivation of the compiler are generic and the techniques used in the derivation are reusable.

Along the way to compiler correctness we have developed a predicative interpretation for machine languages. Although it is illustrated by a simple machine language, it is suitable for machine languages with more complex instruction sets and more complex state spaces. This predicative interpretation may also be employed for other problems such as processor verification and reasoning about hand coded machine code.

Clearly there is work to be done on using the framework presented above for more elaborate and realistic source and target languages, for dealing with optimizing compilers, and for automating some of the theorem proving. These and other topics are further addressed in [Norvell 1993].

Acknowledgements

I would like to thank He Jifeng for helping me understand while loops, and Steve Cook for providing a superior proof of the separation theorem. I especially thank Ric Hehner, not only for many specific contributions to this paper, but also for many years of guidance and support in many ways. I am grateful to the Natural Sciences and Engineering Research Council for financial support, the Computing Laboratory at Oxford for logistical support, and especially to the Department of Computer Science at the University of Toronto for providing both.

References

[Cook 1993] Stephen A. Cook, 1993. Personal Communication.

[Hehner 1984] Eric C.R. Hehner. Predicative programming. *Communications of the ACM*, 27(2):134–151, 1984.

[Hehner 1993] Eric C.R. Hehner. *A Practical Theory of Programming*. Springer-Verlag, 1993.

[Hoare 1990] C.A.R. Hoare. Refinement algebra proves correctness of compiling specifications. Technical Report PRG-TR-6-90, Oxford University Computing Laboratory, Oxford University, 1990.

[Hoare 1992] C.A.R Hoare. Programs are predicates. In *Meeting of the Fifth Generation Project*. ICOT, 1992.

[Jones 1980] Neil D. Jones, editor. *Semantics-Directed Compiler Generation.* Number 94 in Lecture Notes in Computer Science. Springer-Verlag, 1980.

[Manasse and Nelson 1984] Mark Manasse and Greg Nelson. Correct compilation of control structures. Technical Report Technical Memorandum 11272-840909-09TM, AT&T Bell Laboratories, 1984.

[McCarthy and Painter 1967] J. McCarthy and J. Painter. Correctness of a compiler for arithmetic expressions. In *Proceedings of Symposia in Applied Mathematics, Volume XIX*, 1967.

[Milne and Strachey 1974] R. E. Milne and C. Strachey, editors. *A Theory of Programming Language Semantics.* Chapman & Hall, London, 1974.

[Morris 1973] F. Lockwood Morris. Advice on structuring compilers and proving them correct. In *Proceedings of the ACM Conferfence on Principles of Programming Languages*, 1973.

[Mosses 1980] Peter D. Mosses. A constructive approach to complier correctness. In [Jones 1980]. 1980.

[Norvell 1993] Theodore S. Norvell. *A Predicative Theory of Machine Languages and its Application to Compiler Correctness.* PhD thesis, University of Toronto, 1993.

[Polak 1981] Wolfgang Polak. *Compiler Specification and Verification.* Number 124 in Lecture Notes in Computer Science. Springer-Verlag, 1981. Also a Stanford Ph.D. thesis.

[Sampaio 1993] Augusto Sampaio. *An Algebraic Approach to Compiler Design.* PhD thesis, Oxford University, 1993.

[Tarski 1955] Alfred Tarski. A lattice-theoretical fixpoint theorem and its applications. *Pacific Journal of Mathematics*, 5:285–309, 1955.

[Thatcher *et al.* 1980] James W. Thatcher, Eric G. Wagner, and Jesse B. Wright. More advice on structuring compilers and proving them correct. In [Jones 1980]. 1980.

Laws of Parallel Programming with Shared Variables

Xu Qiwen*

Department of Computer Science, Åbo Akademi,
Lemminkainenkatu 14, SF-20520 Turku, Finland

He Jifeng

Oxford University Computing Laboratory,
8-11 Keble Road, Oxford OX1 3QD, England, UK.

Abstract

Extending the laws of sequential programming, we investigate laws of
parallel programs in which processes communicate via shared variables.
A rich and elegant set of laws, which resemble closely the laws of message
passing concurrency, is presented, and this forms an algebraic framework
of refinement and verification.

1   Introduction

In two main paradigms of parallel programming, processes communicate by
passing messages or accessing shared variables. In contrary to the extensive
study of algebraic theories of message passing concurrency [BW90, Ho85, Mi89],
little has been done on the algebraic side of shared variable concurrency. Verification of shared variable parallel programs usually employs an assertional
system (first order or temporal). Such methods have evolved over a period
of more than fifteen years, with one branch of them reported, for example,
in [OG76, Jo81, Br85, Sti88, Stø90, XH91, Jo91] among others. On the one
hand, they seem to be quite effective in dealing with some, even non-trivial,
applications, but on the other hand, using the methods to verify some other
programs, often completely trivial ones, needs human ingenuity.

Driven by this, we set out to investigate algebraic theory as an alternative method to a purely assertional one. We choose as the programming language a variant of the one used by Owicki & Gries in [OG76]. It turns out
that programs in this language are subject to a set of rich and elegant laws,
which, can be regarded as an extension of Hoare and others' work on sequential
programs [Hoare et al 87], and resembles closely the laws of message passing
concurrency. Refinement is expressed through an algebraic equation as in the
sequential case, and can thus be reasoned about by these laws. Moreover, based
on a specification-oriented semantics, refinement and verification can be used
together in showing that a program satisfies its requirements. In this respect,
the algebraic laws seem to be particularly useful, in transforming a program

---

*Partially supported by Esprit-BRA project 6021 (REACT) and Finnish Akademi Project
Irene

from a structure which can be easily verified to have correctly implemented a specification to a more efficient one during top-down design, and in transforming a program the other way round in a-posteriori verification. The close resemblance between the algebraic theories of message passing and shared variable based concurrency has stimulated the integration of these two paradigms [He92].

Different applications of the programs have different correctness requirements, and are therefore subject to different laws. The laws presented in this paper are based on a trace (state transition sequence here) semantics, and were shown to be sound in [Xu92].

An important goal in algebraic theories for concurrency is to find out whether the proposed the set of laws are sufficient to eliminate complex operator, which is usually the parallel composition. In our case, the *await*-statement is also more complicated than other sequential operators, and actually is somehow connected with the parallel composition, which in turn makes removing concurrency less straightforward. In this paper, we limited ourselves to removing parallel and *await* operators only from a flat concurrency program, namely, program that is a parallel composition of a number of sequential programs but will not be used itself in parallel with any other programs. The paper concludes with a discussion, in which the trace model and some related work are mentioned.

2   Language

Let us first introduce the programming language. The syntax and a brief explanation of various language structures is as follows:

$$S ::= skip \mid stop \mid X := E \mid < S > \mid S_1 \sqcap S_2 \mid S_1 ; S_2 \mid if\, G_1 \square \ldots \square G_n\, fi \mid$$
$$while\, b\, do\, S\, od \mid await\, b\, then\, S\, end \mid S_1 \parallel S_2$$
$$G ::= b \rightarrow S$$

The statement *skip* has no effect on any program variables, and terminates immediately. Deadlock is modelled by *stop* which can never be activated. In the assignment statement, X represents a vector of variables $(x_1, ..., x_n)$, and E represents a vector of expressions $(e_1, ..., e_n)$. The computations of expressions $e_1, \cdots, e_n$ in the assignment statement is assumed to be terminating, and moreover the execution of the complete statement is considered as atomic, with $x_1, \cdots, x_n$ being set to the values computed for $e_1, \cdots, e_n$. The atomic execution of P is represented as $< P >$, and is referred to as an atomic command. Other atomic commands are *skip*, *stop* and assignment statements. The nondeterministic choice of P and Q, written as $P \sqcap Q$, behaves either like P or Q. In sequential composition $P;Q$, P is executed first, and when it terminates, Q is executed. When more than one guards hold in the conditional statement $if\, b_1 \rightarrow S_1 \square \ldots \square b_n \rightarrow S_n\, fi$, any of the corresponding programs S_i can be selected for execution; when none of the guards hold, the process is deadlocked. Iteration is represented by *while b do P od* as usual. In both conditional and iteration statements, the evaluation of the boolean test b is atomic, but an environment can interrupt between the boolean tests and the first actions of the corresponding bodies. In order to limit interference, we stipulate that the variables appearing in the boolean test can not be written by other processes. As noted in [St90], this constraint does not reduce the set of possible algorithms.

The two more complicated structures are the parallel composition and the *await*-statement. There are several different views, of which each is suitable for a certain class of applications, regarding the concurrent execution of a system. One often adopted view is to consider the execution of each program as composed of atomic actions, and concurrency is modelled by interleaving. For $P \parallel Q$, P and Q are executed concurrently, with atomic actions from the two processes interleaving each other. Process $P \parallel Q$ is blocked if and only if both of them are blocked. Synchronisation and mutual exclusion are achieved by *await b then P end*, which in turn is the cause of a process to become blocked. When b is true, P will be executed without interruption. If the body P loops forever then the whole process is led to a failure, while if P terminates then the execution of the statement is considered to be atomic. When b does not hold, the process is blocked and can only become active again when an environment has set b to true.

A program in general will be used in parallel with some other programs, and in this case, it is said to be open. In some other cases, we know from the expected application that a program will not be used in parallel with other programs, and we say it is closed. A closed program is denoted by $< P >$, where P can be either an open or a closed program (P in general also contains a number of parallel components). Parallel composition of n processes $S_1, \ldots, S_n$, $S_1 \parallel (S_2 \parallel (\ldots \parallel S_n) \ldots)$, is simply written as $S_1 \parallel S_2 \parallel \ldots \parallel S_n$ or $\parallel_{1 \leq i \leq n} S_i$. The same convention is used for nondeterministic choice $\sqcap$. For notational convenience, let $\parallel_0 = skip$.

3 Algebraic laws

This section presents the main laws governing the language. The laws concerning sequential operators are mostly the same as in [Hoare et al 87].

- Nondeterminism
  Nondeterministic choice is idempotent, symmetric and associative:
  1. $P \sqcap Q = Q \sqcap P$
  2. $P \sqcap (Q \sqcap R) = (P \sqcap Q) \sqcap R$
  3. $P \sqcap P = P$

- Conditional
  When there is only one guarded program to choose, and it is always possible, the conditional behaves the same as that program:
  1. $if\ true \rightarrow P\ fi = P$.
  If one guarded program is always enabled, it can always be chosen:
  2. $if\ true \rightarrow P \Box b_1 \rightarrow P_1 \Box \cdots \Box b_n \rightarrow P_n\ fi$
  $= if\ \neg(b_1 \vee b_2 \vee \cdots \vee b_n) \rightarrow P \Box b_1 \rightarrow P_1 \Box \cdots \Box b_n \rightarrow P_n\ fi \sqcap P$
  When one branch is never enabled, the meaning of the statement remains the same if that branch is deleted:
  3. $if\ false \rightarrow P \Box \underline{gc}\ fi = if\ \underline{gc}\ fi$,   where gc is any guarded command.
  The order of alternative is irrelevant:
  4. $if\ G_1 \Box \cdots \Box G_n\ fi = if\ G_{i_1} \Box \cdots \Box G_{i_n}\ fi$,   provided $i_1, \cdots i_n$

is a permutation of $1, \cdots, n$.

If none of the boolean guards b_1, b_2,...,b_n are true, the statement behaves like *stop*. Thus the alternative with *stop* guarded by $\neg(b_1 \vee \cdots \vee b_n)$ can be freely added or deleted:

5. $if\, b_1 \rightarrow P_1 \square \cdots \square b_n \rightarrow P_n\, fi$
$= if\, b_1 \rightarrow P_1 \square \cdots \square b_n \rightarrow P_n \square \neg(b_1 \vee \cdots \vee b_n) \rightarrow stop\, fi.$

Corollary $if\, fi = stop$

Conditional distributes through nondeterministic choice:

6. $if\, b \rightarrow P \sqcap Q \square \underline{gc}\, fi = if\, b \rightarrow P \square \underline{gc}\, fi \sqcap if\, b \rightarrow Q \square \underline{gc}\, fi.$

Two alternatives with the same guard or program can be merged:

7. $if\, b \rightarrow P \square b \rightarrow Q \square \underline{gc}\, fi = if\, b \rightarrow P \sqcap Q \square \underline{gc}\, fi$
8. $if\, b \rightarrow P \square c \rightarrow P \square \underline{gc}\, fi = if\, b \vee c \rightarrow P \square \underline{gc}\, fi$

The following law allows the removal of the nested conditional statement:

9. $if\, b \rightarrow if\, b_1 \rightarrow P_1 \square \cdots \square b_n \rightarrow P_n\, fi \square \underline{gc}\, fi$
$= if\, b \wedge b_1 \rightarrow P_1 \square \cdots \square b \wedge b_n \rightarrow P_n \square b \wedge \neg(b_1 \vee \cdots \vee b_n) \rightarrow stop \square \underline{gc}\, fi.$

- Sequential composition

  Sequential composition is associative with *skip* as its unit and *stop* as its left zero:

  1. $P; (Q; R) = (P; Q); R$
  2. $skip; P = P; skip = P$
  3. $stop; P = stop$

  It distributes through $\sqcap$:

  4. $(P \sqcap Q); R = (P; R) \sqcap (Q; R)$
  5. $R; (P \sqcap Q) = (R; P) \sqcap (R; Q)$

  It distributes through conditional in its left argument:

  6. $if\, b_1 \rightarrow P_1 \square ... \square b_n \rightarrow P_n\, fi; Q = if\, b_1 \rightarrow P_1; Q \square ... \square b_n \rightarrow P_n; Q\, fi.$

- Assignment

  We have assumed that the execution of an assignment is atomic, therefore assigning the value of a variable to itself does not change anything:

  1. $X := X = skip$

  Moreover, such a vacuous assignment can be added to any other assignment without changing its effect:

  2. $(x, y := e, y) = x := e$

  The list of variables and expressions may be subjected to the same permutation without changing its effect:

  3. $(x, y, z := e, f, g) = (y, x, z := f, e, g)$

- Await

  It distributes over nondeterministic choice:

  1. $await\, b\, then\, P \sqcap Q\, end = await\, b\, then\, P\, end \sqcap await\, b\, then\, Q\, end$

  When the *await* statement is executed, it body is treated as an atomic action:

  2. $await\, b\, then\, S\, end = await\, b\, then\, <S>\, end$
  3. $<X := E; X := F> = <X := F[E/X]>$
  4. $<X := E; if\, b_1 \rightarrow P_1 \square, ..., \square b_n \rightarrow P_n\, fi>$
  $= <if\, b_1[E/X] \rightarrow X := E; P_1 \square, ..., \square b_n[E/X] \rightarrow X := E; P_n\, fi>.$
  5. $<X := E; await\, b\, then\, S\, end>$
  $= <await\, b[E/X]\, then\, X := E; S\, end>$

  If several *await*-statements composed in parallel are able to proceed, then the choice among them is arbitrary:

6. $<\|_{1 \leq i \leq n} (await\ b_i\ then\ P_i\ end;Q_i) >$
$= < if\ b_1 \rightarrow P_1;(\|_{i \neq 1} (await\ b_i\ then\ P_i\ end;Q_i) \| Q_1)$
$\quad \square\ b_2 \rightarrow P_2;(\|_{i \neq 2} (await\ b_i\ then\ P_i\ end;Q_i) \| Q_2)$
$\quad \ldots\ldots$
$\quad \square\ b_n \rightarrow P_n;(\|_{i \neq n} (await\ b_i\ then\ P_i\ end;Q_i) \| Q_n)$
$\quad fi >$

This law is actually a collection of laws rather than a single one, quite like the expansion theorem of CCS [Mi89]. Some special forms of it are as follows:

$< await\ true\ then\ S\ end > = < S >$
$< await\ false\ then\ S\ end > = stop.$

As an unary operator, $<>$ propagates through all combinators but parallel composition:

7. $< P \sqcap Q > = < P > \sqcap < Q >$
8. $< P;Q > = << P >;< Q >>$
9. $< if\ b_1 \rightarrow P_1 \square \cdots \square b_n \rightarrow P_n\ fi >$
$= < if\ b_1 \rightarrow < P_1 > \square \cdots \square b_n \rightarrow < P_n > \ fi >$
10. $< while\ b\ do\ P\ od > = < while\ b\ do\ < P >\ od >$

$<>$ has no effect on atomic commands:

11. $< a > = a$ if a is an atomic command.

- Parallel

  Parallel composition is symmetric and associative:

  1. $P \| Q = Q \| P$
  2. $(P \| Q) \| R = P \| (Q \| R)$

  It distributes over nondeterministic choice:

  3a. $P \| (Q \sqcap R) = (P \| Q) \sqcap (P \| R)$
  3b. $(P \sqcap Q) \| R = (P \| R) \sqcap (Q \| R)$

  $skip$ is the unit of this operator:

  4. $P \| skip = P$

  Because the boolean test does not involve shared variables, parallel composition distributes over conditional:

  5. $if\ b_1 \rightarrow P_1 \square \cdots \square b_n \rightarrow P_n\ fi \| R$
  $= if\ b_1 \rightarrow P_1 \| R \square \cdots \square b_n \rightarrow P_n \| R \square \neg(b_1 \vee \cdots \vee b_n) \rightarrow R; stop\ fi.$

  Corollary $stop \| P = P; stop.$

  In the following a and d are atomic commands. The choice of which one runs first is arbitrary:

  6. $(a;P) \| (d;Q) = (a;(P \| (d;Q))) \sqcap (d;((a;P) \| Q))$

- Iteration

  1. $while\ b\ do\ while\ b\ do\ P\ od\ od = while\ b\ do\ P\ od.$
  2. $while\ b\ do\ P\ od = if\ b \rightarrow P; while\ b\ do\ P\ od \square \neg b \rightarrow skip\ fi$
  3. $while\ b\ do\ P \sqcap Q\ od \sqcap while\ b\ do\ P\ od = while\ b\ do\ P \sqcap Q\ od$

4   Refinement

The intended meaning of $P = Q$ is that the two programs are identical as far as any external observations are concerned. Therefore, they refine each other. If one program is considered to "improve" another when the first one is more determinate than the second, then a usual refinement order $\sqsubseteq$ can be defined as follows.

Definition 1 $P \sqsubseteq Q$ *if* $P \sqcap Q = P$

To distinguish the two refinement notions, we call relation = bi-directional refinement, and $\sqsubseteq$ refinement. The following laws hold:

- Ordering
  $\sqsubseteq$ is a partial order, that is, it satisfies
  1. $P \sqsubseteq P$
  2. If $P \sqsubseteq Q$ and $Q \sqsubseteq P$, then $P = Q$.
  3. If $P \sqsubseteq Q$ and $Q \sqsubseteq R$, then $P \sqsubseteq R$.
  Moreover, $P \sqcap Q$ is the greatest lower bound of P and Q:
  4. $P \sqcap Q \sqsubseteq P$ and $P \sqcap Q \sqsubseteq Q$
  5. If $R \sqsubseteq P$ and $R \sqsubseteq Q$, then $R \sqsubseteq P \sqcap Q$
  Nondeterminism 3 and Ordering 4 imply the expected result that bi-directional refinement is stronger than refinement. Combining this with Ordering 2, it follows that $P = Q$ if and only if $P \sqsubseteq Q$ and $Q \sqsubseteq P$.

With the newly defined relation $\sqsubseteq$, law Iteration 3 can be rewritten as

$$while\, b\, do\, P\, od \;\sqsubseteq\; while\, b\, do\, Q\, od \qquad if\; P \sqsubseteq Q$$

In a program, if we pick out a subprogram of it, then the system is divided into the selected subprogram and the remaining part with a 'hole'. This remaining part is usually called a *context*. Formally, a program context is considered as a function from programs to programs, and is expected to be monotonic with respect to a refinement order.

Proposition 1 *If F is a function from programs to programs, and for all programs P, Q, $F(P \sqcap Q) \sqsubseteq F(P) \sqcap F(Q)$, then F is monotonic.*

Proof. Standard.

Corollary 1 *If F is a function from programs to programs, and for all programs P, Q, $F(P \sqcap Q) = F(P) \sqcap F(Q)$, then F is monotonic.*

Theorem 1 *If $P \sqsubseteq Q$ and C is a program context, $C(P) \sqsubseteq C(Q)$.*

Proof. By induction to show C satisfies the condition in proposition 1.

Corollary 2 *If $P = Q$ and C is a program context, $C(P) = C(Q)$.*

5 Small applications

We now look at some small examples.

Example 1. Consider a simple program $x := x + 1 \parallel x := x + 1$. We can perform the following calculation:

$$
\begin{aligned}
&x := x + 1 \parallel x := x + 1 && \{\text{Parallel 6}\} \\
&= (x := x + 1; x := x + 1) \sqcap (x := x + 1; x := x + 1) && \{\text{Nondeter. 3}\} \\
&= x := x + 1; x := x + 1
\end{aligned}
$$

Furthermore, if the program is closed, we have

$$< x := x + 1 \parallel x := x + 1 > \qquad \{\text{Corollary 2}\}$$
$$=< x := x + 1; x := x + 1 > \qquad \{\text{Await 3}\}$$
$$=< x := x + 2 > \qquad \{\text{Await 11}\}$$
$$= x := x + 2$$

When the program context is of a special form, several reasoning steps can be merged. The following proposition applies to the case that the context is sequential, in the sense that no parts from the context will be executed in parallel with the 'hole'.

Proposition 2 *If C is a sequential context and $< P >=< Q >$, then $< C[P] >=< C[Q] >$.*

Proof. Obvious from the laws about $<>$, which indicate that it propagates through all the sequential combinators.

Example 2. A quick look at the program $< await\ x = 1\ then\ await\ x = 0\ then\ P\ end\ end >$ reveals that it can not proceed, we now prove it is equivalent to *stop*.

$$< await\ x = 1\ then\ await\ x = 0\ then\ P\ end\ end > \qquad \{\text{Await 6}\}$$
$$=< if\ x = 1 \rightarrow await\ x = 0\ then\ P\ end\ fi > \qquad \{\text{Await 6, prop 2}\}$$
$$=< if\ x = 1 \rightarrow if\ x = 0 \rightarrow P\ fi\ fi > \qquad \{\text{Conditional 9}\}$$
$$=< if\ x = 1 \wedge x = 0 \rightarrow P \,\square\, x = 1 \wedge x \neq 0 \rightarrow stop\ fi > \{\text{Logic}\}$$
$$=< if\ false \rightarrow P \,\square\, x = 1 \rightarrow stop\ fi > \qquad \{\text{Conditional 3}\}$$
$$=< if\ x = 1 \rightarrow stop\ fi > \qquad \{\text{Conditional 5}\}$$
$$=< if\ x = 1 \rightarrow stop \,\square\, x \neq 1 \rightarrow stop\ fi > \qquad \{\text{Conditional 8}\}$$
$$=< if\ x = 1 \vee x \neq 1 \rightarrow stop\ fi > \qquad \{\text{Conditional 1}\}$$
$$=< stop > \qquad \{\text{Await 11}\}$$
$$= stop$$

Example 3. Consider another very simple example,

$$< await\ x = 1\ then\ x := 2\ end \parallel x := 1 > .$$

Obviously, this program will not deadlock and the final value of x is either 1 or 2. Note for this purpose, it is sufficient to prove the program is better than $x := 1 \sqcap x := 2$, and we propose to handle this problem by algebraic reasoning, but first let us introduce a derived law.

$$<\|_{1 \leq i \leq n} (await\ b_i\ then\ S_i\ end; Q_i) \parallel (X := E; Q) >$$
$$= <\|_{1 \leq i \leq n} (await\ b_i\ then\ S_i\ end; Q_i) \parallel (await\ true\ then\ X := E\ end; Q) >$$
$$= < if\ b_1 \rightarrow S_1; (\|_{i \neq 1} (await\ b_i\ then\ S_i\ end; Q_i) \parallel Q_1 \parallel (X := E; Q))$$
$$\square\ b_2 \rightarrow S_2; (\|_{i \neq 2} (await\ b_i\ then\ S_i\ end; Q_i) \parallel Q_2 \parallel (X := E; Q))$$
$$\cdots\cdots$$
$$\square\ b_n \rightarrow S_n; (\|_{i \neq n} (await\ b_i\ then\ S_i\ end; Q_i) \parallel Q_n \parallel (X := E; Q))$$
$$\square\ true \rightarrow X := E; (\|_{1 \leq i \leq n} (await\ b_i\ then\ S_i\ end; Q_i) \parallel Q)\ fi >$$
$$= < if\ b_1 \rightarrow S_1; (\|_{i \neq 1} (await\ \bar{b}_i\ then\ S_i\ end; Q_i) \parallel Q_1 \parallel (X := E; Q))$$
$$\square\ b_2 \rightarrow S_2; (\|_{i \neq 2} (await\ b_i\ then\ S_i\ end; Q_i) \parallel Q_2 \parallel (X := E; Q))$$
$$\cdots\cdots$$
$$\square\ b_n \rightarrow S_n; (\|_{i \neq n} (await\ b_i\ then\ S_i\ end; Q_i) \parallel Q_n \parallel (X := E; Q))$$
$$\square\ \neg(b_1 \vee \cdots \vee b_n) \rightarrow X := E; (\|_{1 \leq i \leq n} (await\ b_i\ then\ S_i\ end; Q_i) \parallel Q)\ fi$$
$$\sqcap X := E; (\|_{1 \leq i \leq n} (await\ b_i\ then\ \bar{S}_i\ end; Q_i) \parallel Q) >$$

Therefore,

$$< await \ x = 1 \ then \ x := 2 \ end \ \| \ x := 1 >$$
$=\{$the above derived law$\}$
$$< if \ x = 1 \rightarrow (x := 2; x := 1)$$
$$\square \ x \neq 1 \rightarrow x := 1; await \ x = 1 \ then \ x := 2 \ end \ fi$$
$$\sqcap \ (x := 1; await \ x = 1 \ then \ x := 2 \ end) >$$
$=\{$Await 3, 5 and proposition 2$\}$
$$< if \ x = 1 \rightarrow x := 1 \ \square \ x \neq 1 \rightarrow await \ true \ then \ x := 1; x := 2 \ end \ fi$$
$$\sqcap \ await \ true \ then \ x := 1; x := 2 \ end >$$
$=\{$Await 6 and proposition 2$\}$
$$< if \ x = 1 \rightarrow x := 1 \ \square \ x \neq 1 \rightarrow x := 1; x := 2 \ fi \ \sqcap \ (x := 1; x := 2) >$$
$=\{$Await 3 and proposition 2$\}$
$$< if \ x = 1 \rightarrow x := 1 \ \square \ x \neq 1 \rightarrow x := 2 \ fi \ \sqcap \ x := 2 >$$
$\sqsupseteq\{$Ordering 4$\}$
$$< if \ x = 1 \rightarrow x := 1 \sqcap x := 2 \ \square \ x \neq 1 \rightarrow x := 1 \sqcap x := 2 \ fi \ \sqcap \ x := 2 >$$
$=\{$Conditional 8$\}$
$$< if \ x = 1 \vee x \neq 1 \rightarrow x := 1 \sqcap x := 2 \ fi \ \sqcap \ x := 2 >$$
$=\{$Conditional 1$\}$
$$< x := 1 \sqcap x := 2 \sqcap x := 2 >$$
$=\{$Nondeterminism 3, Await 7, 11$\}$
$$x := 1 \sqcap x := 2$$

Although the calculation here is admittedly quite long, one could notice that after the first three steps, parallel and *await* operators have all been removed.

Example 4. Atomicity refinement (a limited case).
The problem, occurring very often in the transaction-based systems, is this: if there are two transactions S and R in the system, so the system is modelled as $<< S >\|< R >>$, and S and R are each a sequence of atomic actions $S_1;\ldots;S_m$ and $R_1;\ldots;R_n$ respectively, then what are the conditions for the system to be implemented as $< (S_1;\ldots;S_m) \ \| \ (R_1;\ldots;R_n) >$?

Definition 2 *Two atomic actions a and b are commutative if* $< a;b >=< b;a >$.

Proposition 3 *If all the pairs S_i and R_j, except S_1 and R_1, are commutative, then* $<< S_1;\ldots;S_m >\|< R_1;\ldots;R_n >> = < (S_1;\ldots;S_m) \ \| \ (R_1;\ldots;R_n) >$.

Proof. By repeatedly using **Parallel** 6, it is easy to show that

$$< (S_1;\ldots;S_m) \ \| \ (R_1;\ldots;R_n) > = < \sqcap_{1 \leq i \leq m+n}(T_1;\ldots;T_{m+n}) >,$$

where $(T_1;\ldots;T_{m+n})$ is an action sequence interleaved by $(S_1;\ldots;S_m)$ and $(R_1;\ldots;R_n)$. It follows from laws **Await** 7,8,11, **Nondeterminism** 3, and the assumption that S_i and R_j $(i \neq 1 \vee j \neq 1)$ are communicative, that

$$< \sqcap_{1 \leq i \leq m+n}(T_1;\ldots;T_{m+n}) >$$
$$= < (S_1;\ldots;S_m;R_1;\ldots;R_n) \ \sqcap \ (R_1;\ldots;R_n;S_1;\ldots;S_m) > .$$

Finally, from laws **Await** 7 and **Parallel** 6, it follows that

$$< (S_1;\ldots;S_m;R_1;\ldots;R_n) \ \sqcap \ (R_1;\ldots;R_n;S_1;\ldots;S_m) >$$
$$= < (S_1;\ldots;S_m) \ \| \ (R_1;\ldots;R_n) > . \qquad \square$$

As stated earlier, we hope a finite (without iteration statement) parallel program can be transformed by algebraic manipulation to one without parallel combinators. In this section, we limit to the case of flat concurrency. The program that we consider now is of the form $< P_1 \parallel P_2 \parallel \cdots \parallel P_n >$, where each P_i is a sequential program, namely, one generated by the following BNF:

$$P ::= skip \mid stop \mid X := E \mid < P > \mid P_1 \sqcap P_2 \mid P_1;P_2 \mid$$
$$if\ b_1 \rightarrow P_1 \square \cdots \square b_n \rightarrow P_n\ fi \mid await\ b\ then\ P\ end$$

Theorem 2 *For any finite flat concurrency program $< P >$, there is a sequential program Q, such that $< P >=< Q >$.*

Proof. We proceed by induction on the complexity of programs over the parallel composition. First, if any P_i is one of the following:

$$skip,\quad stop,\quad S_1 \sqcap S_2,\quad if\ b_1 \rightarrow S_1 \square \cdots \square b_n \rightarrow S_n\ fi,$$

by laws **Parallel 4, 5**'s corollary, **3a, 3b** and **5** respectively, $< P_1 \parallel P_2 \parallel \cdots \parallel P_n >$ can be transformed to an equivalent one with less complex parallel structures. Hence, the theorem holds by induction. Therefore, we only have to look at the case that P_i is of the following kind:

$$X := E,\quad < S >,\quad S_1;S_2,\quad await\ b\ then\ S\ end \qquad (*)$$

We consider the case that there is an i such that P_i is of the form $S_1;S_2$. By law **Sequential 1**, we can assume that sequential composition is not the main combinator of S_1. In other words, S_1 is of the following form:

$$skip,\quad stop,\quad X := E,\quad < Q >,\quad Q_1 \sqcap Q_2,\quad if\ b_1 \rightarrow Q_1 \square \cdots \square b_n \rightarrow Q_n\ fi,$$
$$await\ b\ then\ Q\ end$$

If S_1 is *skip* or *stop*, then by laws **Sequential 2** and **3**, P_i can be transformed to an equivalent program with simpler structure. For the case that S_1 is a nondeterministic choice or a conditional, from laws **Sequential 4, 6** and **Parallel 3a, 3b, 5**, it follows that $< P_1 \parallel P_2 \parallel \cdots \parallel P_n >$ can be reduced to a simpler structure. The remaining case is that S_1 is one of the following:

$$X := E,\quad < S >,\quad await\ b\ then\ S\ end$$

Therefore, among the cases in (*), we only need to consider the situations that every P_i is of the form:

$$X := E,\quad < S >,\quad S_1;S_2,\quad await\ b\ then\ S\ end,$$

where S_1 is either an atomic statement or an *await*–statement. If there are two processes started with atomic statements, applying law **Parallel 6** leads to a reduction in complexity of parallel structures. For the last case, that is, at most one process is started with an atomic statement and all the other processes are started with *await*–statements, law **Await 6** suffices for this purpose. $\square$

6   Discussion

This study was started with reasoning total correctness of programs. Although the overall behaviours for such systems can be given as mappings from the initial states to the final ones, the constitute components of the system interact with one another. Therefore, to develop these components, a semantical model must take into account of the on-going behaviours. Following [AL89], a trace semantics is proposed in [XH91]. For our purpose, a trace is a finite or infinite labelled state transition sequence:

$$\eta_0 \xrightarrow{\delta_1} \eta_1 \cdots \xrightarrow{\delta_n} \eta_n \cdots,$$

where a label is either E or C to indicate whether it is an environment or a component transition, and a state records values of the variables as well as the status of the process. A process status could be *running*, *blocked*, *failed* or *terminated*, and can thus be viewed as a limited form of *Ready* or *Refusal* set in CSP semantics [Ho85]. The semantics of a program P, $M(P)$, is a set of traces, under the following closure property:

- for any computation σ in $M(P)$, any σ' obtained from σ by adding or removing a 'stuttering' transition is also in $M(P)$.

All the laws presented so far can be justified in this model.
Without an additional closure property:

- for any computation σ in $M(P)$, any σ' obtained from σ by merging two C–consecutive transitions of P is also in $M(P)$,

the semantics is not fully abstract with respect to partial correctness [Br93]. Looking from the algebraic angle, the following law should hold:

$$X := E; X := F \sqsubseteq X := F[E/X],$$

and the same closure property was introduced in [XH91] to justify it.

A fully abstract model for total correctness is currently under investigation by Back and Jonsson [BJ93]. They indicate that apart from the above two closure conditions, a third one is required. It might be interesting to study what kind of additional laws hold in such a model.

An assertional verification method was also formalised in the same model [XH91], and this provides a formal justification for combined use of the assertional and the algebraic methods. In an assertion based verification method, a specification is given by a formula, say, $SPEC$, and proof rules are provided to establish the fact that a program P satisfies such a specification, denoted by $P \; \underline{sat} \; SPEC$. Our results indicate that for any specification S,

- if $P = Q$, then $P \; \underline{sat} \; SPEC \;\; \Leftrightarrow \;\; Q \; \underline{sat} \; SPEC$,

- if $P \sqsubseteq Q$, then $P \; \underline{sat} \; SPEC \;\; \Rightarrow \;\; Q \; \underline{sat} \; SPEC$.

Experiments show that it is often more convenient to allow both message passing and shared variable formalisms in parallel programming, for example, in the implementation of message passing primitives either in a machine language or by hardware directly. The close resemblance between the two algebraic theories have stimulated their integration. Some nontrivial applications based on both laws of OCCAM and shared variable concurrency have been attempted in [He92] and [HPB92]. It is noticed that the general model and laws involving unrestricted interference on shared variables are in general too weak for specific applications, and it seems worthwhile to investigate special theories connected to particular applications.

Acknowledgement We are grateful to Tony Hoare, Chris Holt, Michael Butler and the referees for helpful comments.

References

[AL89] M. Abadi and L. Lamport. Composing specifications. In *Proc. of the REX Workshop on Stepwise Refinement of Distributed Systems, models, formalisms, correctness*. LNCS 430, Springer-Verlag, 1989.

[BJ93] R.J.R. Back and B. Jonsson. Fully abstract semantic ordering for shared–variable concurrent programs. Manuscript, 1993.

[BW90] J.C.M. Baeten and W.P. Weijland. *Process Algebra*. Cambridge University Press, 1990.

[Br85] S.D. Brookes. An axiomatic treatment of a parallel programming language. In R. Parikh, editor, *Proc. of Logics of Programs*, LNCS 193, 1985.

[Br93] S.D. Brookes. Full abstraction for a shared variable parallel language. In *Proc. 8th IEEE Int. Symp. on Logic in Computer Science*, 1993.

[HPB92] He Jifeng, I. Page and J. Bowen. Normal form approach to FPGA implementation of occam. Report, ESPRIT Basic Research Actions ProCoS 1992.

[He92] He Jifeng. Introduction of hybrid parallel programming. Report, ESPRIT Basic Research Actions ProCoS 1992.

[HX91] He Jifeng and Xu Qiwen. Algebraic semantics of shared variable concurrency. Report, ESPRIT Basic Research Actions ProCoS 1991.

[Ho85] C.A.R. Hoare. *Communicating Sequential Processes*. Prentice Hall, London. 1985.

[Hoare et al 87] C.A.R. Hoare et al. Laws of programming. *Commun. ACM 30*, 8 672-686 1987.

[Jo81] C.B. Jones. Development methods for computer programs including a notion of interference. Dphil. Thesis, Oxford University Computing Laboratory, 1981.

[Jo91] C.B. Jones. Interference resumed. in P. Bailes, editor, *Australian Software Engineering Research 1991*.

[LS89] L. Lamport and F.B. Schneider. Pretending atomicity. Research report 29, Digital System Research Center 1989.

[Mi89] R. Milner. *Communication and Concurrency*. Prentice-Hall International Series in Computer Science, 1989.

[OG76] S. Owicki and D. Gries. An axiomatic proof technique for parallel programs. *Acta Inform. 6* 319-340 Springer-Verlag 1976.

[Sti88] C. Stirling. A generalization of Owicki-Gries's Hoare logic for a concurrent while language. *Theoretical Computer Science* 58 347-359 1988.

[Stø90] K. Stølen. *Development of Parallel Programs on Shared Data-structures*. Ph.D Thesis, Computer Science Department, Manchester University, 1990.

[Stø91] K. Stølen. A method for the development of totally correct shared-state parallel programs. In J.C.M. Baeten and J.F. Groote, editors, *Proceedings of CONCUR 91*, LNCS 527, Springer-Verlag, 1991.

[XH91] Xu Qiwen and He Jifeng. A theory of state-based parallel programming: Part 1. in J. Morris, editor, *Proceedings BCS FACS 4th Refinement Workshop* January 1991, Cambridge, 326-359 Springer-Verlag.

[Xu92] Xu Qiwen. *A theory of state-based parallel programming*. DPhil. Thesis, Oxford University Computing Laboratory, 1992.

Environment-based Development of Reactive Systems

Yves Ledru[1]

Service d'Informatique, Faculté Polytechnique de Mons
Mons (Belgium)

Pierre Collette[2]

National Fund for Scientific Research, Université Catholique de Louvain
Louvain-la-Neuve (Belgium)

Abstract

This paper presents an approach for the specification and design of reactive systems where the environment is the starting point of the development process. This environment subsequently provides a proving context for the design and validation activities. In this paper, the approach is used within Lamport's TLA framework. A case study clearly shows the benefits of the method at the specification stage where it prevents overspecification. The paper then explores and discusses the design and validation of a program for the controller. The discussion tries to make more precise the nature of the elementary development steps and to point out specific steps in the development of reactive applications.

1 Introduction

The specification and design of reactive systems has been a subject of intensive research in the recent years. Major advances have been made in the domain of specification and programming languages. Typical specification languages include the STATECHARTS [Har87], LOTOS [ISO88], or ESTELLE [DAC+89]. Specific programming languages like Esterel [BC85] or LUSTRE [CPHP87] have also been defined. In parallel, research is led in order to define effective methods for the design and validation of reactive systems. The major methods are UNITY [CM88] and the "transition axiom method" [Lam89]. Other efforts include [LT90, Bro89, MP92].

A reactive system is *"a system which interacts with its environment"* [Pnu86] (figure 1). The characteristics of this environment should thus be taken into account during the development of a reactive system. There are three ways to specify a reactive system with some respect to its environment.

    Direct approach. Most development methods take the reactive system itself as the central object in the specification process. The environment is

---

[1]Current affiliation: LGI/IMAG, Bat. D bureau 316, BP 53x, F-38041 Grenoble Cedex, FRANCE; Tel: + 33 76 51 45 76, Fax: + 33 76 51 33 79, e-mail: Yves.Ledru@Imag.Fr
[2]Address: Unité d'Informatique, Place Sainte-Barbe 2, B-1348 Louvain-la-Neuve, BELGIUM; Tel: + 32 10 47 31 50, Fax: + 32 10 45 03 45, e-mail: pc@info.ucl.ac.be

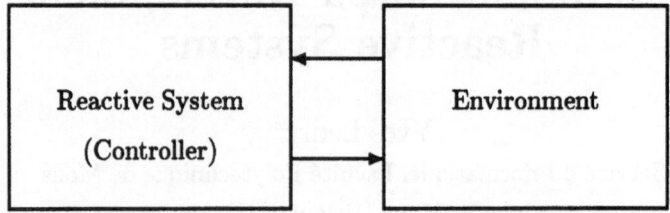

Figure 1: The reactive system and its environment

only seen from the point of view of the system to develop. The specification thus only refers to those aspects of the environment that are involved in interactions with the reactive system. So, in [Bro90, Lam89, CM88], specifications include assumptions on the interface behaviour of the environment.

Closed-system approach. Other methods [Fea87, Ded90, FM92] consider the global system (reactive system + environment) as a starting point. After a specification of the result of their interactions, the development progressively splits the specification into parts corresponding to the environment and those parts that constitute the reactive system to implement.

Environment-based approach. A third approach takes the environment as the starting point of the development. The specification of the environment provides then a context for the specification of the reactive system and its subsequent design and validation. This context allows to *reduce the specification of the reactive system itself to a minimum* and hence to *prevent overspecification* which often leads to premature design decisions. This approach often corresponds to the way problems are initially stated. For example, the initial specification of a bridge is often given by the river it crosses and the traffic it should support. The idea of specifying the environment instead of the system has been suggested previously in the JSD [Jac83] and CORE [Mul85] methods but its particular application in the context of reactive systems [RE87, DH87, Led91] still requires further researches.

The present paper explores this third approach at the specification, design and validation stages of the life-cycle. With respect to previous work [RE87, DH87, Led90, Led91, Led93], the originality of this paper lies in:

- the application of the approach *beyond the specification stage.* The case study evaluates the suitability of an environment-based specification for the subsequent design and validation stages.

- the use of the Temporal Logic of Actions (TLA) of Lamport [Lam91] as an alternate formal framework.

Based on a case study, section 2 discusses the expected advantages of an environment-based approach to specifications. Section 3 then presents a classification of the design steps that occured in the construction of a solution from that specification. Finally, section 4 draws the conclusions of this work.

2 Environment-based specification

2.1 The proposed approach

In the environment-based approach, writing a specification mainly consists of two tasks.

- **Specification of the environment.** It is a modeling task that takes an *existing* environment as input and produces a formal representation of its behaviour.

- **Specification of the goals.** Based on the specification of the environment, it is a list of requirements that must be enforced by the controller, i.e. the reactive system.

Both specifications refer to environment entities only, i.e. none refers to controller entities.

2.2 A case study: the dining philosophers

N philosophers are sitting around a table where N forks are available. Forks are located between philosophers (see figure 2). Philosophers share their time between two major activities: to think and to eat. In order to eat, a philosopher needs two forks, i.e. the ones located at its left and right hand sides. It is guaranteed that an eating philosopher eventually stops eating and starts thinking again. The problem to solve is to ensure that "hungry" philosophers eventually eat.

One might argue about the choice of a classical case study to illustrate the approach. However, this problem [Dij71] is generally chosen to illustrate the development of distributed programs, i.e. the design of programs that implement *the philosophers* [Dij78]. In contrast, figure 2 shows that the philosophers are part of the environment, which is *well known* to the designer: the philosophers play the same role as industrial devices for which a controller must be designed.

A somewhat similar concern has been followed by Chandy and Misra in [CM88], and Dederichs in [Ded90]. The main difference with their treatment of the dining philosophers problem resides in the communication mechanism between the environment and the controller. For example, Chandy and Misra assume that communication occurs through unrestricted access to arbitrary shared variables. In our view of what a controller is for industrial devices, the controller receives information through *sensors* and reacts through *actuators*; the sensor 'variables' do not influence the behaviour of the environment and the actuator 'variables' can be written by the controller only. This restriction

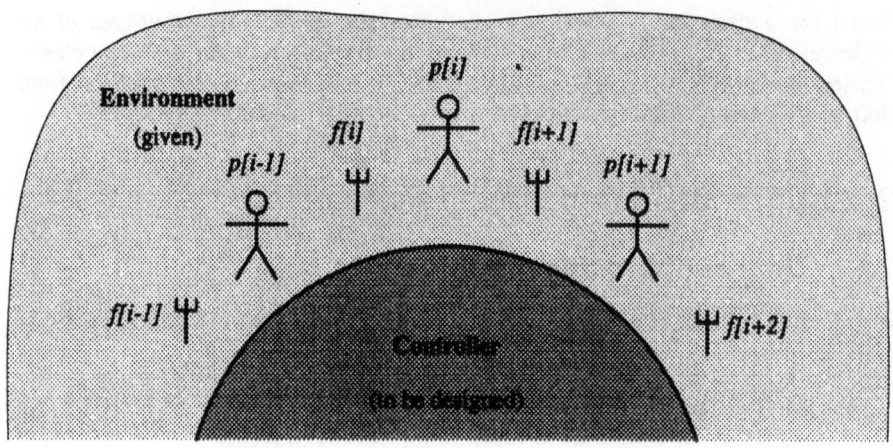

Figure 2: The philosophers and the forks

certainly impacts on the complexity of the development. Moreover, the developments of [CM88, Ded90] use the following shortcut: the transition between the 'hungry' and 'eating' states of a philosopher is performed by the controller. In the presentation of this section, the controller *allows* this transition but it is indeed performed by the environment (philosophers). This additional asynchronism also makes this case study less classical than expected.

2.3 A formal specification of the problem

2.3.1 Description of the environment

In order to specify the controller, the environment-based approach suggests that the environment of the controller, i.e. the philosophers, should be modeled. As a first modeling step, the environment variables are defined. These are p, an array which stores the current state of each philosopher, and f, an array which stores the current state of forks (down, in a left hand, in a right hand):

$p[i]$: philosopher state
$f[i]$: $\{D, L, R\}$

where i is in the range $0..N-1$, N being the number of philosophers. In contrast with e.g. [CM88], these environment variables can not be modified by the controller.

A graphical description of the behaviour of the philosophers is given at figure 3. Each philosopher may be in one of the following states: *Thinking, Hungry, Eating, Has_Left_Fork, Has_Right_Fork, Still_has_Left_Fork*, and *Still_has_Right_Fork*, abbreviated as T, H, E, HLF, HRF, SLF, and SRF respectively. In TLA, state transitions can be specified by *actions*. An action is a boolean-valued expression that is evaluated on a pair of states; primed and unprimed variables refer to the 'new' and 'old' state respectively. For example,

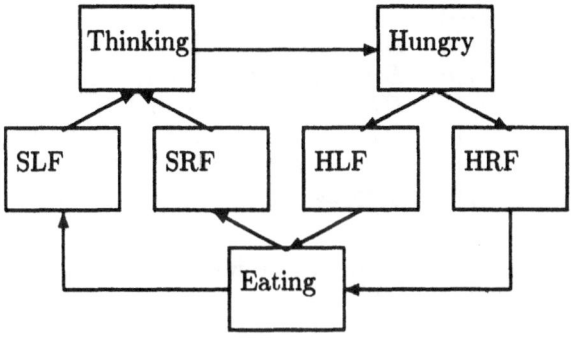

Figure 3: State-based description of the environment

the action $x' \geq x$ holds on the pair (s, t) if and only if the value of x in state t is greater than the value of x in state s. The transition from the *Thinking* to the *Hungry* state of philosopher i can thus be specified by the TLA action $p[i] = T \wedge p'[i] = H$; this action is referred as $T\_to\_H_i$. All the environment actions associated to figure 3 are now summarized:

$$
\begin{array}{llllll}
T\_to\_H_i & \triangleq & p[i] = T & \wedge & p'[i] = H & \\
H\_to\_HLF_i & \triangleq & p[i] = H & \wedge & p'[i] = HLF & \wedge & f[i+1] = D \\
H\_to\_HRF_i & \triangleq & p[i] = H & \wedge & p'[i] = HRF & \wedge & f[i] = D \\
HLF\_to\_E_i & \triangleq & p[i] = HLF & \wedge & p'[i] = E & \wedge & f[i] = D \\
HRF\_to\_E_i & \triangleq & p[i] = HRF & \wedge & p'[i] = E & \wedge & f[i+1] = D \\
E\_to\_SLF_i & \triangleq & p[i] = E & \wedge & p'[i] = SLF & \\
SLF\_to\_T_i & \triangleq & p[i] = SLF & \wedge & p'[i] = T & \\
E\_to\_SRF_i & \triangleq & p[i] = E & \wedge & p'[i] = SRF & \\
SRF\_to\_T_i & \triangleq & p[i] = SRF & \wedge & p'[i] = T & \\
\end{array}
$$

where primed and unprimed variables refer to the state after and before the transition respectively; addition on i is always modulo N. The actions from H to E also state that philosophers may only take a fork when it is *Down* on the table; a philosopher may not steal a fork from his neighbour's hand. Figure 3 distinguishes between states where a philosopher is hungry and has not yet both forks and states where he is in the process of releasing a second fork. Whether this distinction can be observed by the controller is irrelevant at this stage: the process of describing the environment is carried out without such concerns.

State Invariant. A state invariant, expresses the relation between philosophers and forks: eating philosophers hold two forks, thinking philosophers do not hold any, ...

$$
\begin{aligned}
Inv_i \quad \triangleq \quad & (p[i] = T \Rightarrow f[i] \neq R \wedge f[i+1] \neq L) \\
\wedge \quad & (p[i] = H \Rightarrow f[i] \neq R \wedge f[i+1] \neq L) \\
\wedge \quad & (p[i] = E \Rightarrow f[i] = R \wedge f[i+1] = L) \\
\wedge \quad & (p[i] = HLF \Rightarrow f[i] \neq R \wedge f[i+1] = L) \\
\wedge \quad & (p[i] = HRF \Rightarrow f[i] = R \wedge f[i+1] \neq L) \\
\wedge \quad & (p[i] = SLF \Rightarrow f[i] \neq R \wedge f[i+1] = L) \\
\wedge \quad & (p[i] = SRF \Rightarrow f[i] = R \wedge f[i+1] \neq L)
\end{aligned}
$$

Initial State. Philosophers are initially thinking and forks are initially down; state invariants hold initially.

$$
Init_\epsilon \quad \triangleq \quad \wedge_{i=0}^{N-1} (Inv_i \wedge p[i] = T \wedge f[i] = D)
$$

The formula $Init_\epsilon$ holds on the state sequence $s_0 s_1 s_2 \ldots$ if it holds on s_0.

Fairness. Up to now, the description of the environment gives conditions under which philosophers *may* change their state. The actual problem requires that some state changes *must* occur. In particular, philosophers eventually stop eating and put their forks down. This is expressed by *weak fairness* requirements on the transitions from E to T. Similarly, weak fairness requirements on the transitions from H to E express that hungry philosophers eventually eat if these transitions are enabled.

$$
\begin{aligned}
H\_to\_E_i \quad &\triangleq \quad H\_to\_HLF_i \vee H\_to\_HRF_i \vee HLF\_to\_E_i \vee HRF\_to\_E_i \\
E\_to\_T_i \quad &\triangleq \quad E\_to\_SLF_i \vee E\_to\_SRF_i \vee SLF\_to\_T_i \vee SRF\_to\_T_i \\
Fair_i \quad &\triangleq \quad WF_{p[i]}(E\_to\_T_i) \wedge WF_{p[i]}(H\_to\_E_i)
\end{aligned}
$$

Weak fairness requirements prevent an action from being continuously enabled beyond some point in a run without being executed. The TLA formula **enabled**(A) holds on state s if there exists a state t such that the action A holds on the pair (s,t); the TLA formula $WF_v(A)$ holds on the state sequence $s_0 s_1 s_2 \ldots$ if: either there are infinitely many k such that the formula $\neg$**enabled**$(A \wedge v' \neq v)$ holds on state s_k or there are infinitely many k such that the action $A \wedge v' \neq v$ holds on the pair (s_k, s_{k+1}).

Actuators. As discussed in section 2.2, the interface between the environment and the controller consists of a set of *actuators* and a set of *sensors*. Defining the set of actuators is a design decision that occurs within this specification stage. It can not be postponed until the task of modeling the behaviour of the environment is completed because an actuator influences this behaviour. In contrast, the choice of the set of sensors is a design decision that can be postponed until the designer has identified the relevant features of the environment (see section 3). In this case study, the array *go* of actuators gives a way for the controller to influence the behaviour of the philosophers: the transition from *Hungry* to *Eating* is conditioned by *go*. The modified actions are:

$$
\begin{aligned}
H\_to\_HLF_i \quad &\triangleq \quad p[i] = H \wedge p'[i] = HLF \wedge f[i+1] = D \wedge go[i] \\
H\_to\_HRF_i \quad &\triangleq \quad p[i] = H \wedge p'[i] = HRF \wedge f[i] = D \wedge go[i] \\
T\_to\_H_i \quad &\triangleq \quad p[i] = T \wedge p'[i] = H \wedge \neg go[i]
\end{aligned}
$$

where $go[i] : Bool$

Indeed, avoiding deadlocks without such actuators would be impossible: all philosophers might take their left fork at the same time. Since *go* must be set to allow a philosopher to eat, it should also be reset at some point. In this specification of the philosophers, the additional synchronisation point has been located in the $T\_to\_H_i$ transition, i.e. in the last transition before state *Hungry*. This design decision puts thus the least restriction on the behaviour of the controller.

Summary. The environment description is summarized in figure 4. First, the actions performed by philosopher i are grouped into the action Ph_i:

$$Ph_i \quad \triangleq \quad (T\_to\_H_i \vee H\_to\_E_i \vee E\_to\_T_i)$$
$$\wedge Inv_i \wedge Inv'_i \wedge \textbf{unchanged}(Var \setminus \{p[i], f[i], f[i+1]\})$$

where Var is the set of environment and controller variables; the latter are unknown at this stage. The TLA action $\textbf{unchanged}(V)$ asserts that the variables in V are not modified. This corresponds to an interleaving model of the environment where only one philosopher acts at a given time. All the environment actions are then grouped into the action Act_ϵ:

$$Act_\epsilon \quad \triangleq \quad Ph_0 \vee Ph_1 \vee \ldots \vee Ph_{N-1}$$

In summary, the description of the environment is given by the TLA formula

$$D \quad \triangleq \quad Init_\epsilon \wedge \Box[Act_\epsilon]_{\{p[0],p[1],\ldots p[N-1]\}} \wedge Fair_\epsilon$$

where $\Box[A]_V$ holds on the state sequence $s_0 s_1 s_2 \ldots$ if, for all k, the action $A \vee \textbf{unchanged}(V)$ holds on (s_k, s_{k+1}). Observe that this formula constrains only those steps where some variable $p[i]$ is modified, i.e. steps of the environment.

2.3.2 Goals

The goals specify how the previously described environment should behave when it interacts with the controller. This second part of the specification thus constrains the behaviour of the controller. Actually, the role of the controller is to ensure that hungry philosophers eventually eat: the first goal expresses that the state where a philosopher is hungry "leads to" a state where he is eating.

$$\wedge_{i=0}^{N-1}(p[i] = H \rightsquigarrow p[i] = E)$$

The TLA formula $p \rightsquigarrow q$, i.e. $\Box(p \Rightarrow \Diamond q)$, holds on the state sequence $s_0 s_1 s_2 \ldots$ if: whenever p holds on state s_k, there exists $j \geq k$ such that q holds on state s_j.

The problem also requires that the transition from T to H is enabled to allow *Thinking* philosophers to become *Hungry*: the next goals express that the transition is eventually enabled and remains enabled unless the philosopher reaches state H.

$$\wedge_{i=0}^{N-1}(p[i] = T \rightsquigarrow \textbf{enabled}(T\_to\_H_i))$$
$$\wedge_{i=0}^{N-1}\Box[\textbf{enabled}(T\_to\_H_i) \wedge \neg\textbf{enabled}'(T\_to\_H_i) \Rightarrow p'[i] = H)]_{Var}$$

In summary, the meaning of the specification is given by the TLA formula $D \Rightarrow G$ where G is the conjunction of the above goals. It must be noted how simple the goals G are when compared to the description D of the environment. Moreover, these goals refer to environment variables only.

Variables

$p[i]$: $\{T, H, HLF, HRF, E, SLF, SRF\}$
$f[i]$: $\{D, L, R\}$
$go[i]$: $Bool$

State Invariant

$Inv_i \triangleq \quad (p[i] = T \Rightarrow f[i] \neq R \land f[i+1] \neq L)$
$\land (p[i] = H \Rightarrow f[i] \neq R \land f[i+1] \neq L)$
$\land (p[i] = E \Rightarrow f[i] = R \land f[i+1] = L)$
$\land (p[i] = HLF \Rightarrow f[i] \neq R \land f[i+1] = L)$
$\land (p[i] = HRF \Rightarrow f[i] = R \land f[i+1] \neq L)$
$\land (p[i] = SLF \Rightarrow f[i] \neq R \land f[i+1] = L)$
$\land (p[i] = SRF \Rightarrow f[i] = R \land f[i+1] \neq L)$

Initial Condition

$Init_\epsilon \triangleq \land_{i=0}^{N-1} (Inv_i \land p[i] = T \land f[i] = D)$

Environment Actions

$T\_to\_H_i \triangleq p[i] = T \land p'[i] = H \land \neg go[i]$
$H\_to\_HLF_i \triangleq p[i] = H \land p'[i] = HLF \land f[i+1] = D \land go[i]$
$H\_to\_HRF_i \triangleq p[i] = H \land p'[i] = HRF \land f[i] = D \land go[i]$
$HLF\_to\_E_i \triangleq p[i] = HLF \land p'[i] = E \land f[i] = D$
$HRF\_to\_E_i \triangleq p[i] = HRF \land p'[i] = E \land f[i+1] = D$
$E\_to\_SLF_i \triangleq p[i] = E \land p'[i] = SLF$
$SLF\_to\_T_i \triangleq p[i] = SLF \land p'[i] = T$
$E\_to\_SRF_i \triangleq p[i] = E \land p'[i] = SRF$
$SRF\_to\_T_i \triangleq p[i] = SRF \land p'[i] = T$

$H\_to\_E_i \triangleq H\_to\_HLF_i \lor H\_to\_HRF_i \lor HLF\_to\_E_i \lor HRF\_to\_E_i$
$E\_to\_T_i \triangleq E\_to\_SLF_i \lor E\_to\_SRF_i \lor SLF\_to\_T_i \lor SRF\_to\_T_i$

$Ph_i \triangleq (T\_to\_H_i \lor H\_to\_E_i \lor E\_to\_T_i)$
$\land Inv_i \land Inv_i' \land \textbf{unchanged}(Var \setminus \{p[i], f[i], f[i+1]\})$
$Act_\epsilon \triangleq Ph_0 \lor Ph_1 \lor \ldots \lor Ph_{N-1}$

Fairness requirements

$Fair_\epsilon \triangleq \land_{i=0}^{N-1} (WF_{p[i]}(E\_to\_T_i) \land WF_{p[i]}(H\_to\_E_i))$

Environment Description

$D \triangleq Init_\epsilon \land \Box[Act_\epsilon]_{\{p[0], p[1], \ldots p[N-1]\}} \land Fair_\epsilon$

Figure 4: The specification of the environment

2.4   Discussion

In the 'direct' approach (the controller is the central object), a classical distinction is between *problem specification* and *system specification*. A problem specification states what should be done while a system specification states how to do it [Pnu86, Pnu92]. The latter can usually be recognized by their operational flavour. Consequently, the use of system specification formalisms at the early stages of a development in the direct approach often leads to an overspecification of the controller by the addition of premature details about its intended behaviour. But, even the use of problem specification formalisms (e.g. temporal logic) at these early stages may result in overspecification, mainly because many analysts and developers use to think about problems in terms of possible solutions.

The environment-based approach tends to take advantage of the availability of a large number of system specification formalisms and of the fact that developers tend to think operationally. The key issue is to replace the problem specification of the controller with the *system specification of its environment*: the TLA specification of the environment in the previous section clearly has an operational flavour. The example presented in this section demonstrates the expected benefits of this approach at the specification stage: modeling process, conciseness of the goals, customer orientation, . . .

A modeling process.   The specification of this problem was mainly concerned with building a model of philosophers. Although this modeling activity is not necessarily a trivial task, the approach postulates that it is often easier to perform a system specification of the environment than to provide a direct specification of the controller which preserves implementation freedom. This property is definitely verified in cases where a reactive system must be designed for an existing system whose specification is already available. In the more general case, a model of the environment is not harder to construct than a direct specification of the reactive system because the latter usually "mirrors" the behaviour of the environment.

Conciseness of the goals.   This case study and other examples previously developed [Led91] show that the expression of the goals (section 2.3.2) is significantly shorter than the specification of the environment (section 2.3.1). Actually, the controller is indirectly specified through goals that refer to environment entities only. This definitely reduces the risk of overspecification and premature design decisions. In cases where a specification of the environment exists before the development starts, the specification activity can so be drastically reduced.

One might also argue that overspecification of the environment is still possible. This is true. But this kind of overspecification only impacts on the modeling process and does not introduce bias in the design process. To some extent, overspecification of the environment is inevitable because it is difficult to precisely figure out at these early stages of the development what are the relevant features of the environment in the perspective of the system under development. Avoiding overspecification of the environment increases the risk to introduce bias in the development of the system.

Customer orientation and completeness. A major issue is the completeness of the formal specification w.r.t. the initial informal description of the problem. The fact that the whole specification (environment + goals) only refers to the environment makes it easier to validate by the customer of the development. Actually, the customer has a better understanding of this existing environment than of the program he needs. Moreover, the use of simulation and animation techniques allows to compare the specification with the actual environment it models. This customer orientation is also one of the underlying ideas of the specification approach of Dubois and Hagelstein [DH87].

Specification frameworks. The specification activity can take benefit of the availability of numerous formalisms, especially for system specification. The choice of TLA appears as interesting at this stage of the development because it allows to combine state formulae with transition formulae (actions) in the same framework. In [Led93] and [Led91], the approach was supported by an extension of VDM which associates the STATECHARTS and VDM [Jon90] formalisms at the specification stage. The technical aspects of this combination of VDM with state machines were the major topic of [Led93]. This evolution towards the use of TLA brings up several benefits to the approach:

1. It demonstrates the portability of the method across formalisms and logics. From this point of view, TLA was chosen because of its growing influence in this research area.

2. The language also benefits of a well defined semantics and is better suited for concurrency than VDM. Moreover, TLA allows to keep state machine notations which are thus close to the STATECHARTS.

3 Environment-based design

The design phase aims at developing a program that satisfies the specification. As discussed previously, the goals are properties of the environment that must be respected when the environment is under control. Thus, in our case, the design phase aims at developing a controller whose interaction with the environment enforces these goals.

While the specification refers to entities of the existing environment only, the subsequent development must progressively refine this specification into a specification that refers to entities of the controller only. The major topic of this section is a classification of the design steps that occured in this refinement process. This classification, which results from our case study, is an analysis of how the development of a solution to a rather complex problem has been influenced by an environment-based approach. This analysis must be considered as a starting point for the statement of a design method.

Although the purpose of this section is not to present a new solution to the dining philosophers problem, the methodological discussion of section 3.2 is based on simple excerpts from the actual development. Thus, an outline of the development is first presented in section 3.1.

3.1 Development Outline

The development has been entirely carried out in a stepwise fashion. At each step, a few goals have been replaced with new goals until the list of goals is precise enough to derive a program for the controller. Thus, this development can be viewed as a stepwise transformation of environment goals into controller actions. All these transformations have been carried out in a formal way; detailed proofs are available for each design step and can be found in [CL93].

3.1.1 Design decisions

The development of a solution was based on three major design steps:

A dynamic ordering. The proposed solution to the dining philosophers problem is based on the construction of a dynamic partial ordering between *sad* philosophers. As such, it follows the ideas of Chandy and Misra [CM88]. In the present development, a hungry philosopher is and remains sad until he has eaten. A sad philosopher at the top of the ordering eventually eats; it then goes to the bottom of the ordering. Therefore, every sad philosopher eventually eats. Thus, the first design steps transform the goal

$$p[i] = H \rightsquigarrow p[i] = E$$

into, among others, the goals

$$sad[i] \wedge top[i] \quad \rightsquigarrow \quad \neg(sad[i] \wedge top[i]) \tag{1}$$
$$haseaten[i] \quad \rightsquigarrow \quad low[i] \tag{2}$$

where $top[i]$ and $low[i]$ respectively denote that philosopher i is at the top or at the bottom of the partial ordering; $haseaten[i]$ is a *sensor* that has been added to detect when a philosopher has eaten. Adding a sensor does not modify the behaviour of the existing environment but increases the amount of information available to the controller.

In [CM88], a centralized controller is easily derived from the above goals because the transition from *Hungry* to *Eating* is performed by the *controller* as an atomic step. Here, this transition is performed by the *environment* in several steps and deadlocks may occur between the *Hungry* and *Eating* states. Therefore, other important development steps were necessary.

Mutual exclusion. Although some mutual exclusion is already enforced by the forks, the proposed solution adds a mutual exclusion constraint on the HLF and HRF states. Let $in\_HF[i]$ be a shorthand for $p[i] = HLF \vee p[i] = HRF$.

$$\Box(in\_HF[i] \Rightarrow \neg in\_HF[i+1] \wedge \neg in\_HF[i-1]) \tag{3}$$

where the TLA formula $\Box p$ holds on the state sequence $s_0 s_1 s_2 \ldots$ if, for all k, the state formula p holds on state s_k.

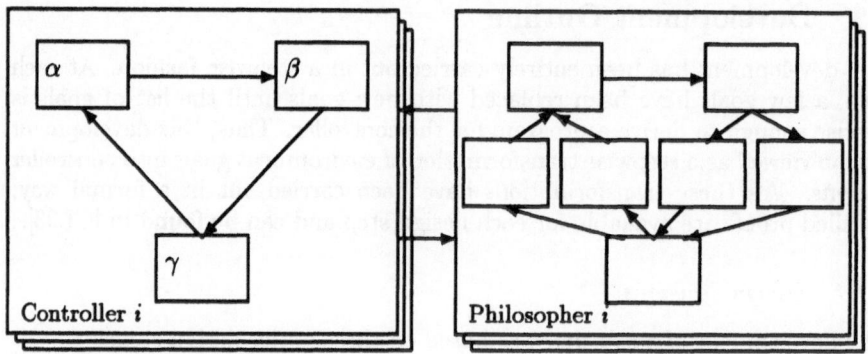

Figure 5: Interactions between controllers and philosophers

This mutual exclusion constraint is later implemented by a mutual exclusion on go: $go[i]$ is only set when the neighbours of philosopher i have their go reset.

$$\Box(go[i] \Rightarrow \neg go[i-1] \wedge \neg go[i+1]) \tag{4}$$

$$\Box(p[i] = HLF \vee p[i] = HRF \Rightarrow go[i]) \tag{5}$$

These are invariant properties of both the environment and the controller. They ensure the absence of deadlocks between philosophers, since a philosopher has the guarantee that none of his neighbours is in any critical state whenever he gets the permission to eat.

The $go[i]$ variable remains true long enough. Based on this mutual exclusion constraint, a third design decision states that $go[i]$, once set, must remain true while philosopher i is sad. This can be expressed as:

$$\Box[go[i] \wedge sad[i] \Rightarrow go'[i]]_{Var}$$

3.1.2 The resulting program

The development guided by these three design decisions has led to a concurrent program, distributed among philosophers. Variable $c[i]$ stores the current state of controller i. As shown in figure 5, it ranges in $\{\alpha, \beta, \gamma\}$. Let *check* and *allow* stand for the following formulae:

$$
\begin{aligned}
check[j] \quad &\triangleq \quad \neg go[j] \wedge (haseaten[j] \vee \neg hungry[j] \vee (i \rhd j)) \\
allow[i] \quad &\triangleq \quad hungry[i] \wedge check[i+1] \wedge check[i-1]
\end{aligned}
$$

where

- the sensor $hungry[i]$ detects if philosopher i is hungry;

- $i \rhd j$ indicates that i is "higher" than its neighbour j in the partial ordering.

Based on this definition of *allow*, the controller actions associated to figure 5 are defined as follows:

$$\alpha\_to\_\beta_i \quad \triangleq \quad c[i] = \alpha \wedge c'[i] = \beta \wedge allow[i] \wedge go'[i]$$
$$\beta\_to\_\gamma_i \quad \triangleq \quad c[i] = \beta \wedge c'[i] = \gamma \wedge haseaten[i] \wedge \neg go'[i]$$
$$\gamma\_to\_\alpha_i \quad \triangleq \quad c[i] = \gamma \wedge c'[i] = \alpha \wedge low'[i] \wedge \neg haseaten'[i]$$

$$Init_\pi \quad \triangleq \quad \text{acyclic}(\triangleright) \wedge (\wedge_{i=0}^{N-1} c[i] = \alpha \wedge \neg go[i] \wedge \neg haseaten[i])$$

where each action only modifies primed variables. The first transition sets $go[i]$ if $allow[i]$ is verified. The second transition waits for $haseaten[i]$ to become true before resetting $go[i]$. The third transition resets both $haseaten[i]$ and the priority of i ($low[i]$) in the partial ordering. Finally, the transitions of the controller are submitted to a weak fairness constraint.

3.2   Methodological observations

The development of a program for the controller from the abstract specification of the problem has been conducted formally as a series of refinement steps. This section analyses the nature of these steps and points out steps which are specific to an environment-based approach.

As for the assumption-commitment style of [AL93, Bro89], a specification can be viewed as a pair (D, G) where D and G respectively denote the description of the environment and the goals to be achieved. A refinement step thus transforms a so-called abstract specification (D_a, G_a) into a refined specification (D_r, G_r). The development may thus be seen as a series of progressively more concrete specifications linked by refinement steps:

$$(D_0, G_0) \to \ldots \to (D_a, G_a) \to (D_r, G_r) \to \ldots \to (D_n, G_n)$$

Figure 6 identifies two major classes of steps: rewriting steps and strengthening steps. Both classes include steps that are specific to the approach. The corresponding proof obligations are deduced from [AL93].

Rewriting steps	Strengthening steps
(1) $(D_a, G_a) \to (D_a, G_r)$ with $G_a \Leftrightarrow G_r$	(4) $(D_a, G_a) \to (D_a, G_r)$ with $G_r \Rightarrow G_a$
(2) $(D_a, G_a) \to (D_r, G_a)$ with $D_a \Leftrightarrow D_r$	(5) $(D_a, G_a) \to (D_r, G_a)$ with $D_a \Rightarrow D_r$
(3) $(D_a, G_a) \to (D_a, G_r)$ with $D_a \Rightarrow (G_a \Leftrightarrow G_r)$	(6) $(D_a, G_a) \to (D_a, G_r)$ with $D_a \Rightarrow (G_r \Rightarrow G_a)$

Figure 6: Refinement steps

3.2.1 Rewriting steps

In a rewriting step, the refined specification (D_r, G_r) is equivalent to the abstract specification (D_a, G_a). The new TLA formulae do not increase the amount of information provided by the specification but clarify it and reorganize it so that subsequent design steps are easier to introduce. Only three kinds of rewriting steps occur in the development process.

1. $D_a = D_r$ and $G_a \Leftrightarrow G_r$: the goals are replaced with equivalent new ones, without taking into account the description of the environment. For example, the goal

$$\Box[\mathbf{enabled}(T\_to\_H_i) \wedge \neg\mathbf{enabled}'(T\_to\_H_i) \Rightarrow p'[i] = H]_{Var}$$

can be replaced with

$$\Box[p[i] = T \wedge \neg go[i] \wedge p'[i] \neq T \Rightarrow p'[i] = H]_{Var} \tag{6}$$
$$\Box[p[i] = T \wedge \neg go[i] \wedge go'[i] \Rightarrow p'[i] = H]_{Var} \tag{7}$$

because $\mathbf{enabled}(T\_to\_H_i)$ is equivalent to $p[i] = T \wedge \neg go[i]$.

2. $D_a \Leftrightarrow D_r$ and $G_a = G_r$: the assumptions on the environment are replaced with equivalent new ones. Usually, D_r includes more properties of the environment than D_a. These additional properties represent information that is *derived* from the specification D_a of the environment. For example, a refinement step derives the property

$$p[i] = HLF \wedge f[i] = D \rightsquigarrow f[i] \neq D \vee p[i] = E$$

from the weak fairness requirement on the environment actions: if the right fork is continuously *Down*, it is eventually taken by a hungry philosopher.

3. $D_a = D_r$ and $D_a \Rightarrow (G_a \Leftrightarrow G_r)$: some goals are replaced with new goals that are equivalent to the abstract ones *in the context* of the specified environment, i.e. $G_a \not\Leftrightarrow G_r$. Especially, properties of the environment may be used to discharge parts of the goals. For example, goal (6) above can be removed because it is a straightforward consequence of the environment description: state *Hungry* follows state *Thinking*. As another example, the goal

$$p[i] = T \rightsquigarrow \mathbf{enabled}(T\_to\_H_i)$$

is first transformed into

$$
\begin{aligned}
&\quad p[i] = T \rightsquigarrow p[i] = T \wedge \neg go[i] \\
\Leftrightarrow\ &\quad p[i] = T \wedge (go[i] \vee \neg go[i]) \rightsquigarrow p[i] = T \wedge \neg go[i] \\
\Leftrightarrow\ &\quad p[i] = T \wedge go[i] \rightsquigarrow p[i] = T \wedge \neg go[i]
\end{aligned}
$$

by rewriting steps of type 1. Since $\Box[p[i] = T \wedge go[i] \Rightarrow p'[i] = T]_{Var}$ follows from the description of the environment, an environment-based rewriting step then transforms the goal into

$$p[i] = T \wedge go[i] \rightsquigarrow \neg go[i] \tag{8}$$

3.2.2 Strengthening steps

Strengthening steps correspond to the expression of design decisions which restrict implementation freedom until the goals correspond to a program. The refined specification (D_r, G_r) is stronger than the abstract specification (D_a, G_a). This means that either the goals are more precise or less hypotheses are made on the environment. The rest of this section details the three kinds of strengthening steps and discusses how the selection of stronger goals is guided by the need to progress towards an implementation.

4. $D_a = D_r$ and $G_r \Rightarrow G_a$: some goals are replaced with stronger ones. The description of the environment is not taken into account. In the development of the dining philosophers, steps of this kind may be classed into two major categories.

Creative steps. Creative steps carry some level of invention to refine goals into new ones. Most developments include this kind of steps. Although they appear as "magic", they often improve the efficiency or the elegance of the proposed solution significantly. Finding these steps is beyond the scope of development methods but methods must be flexible enough to allow their introduction. Typical examples have been presented in section 3.1: the introduction of a dynamic ordering to deal with conflicts between sad philosophers, or the introduction of invariants to reduce the set of reachable states (first and second design decisions). Such steps are obviously not specific to an environment-based approach.

Observation concerns. Goals refinement is also guided by the ability of the controller to *observe* properties of the environment. For example, it may only observe the *Hungry* state of philosophers. Thinking states are thus not observable by the controller and goal (8) is replaced with:

$$go[i] \rightsquigarrow \neg go[i]$$

Other steps introduce new sensors to make more information available to the controller. Typically, the controller must be aware of when a philosopher has eaten; the goal $sad[i] \rightsquigarrow p[i] = E$ is thus transformed into

$$\Box(sad[i] \Rightarrow \neg haseaten[i])$$
$$sad[i] \rightsquigarrow haseaten[i]$$

where $haseaten[i]$ is a sensor that becomes *true* when philosopher i enters its eating state. It remains true until it is reset by the controller. Requiring that $haseaten[i]$ holds beyond a point where it does not hold is equivalent to requiring that $p[i] = E$ holds meanwhile.

5. $D_a \Rightarrow D_r$ and $G_a = G_r$: the assumptions on the environment can be weakened. In particular, useless assumptions or irrelevant details can be discarded. In the development of the dining philosophers, this step was never taken, so that at each development step, the full description of the environment was available to demonstrate refinements.

6. $D_a = D_r$ and $D_a \Rightarrow (G_r \Rightarrow G_a)$: some goals are replaced with goals that are stronger *in the context of* the specified environment. This means that the refinement "relies" on properties of the environment. In the development of the dining philosophers, the following motivations have been observed for such steps:

Targeting the development. At the early stages of the development, the goals are expressed in terms of environment variables only. Design steps progressively refine these into constraints on the sole behaviour of the controller, i.e. the target of the development. For example, at the last stage of the development process, goals expressed in terms of "leads to" are replaced with weak fairness requirements on the controller actions. Another example is the refinement of the mutual exclusion property (3) into properties (4) and (5) in the context of the specified environment. These refined invariants depend on the controller only because they are preserved by any environment action: $go[i]$ is not modified and the HLF/HRF states are reached only when $go[i]$ holds.

Rely steps. Several design steps take their underlying intuition from properties of the environment. For example, the third major design decision replaces the goal

$$go[i] \wedge sad[i] \rightsquigarrow go[i] \wedge \neg sad[i] \quad \text{with} \quad \Box[go[i] \wedge sad[i] \Rightarrow go'[i]]_{Var}$$

The refinement relies on the weak fairness properties and on the design decision to put a mutual exclusion constraint between philosophers (3). Indeed, if $go[i]$ remains continuously enabled, no neighbour of i is allowed to take forks. Hence the transitions from H to E become continuously enabled and weak fairness ensures that philosopher i eventually eats.

3.2.3 Comments

Specific design steps. Steps of type 2, 3, 5, and 6 explicitly involve the description of the environment (D) and are thus specific to an environment-based approach. However, the specificity of the approach may also impact on steps 1 and 4. As discussed in section 2.4, the initial specification is described in terms of environment-related concepts. On the contrary, the final program given in section 3.1, is expressed in terms of controller-related concepts only (program variables, sensors, actuators). The induced transformation process involves steps of all types, including 1 and 4. For example, observation concerns motivate the introduction of sensors within steps of type 4.

From that point of view, this approach is rather close to Feather's [Fea87] where the design phase involves the transformation of overall goals into local behaviours of a component in a stepwise fashion. Both approaches share the objective to preserve implementation freedoms at the specification stage. In the design process, a common advantage of both approaches is the liberal use of references to entities of the overall system without regard to the boundary between the controller and its environment.

Consistency of environment descriptions. The logical framework (figure 6) does not feature steps which transform D in the context of G. Modifications of D may only result from its logical consequences (steps 2 and 5). This guarantees that the assumptions (D_n) under which the final program implements the abstract goals (G_0) are compatible with the initial description of the environment (D_0): $D_0 \Rightarrow D_n$. In this case study, the equivalence between descriptions of the environment $(D_0 \Leftrightarrow D_n)$ was kept through the whole development. This potentially provides the developer with the widest validation context for the proof of steps 3 and 6.

4 Conclusions

This paper has presented an environment-based approach to the development of reactive systems. The approach offers advantages at both the specification and design/validation phases of the development.

The specification stage is mainly turned into a modeling activity. The availability of this context allows a concise expression of the goals and hence reduces overspecification. In section 2, the goals of the controller are expressed in 3 formulae while the environment is described in about 20 formulae. Moreover, the whole specification is expressed in terms of the environment which are familiar to the customer of the development. This eases thus the validation of the specification.

At the design phase, the goals are progressively transformed in terms of variables, sensors and actuators which are accessible by the controller. Still, the description of the environment provides a context which can be referred to through the whole design/validation activity. It thus allows the developer to refer to a wide variety of concepts and to relate controller events to environment events. This paper has tried to understand and classify the elementary refinement steps involved in this design process. This kind of understanding is a prerequisite to the definition of an effective method and the development of its associated tool support.

References

[AL93]   M. Abadi and L. Lamport. Composing specifications. *ACM Transactions on Programming Languages and Systems*, 15(1):73–132, january 1993.

[BC85]   G. Berry and I. Cosserat. The ESTEREL synchronous programming language and its mathematical semantics. In S. Brookes and G. Winskel, editors, *Seminar on Concurrency*, volume 197 of *Lecture Notes in Computer Science*, pages 389–449. Springer-Verlag, 1985.

[Bro89]   M. Broy. Functional specification of communicating systems. In G.X. Ritter, editor, *IFIP 89*, pages 851–856. North-Holland, 1989.

234

[Bro90]   M. Broy. On bounded buffers: Modularity, robustness, and reliability in reactive systems. In W. H. J. Feijen, A. J. M. Van gasteren, D. Gries, and J. Misra, editors, *Beauty is our business - a birthday salute to Edsger W. Dijkstra*, pages 83–93. Springer Verlag, 1990.

[CL93]   P. Collette and Y. Ledru. From environment to system specifications: Dining philosophers revisited. Technical report, Université Catholique de Louvain, Unité d'Informatique, 1993.

[CM88]   K. Chandy and J. Misra. *Parallel Program Design: A Foundation*. Addison-Wesley, 1988.

[CPHP87]   P. Caspi, D. Pilaud, N. Halbwachs, and J. A. Plaice. LUSTRE: A declarative language for programming synchronous systems. In *Proceedings of the 14th POPL*, pages 178–188. ACM, 1987.

[DAC+89]   M. Diaz, J.-P. Ansart, J.-P. Courtiat, P. Azema, and V. Chari. *The formal description technique Estelle - Results of the ESPRIT/SEDOS project*. North Holland, 1989.

[Ded90]   F. Dederichs. System and environment: the philosophers revisited. Technical Report TUM-I9040, Technische Universität München, 1990.

[DH87]   E. Dubois and J. Hagelstein. Reasoning on formal requirements: a lift control system. In *Proceedings of the fourth International Workshop on Software Specification and Design*. IEEE Computer Society, 1987.

[Dij71]   E.W. Dijkstra. Hierarchical ordering of sequential processes. *Acta Informatica*, 1(2):115–138, 1971.

[Dij78]   E.W. Dijkstra. Two starvation free solutions to a general exclusion problem. Technical Report EWD 625, Plataanstraat 5, 5671 Al Nuenen, 1978.

[Fea87]   M.S. Feather. Language support for the specification and development of composite systems. *ACM Transactions on Programming Languages and Systems*, 9(2):198–234, april 1987.

[FM92]   J. Fiadeiro and T. Maibaum. Temporal theories as modularisation units for concurrent system specification. *Formal Aspects of Computing*, 4(3):239–272, 1992.

[Har87]   D. Harel. STATECHARTS: a visual formalism for complex systems. *Science of Computer Programming*, 8(3), 1987.

[ISO88]   ISO. Lotos, a formal description technique based on the temporal ordering of observational behaviour. Technical Report ISO-DP-8807, International Organization for Standardisation, 1988.

[Jac83]   M.A. Jackson. *System development*. Prentice-Hall, 1983.

[Jon90]   C. B. Jones. *Systematic Software Development Using VDM (Second Edition)*. Prentice-Hall, London, 1990.

[Lam89]   L. Lamport. A simple approach to specifying concurrent systems. *Communications of the ACM*, 32(1):32–45, 1989.

[Lam91]   L. Lamport. The temporal logic of actions. Technical Report SRC-79, DEC Systems Research Center, Palo Alto, december 1991.

[Led90]   Y. Ledru. Hierarchical Specification of Reactive Systems : a case study. In *Proceedings of the CompEuro'90 Conference*, pages 109–116. IEEE Computer Society Press, 1990.

[Led91]   Y. Ledru. *Towards the formal development of terminating reactive systems*. PhD thesis, Université Catholique de Louvain, Unité d'Informatique, 1991.

[Led93]   Y. Ledru. Developing reactive systems in a VDM framework. *Science of Computer Programming*, 20(1-2):51–71, 1993.

[LT90]   N.A. Lynch and M.R. Tuttle. Hierarchical correctness proofs for distributed algorithms. In *Proceedings of the ACM Symposium on Principles of Distributed Computing*. ACM, 1990.

[MP92]   Z. Manna and A. Pnueli. *The temporal logic of reactive and concurrent systems*. Springer-Verlag, 1992.

[Mul85]   Geoff Mullery. Acquisition - environment. In M. Paul and H.J. Siegert, editors, *Distributed Systems - Methods and Tools for Specification - An Advanced Course*, volume 190 of *Lecture Notes in Computer Science*. Springer-Verlag, 1985.

[Pnu86]   A. Pnueli. Specification and development of reactive systems. In H.-J. Kugler, editor, *IFIP 86*, pages 845–858. North-Holland, 1986.

[Pnu92]   A. Pnueli. System specification and refinement in temporal logic. In R. Shyamasundar, editor, *Software technology and Theoretical Computer Science*, volume 652 of *Lecture Notes in Computer Science*. Springer-Verlag, 1992.

[RE87]   G.-C. Roman and M.E. Ehlers. System specifications and physical relevance. In *Proceedings of the fourth International Workshop on Software Specification and Design*. IEEE Computer Society, 1987.

Refinement in Object-Oriented Specification Languages

K. Lano,

Lloyd's Register,
Croydon, UK

Abstract

This paper addresses the issues related to the development of a formal semantic framework, oriented around refinement, for object-oriented specification languages, particularly those based upon the Z specification language [27]. A proposal for a systematic mapping of object-oriented Z into standard Z is presented, and is then extended to include treatment of object identity. Throughout, we stress the importance of a formal semantics and a related reasoning system to the correct development and verifiability of software systems using formal methods. This work is a product of investigations into the use of formal methods and semantic analysis in assessment and arises from the need to provide a precise meaning to formal specifications extracted from imperative programs as part of a process of static and semantic analysis. The 'reference Z' style of specification has been applied in particular to the functional specification of parsing and translation components of a program analysis tool [12, 17]. Examples from this specification are provided.

A 'transformational' semantics approach will be taken, whereby the semantics of Z extensions are defined via interpretation into standard Z, so that the well-defined and widely assumed semantics for this language can be used.

1 Introduction

Lloyd's Register is concerned with assessing safety critical software systems, and is also conducting research aiming at using reverse engineering to improve dependability of existing systems or to bring them under proper quality control in accordance with emerging software engineering standards. The current paper has emerged from both of these concerns: providing a framework for the verification of formal object oriented specification languages, which are becoming increasingly used for high-integrity and safety critical systems, and with the design of rigorously developed program analysis and reverse engineering tools.

Object-oriented specification languages are becoming more widely adopted and accepted, with the contributions that they can make to the rigorous development of large high-integrity systems being recognised. The advantages that these languages offer over non-object-oriented specification languages, in improving the comprehensibility, modularisation and validatability of specifications has been shown in a number of practical trials ([29] demonstrated that Object-Z was learned and applied significantly more rapidly than Z, despite the relative lack of tutorial material, and [7] discusses the improvements in usability found through the use of ZEST for communications systems, rather than languages specifically aimed at this domain, such as LOTOS).

Applications to safety critical and real time systems are also being carried out [24, 5, 9], and object oriented formal languages are a natural approach to the specification of real time systems, since these systems are often effectively structured around the real-world elements which they control [18, page 54].

However, although a number of such languages exist (eg, Fresco [30], OOZE [2], Z^{++} [14], ZEST [6], MooZ [21], Object-Z [4]) these are either based upon specification languages with a different semantics to Z (Fresco and OOZE) or do not yet have a readily usable or fully developed semantics. This is a hindrance to their acceptance for high-integrity and particularly safety-critical systems, since such systems must be assessable and must be developed to a high degree of confidence. We believe that Z is an excellent basis for a formal object-oriented specification language, and that its wide and increasing uptake, together with a long history of practical application, and its progress towards standardisation, gives it a strong position with regard to the market for formal methods. Thus a semantics for an object-oriented Z should be compatible with that for standard Z, as should the mode of use of the language.

Of importance also is the need for a practical reasoning system based on the specification language. This is an area where Z is comparatively weak with respect to the languages B [1] and RSL [10]. The encapsulation offered by object-oriented specification is one way in which the practicality of reasoning using Z can be enhanced, since classes and class composition operations provide a means by which the mathematical context involved in each proof can be constrained to that strictly required, and by which proof obligations can be partitioned into manageable subsets. This latter benefit of semantically restrictive specification structuring mechanisms was the major incentive behind the 'machine' composition constructs of B AMN, and some of these mechanisms would also be of use for object-oriented Z.

Major obstacles to a coherent semantics for object-oriented Z are:

- the need to treat object identity – which introduces problems related to aliasing and sharing which do not arise in specification languages whose data items have only mathematical values without identity;

- the need to consider specification of timing and of concurrent and dynamic behaviour and to integrate this with specification of sequential behaviour.

Each of these issues will be addressed below. In section 2 we give a semantic framework for an object-oriented Z without object identify, and illustrate how this semantics is applied to proof and refinement. We identify a series of properties for refinement which we believe are essential for practical use, and show that our framework satisfies these. In section 3 we extend the framework to treat reference semantics for objects, ie, objects with a persistent identity. In section 4 we give applications of the semantics to reasoning about refinement and properties of classes. In section 5 we give examples of the application of the semantics to support the specification of a large high-integrity system.

2 A Semantic Framework for Object-Oriented Formal Specification in Z

In this section we describe how a notation for specifying objects and classes in Z can be interpreted in standard Z, and will define concepts of internal consistency of classes and refinement between classes which are of use in specification and development using these languages. We will use the notation of Z^{++} [13] for simplicity – a notation such as Object-Z could equally well be used in place of this. A syntax summary is given in the appendix.

2.1 Representing Object-Oriented Z in Z

2.1.1 Classes

Let C be a class defined as follows:

```
CLASS C
OWNS
    c
INVARIANT
    Inv_C
OPERATIONS
    m : IN → OUT;
    ....
ACTIONS
    Pre_{m,C} &
        m x y ==> Def_{m,C};
    ....
HISTORY
    H_C
END CLASS
```

History constraints will not be considered in detail in this paper. In such a class there may be a set of methods of the form of m. For C we can define the following schemas.

$$\boxed{\begin{array}{l} State_C \\ \hline c \\ \hline Inv_C \end{array}}$$

specifies the state of the class.

For each method m of the class we also define:

$$\boxed{\begin{array}{l} In_m \\ \hline x : IN \end{array}}$$

$$\boxed{\begin{array}{l} Out_m \\ \hline y : OUT \end{array}}$$

In these last two schemas, variables and types will be listed in pairs in the conventional Z style. That is, the sequence IN of types will be matched with the sequence x of input parameters to produce a Z declaration. Similarly for OUT and y.

Note that $Pre_{m,C}$ is a predicate on the state of the class and the input parameters only, whereas $Def_{m,C}$ is a predicate on $\Delta State_C$, and the input and output parameters of the method.

$$
\begin{array}{|l}
\underline{SPre_{m,C}} \\
State_C; \\
In_m \\
\hline
Pre_{m,C} \\
\end{array}
$$

This schema represents the 'precondition' of the method – outside of the condition represented by the predicate the method should not be executed (strictly, an implementation for the method is not required to be able to deal with states and inputs not satisfying this condition).

$$
\begin{array}{|l}
\underline{Schema_{m,C}} \\
\Delta State_C \\
In_m \\
Out_m \\
\hline
Def_{m,C} \\
\end{array}
$$

2.1.2 Objects and Methods

If C is a class, the declaration $a : C$ is interpreted as $a : State_C$ in standard Z, with the following additional translations of methods. If m is a method of C, with definition in the form given above, $a.m$ expands to

$$a.m_{full} \setminus (\Delta State_C)$$

where

$$
\begin{array}{|l}
\underline{a.m_{full}} \\
a : C; \\
a' : C; \\
Schema_{m,C}; \\
SPre_{m,C} \\
\hline
a = \theta C\ \wedge \\
a' = \theta C' \\
\end{array}
$$

Only identifiers can be used in this form of method application. If we have, for example, $fc : Cid \rightarrow C$, we need to write suitable circumlocutions of the method application $fc(c).m$ in order to reduce it to the above form. Renaming of schema variables is used to supply 'actual parameters' to a method application: $a.m[vv/ww]$ denotes the above schema with the variable ww replaced by the expression vv. ww must be an input or output variable of the schema. This extends standard Z in the case that vv is not a variable name, in that declarations $ww : T$ will now be syntactically invalid in the substituted schema. In this case the declarations are omitted and the corresponding set membership assertions are used in the predicates of schema texts in which the substitution takes place.

2.2 Internal Consistency

Internal consistency of the class C is then expressible as follows:

$$(i): \quad \vdash \exists State_C \bullet true$$

That is, there is an element in the state space. This corresponds to the criterion of non-triviality of a specification in the 'established strategy' for Z [3].

$$(ii): \quad \vdash SPre_{m,C} \Rightarrow pre\ Schema_{m,C}$$

That is, the explicit precondition of the method implies its implicit precondition.

$$(iii): \quad \vdash \forall c;\ c' \bullet SPre_{m,C} \wedge$$
$$[State_C;\ c';\ In_m;\ Out_m \mid Def_{m,C}] \Rightarrow State'_C$$

That is, each method, when executed within its precondition, guarantees to produce a state satisfying the invariant of the class.

If an initialisation operation

$$
\begin{array}{|l}
\_Init_C _____ \\
\ State_C \\
\hline
\ \psi \\
\end{array}
$$

is specified, we must have:

$$(iv): \quad \vdash \exists State_C \bullet \psi$$

2.3 Refinement

The refinement relation $\sqsubseteq$ ('is refined by') between specifications and between specifications and implementations is a key concept in any formal approach which aims at the development of executable systems from specifications using rigorous processes. At the same time, proof of refinements between specifications are acknowledged to be extremely expensive and difficult to perform. A definition of refinement for a formal language must therefore satisfy a number of criteria:

- it must be semantically valid – any implementation of a refined specification D must be valid as an implementation of the specification C it refines, ie, $C \sqsubseteq D$ and $code \models D \Rightarrow code \models C$, where $code \models S$ is an implementation relation 'code implements S';

- a more philosophical version of the above criteria is that a user of class C should be unable to determine if an instance of D is provided in place of an instance of C – externally visible behaviour of D instances should be entirely compatible with that of C instances;

- the definition should include all valid forms of refinement which are used in industrial practice for the language in question;

- refinement proof obligations must be directly calculatable from the visible components of the specifications;

- these proof obligations should be decomposable into sub-ordinate conditions, to allow partitioning of the proof effort (rather than these obligations being presented as one monolithic condition);

- it should be reflexive ($C \sqsubseteq C$) and transitive ($C \sqsubseteq D \wedge D \sqsubseteq E \Rightarrow C \sqsubseteq E$);

- ideally, it should define a finitely complete lattice of specifications.

Additional criteria, more specifically related to object-oriented formal languages, will be given below.

We will define a concept of refinement which appears to satisfy most of these criteria. It is adapted directly from the Z concept of refinement between specifications, which itself arose from a need to represent the forms of refinement reasoning which were used in industrial practice.

Our refinement relation is denoted by

$$C \sqsubseteq_{\phi, R} D$$

where C and D are defined classes, R is a predicate upon the states of C and D, and ϕ is a finite map from the names of methods of C to the names of methods of D. The finiteness of ϕ is in contrast to the concept of refinement which has been used in ZEST [6]. ϕ need not be surjective since adding extra methods is considered to produce a refinement, and it need not be injective, since it may be possible for two distinct operations to be implemented using a single more general operation in a refinement.

It is defined by the conditions (i) – (v) below, where C is defined as above, and D has corresponding definitions d, Inv_D, $State_D$, etc, and with a corresponding operation $n = \phi(m)$ with $In_n \hat{=} In_m$, $Out_n \hat{=} Out_m$ for each operation m of C.

The requirement (i) is not strictly necessary for the results of this paper, however it is a quality constraint which prevents certain pathological situations. The restriction that input and output schemas should be identical still allows a limited form of operation polymorphism, since, as a result of axiom (ii), we can consider that each element $a \in D$ corresponds to some element $a^R \in C$, hence an operation may always be applied to elements of subtypes of its declared input types.

We encapsulate the refinement relation into a schema:

```
┌─ RSchema ─────────────────────────────────────────────
│  c;
│  d
│ ──────────
│  R
│
└───────────────────────────────────────────────────────
```

The conditions for refinement of C by D via R and ϕ are then:

(i) : $\vdash State_D \wedge RSchema \Rightarrow State_C$

That is, for every concrete state d and every abstract state c related to this state by R, c is actually in the state space of C.

(ii) : $\vdash State_D \Rightarrow \exists State_C \bullet RSchema$

This is a consistency constraint: it rules out $R \equiv false$ for instance. It is also related to the requirement that refinement implies subtyping: every instance of D has a corresponding (R-related) instance of C.

(iii) : $\vdash RSchema \wedge SPre_{m,C} \Rightarrow SPre_{n,D}$

That is, the precondition of the refined operation may be weaker than the precondition of the original operation, under the refinement relation.

Note that the precondition of an operation implicitly contains the state invariant of its class.

(iv) :

$$\vdash RSchema \wedge SPre_{m,C} \wedge Schema_{n,D} \Rightarrow$$
$$\exists State'_C \bullet RSchema' \wedge Schema_{m,C}$$

That is, the postcondition of the refined method may be stronger.

(iii) and (iv) must hold for each pair (m, n) of methods, where m is a method of C and $n = \phi(m)$ is a method of D.

The final condition for refinement relates to temporal logic predicates:

(v) : $\vdash H_D \Rightarrow \phi(H_C)$

where application of ϕ denotes renaming of the names for methods of C in H_C by the names of corresponding methods under ϕ of D. A semantics for history constraints is given in the appendix.

We may drop one or both of ϕ and R from the statement $C \sqsubseteq_{\phi,R} D$ when they correspond to the default values: the identity mapping and the *true* predicate.

2.3.1 Refinement and Subtyping

The concept of refinement used in Z^{++} has been chosen in order to have a close link with *subtyping*. If a user of an instance of specification (class) C instead received an instance of D, where

$$C \sqsubseteq_{\phi,R} D$$

then they should be able to safely use this instance as if it were an instance of
C, remembering only to perform a suitable substitution of method names of C
for the corresponding names of D.

This is a further requirement upon a definition of refinement, specific to
object-oriented languages where specification modules can be regarded as types.
It is almost satisfied in the presented framework, although there are limitations
concerned with temporal constraints and the emulation of two different methods
by a single method in a refinement. These are discussed in section 2.4. The
above requirement is also specified in the Object Management Group's Object
Model [23].

2.3.2 Transitivity and Reflexivity of Refinement

If C is a consistent class then it is clear that $C \sqsubseteq C$.

It is direct also to show that refinement is transitive, in particular, that:

$$\frac{C \sqsubseteq_{\phi,R} D \qquad\qquad D \sqsubseteq_{\psi,S} E}{C \sqsubseteq_{\phi;\ \psi,\exists\ State_D \bullet R \wedge S} E}$$

where the sets of variables of C, D and E are disjoint.

2.3.3 Existence of Co-products

We can define a syntactic operation upon two classes which defines a 'least
common refinement' of both. This is clearly important in a development, where
we may wish to save effort in separate development and refinement to code
of two similar specification components. It is related to the use of theory
combination operators in algebraic specification languages.

First, notice that if C and D are two classes whose only difference is a one-
one renaming of attribute names and a one-one renaming of method names,
then C and D are mutual refinements. Thus we can always assume that the
respective sets of attribute names and method names of two different classes
are disjoint.

The co-product (least common refinement) construction on classes can be
defined as follows. Let C and D be classes with no common variables or
operations. The strict inheritance [13] E of both in the empty class is the class
with attributes those of both C and D, invariant the conjunction of Inv_C and
Inv_D, and for each operation m of C, an operation m defined as for m in C
but with $Schema_{m,E} \mathbin{\widehat{=}} Schema_{m,C} \wedge \Delta State_D$. Similarly, for every operation
n of D there is a corresponding operation n of E which is completely nondeterministic on $State_C$.

Then E is a refinement of both C and D, using the refinement schema
$State_C \wedge State_D$.

This construction is the least refined class refining C and D in the following
sense. If E is any class (with variables disjoint from those of C and D, without
loss of generality) then:

$$\frac{C \sqsubseteq_{\phi,R} E \qquad\qquad D \sqsubseteq_{\psi,S} E}{C \pm D \sqsubseteq_{\phi \cup \psi, R \wedge S} E}$$

Note that the 'initial object' in the category of classes and refinements is the empty class $\emptyset$. The 'terminal object' is any class with a false invariant and history constraint, and at least one method. These are pseudo-initial and terminal since uniqueness of the resulting refinements is not obtained.

2.4 Limitations of Refinement Concept

There are two specific problems which can be identified with the above definition $C \sqsubseteq_{\phi,R} D$ of refinement:

- strengthening a history invariant leads to a refinement, however this does not imply type compatibility, since a user of C may exercise sequences of operation invocations which are disallowed by the stronger history constraint of D;

- ϕ is allowed to be non-injective, ie, we can refine two distinct methods in C by a single method in D. This is not legitimate if we are in an implementation environment where more than one method of a class can be executing concurrently, but where no more than one invocation of a given method can be executing at one one time (it may be a non-re-entrant procedure).

Related to these problems is the choice to be made regarding the dynamic semantics of the methods of a class. In Z specifications it is often implicitly assumed that operations are scheduled in a strictly interleaved fashion: one operation must complete before another can be invoked. This is the semantics proposed for temporal logic in Object-Z and it is the interpretation we have adopted. However, other approaches to the use of Object-Z notation, such as [20], have allowed many invocations of a method and invocations of distinct methods of a class, to be executing concurrently. This requires an alternative interpretation of temporal logic formulae, or, as in [20], the use of a different formalism for concurrent behaviour, such as RTL (Real Time Logic), which allows discussion of the i'th invocation of a method, rather than the unit of time in which a method occurs. A further possibility is to use an alternative concept of subtyping for processes, as is discussed for ZEST in [8].

3 Objects with Identity

Although the above approach is adequate for the use of object classes as an enhanced structuring mechanism for Z specifications, encapsulating state and operations into a single unit, and for supporting global reasoning about the relationships between such units, this form of specification is not adequate to represent objects with a persistent identity.

Object identity introduces problems of aliasing – two variables denoting identical objects, so that an application of a method to one variable changes the contents of the other, of ownership – one object being shared between more than one other object, and of clusters of interconnected objects – where the unit of modularity is not a class but instead a logically linked collection of objects of (potentially) several classes.

In the following sections we examine existing approaches to this problem. We will propose a particular Z-like notation, which we will term 'reference Z' that provides some syntactic sugar for treatment of object identities within Z or Z^{++}.

3.1 Existing Approaches

There are three current approaches to the treatment of object identity in an object-oriented specification language: (i) 'ignore' (ie, treat objects as values only); (ii) model implicitly; (iii) model explicitly.

The first option was taken by early versions of Object-Z and Z^{++}. In this approach class types are identified with the schema type of their state schema, or a set of *histories* of state schema values. There is no inherent concept of identity for objects, other than equality as values of a schema type or sets of sequences of elements of a schema type.

A substantial drawback of this approach is that sharing of objects is not correctly expressed: copy semantics is used when an assignment of one variable to another is performed, rather than an aliasing association (a copy of identity).

The second approach (implicit modelling) involves the use of the same surface syntax as Z or object-oriented Z as described above, but this syntax is given a new semantics which regards elements of a class type as denoting objects with a persistent identity in addition to being associated with a member of the schema type of the state schema of the class. The approach further sub-divides into two approaches:

- allowed access to the set of existing objects and other non-standard specification items;

- no direct access (in unexpanded notation) to non-standard specification items.

The former approach is adopted by OOZE and reference Z, the latter by the current version of Object-Z. In either approach, we have the intuitive situation that each class type C (strictly, the set $@C$ of identities of objects of C) is partitioned into two sets – those elements which are purely 'potential' instances, and those which are actual instances.

Creation of an object moves an element from the potential object set to the actual object set. In Object-Z there is only limited control over allocation – the set of object-id's of existing objects is not available directly. In the OOZE and reference Z approaches it is. We expand on this approach in section 3.2 below. The drawbacks of this approach are:

- it may be unclear to a reader when value or reference semantics is being used;

- it creates a larger gap between the notation and conventional Z;

- it may bias implementation of specification aspects (for example associations) towards the use of object id's and pointers.

The final approach (explicit modelling) uses a (possibly non-object-oriented) specification language to directly represent the object concept. There is no need to translate the surface syntax into a more basic notation. B Abstract Machine Notation [1] has been used effectively for this approach, using a systematic translation of domain and analysis models into B specifications [15]. The approach of Hall [28] also fits into this category, although it uses some syntactic sugar to avoid excessive low-level specification machinery.

The explicit approach can lead to the drawbacks of being notationally cumbersome, its use of global variables re-introduces violation of encapsulation, and it is removed from OO language notation (but not concepts). The case study of Section 5 uses the reference Z notation in a relatively explicit way.

3.2   A Reference Semantics for Z

We will now define an alternative interpretation of the class / object / method syntax described in Section 2 in order to reflect the existence of object identities.

Defining a class C defines a set of identities (a given set in Z terms) $@C$ for the schema type of C (which will itself be named C), and a global map

$$*_C : @C \nrightarrow C$$

We write $a : @C$ for 'a has value an object (identity) of C'. $\overline{C}$ is used to denote $dom *_C$, the set of currently existing instances of C.

By convention, in an implicit approach using reference Z, the differences between $@C$ and C in state declarations, between $\overline{C}$ and C in method parameter definitions, and between $*_C(x).v$ and $x.v$ are ignored.

The global state referring to elements of C is:

$$
\begin{array}{|l}
\hline
\textit{Instances}_C \\
\hline
*_C : @C \nrightarrow C \\
\overline{C} : \mathbf{P}(@C) \\
\hline
\overline{C} = dom *_C \\
\hline
\end{array}
$$

An operation to create an instance $c!$ of C is given by:

$$
\begin{array}{|l}
\hline
\textit{Create}_C \\
\hline
\Delta \textit{Instances}_C \\
c! : @C \\
\hline
\exists\, c : C \bullet \\
\quad c! \notin \overline{C} \ \wedge \\
\quad *_C' = *_C \oplus \{c! \mapsto c\} \\
\hline
\end{array}
$$

This standard schema can be replaced by specific schemas to (for instance) assign default values to the attributes of a new instance of a class. This operation must occur before any initialisation operation of the class is applied: it creates an object which satisfies the class invariant, but no other details of its attribute values are determined.

For $a : @C$, $a.m$ expands to:

$$a.m_{full} \setminus (\Delta State_C; \ \Delta[a_{val} : C])$$

where:

$$
\begin{array}{|l|}
\hline
\;a.m_{full} \\[-1pt]
\hline
a,\, a' : @C; \\
a_{val},\, a'_{val} : C; \\
\Delta\, Instances_C; \\
Schema_{m,C}; \\
SPre_{m,C} \\
\hline
a' = a \\
a \in \overline{C} \\
a_{val} = \theta C \\
a'_{val} = \theta C' \\
a_{val} = *_C(a) \\
*'_C = *_C \oplus \{a \mapsto a'_{val}\} \\
\hline
\end{array}
$$

Note that here the object identity a is unchanged – the value pointed to is modified. Objects are pointers to (schema type) values, and this has advantages in defining promoted applications of schemas, as discussed for Object-Z in [16, Chapter 5].

No method can change the identity of the object it operates on, but this identity can be set explicitly by assignment (as with $xx' = cc$).

In OOZE, the notation $\overline{X} \bullet objs$ denotes the sequence of currently existing objects for each class X, considered as an attribute of a meta-class $\overline{X}$ managing the allocation and de-allocation of instances of X. There is a meta-class method Del used to remove a particular object (identity) from this sequence.

Note that the reference semantics approach resolves a significant problem with existing object-oriented specification languages, which is the representation of mutually recursive class types. This problem was highlighted by [19], which proposed the use of non-well-founded set theory as a solution. We feel the reference semantics approach is a less drastic solution, and is more general (infinitary type constructions such as P can be used in conjunction with class-valued attributes in a self-reference cycle, and a class can contain an attribute of its own type). The reason this works is illustrated by the following example of mutually recursive schemas:

$$
\begin{array}{|l|}
\hline
\;C \\[-1pt]
\hline
a : D; \\
t : Z \\
\hline
\end{array}
$$

$$
\begin{array}{|l|}
\hline
\;D \\[-1pt]
\hline
b : C; \\
s : N \\
\hline
\end{array}
$$

These are interpreted as the specification:

$[@D, @C]$

$$
\begin{array}{|l}
\hline
\;C \underline{\hspace{8cm}} \\
\; a : @D; \\
\; t : \mathbf{Z} \\
\hline
\end{array}
$$

$$
\begin{array}{|l}
\hline
\;D \underline{\hspace{8cm}} \\
\; b : @C; \\
\; s : \mathbf{N} \\
\hline
\end{array}
$$

$$
\begin{array}{|l}
\hline
\;GlobalState \underline{\hspace{6cm}} \\
\; *_C : @C \twoheadrightarrow C; \\
\; *_D : @D \twoheadrightarrow D \\
\hline
\end{array}
$$

(Omitting $\overline{C}$, etc).

Such a situation is common in data models of real-world systems, and the use of relationships and associations between classes is a major part of such techniques as OMT [25]. Commonly, there will be a pair of links between classes, which are intended to be mutually inverse. This constraint can be formally stated as follows:

$$
\forall c : \overline{C}; \; d : \overline{D} \bullet \\
\qquad d = *_C(c).a \;\equiv\; \\
\qquad c = *_C(d).b
$$

in the above case.

Thus this approach supports the direct interpretation of OMT data models as sets of (possibly mutually referring) classes, and therefore supports the integration of formal and structured methods.

We adopted this approach, rather than the somewhat more abstract approach of defining relationships between classes as conventional relationships between their object identity sets, since it created a closer correspondence between the explicit specification text and the expanded Z specification it defines. In addition, both parts of a relationship are often named in informal models, with neither being regarded as derived.

3.3 Object Identity versus Object Equality

In this interpretation we have two different concepts of equality: *identity* between two variables x, y with values in $@C$, simply expressed by

$$
x = y
$$

and *equality* of values x, $y : \overline{C}$:

$$
*_C(x) = *_C(y)
$$

It is possible therefore for these two object-valued variables to represent equal but non-identical objects (when the latter equation holds but the former does not) and for them to represent identical objects (when both equations hold).

If the attributes of an object are themselves object-valued, then equality of objects means that the object values of corresponding attributes are identical, and so forth recursively. Thus object equality, which could be written as $x \sim y$ in a purely implicit notation, really means that x and y share some storage locations if either involves (at any level) object class types.

As an example, consider defining a *Point* class with an attribute

$$owner : Shape$$

where

$$
\begin{array}{|l}
\hline
\quad Shape \\\hline
type\_of\_shape : SHAPE\_TYPE \\
owns\_points : \mathbf{P}(Point) \\
\hline
\end{array}
$$

and *owns_points* and *owner* are mutually inverse.

Then if $s1, s2 : \overline{Shape}$, we have that

$$s1 \sim s2 \Rightarrow$$
$$*_{Shape}(s1).owns\_points = *_{Shape}(s2).owns\_points$$

ie, that these sets have the same (identical object) members.

Note that when we create a point instance, we have to create a shape instance for it to belong to – or adopt an existing shape and modify its *owns_points* attribute.

It is possible to define objects which always 'know their own identity', that is, each class C by convention would contain an attribute

$$self : @C$$

and

$$
\begin{array}{|l}
\hline
\quad Instances_C \\\hline
\overline{C} : \mathbf{P}(@C) \\
*_C : @C \twoheadrightarrow C \\
\hline
\overline{C} = dom(*_C) \\
\forall c : \overline{C} \bullet \\
\qquad *_C(c).self = c \\
\hline
\end{array}
$$

which may lead to a more natural specification style in some cases. However in this case object equality implies object identity.

4 Reasoning Techniques for Object-Oriented Z

As a consequence of the above definition of refinement, we can define a number of simple rules for proving that certain transformations upon classes are refinements. These general rules remove the need to prove refinement in a number of cases, thus increasing the practicality of fully formal development from specification to code. In addition, the language provides a framework for the specification of reusable software modules, both for semantic analysis during assessment, and for the rapid and reliable development of new systems.

4.1 Generic Refinement Rules

A number of rules, such as that strict inheritance is a refinement, are given in
[14]. In addition we can derive the following:

(*Cond*) : $\quad\quad$ C and D are classes with the same methods and
state, except that the method m of C, defined by:

$$E \ \& $$
$$m \ x \ y \quad ==> \quad P_1$$

is replaced by the method

$$r \ x \ y \ ==> \ (E \ \wedge \ P_1) \ \vee$$
$$(\neg \ E \ \wedge \ P_2)$$

of D, with the same input and output types as m.

ϕ is $id_{\underline{methods}(C)} \oplus \{m \mapsto r\}$, R is *true*.

The same rule is true if m were defined by

$$\neg \ E \ \& $$
$$m \ x \ y \ ==> \ P_2$$

Similarly, we have the rule that a weakening of the precondition . . . .
leads to a refinement:

(*WeakenPre*) :

$$\frac{\vdash SPre_{m,C} \Rightarrow SPre_{n,D}}{C \sqsubseteq_{\phi, true} D}$$

where $\phi = id_{\underline{methods}(C)} \oplus \{m \mapsto n\}$, and D and C are identical apart from the
changed precondition and name of m.

Refinement and reasoning techniques for Z specifications involving the explicit manipulation of memory addresses as pointers are given in [26]. These
can be adopted for the specification style described in this paper.

4.2 Specific Refinement Processes

Certain 'standard' refinements can be shown to be refinements in this context.
For instance, the refinement of a class $Set[X]$ by a corresponding sequence class:

```
CLASS Set[X]                      CLASS Seq₁[X]
OWNS                              OWNS
  s  :  P(X)                        sq  :  seq(X)
OPERATIONS                        OPERATIONS
  add  :  X  →;                     add  :  X  →;
  init  :  →;                       init  :  →;
  del  :  X  →;                     del  :  X  →;
  is_in  :  X  →                    is_in  :  X  →
ACTIONS                           ACTIONS
  add x  ==>                        add x  ==>
    s' = s ∪ { x };                   sq' = sq ⌢ ⟨ x ⟩;
  init ==>                          init ==>
    s' = { };                         sq' = ⟨ ⟩;
  del x ==>                         del x ==>
    s' = s − { x };                   sq' = squash(sq, x);
  is_in x  ==>                      is_in x  ==>
    x ∈ s                             x ∈ ran(sq)
END CLASS                         END CLASS
```

$squash$ removes all occurrences of x from the sequence sq, returning a sequence.

This refinement is implemented by:

$$Set[S] \sqsubseteq_{s=ran(sq)} Seq_1[S]$$

for any type S. Note that the signature and external behaviour of the class $Set[S]$ is maintained by $Seq_1[S]$, but the internal implementation has changed – to support more effective implementation or analysis.

Similarly we have a refinement of a bag class (with operations of add, $init$ and del) by a sequence class:

```
CLASS Bag[X]                      CLASS Seq₂[X]
OWNS                              OWNS
  b  :  bag(X)                       sq  :  seq(X)
OPERATIONS                        OPERATIONS
  add  :  X  →;                      add  :  X  →;
  init  :  →;                        init  :  →;
  del  :  X  →;                      del  :  X  →
  is_in  :  X  →                   ACTIONS
ACTIONS                             add x  ==>
  add x ==>                            sq' = sq ⌢ ⟨ x ⟩;
    b' = b ⊎ [ x ];                  init ==>
  init ==>                             sq' = ⟨ ⟩;
    b' = [ ];                        del x ==>
  del x ==>                            sq' = squash₁(sq, x)
    b' = b ~ [ x ];              END CLASS
END CLASS
```

We need an operation $squash_1$ which removes one occurrence of x from the sequence sq, returning a sequence, in order to implement del. The refinement in this case is:

$$Bag[S] \sqsubseteq_{b=\{x:S|x\in ran(sq)\bullet(x,\#sq^{-1}(x))\}} Seq_2[S]$$

Note however, that there are operations on sequences for which there is no corresponding equivalent for a bag or set. For instance:

$$
\begin{aligned}
&get\_oldest \; : \; \rightarrow \; X \\
&sq \; \neq \; \langle \; \rangle \; \& \\
&\qquad get\_oldest \; a! \; ==> \\
&\qquad\qquad\qquad a! \; = \; head(sq)
\end{aligned}
$$

Thus if we added this operation to either version of $Seq[X]$, we would lose the ability to find a suitable set or bag-based refinement.

5 Application: Specification of a Program Analysis Tool

The following examples are taken from a substantial (250 page) specification of an analysis tool for full IBM OS/VS COBOL (COBOL '74). This tool translates the abstract syntax of COBOL programs into a semantic representation, and populates a database with information derived from the program.

The abstract representation of the semantics expresses COBOL constructs in more familiar third generation language constructs, and is intended to be the first step towards an 'intermediate language' which would serve to represent, and support the analysis of, a wide variety of COBOL dialects, and auxilliary languages such as JCL (Job Control Language).

The representation is specified by an ERA model in an object oriented notation with inheritance, relationships with various cardinalities, and abstract and concrete entity types.

An example of this notation is given in Figure 1, which describes an *Iterative_statement*, a generic loop representation.

The need for formal specification of the translation process arises from the need to establish the correctness of the translation: or high-integrity applications, the validity of any results from semantic analysis of these applications must themselves have a high degree of assurance. The integrity requirements upon tools used to analyse safety-critical systems in particular are nearly as rigorous as for the systems themselves, in standards such as DEF STAN 00-55 [22].

The above entity description has the corresponding formal description in the fully expanded reference Z style:

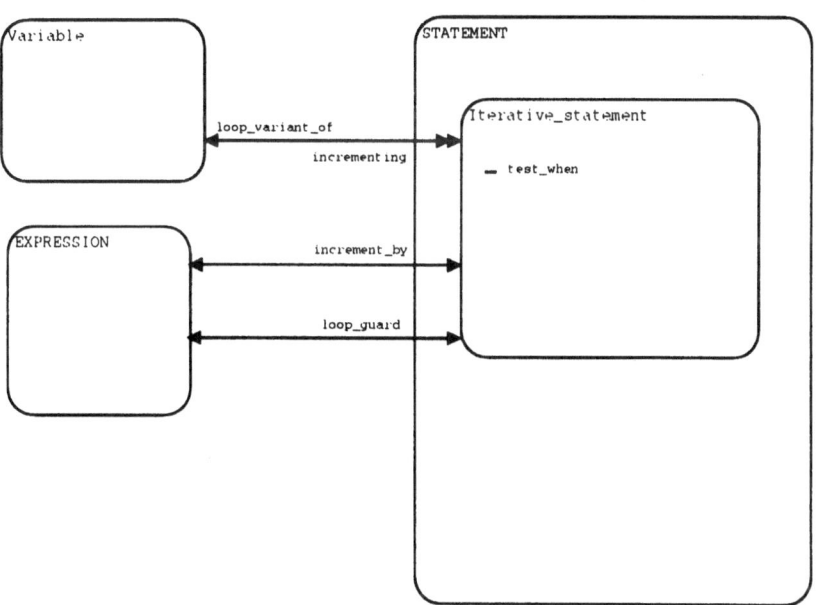

Figure 1: ERA specification of Iterative Statements

254

```
┌─ Iterative_statement ──────────────────────────────────
│  COMMENTED
│  CONTROL_FLOW_NODE
│  CONTROL_FLOW_PARENT
│  EXPRESSION_USER
│  PROCEDURAL_MODULE_COMPONENT
│  STATEMENT
│  SYMBOL
│  VARIABLE_DECLARER
│  test_when : TEST_WHEN
│  increment_by : @EXPRESSION
│  incrementing : @Variable
│  loop_guard : @EXPRESSION
└────────────────────────────────────────────────────────
```

where:

$$TEST\_WHEN ::= TEST\_WHEN\_NULL$$
$$|\ \ DO\_WHILE\_BEFORE$$
$$|\ \ REPEAT\_UNTIL\_AFTER$$

Each concrete and abstract type C has a corresponding creation schema $Create_C$ which assigns default values to links and attributes (the empty sequence or set to many-valued links, a non-assigned object identity to a entity-valued attribute, and the empty string to string-valued attributes. The default value of an enumerated type is the first element).

The operations to translate COBOL source code items into such entity types are specified as operations acting upon the $Instances_C$ schemas of these types. That is, they can be regarded as methods of the classes which correspond to the ERA entity types.

As an example, we consider the representation of a particular COBOL loop construct.

5.1 Translation of PERFORM statements

There are a number of loop-like constructs in COBOL. The PERFORM statement in particular has a number of variants which are semantically loops. One particular format is the PERFORM UNTIL statement, which has the syntax:

```
PERFORM proc_1 [ { THRU | THROUGH } proc₂ ]
   UNTIL cond
```

This is interpreted as the statements:

```
WHILE ¬ cond
DO
   perform_stat
END
```

Where *perform_stat* represents the perform through clause.

Its creation operation involves the following actions:

```
┌─ Create_Perform_Until ─────────────────────────────────────
│  Create_Basic_Perform
│  Δ Instances_Boolean_uni_expression
│  Δ Instances_Iterative_statement
│  Δ Instances_Factored_iteration
│
│  buexp : Boolean_uni_expression
│  exp : EXPRESSION
│
│  Create_Boolean_uni_expression[buexp/boolean_uni_expression!]
│  Create_Iterative_statement
│  Create_Factored_iteration
│  Create_EXPRESSION[exp/expression!]
├─────────────────────────────────────────────────────────────
│  factored_iteration!′.iterative_type = ITERATIVE_UNTIL
│  iterative_statement!′.test_when = DO_WHILE_BEFORE
│  iterative_statement!′.loop_guard = buexp
│  buexp′.used_within = {iterative_statement!}
│  buexp′.bool_uni_op = NOT
│  buexp′.first_factor = exp
│  exp′.used_within = {buexp}
│  iterative_statement!′.nodes_are_seq = ⟨perform_statement!⟩
│  perform_statement!′.node_of = iterative_statement!
└─────────────────────────────────────────────────────────────
```

This operation is an expanded sequential composition of actions upon the individual objects exp, $buexp$, $factored\_iteration!$, $perform\_statement!$ and $iterative\_statement!$. The invariant that (for example) $nodes\_are\_seq$ is an inverse to $node\_of$ is maintained as a result of the execution of the complete operation, rather than of its individual components.

The expression exp is created for *cond* according the definition of creation operations for expressions.

Create_Basic_Perform creates the statement

$$perform\_statement! : \overline{Perform\_statement}$$

which represents the

PERFORM $proc\_1$ [{ **THRU** | **THROUGH** } $proc_2$]

clause.

Each attribute update

$$instance'.attr = val$$

is an abbreviation for the requirement:

$$*'_{Class}(instance).attr = val$$

Where *Class* is the class of *instance*. Note that attributes not explicitly changed are assumed to remain unchanged: here there are no invariants linking distinct attributes of the same object, so that the requirements of internal consistency are simple to discharge.

5.2 Results

The parser and populator is currently being implemented in C, on the TBK object-oriented database [11]. The close link between the structure of the specification and the structure of the implementation has resulted in a faster refinement step than is normally possible. This is due to the abstract nature of the database interface operations, which directly correspond to operations for manipulating sets of object instances.

We would have found the animation facilities of tools such as the B Toolkit for B AMN useful in developing the specification, however, the scale of the specification would have been at the limit of those specifications for which B has been used, and we felt it was less of a risk to adopt a version of Z. In addition, the B approach to explicit representation of object identities would have been more prolix and cumbersome to use. Thus a more implicit style of treatment of object identities was used.

6 Conclusions

We have shown that development of a clear semantic framework for object-oriented specification is possible, based upon the standardised specification language Z. This framework can include simple forms of temporal reasoning and treatment of object identity. It supports global and local reasoning about the properties of specifications. Outstanding issues remaining are:

- integration of more complex forms of concurrent and dynamic behaviour specification, such as real time logic [20];

- development of tools to support specification expansion to Z;

- development of tools and techniques to support proof of internal consistency and refinement – particularly in the case of reference Z, to avoid where possible the need to expand the notation to the pure standard Z form.

Progress has however been made in using the language with informal diagrammatic notations, such as Rumbaugh's OMT [16, Chapter 3], and in using it to define substantial functional specifications of program analysis tools [12, 17].

Acknowledgement

The research conducted in this paper was performed under the REM Eureka project. The author wishes to thank the Committee at Lloyd's Register for permission to submit this paper for publication. The views expressed in the paper are the opinions of the author and are not necessarily the views of Lloyd's Register. The contributions of G. Ostrolenk and H. Haughton are acknowledged.

References

[1] J R Abrial. *Assigning Programs to Meaning*. Prentice Hall International, 1994. To appear.

[2] A J Alencar and J A Goguen. OOZE: An Object-Oriented Z Environment. In P America, editor, *ECOOP '91 Proceedings, LNCS 512*, pages 180-199. Springer-Verlag, July 1991.

[3] R Barden, S Stepney, and D Cooper. *Z in Practice*. Logica Cambridge, 1993.

[4] D Carrington, D Duke, R Duke, P King, G A Rose, and G Smith. Object-Z: An object-oriented extension to Z. In *Formal Description Techniques, II (FORTE'89)*, pages 281 - 296. North-Holland, 1990.

[5] C Carter. Object-Oriented Analysis and Recursive Development in Safety-Critical System Development. In *Proceedings of Object Technology '93*, 1993.

[6] E Cusack. Object-oriented modelling in Z. In P America, editor, *ECOOP '91 Proceedings*, Springer-Verlag Lecture Notes in Computer Science. Springer-Verlag, 1991.

[7] E Cusack. Using z in communications engineering. In J Nicholls, editor, *Z User Meeting 1992*, Workshops in Computer Science. Springer-Verlag, 1993.

[8] E Cusack and C Wezeman. Deriving tests for objects specified in Z. In J Nicholls, editor, *Z User Meeting 1992*, Workshops in Computer Science. Springer-Verlag, 1993.

[9] E Foster et al. PoeT: Object Engineering in Public Transport. In *Proceedings Object Technology '93*, 1993.

[10] The RAISE Language Group. *The RAISE SPECIFICATION LANGUAGE*. Prentice Hall, 1992.

[11] IPSYS Limited. *TBK Version 2.5 Manual (3 Volumes)*, 1991.

[12] K Lano. Functional Specification of Mapping of MVS and DOS JCL into the JCL Schema. Technical report, Applied Information Engineering, Lloyd's Register, Feb 1993.

[13] K Lano and H Haughton. Reasoning and refinement in object-oriented specification languages. In *ECOOP '92 Conference Proceedings*. Springer Verlag, 1992.

[14] K Lano and H Haughton. Reuse and adaptation of Z specifications. In *Proceedings of Z User Meeting 1992*. Springer Verlag, 1992.

[15] K Lano and H Haughton. Approaches to object identity. In *EROS II Workshop*. LBMS London, 1993.

[16] K Lano and H Haughton. *Object-Oriented Specification Case Studies*. Lloyd's Register of Shipping, 1993.

[17] K Lano and G. Ostrolenk. The Mapping of OS/VS COBOL into the COBOL Schema. Technical Report CHASE-LR-32, Applied Information Engineering, Lloyd's Register, June 1993.

[18] A W Leigh. *Real Time Software for Small Systems*. Halstead Press, 1988.

[19] I Maung and J R Howse. Introducing Hyper-Z: A new approach to object-orientation in Z. In *Z User Meeting 1992, Springer-Verlag Workshops in Computer Science*. Springer-Verlag, 1993.

[20] J McDermid. An approach to the specification of real time systems, York University, 1992.

[21] S R L Meira and A L C Cavalcanti. Modular Object-Oriented Z Specifications. In *Z User Meeting 1990, Workshops in Computing Series*, pages 173 – 192. Springer-Verlag, 1991.

[22] Ministry of Defence. *The Procurement of Safety Critical Software in Defence Equipment*. Interim Defence Standard 00-55 Issue 1.

[23] Object Management Group. *OMG Architecture Guide*, 1992.

[24] J. Robinson and S. Menani Menad. Developing an environment for computer-based automative suspension and steering systems. In *Directions in Safety Critical Systems*, pages 150 – 167. Springer-Verlag, 1993.

[25] J Rumbaugh, M Blaha, W Premerlani, F Eddy, and W Lorensen. *Object-Oriented Modelling and Design*. Prentice-Hall International, Englewood Cliffs, NJ (USA), 1991.

[26] C T Sennett. Formal specification and implementation. In C T Sennett, editor, *High Integrity Software*, Computer Systems Series. Pitman, 1989.

[27] M Spivey. *The Z Notation: A Reference Manual, 2nd Edition*. Prentice Hall, 1992.

[28] S Stepney, R Barden, and D Cooper, editors. *Object Orientation in Z*. Springer-Verlag Workshops in Computer Science, 1992.

[29] P A Swatman. Using formal specification in the acquisition of information systems: Educating information systems professionals. In *Z User Meeting 1992*, Workshops in Computer Science. Springer-Verlag, 1993.

[30] A Wills. Capsules and types in Fresco: Program verification in Smalltalk. In P America, editor, *ECOOP '91 Proceedings, LNCS Vol. 512*, pages 59 – 76. Springer-Verlag, 1991.

A Z++

A.1 BNF Syntax Description

The general description of a Z++ class specification is as follows:

$Object\_Class$ ::= **CLASS** $Identifier$ $TypeParameters$ [**EXTENDS** $Imported$]
[**TYPES** $Types$] [**FUNCTIONS** $Axdefs$]
[**OWNS** $Locals$]
[**RETURNS** $Optypes$]
[**OPERATIONS** $Optypes$]
[**INVARIANT** $Predicate$]
[**ACTIONS** $Acts$]
[**CONSTRAINTS** $Constraints$]
[**HISTORY** $History$]
END CLASS

where:

$TypeParameters$ ::= ["[" $Parlist$ "]"]

$Parlist$ ::= $Identifier$ [, $Parlist$]
 | $Identifier$ $\ll$ $Identifier$
   [, $Parlist$]

$Imported$ ::= $Idlist$

$Types$ ::= $Type\_Declarations$

$Locals$ ::= $Identifier$: $Type$; $Locals$
 | $Identifier$: $Type$

$Optypes$ ::= [*] $Identifier$: $Idlist$ $\rightarrow$
    $Idlist$; $Optypes$
 | [*] $Identifier$: $Idlist$ $\rightarrow$
    $Idlist$

$Acts$ ::= [*] [$Expression$ **&**] $Identifier$
    $Idlist$ ==> $Code$; $Acts$
 | [*] [$Expression$ **&**] $Identifier$
    $Idlist$ ==> $Code$
$Constraints$ ::= $Equation$
 | $Equation$; $Constraints$
$History$ ::= $Fmla_{LTL}$

The **HISTORY** predicate specifies the admissible execution sequences of objects of the class, using linear temporal logic formulae with operators [] (henceforth), $\bigcirc$ (next), and $\diamond$ (eventually). Further temporal logic operators, such as ; (chop), * (iterate), _before_ (before) and _until_ (until), can also be defined. The default temporal predicate is []$true$.

Operations which are prefixed by the * symbol are spontaneous internal actions: they cannot be called by clients or descendants of the class, although they become spontaneous internal actions of the descendants in turn. They correspond to _daemons_ in object-oriented terminology. Explicit preconditions of methods can be declared via the **&** syntax.

Operation Semantics with Read and Write Frames

Juan Bicarregui

Systems Engineering Division

S.E.R.C. Rutherford Appleton Laboratory, UK

Abstract

The read and write "externals" clauses in VDM implicit operation definitions play two distinct roles. On the one hand, they bind the free variables that appear in the preconditions and postconditions, whilst on the other hand, they can be understood to indicate the sets of state variables that an implementation of the operation can be permitted to "read" and "write". However, in the case of the read frame, existing semantic models for VDM give no formal interpretation to this latter role.

This paper investigates an extension to the denotational model of operations which captures this informal understanding of the read frame. It interprets the read frame via an extra constraint on the semantics of operations which formalises the idea that the behaviour of an operation should not depend on the variables outside the read frame. This semantics is shown to justify a new formalisation of the satisfiability obligation and to yield a property of non-interference between operations with sufficiently disjoint frames. However, some difficulties remain with this approach as a means of justifying algorithm refinement with read frames the resolution of which would require more substantial changes to the semantic model.

1 Introduction

The semantic role of the "read frame" in operation specifications is often underplayed. In VDM, implicit operation definitions have "read" and "write" clauses which serve two purposes. On the one hand, they bind the free variables that appear in the preconditions and postconditions, whilst on the other hand, they can be understood to indicate the largest sets of state variables that any implementation of the operation can be permitted to "read" and "write". Whilst for the write frame this role is formally interpreted by defining the meaning relation as if the postcondition were augmented with "rest unchanged" clauses; it is not the case that the read frame is interpreted as having any semantic meaning whatsoever. However, an informal understanding of what it means for an implementation to restrict its read accesses to a given set of state variables is clear.

If we are to maximise the benefit of formal notations and formal reasoning in the development of realistically sized systems, compositionality in design must be a primary concern. Modularisation of specifications, where the definition of the overall system state and operations is partitioned into modules with formal interfaces defined between them, can be the source of coarse-grained compositionality provided the modularisation mechanisms are sufficiently powerful to allow independent development of separate modules. However, this degree of independence between modules can lead to individual modules which are themselves complex systems.

Compositionality *within* modules, that is, independence in the development of operations (or parts of operations) that share a common state is also a possibility provided some means is given to define the areas of influence of individual operations. Just as the write frame determines the maximal set of state variables that the execution of an operation can influence, the read frame can define the maximal set of state variables by which the behaviour of an operation can be influenced. Properties of non-interference can then be defined for operations with sufficiently disjoint frames and these properties can be exploited to yield greater compositionality in the development of those operations. Thus read and write frames can be seen as a fine-grained counterpart to modularisation which provide for the compositional development of operations that share state within modules.

1.1 Background

Existing formalisations of operation decomposition in model-oriented specification pay little attention to the read frame, in particular, no formal interpretation has been given to the idea that an implicit operation specification might declare that only certain variables should be "read" by any implementation of it.

Jones [Jon87] gives a formalisation of operation decomposition in VDM incorporating some Hoare/Jones style rules describing valid decomposition steps which are justified against a denotational semantics based on relational algebra. This treatment deals in terms of the whole state and, whilst the write frame is interpreted as if the postcondition were augmented with "rest unchanged" clauses, that paper does not consider constraints on implementations imposed by the read frame. The same approach to read and write frames is also taken in the semantics for operations given in [VDM-SL].

In Z [Spi88], the distinction between read-only and read-write variables can be made in the declaration part of a schema through the use of Δ and Ξ in schema inclusion. The syntactic role of binding the variables in schema predicates is played by these declarations and an "open-world" interpretation is given to variables outside this scope (outside this frame anything can happen). This interpretation is useful for the incremental development of specifications as it provides for elegant interpretations of the schema combinators. However, no programming counterparts exist for some of these combinators and so the structure of the specification cannot necessarily be carried down into a structuring of the code. Hence such structuring is not a source of compositionality in development. Furthermore, no explicit treatment of the semantic role of the read frame is given as specifications are flattened before refinement occurs and hence read framing information is lost.

In the Refinement Calculus on the other hand [Mor88, Mor90], where the development of explicit operations is the primary concern, a "closed-world" assumption (outside this frame nothing changes) is made to enable convenient use of coding combinators. Here too, write frames are given an explicit treatment, but no attention is paid to the read frame.

Recent attempts to reconcile these two world views [Kin90, War93] have proposed some intermediate stances. In practice, a switch at some stage in the development from an open world view to a closed world view may suffice, but such a dichotomous approach would seem to be rather artificial.

In B's "Abstract Machines" [Abr93, ALNS91], the use of generalised substitutions as a means of specifying operations brings read and write information to the fore. Furthermore, the extensive facilities available for the structuring of specifications through various forms of machine composition, and the full-hiding and semi-hiding principles that arise from these structuring mechanisms, provide syntactic constraints to the state accesses that can be made by operations. In effect, this provides a form of read and write frames for the operations. Although these syntactic constraints do yield some degree of compositionality in development, no direct interpretation in the semantics is given and so the exact correspondence to the VDM style read and write frames discussed here is not clear.

[Bic93] gives a treatment of operation decomposition where the read and write frames are interpreted as "advanced information" about the state access that any eventual implementation of an operation can be permitted to make. This interpretation is formalised by a set of rules for algorithm refinement where each decomposition step respects the constraints imposed by the read and write frames. In effect, these rules give a definition of satisfaction that is a restriction of the usual refinement relation. However, no interpretation of the read frame in a relational semantics is given.

1.2 This paper

This paper develops a denotational semantics for operations where an interpretation is given to both read and write frames as constraints on the interpretation of operations. Thus it provides a semantic model which might form the foundation of a rule-based definition of algorithm refinement with read frames such as that given in [Bic93].

The next section recaps on the key definitions of [Jon87] and [Bic93] and section 3 gives some simple motivating examples. Section 4 gives a more formal presentation of this semantics and uses it justify a new definition of satisfiability and a property of non-interference. Finally, section 5 discusses some shortcomings of this formalisation and suggests some possible extensions to the work.

2 Recap

2.1 Relational semantics for operations

The interpretation of operations in [Jon87] is given by a pair of semantic functions. The first gives the termination set (of values of the state for which termination is guaranteed) and the second gives the set of possible state transitions (a relation on states).

$$T: Stmt \rightarrow \mathcal{P}(\Sigma)$$
$$M: Stmt \rightarrow \mathcal{P}(\Sigma \times \Sigma)$$

For any statement S, the domain of $\mathcal{M}(S)$ can be thought of as the set of states over which termination is possible and it is required that for all statements

$$T(S) \subseteq \text{dom } \mathcal{M}(S)$$

Refinement is defined in the usual way as a reduction in either non-determinism or undefinedness. For two statements S_1 and S_2, let

$$T_i = T(S_i) \text{ and}$$
$$M_i = \mathcal{M}(S_i)$$

then S_1 being refined by S_2 is defined as follows[1]

$$S_1 \sqsubseteq S_2 \quad \triangle \quad T_1 \subseteq T_2 \quad \wedge \quad M_1 \supseteq (T_1 \triangleleft M_2)$$

Proof rules for operation decomposition are given and justified against this semantics and compositionality and monotonicity are proven.

No treatment is given to parameters and results and the same simplification is taken here. Their treatment can be considered independently of the ideas developed here.

For the purposes of this paper the question of termination is not the focus of interest and thus T is not considered, rather it is assumed that

$$T = \text{dom } M$$

and does not change during refinement.

2.2 Algorithm refinement with read and write frames

In [Bic93] it is argued that the syntactic and semantic roles of read and write frames can be usefully distinguished and an extra syntactic frame is proposed which binds the free variables that appear in the pre and postconditions and hence liberates the read and write frames to play their semantic role.

Thus an operation definition is composed of six components

$$
\begin{array}{rll}
OpDef :: & frame & : \text{ map } Id \text{ to } Type \\
& invariant & : Exp \\
& reads & : Id\text{-set} \\
& writes & : Id\text{-set} \\
& pre & : Exp \\
& post & : Exp
\end{array}
$$

The first component is a declaration and binding of the variables appearing in the operation. The second records the pertinent clauses of the invariant. Third and fourth components give the "semantic" read and write frames, and the last two are pre and postcondition as usual.

Note that we do not insist on any relationship between the "externals" (the *reads* and *writes*) and the free variables of *pre* and *post*. Unlike the standard usage, here variables that can be read and written appear in both *reads* and *writes* clauses.

The paper gives a modified definition of satisfiability which takes account of the read and write frames and also defines some Hoare/Jones style rules

---

[1]Recall that $\triangleleft$ is domain restriction: for any set S and binary relation R over the same type, define the domain restriction of R to S to be the relation $S \triangleleft R \quad \triangle \quad \{(s_1, s_2) \in R \mid s_1 \in S\}$

for operation decomposition where extra constraints ensure that requirements encoded in the read and write frames are respected during refinement. Thus the satisfaction relation defined by these rules depends on the operation's read and write frames.

We recall the modified definition of satisfiability where the position of an extra universal quantifier inside the existential quantifier formalises the idea that the choice of new values for the writes must be valid whatever the value of the unread variables. For an operation $mk\text{-}OpDef(M, I, R, W, P, Q)$ we have[2]

$$\overleftarrow{\forall R} \cdot \exists W \cdot \overleftarrow{\forall F - R} \cdot \overleftarrow{P} \wedge \overleftarrow{I} \Rightarrow \overleftarrow{Q}^{F-W} \wedge \overleftarrow{I}^{F-W}$$

3 Examples

We now present two simple examples which are sufficient to expose the key issues that will arise in the sequel.

Example 1

The first example has a state with two components and an invariant that restricts the state space to three possible values

$$\Sigma :: \ a \ : \ \mathbf{N}$$
$$b \ : \ \mathbf{N}$$

$$inv\text{-}\Sigma(a, b) \ \triangleq$$
$$a \in \{0, 1\} \wedge$$
$$b \leq a$$

Thus, the only possible states are

$$\{mk\text{-}\Sigma(0, 0), mk\text{-}\Sigma(1, 0), mk\text{-}\Sigma(1, 1)\}$$

First consider the operation that simply assigns an arbitrary value to b (whilst respecting the invariant, naturally).

$choose\_b$
ext rd b : $\mathbf{N}$
   wr b : $\mathbf{N}$
pre true
post true

Clearly, if both read and write frames are ignored, then the trivial predicates permit any transition between the three states that satisfies the invariant. Thus the interpretation is simply the trivial relation, $\Sigma \times \Sigma$.

It is a simple matter to interpret the write frame as a restriction of this relation by requiring that the a value cannot change. Thus, the four transitions that change the value of a are removed from the interpretation. In the following diagram these transitions are marked with an $\times$.

---

[2] The notation is explained in detail in sections 4.1 and 4.2.

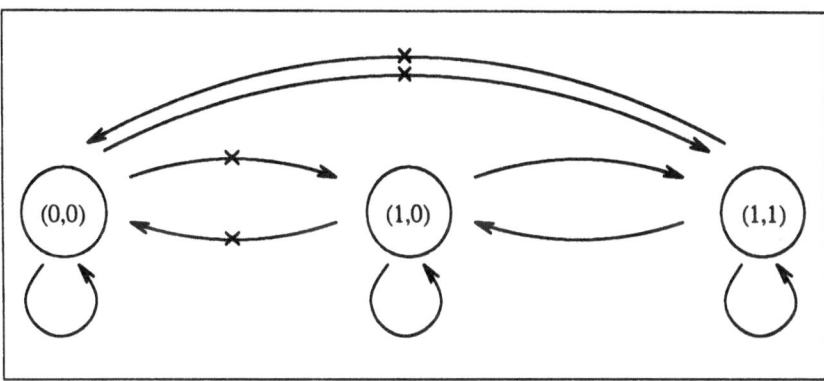

Now the central question addressed by this paper is whether it is possible to interpret the read frame by a similar constraint on the possible transitions? Or more precisely, whether those sets of transitions which *can* arise from code that respects the read frame can be characterised by some restriction of the usual semantics and the normal definition of satisfaction. This would in turn lead to a direct interpretation of the read frame in the semantics of the operation specification, rather than as a restriction on the definition of satisfaction.

In order to see how this might be possible, let us consider the validity of some possible implementations:

$skip$ - valid
$b := a$ - not valid, read frame not respected
$a := b$ - not valid: write frame not respected
$b := 1$ - not valid: invariant not respected
$b := 0$ - valid

It is in fact quite simple to list all the possible denotations of implementations which refine this specification. They are simply all the subsets of the relation which preserve its domain and are depicted in figure 1 (next page). Now trial and error will quickly establish that some of these interpretations can arise from code that respects the read frame whereas others cannot. These are indicated in the figure along with some example code that yields the valid interpretations.

It is claimed that any code yielding one of the interpretations marked as not valid cannot respect the read frame.

An inspection of these tentative implementations will quickly establish that the valid denotations are precisely those which do not contain the transition from $(1, 0)$ to $(1, 1)$. Thus the removal of this transition from the interpretation of the operation specification encodes the intention described by the read frame.

To understand more fully why this is the case, it might be helpful to picture the state-space and state-transitions in two dimensions as follows:

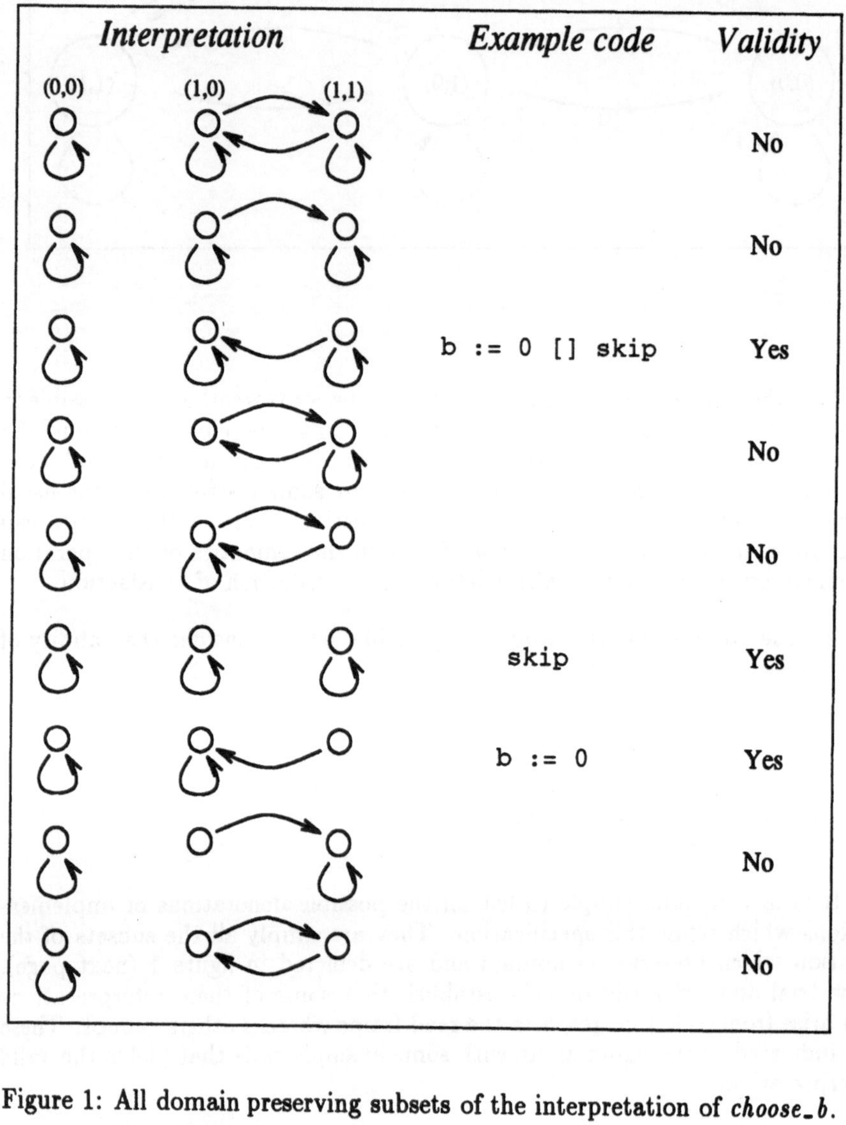

266

Figure 1: All domain preserving subsets of the interpretation of *choose_b*.

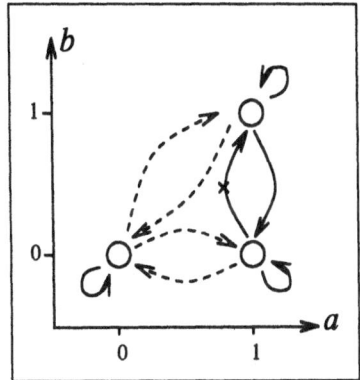

The write frame constrains the transitions so that no movement in the a direction is possible. The read frame requirement removes one extra transition. This constraint on the semantic interpretation can be rationalised as follows:

> "Because, when $b = 0$, it is impossible, without looking at the a value, to establish whether the original state is $(0, 0)$ or $(1, 0)$, and because no change in the b value is possible in the case where the original state is $(0, 0)$, therefore any such change in b must also be prohibited from state $(1, 0)$."

With this constraint applied to the interpretation of operation specifications *at each stage in the decomposition process*, the usual refinement relation ensures that the read frame is respected.

Example 2

The second example is similar in nature to the first but has a slightly more complex state. The state has three components and an invariant which permits four valid states.

$$\Sigma :: \; a \; : \; \mathbf{N}$$
$$b \; : \; \mathbf{N}$$
$$c \; : \; \mathbf{N}$$

$$inv\text{-}\Sigma(a, b) \;\; \triangleq$$
$$a \in \{0, 1\} \wedge$$
$$b \leq a \wedge$$
$$c \leq b$$

In this case the only possible states are

$$\{ mk\text{-}\Sigma(0, 0, 0), mk\text{-}\Sigma(1, 0, 0), mk\text{-}\Sigma(1, 1, 0), mk\text{-}\Sigma(1, 1, 1) \}$$

Let us consider the operation that can read and write b only

choose_b
ext rd b : $\mathbf{N}$
   wr b : $\mathbf{N}$
pre true
post true

Again ignoring the read frame in the first instance (but respecting the write frame), leads to six possible state transitions (including the four identity transitions or stuttering steps).

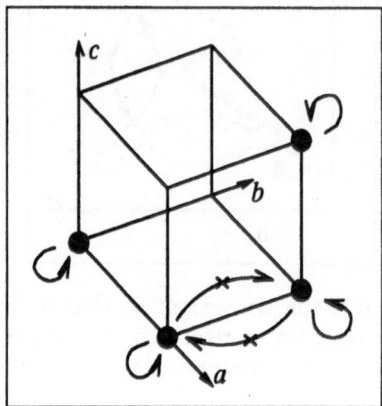

In this case, no state transitions (other than the stuttering steps) can arise from code that respects the read frame. Movement in each direction being prohibited by the existence of another state with the same unread values where that movement is not possible. Thus the only implementation that respects the read frame is skip.

(The reader may find it instructive to experiment further with this example by considering possible implementations for other combinations of variables in the read and write frames.)

4   Relational semantics with read and write frames

This section defines a denotational semantics for operations as relations on the state space (after the style of [Jon87]) but with an extra complexity introduced to formalise the interpretation of the read frame.

4.1   Notation

Some notation introduced in [Bic93] is summarised again here.

Hooking.

If S is any set of identifiers, say

$$S = \{x_a \mid a \in \alpha\}$$

then $\overleftarrow{S}$ is the set with each identifier in S distinguished in some way, with a ⟵ say. That is,

$$\overleftarrow{S} = \{\overleftarrow{x_a} \mid x_a \in S\}$$

More generally if we want to distinguish just some of the members of S, those in $S_1 \subseteq S$ say, then we write

$$\overleftarrow{S}^{S_1} \triangleq \{\overleftarrow{x_a} \mid x_a \in S_1\} \cup \{x_a \mid x_a \in S - S_1\}$$

Similarly, if E is an expression with free variables in S, written

$$E : Exp(S)$$

and $S_1 \subseteq S$, then

$$\overleftarrow{E}^{S_1} \triangleq E[\overleftarrow{\sigma_i}/\sigma_i]_{\sigma_i \in S_1}$$

Thus

$$\overleftarrow{E}^{S_1} : Exp(\overleftarrow{S}^{S_1})$$

Quantification.

Let F be a composite type

$$F :: f_1 : T_1$$
$$\vdots$$
$$f_n : T_n$$

and let S be a subset of the field names of F

$$S = \{f_{S_1}, \ldots, f_{S_k}\} \subseteq \{f_1, \ldots, f_n\}$$

Let E be an expression with the field names in S appearing as free variables

$$E : Exp(f_{S_1}, \ldots, f_{S_k})$$

then we use the notations

$$\forall S \cdot E \quad \text{and} \quad \exists S \cdot E$$

to stand for the quantifications over the free variables from S. For example:

$$\forall S \cdot E \triangleq \forall v_1 : T_{S_1}, \ldots, v_k : T_{S_k} \cdot E[v_i/f_{S_i}]_{i=1,\ldots,k}$$

where the v_i are fresh variables.
Similarly

$$\forall \overleftarrow{S} \cdot \overleftarrow{E}$$

is a shorthand for the corresponding hooked formula.

Projection.

For an element of a composite type, define the projection onto a subset of the fields as the tuple composed of only those fields. For example

$$(a, b, c, d)\Big|_{(b,d)} \triangleq (b, d)$$

Thus, for example, we have[3]

$$\overleftarrow{\sigma_i}^S = (\overleftarrow{\sigma_i}\Big|_S, \sigma_i\Big|_{F-S})$$

---

[3] Two minor syntactic liberties are taken with the presentation here. Firstly no account is taken of the order of the fields in the state and secondly the constructor function is omitted when convenient.

4.2   Semantic models

For a given operation, $mk\text{-}OpDef(M, I, R, W, P, Q)$, we define three relations on the state space giving interpretations for operations respecting none, one or both frames. Let $F = \text{dom } M$ and Σ be the state space spanned by F, then we will define three meaning relations as follows

$\Sigma \overset{o}{\longrightarrow} \Sigma \subseteq \Sigma \times \Sigma$ is the meaning relation not respecting either frame,

$\Sigma \overset{w}{\longrightarrow} \Sigma \subseteq \Sigma \times \Sigma$ which respects, in addition, the write frame and

$\Sigma \overset{RW}{\longrightarrow} \Sigma \subseteq \Sigma \times \Sigma$ which respects, in addition, the read frame.

For any $(\overleftarrow{\sigma}, \sigma) \in \Sigma \times \Sigma$ we write $\overleftarrow{\sigma} \overset{o}{\longrightarrow} \sigma$ for $(\overleftarrow{\sigma}, \sigma) \in \Sigma \overset{o}{\longrightarrow} \Sigma$, and similarly for $\overleftarrow{\sigma} \overset{w}{\longrightarrow} \sigma$ and $\overleftarrow{\sigma} \overset{RW}{\longrightarrow} \sigma$. Note that although single headed arrows are used in the relations above none of these relations are necessarily functions.

Thus we have

$$\Sigma \overset{o}{\longrightarrow} \Sigma \ \triangleq \ \left\{ (\overleftarrow{\sigma}, \sigma) \in \Sigma \times \Sigma \,\middle|\, Predicates(\overleftarrow{\sigma}, \sigma) \right\}$$

where

$$Predicates(\overleftarrow{\sigma}, \sigma) \ \triangleq \ \overleftarrow{P} \wedge \overleftarrow{I} \Rightarrow Q \wedge I$$

It is a simple matter to extend this definition to incorporate the semantics of the write frame. The write frame is interpreted as if the postcondition were extended with "rest unchanged" clauses.

$$\Sigma \overset{w}{\longrightarrow} \Sigma \ \triangleq \ \left\{ (\overleftarrow{\sigma}, \sigma) \in \Sigma \overset{o}{\longrightarrow} \Sigma \,\middle|\, NoWrite((\overleftarrow{\sigma}, \sigma), F - W) \right\}$$

where

$$NoWrite((\overleftarrow{\sigma}, \sigma), F - W) \ \triangleq \ \sigma\big|_{F-W} = \overleftarrow{\sigma}\big|_{F-W}$$

The task now remaining, is to define an extra predicate that constrains the semantics as required by the read frame. However this predicate is not simply a predicate on individual transitions, but also depends on the whole set of transitions. Thus the intention in the following sections is to define the predicate *NoRead* taking a transition, a relation on the state space and a set of fields such that

$$\Sigma \overset{RW}{\longrightarrow} \Sigma \ \triangleq \ \left\{ (\overleftarrow{\sigma}, \sigma) \in \Sigma \overset{w}{\longrightarrow} \Sigma \,\middle|\, NoRead((\overleftarrow{\sigma}, \sigma), \Sigma \overset{w}{\longrightarrow} \Sigma, F - R) \right\}$$

4.3   First Simplification

First consider the case where read and write frames are equal, $W = R \subseteq F$, and let $U = F - R$ be the unread part of the state.

From the examples above it is possible to describe informally the condition for respecting read frame as follows:

> "For any two states that differ only in the values of unread components, the possible final states must also differ only in the unread components (which cannot themselves change)".

This idea is depicted in the following diagram:

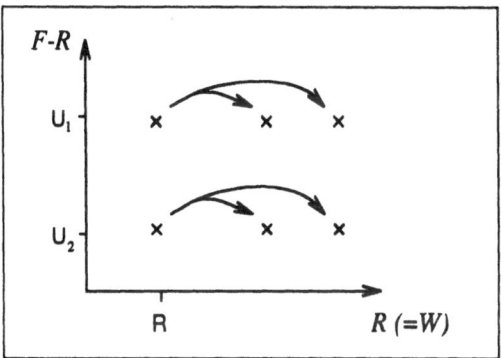

Movement in the $F-R$ direction is prohibited by the write frame, whereas the read frame constraint can be interpreted as saying that for any two starting states with the same R component, the same final values for the R component must be possible.

Thus, we require that $\Sigma \xrightarrow{RW} \Sigma$ be the largest subset of $\Sigma \xrightarrow{W} \Sigma$ such that

$$\forall \overleftarrow{R}, \overline{U}_1, \overline{U}_2 \cdot \left\{ R_1 \,\middle|\, (\overleftarrow{R}, \overline{U}_1) \xrightarrow{W} (R_1, \overline{U}_1) \right\} = \left\{ R_2 \,\middle|\, (\overleftarrow{R}, \overline{U}_2) \xrightarrow{W} (R_2, \overline{U}_2) \right\}$$

which can be reexpressed as

$$\forall \overline{\sigma}_1, \overline{\sigma}_2 \cdot \overline{\sigma}_1 \Big|_R = \overline{\sigma}_2 \Big|_R \Rightarrow \left\{ \sigma_1 \Big|_R \,\middle|\, \overline{\sigma}_1 \xrightarrow{W} \overline{\sigma}_1^{F-R} \right\} = \left\{ \sigma_2 \Big|_R \,\middle|\, \overline{\sigma}_2 \xrightarrow{W} \overline{\sigma}_2^{F-R} \right\}$$

This can be ensured by defining the *NoRead* predicate as follows

$$NoRead((\overleftarrow{\sigma}_1, \sigma_1), \Sigma \xrightarrow{W} \Sigma, F-R) \;\triangleq$$
$$\forall \overline{\sigma}_2 \cdot \overline{\sigma}_1 \Big|_R = \overline{\sigma}_2 \Big|_R \Rightarrow \sigma_1 \Big|_R \in \left\{ \sigma_2 \Big|_R \,\middle|\, \overline{\sigma}_2 \xrightarrow{W} \overline{\sigma}_2^{F-R} \right\}$$

4.4 First generalisation

The case where $W \subseteq R \subseteq F$ is really very similar. Simply, the R components are split in two parts. RO are the read-only components and RW are the read-write components. (U is still the unread part.)

The transitions can be pictured in three dimensions as follows:

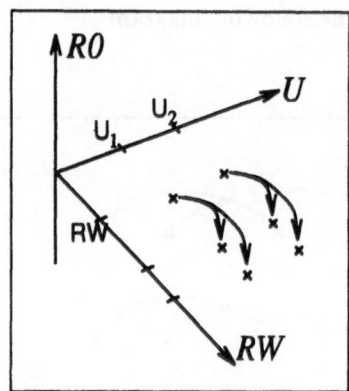

Each transition lies in a horizontal plane, each horizontal plane satisfies the constraints of the previous section, but there is not necessarily any correspondence between planes.

Thus, we require that $\Sigma \xrightarrow{RW} \Sigma$ is the largest subset of $\Sigma \xrightarrow{w} \Sigma$ such that:

$$\forall \overleftarrow{RW}, \overleftarrow{RO}, \overleftarrow{U_1}, \overleftarrow{U_2} \cdot \left\{ RW_1 \,\middle|\, (\overleftarrow{RW}, \overleftarrow{RO}, \overleftarrow{U_1}) \xrightarrow{w} (RW_1, \overleftarrow{RO}, \overleftarrow{U_1}) \right\}$$

$$= \left\{ RW_2 \,\middle|\, (\overleftarrow{RW}, \overleftarrow{RO}, \overleftarrow{U_2}) \xrightarrow{w} (RW_2, \overleftarrow{RO}, \overleftarrow{U_2}) \right\}$$

Which again can be reexpressed

$$\forall \overleftarrow{\sigma_1}, \overleftarrow{\sigma_2} \cdot \overleftarrow{\sigma_1}\bigg|_R = \overleftarrow{\sigma_2}\bigg|_R \Rightarrow \left\{ \sigma_1\bigg|_{\_w} \,\middle|\, \overleftarrow{\sigma_1} \xrightarrow{w} \overleftarrow{\sigma_1}^{F-W} \right\} = \left\{ \sigma_2\bigg|_{\_w} \,\middle|\, \overleftarrow{\sigma_2} \xrightarrow{w} \overleftarrow{\sigma_2}^{F-W} \right\}$$

Note the judicious use of Rs and Ws in the subscripts and superscripts.

Thus, in this case we require

$$NoRead((\overleftarrow{\sigma}_1, \sigma_1), \Sigma \xrightarrow{w} \Sigma, F-R) \quad \triangleq$$

$$\forall \overleftarrow{\sigma_2} \cdot \overleftarrow{\sigma_1}\bigg|_R = \overleftarrow{\sigma_2}\bigg|_R \Rightarrow \sigma_1\bigg|_{\_w} \in \left\{ \sigma_2\bigg|_{\_w} \,\middle|\, \overleftarrow{\sigma_2} \xrightarrow{w} \overleftarrow{\sigma_2}^{F-W} \right\}$$

Note that, since

$$\sigma_2\bigg|_{\_R-w} = \overleftarrow{\sigma_2}\bigg|_{\_R-w} = \overleftarrow{\sigma_1}\bigg|_{\_R-w} = \sigma_1\bigg|_{\_R-w}$$

we can replace the Ws in the subscripts (and superscripts) by Rs, and so this predicate reduces to the one given for the case $R = W$.

4.5 Full generalisation

Before proceeding to consider the implications of this definition, we consider one more generalisation that goes beyond the normal usage in VDM. We remove the constraint that the reads must contain the writes.

The interpretation that will be taken here for variables in the write frame but not the read is that they *must* be written with a value calculated from the reads. This "must-write" semantics is useful for formalising the initialisation of state and local variables and may also have some applications in security requirements (c.f. the Bell and LaPadula Model for confidentiality).

For this section we partition the state into four sets of fields. Now U is unread and unwritten, RO is read only, WO is write-only and RW is read-write:

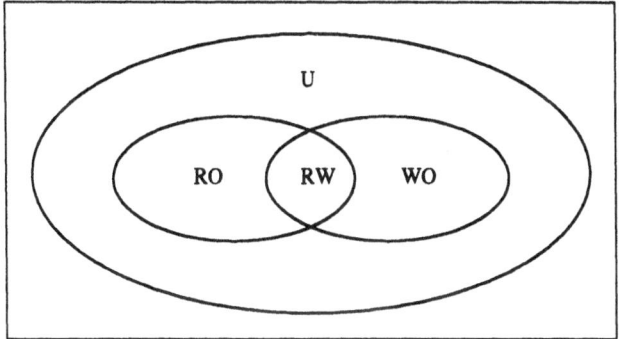

In this general case, the transition diagram should best be drawn in four dimensions (one for each of U, RO, RW and WO). Fortunately, as no change is possible to either the RO or U components (that is there is no movement in the RO or U directions) each $RW \times WO$ plane can be pictured as a separate diagram. Planes separated by a change in U need satisfy the condition in section 4.3. Planes separated by a change in RO need have no correspondence.

Now within a $RW \times WO$ plane, two starting states which differ only in the WO component must have exactly the same possible final states - not just the same RW components:

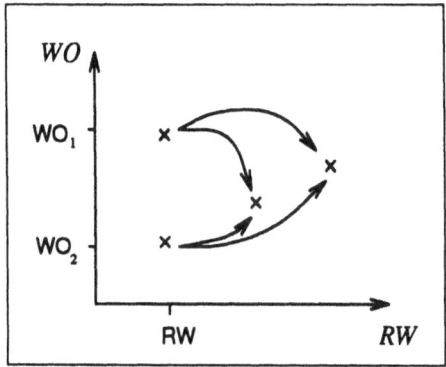

Thus $\Sigma \xrightarrow{RW} \Sigma$ is the largest subset of $\Sigma \xrightarrow{w} \Sigma$ such that:

$\forall \overleftarrow{RO}, \overleftarrow{RW}, \overleftarrow{U_1}, \overleftarrow{U_2}, \overleftarrow{WO_1}, \overleftarrow{WO_2} \,.$

$$\left\{ (WO_1, RW_1) \,\middle|\, (\overleftarrow{RO}, \overleftarrow{RW}, \overleftarrow{U_1}, \overleftarrow{WO_1}) \xrightarrow{w} (\overleftarrow{RO}, RW_1, \overleftarrow{U_1}, WO_1) \right\}$$

$$= \left\{ (WO_2, RW_2) \,\middle|\, (\overleftarrow{RO}, \overleftarrow{RW}, \overleftarrow{U_2}, \overleftarrow{WO_2}) \xrightarrow{w} (\overleftarrow{RO}, RW_2, \overleftarrow{U_2}, WO_2) \right\}$$

This says that for starting states with same read part (RO and RW) but different unread parts (U and WO): each transition keeps the unwritten (RO and U) components unchanged, whilst the possibilities for new values of the written components (WO and RW) must not depend on the old values – for the RW components, which are the same already this is ensured *a priori*, but for the WO component it means that any difference there may have been originally should be ignored. Thus the old values of WO components have no effect on the outcome.

Again this can be re-expressed as a quantification over states and, interestingly, this case also yields the same predicates as in the $W \subseteq R$ case.

However, as the standard usage in VDM does not consider write-only variables, the rest of this paper will concentrate on the case where $W \subseteq R$.

4.6 Satisfiability

In this section we sketch a justification for the modified definition of satisfiability defined in [Bic93].

The usual definition of satisfiability (not respecting the read frame) can be written

$$(1) \qquad \forall \overleftarrow{R}, \overleftarrow{F-R} \cdot \exists W \cdot \overleftarrow{P} \wedge \overleftarrow{I} \; \Rightarrow \; \overleftarrow{Q}^{F-W} \wedge \overleftarrow{I}^{F-W}$$

The modified definition of satisfiability respecting frames is

$$(2) \qquad \forall \overleftarrow{R} \cdot \exists W \cdot \forall \overleftarrow{F-R} \cdot \overleftarrow{P} \wedge \overleftarrow{I} \; \Rightarrow \; \overleftarrow{Q}^{F-W} \wedge \overleftarrow{I}^{F-W}$$

Under the present semantics we have the following extra property that

$$(3) \qquad \forall \overleftarrow{RW}, \overleftarrow{RO}, \overleftarrow{U_1}, \overleftarrow{U_2} \cdot \left\{ RW_1 \,\middle|\, (\overleftarrow{RW}, \overleftarrow{RO}, \overleftarrow{U_1}) \overset{W}{\longrightarrow} (RW_1, \overleftarrow{RO}, \overleftarrow{U_1}) \right\}$$

$$= \left\{ RW_2 \,\middle|\, (\overleftarrow{RW}, \overleftarrow{RO}, \overleftarrow{U_2}) \overset{W}{\longrightarrow} (RW_2, \overleftarrow{RO}, \overleftarrow{U_2}) \right\}$$

where

$R = RW \cup RO,$
$W = RW,$ and
$F-R = U$

In order to justify the new definition of satisfiability (2), we have to show that assuming (3), (1) $\Leftrightarrow$ (2).

The case (2) $\Rightarrow$ (1) is completely trivial. To see that (1) $\Rightarrow$ (2), we argue as follows. If for a particular $\overleftarrow{R}$ and $\overleftarrow{U_1}$ there is a suitable W, then by (3), the same W suffices for $\overleftarrow{R}$ and $\overleftarrow{U_2}$, which is (2).

4.7 Non-interference

One major motivation for the use of read frames in implicit operation definitions is to specify properties of non-interference that are to be achieved in implementations.

If we are to exploit the read and write frames fully, we would wish to have the following non-interference property for operations with sufficiently disjoint frames.

Theorem   *Non-interference*

For two total operations on the same context, F and I,

$$Op_i \; \triangleq \; (F, I, R_i, W_i, P_i, Q_i) \quad i \in \{1, 2\}$$

if the frames are sufficiently disjoint, that is if[4]

$$R_1 \cap W_2 = \{\} = R_2 \cap W_1$$

then we have

(1) $[Op_1]; [Op_2] = [Op_2]; [Op_1]$

where $[Op_1] = \mathcal{M}(Op_1)$ (see section 2.1) and ";" is sequential composition of relations as defined for example in [Jon87].

Furthermore, if each Op_i is refined by Op_i'

$$Op_i \sqsubseteq Op_i'$$

then we also have

(2) $[Op_1']; [Op_2'] = [Op_2']; [Op_1']$

To see (1), note that the state space is spanned by six components:

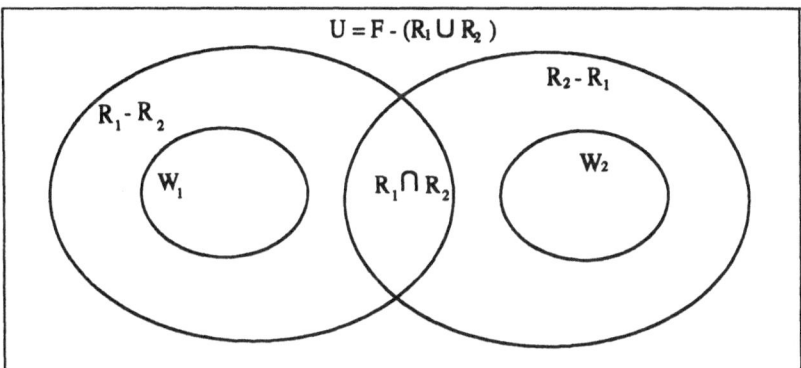

The only possible changes of state are in the plane spanned by the two write components. Let us picture this plane and consider an arbitrary transition from the sequential composition of the two operations $[Op_1]; [Op_2]$. Such a transition must clearly be the composition of one transition solely in the W_1 direction and another in the W_2 direction:

---

[4]A similar condition called soft interference arises in process plant design. Each piece of equipment has a physical volume and a clearance volume. The latter being the space required for access and maintenance. Hard interference occurs if the physical volumes of two pieces of equipment intersect and soft interference if the physical volume of one piece intersects the clearance volume of the other. Two clearances are however allowed to intersect.

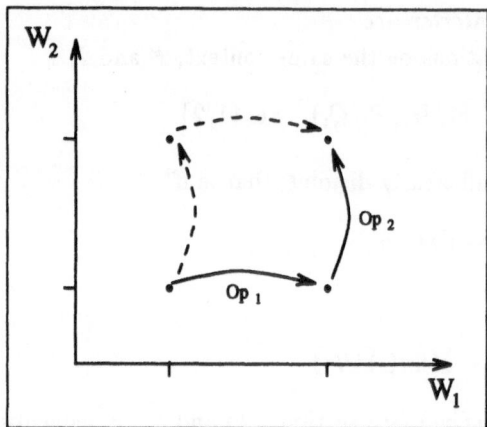

Clearly, the requirement is to show that there are necessarily transitions in the other order as depicted by the dotted arrows.

This follows since each write frames is contained within the unread component of the other operation and so the no-read property is sufficient to ensure the existence of the other transitions.

However, the second part of the theorem, that non-interference is preserved by refinement, raises some interesting issues which are discussed in the following section.

5   Discussion: Read Frames and Satisfaction

This paper has outlined a denotational semantics for operations that gives a formal interpretation to both the read and write frames and has shown how this formalisation of the read frame yields some new properties of satisfiability and non-interference. However it has still not addressed the interaction of this semantics with the satisfaction relation.

Let us return to the "central question" formulated in Section 3. Is it the case that with this modification to the interpretation of operations, the usual definition of refinement characterises the interpretations that can arise from implementations that respect the read frame?

To understand the question more fully, we need to consider the very basis for the semantic models and notion of refinement being used. In each of the three semantic models introduced in Section 4.2, the denotation of an operation as a relation on states is intended to characterise, via the refinement relation, the set of interpretations of its valid implementations. This is done by choosing as a representative of this set, the most general of its members. (In the lattice of the semantic domain under refinement, we take the meet of the set of refinements.) The refinement relation then determines whether any other interpretation is a member of this set, that is, whether it denotes a valid implementation.

In the case of the first two models, this approach is perfectly adequate since for any operation, the interpretation of any refinement is a refinement of the interpretation. (The set of interpretations of implementations is downwards closed in the lattice.) For the read-frame-respecting interpretations, the matter is not so simple.

When motivating the semantic interpretation of the read frame presented here, a crucial proviso was made in the claim that under this interpretation the usual definition of refinement would respect the read frame. It was stated in Section 3, that in order for the definition of refinement to respect the read frame, the constrained interpretation would have to be used *at each stage of the decomposition process*. Recall however, that the constraint itself depends on the read frame and thus we are assuming that some external mechanism is being employed to record this frame and apply *the same* constraint at later stages.

Unlike the *Predicates* and *NoWrite* conditions, the *NoRead* condition does not automatically carry down to all refinements of an interpretation. That is, not all refinements of an interpretation satisfying the *NoRead* predicate, necessarily satisfy the predicate themselves. Thus, it is not the case that the information in the frame is being captured in its entirety by the semantic model of the operation and hence the answer to the question posed above is *No*! It is not possible to characterise the interpretations of read-frame-respecting implementations as the refinements of a restricted interpretation of the operation specification. Thus, it is not possible to give a full interpretation to the read frame in the current semantic framework.

If we are to formalise the role of the read frame in refinement, we are left with two possibilities. Either we accept that the refinement relation must depend on the read frame and parameterise its definition accordingly, or we enrich the semantic model of operations to record more read information. Despite the fact that the read frame is part of the emerging standard for the VDM language [VDM-SL], neither of these two approaches has to date received any attention.

This latter approach is the subject of ongoing investigations by the author. The natural choice for a richer semantic model, which does indeed take full account of the information in the read frame, is to take as interpretation for an operation specification the set of relations on states that corresponds to its valid implementations. By filtering this set by the *NoRead* predicate, the role of the read frame as "advanced information" about the state accesses of valid implementations can be encoded in the interpretation of the operation specification. In effect, we have moved the definition of refinement into the semantics of the individual operations and refinement now becomes simply containment of sets of implementations. Although clearly we now have a more complex semantic model, this extra complexity is counterbalanced by a simplification of the refinement relation.

Of course, it should be remembered that such a semantics is not intended as a basis for the specifier's informal understanding, but rather as a basis for the justification of refinement rules with which it is possible to reason about frames. It is interesting to note that once again, syntactic devices for reasoning have developed well in advance of a formal understanding of their semantics. Although not an unusual occurrence this is perhaps surprising for a supposedly formal notation. As Wittgenstein concludes in his *Tractatus Logico-Philosophicus*[Wit22]

"Whereof one cannot speak, thereof one must be silent."

278

References

[Abr93] *Abstract Machines, Parts I, II and III.* J. R. Abrial. Unpublished, 1993.

[ALNS91]
   The B Method, J. R. Abrial, M. K. O. Lee, D. S. Neilson and P. N. Scharbach. VDM '91, Formal Software Development Methods (Tutorials), LNCS 552, Springer-Verlag (1991).

[Bic93] *Algorithm Refinement with Read and Write Frames,* J.C.Bicarregui, Proceedings of FME'93, LNCS 670, Springer-Verlag, 1993.

[Jon87] *VDM Proof Obligations and their Justification,* C.B.Jones, Proceedings of the VDM '87 Symposium, LNCS 252, Springer-Verlag(1987).

[Kin90] *Z and the Refinement Calculus,* S. King. Proceedings of VDM '90, pp. 164-188, LNCS 428, Springer-Verlag, 199.

[Mor88] *On the Refinement Calculus.* C. Morgan, K. Robinson and P. Gardiner. Oxford University Technical Monograph, PRG-70, 1988.

[Mor90] *Programming from Specifications* C. Morgan, Prentice Hall, 1990.

[Spi88] *Understanding Z,* J.M. Spivey. Cambridge University Press, 1988.

[VDM-SL] VDM-SL, ISO Draft standard. ISO/IEC JTC1/SC22. N1346. April 1993. Also BSI IST/5/50. Draft 1st Decemeber 1992.

[War93] *Adding Specification Constructors to the Refinement Calculus,* N. Ward, Proceedings of FME '93, LNCS 670, Springer-Verlag, 1993.

[Wit22] *Tractatus Logico-Philosophicus,* Wittgenstein, L. Routledge and Kegan Paul, First published 1922, translation by C.K. Ogden.

Proof Obligations for Real-Time Refinement

Colin Fidge

Software Verification Research Centre
Department of Computer Science
The University of Queensland
Queensland 4072, Australia

Abstract

Existing "algorithm design" rules, for refining Z specifications to structured high-level language code, are extended with proof obligations that preserve specified real-time, as well as functional, behaviour.

1 Introduction

Existing refinement methods provide a means of developing programs in such a way that specified functional requirements are preserved as the design evolves. In safety-critical applications, however, code correctness is measured not only by the ability of the system to perform the right actions, but also by the ability to perform them at the right time.

Extending a refinement calculus to encompass timing behaviour offers several profound challenges, including

- the lack of agreed-upon notations for specifying timing behaviour,

- the immaturity of theories for predicting the real-time behaviour of high-level language code, and

- the tension between the desire for specification abstractness and the grounding of real-time behaviour in low-level architectural details.

Accordingly, we believe it is necessary to approach these challenges at a fundamental level.

As a first step towards this we present a minimal set of refinement-like rules in which all timing obligations are explicitly listed. This is not intended to be a practical refinement calculus *per se*, but a convincing foundation for later work on a "real-time refinement calculus".

The approach is based on Wordsworth's "algorithm design" rules for converting Z specifications into guarded command language code [8]. In the interests of brevity some knowledge of Z is assumed. Familiarity with Wordsworth's rules would be helpful.

2 Background

Formal methods for incorporating "timeliness" into the software development process have proven notoriously elusive. Numerous notations have been suggested for specifying timing requirements but no agreed-upon one has emerged. At the other extreme, methods of defining the real-time characteristics of program code have been proposed but they remain inaccurate and restricted to small language subsets. Most disturbingly, formal methods of real-time software development seem to be entirely absent. "Code first and tweak performance later" is still the dominant paradigm in practice.

2.1 Previous work

As a response to this we recently presented a "real-time refinement calculus" [1] consisting of selected rules from Morgan's refinement calculus augmented with extra side-conditions for preserving real-time behaviour. Although successful for the small examples considered, this initial attempt suffered from several problems, including

- the need to change notations from the specification, written in Z, to the language used during refinement, *i.e.*, specification statements [4],

- a restricted form of specification notation that allowed only action durations to be specified,

- the lack of a general rule for iteration, and

- failure to account for all overheads associated with branching around alternatives in conditional statements, *etc.*

Our experiences with this calculus convinced us that the challenges of developing such a real-time calculus need to be treated from the bottom-up, if we are to accurately solve the problems of dealing with low-level, concrete timing behaviour in a high-level, abstract refinement setting.

2.2 Algorithm design rules

Our starting point is the set of basic "algorithm design" rules proposed by Wordsworth [8, ch. 7]. For our needs these rules have the advantages of performing all reasoning using the Z notation, and making all proof obligations explicit.

In the general case, Wordsworth notes that a specification, representable by a Z schema *Spec*, is shown to be correctly implemented by a program, representable as a Z schema *Ref*, *i.e.*,

$$Spec \sqsubseteq Ref ,$$

if we can satisfy the following two proof obligations [8, p. 200].

Safety. Any circumstance acceptable to *Spec* is acceptable to *Ref*.

$$\text{pre } Spec \vdash \text{pre } Ref$$

Liveness. In any circumstance acceptable to *Spec*, the behaviour of *Ref* must be allowed by *Spec*.

$$(\text{pre } Spec) \wedge Ref \vdash Spec$$

The declarations and predicate in the hypothesis, and the predicate in the conclusion, are expressed as Z schemata. He then goes on to develop specific rules for basic structured programming concepts expressed in the guarded command language. Our rules in section 3 are extensions of these.

2.3 High-level language timing prediction

If we are to claim that our refinement steps produce code with correct timing behaviour we must have a way of assessing the execution time of high-level language code. Rules for doing this have been suggested by Shaw & Park [7, 5] and the "Mars" group [6, 3]. Execution times for primitives, such as loading the value of an integer variable or performing an arithmetic operation, are determined, either experimentally, or from the manufacturer's specification of the target architecture. These primitive times are then used to calculate the execution time of structured statements. For instance, the rule for assignment,

$$T(v := E) = T(\text{gadd}) \dotplus T(E) \dotplus T(\text{stor}) ,$$

states that the time taken to execute the assignment $v := E$ is the time required to get the address of the target variable, $T(\text{gadd})$, the time required to evaluate the expression, $T(E)$, and the time required to store the result, $T(\text{stor})$. Our proof obligations in section 3 are loosely based on these techniques.

Apart from primitive operations and target language code fragments, we also apply function T to Z operation schemata; in this case it returns the execution time specified in the schema.

In general, however, such times are not known precisely. For instance, the time required to load the value of a variable depends on whether it is already in a register, or needs to be loaded from primary or secondary memory; compiler optimisation strategies and run-time operating system behaviour greatly affect real-time performance. We therefore assume that function T returns not a single time, but a set of possible execution times. (Other authors use time intervals, but we prefer sets because they retain more information—a non-contiguous set of execution times often offers clues as to how to optimise code [1, §4.5].) We define a "set addition" operator, denoted using an accent as $\dotplus$, to add every pair of times from two non-empty sets, in order to account for every possible combination of execution times.

$$absTime == \mathbb{N}$$

$$exTimes == \mathbb{P}_1 \, absTime$$

$$\begin{array}{|l}
\_ \dotplus \_ : exTimes \times exTimes \to exTimes \\
\hline
\forall X, Y : exTimes \bullet X \dotplus Y = \{x : X, y : Y \bullet x + y\}
\end{array}$$

For example,

$$\{7, 10\} \dotplus \{2, 3\} = \{9, 10, 12, 13\} .$$

3 Rules

This section extends the proof obligations for basic structured programming constructs, assignment, sequence, alternatives and iteration [8], so that they also account for real-time behaviour. Examples of the use of each obligation can be found in section 4.

3.1 Definitions for time

We assume that each occurrence of a Z operation is to be associated with a moment in absolute time. This denotes the time at which the effects of the state change defined by the operation become visible.

For the purposes of this presentation we assume variable *now*, the value of which is used to hold the time at which the current state came into being, is declared in all operation schemata.

$$
\begin{array}{|l}
\hline
\_Time_____ \\
now : absTime \\
\hline
\end{array}
$$

Time at which state change occurred.

This is a standard Z variable with no distinguished properties. If a complex timing relationship is required it could be defined via a function on other state variables.

In proper use, the only restriction is that time cannot go backwards.

$$
\begin{array}{|l}
\hline
\_\Xi Time_____ \\
now, now' : absTime \\
\hline
now' = now \\
\hline
\end{array}
$$

Leave time unchanged.

$$
\begin{array}{|l}
\hline
\_\Delta Time_____ \\
now, now' : absTime \\
\hline
now' \geqslant now \\
\hline
\end{array}
$$

Ensure that time cannot flow in reverse.

In the following rules we frequently want to specify the passage of some duration from a given constant set d, but no changes to the remainder of the system state. Therefore, assuming that *PSpace* is the collection of program variables [8, §7.4.1], this is defined as follows.

$$
\begin{array}{|l}
\hline
\_ChangeTime_____ \\
\Delta Time \\
\Xi PSpace \\
d : exTimes \\
\hline
now' - now \in d \\
\hline
\end{array}
$$

Change the current time only.

In particular, we frequently use this schema to denote the passage of a known amount of time. For conciseness we therefore introduce the following schema-valued function.

$$
\begin{array}{|l}
\hline
age : exTimes \rightarrow ChangeTime \\
\hline
\forall t : exTimes \bullet age(t).d = t \\
\hline
\end{array}
$$

For instance, $age(\{4, 6\})$ returns an instantiation of schema *ChangeTime* which specifies the passage of 4 or 6 units of time.

3.2 Assignment

As usual, the assignment statement is fundamental [8, §7.4.2]. Its introduction is based on the observation that the effect of an assignment

$$x := E$$

is defined by the schema

```
__ assx _____
  ΔPSpace
  ΞOthers
  ΔTime
 _____
  x' = E
  now' − now ∈ T(gadd) ∔ T(E) ∔ T(stor)
```

where *Others* consists of the declarations of all other variables in *PSpace* except x, and the T function returns set constants for the target language "get address" and "store result" primitives and the target language code equivalent to expression E (see appendix A for particular examples).

Since *now* is a standard Z variable no special proof obligations are required to show that *assx* is a refinement of some original specification. The standard **safety** and **liveness** obligations presented in section 2.2 are sufficient.

3.3 Sequence

A sequence of two programs, expressible as schemata A_1 and A_2, is a valid refinement of a specification, expressed as schema S, *i.e.*,

$$S \sqsubseteq A_1 ; A_2 ,$$

if the following three proof obligations can be satisfied.

Seq-safety1. Any circumstance acceptable to the specification is acceptable to the first program.

$$\text{pre } S \vdash \text{pre } A_1$$

Seq-safety2. Executing the first program in circumstances acceptable to the specification, and accounting for the overheads associated with the sequence operator, must result in states acceptable to the second program.

$$(\text{pre } S) \wedge (A_1 \, \S \, age(T(;))) \vdash (\text{pre } A_2)'$$

Seq-liveness. Executing A_1 and then A_2, starting in a state acceptable to the specification, must produce a result acceptable to the specification.

$$(\text{pre } S) \wedge (A_1 \, \S \, age(T(;))) \wedge A_2'$$
$$\vdash S[\_''/\_']$$

The priming notations are defined by Wordsworth as a means of systematically renaming variables [8, §7.6.1]. In this instance, unprimed variables represent the starting state, singly primed variables represent the mid-state (*i.e.*, the state between A_1 and A_2), and doubly primed variables denote the final state. Notation

$$S[\_''/\_']$$

represents the predicate obtained from S by replacing all singly primed variables by their doubly primed equivalents, leaving unprimed variables unchanged.

The obligations above differ from those presented for sequence by Wordsworth [8, p. 211] only in their allowance for the execution time required by the ";" operator. This is achieved by interposing an operation $age(T(;))$ between A_1 and A_2 that changes nothing other than incrementing the time by $T(;)$. In fact, since the sequence operator normally incurs no run-time overhead, this extension usually has no effect and we can use the standard sequence obligations.

3.4 Alternatives

A specification S can be refined by a choice between several operations A_i, each guarded by a target language boolean expression, expressible as a Z schema B_i; *i.e.*,

$$S \sqsubseteq \text{if } ([]_{i \in I} B_i \rightarrow A_i) \text{ fi}$$

if the following two proof obligations are satisfied.

Alt-safety. Any circumstance acceptable to the specification must make at least one of the guards true, allowing for the time taken to evaluate the guard.

$$\text{pre } S \vdash \bigvee {}_{i \in I} (age(T(\mathbf{if}_i)) \, \mathring{,} \, B_i)$$

Alt-liveness. When some B_i is true, A_i must be a refinement of S, when the overheads of selecting the alternative are taken into consideration.

$$\forall i \in I \bullet S[\_''/\_'] \wedge (age(T(\mathbf{if}_i)) \wedge B_i')$$
$$\sqsubseteq (age(T(\mathbf{if}_i)) \, \mathring{,} \, A_i \, \mathring{,} \, age(T(\mathbf{fi}_i)))[\_''/\_']$$

These obligations look more complicated than the standard ones [8, §7.5.1] because they accommodate the overheads associated with the alternative code and the possibility that one or more of the guards may be time dependent.

$T(\mathbf{if}_i)$ represents the real-time overhead associated with reaching the ith alternative. This includes the time required to evaluate and branch past preceding false guards (if any), evaluate B_i and branch to the start of the code for alternative A_i. A formal definition is given in section B.4. Thus, where the usual safety obligation merely asserts that one of the guards must be true, the obligation above ensures that there exists a guard B_i which is true in the state following the passage of time required to evaluate it. This is done to allow for boolean expressions that involve the current time, *e.g.*, as may be used in a "timeout" alternative. It is of no use evaluating a time-dependent expression in the "starting" state if the value of the expression may change due to the time required to evaluate it! Therefore, the state in which a boolean expression B_i must hold above, represents the state at the time alternative A_i is ready to begin executing.

This extension flows through to the liveness obligation. Here the singly-primed state represents the time at which a true guard has been successfully evaluated, and the doubly-primed state is the final one for the entire alternative statement. We can read the LHS as defining a specification between two states, "no prime" and "double prime", where a boolean guard B_i is true at an intermediate time "single prime". The RHS says that alternative A_i must be a refinement of this specification when the initial time required to reach the alternative, $T(\mathbf{if}_i)$, and the final time required to branch past other alternatives, $T(\mathbf{fi}_i)$ (see section B.4), is allowed for.

3.5 Iteration

A specification S on a state X can be refined by an "initialised do-while" loop [8, §7.7.1], consisting of some preceding initialisation code, expressible by schema I, a boolean guard, expressible by a schema B on state X, and a loop body, expressible by schema A, *i.e.*,

$$S \sqsubseteq I \; ; \; \mathbf{do} \; B \to A \; \mathbf{od}$$

assuming a given loop invariant, expressible by schema *inv*, and bound function on state X, declared as

$$bf : X \nrightarrow \mathbb{N},$$

if the following seven proof obligations can be satisfied.

Init-safety. Any circumstance acceptable to the specification must be acceptable to the initialisation program.

$$\text{pre } S \vdash \text{pre } I$$

Init-liveness. When executed in a circumstance satisfying the specification, the initialisation program must establish the invariant, allowing for the overhead of sequence.

$$(\text{pre } S) \wedge (I \; \S \; age(T(;))) \vdash inv$$

Final-condition. When the guard is false the invariant must be an implementation of the specification, allowing for the time required to evaluate the (false) loop guard and branch out of the loop.

$$(\text{pre } S) \wedge (inv \; \S \; age(T(\mathbf{do}))) \wedge \neg B'$$
$$\vdash S$$

Termination. The bound function must be positive in a state satisfying the invariant, when the guard is true, allowing for the time required to evaluate the guard.

$$(\text{pre}\,S) \wedge inv \wedge (age(T(\text{do})) \wedge B')'$$
$$\vdash bf\theta X' > 0$$

Progress. The loop body, plus the time required to evaluate the guard and branch back to the beginning of the loop, must reduce the bound function.

$$(\text{pre}\,S) \wedge inv \wedge (age(T(\text{do})) \wedge B')' \wedge (A \,\natural\, age(T(\text{od})))''$$
$$\vdash bf\theta X''' < bf\theta X'$$

Body-safety. If the invariant holds and the guard is true, at a time at which the body is ready to commence execution, then the body must be safe.

$$(\text{pre}\,S) \wedge inv \wedge (age(T(\text{do})) \wedge B')'$$
$$\vdash (\text{pre}\,A)''$$

Body-liveness. When executed in a safe state the body must preserve the invariant, when the time required to evaluate the guard and branch back to the beginning of the loop is taken into consideration.

$$(\text{pre}\,S) \wedge inv \wedge (age(T(\text{do})) \wedge B')' \wedge (A \,\natural\, age(T(\text{od})))''$$
$$\vdash inv[\_'''/\_']$$

Again these obligations are based on those of Wordsworth [8, §7.7.2] with extensions to allow for the consumption of time. $T(\text{do})$, formally defined in section B.5, accounts for the time required to evaluate the loop guard and conditionally branch (either to the loop body or out of the loop). $T(\text{od})$, also defined in section B.5, accounts for the time required to branch back to the start of the loop. Thus the while-test B must be true at the time when the loop body is ready to begin execution in obligations **final-condition** to **body-liveness**, to allow for the possibility that it is a time-dependent expression. Obligations **progress** and **body-liveness** allow for the delay associated with branching back to the top of the loop at the end of the loop body. Obligation **init-liveness** allows for the possible overhead associated with the sequence operator, if any.

Again priming is used to distinguish distinct intermediate states. In **progress** and **body-liveness**, for example, the singly primed state denotes the moment when the while-test is about to be made, the doubly primed state denotes the moment when the loop body is about to begin execution and the trebly primed state is the final one (representing a return to the start of the loop).

Care has been taken to allow for the possibility that the invariant and bound function expressions may be time-dependent. This forces us to adopt a slightly different view of "invariant" than is usually the case. Wordsworth defines the invariant via a schema in which unprimed variables represent the initial state (*i.e.*, before S begins) and primed variables represent the state "at the time the while-test is evaluated" [8, p. 222]. If the while-test is false then the loop construct terminates and the primed variables thus also represent the final state. This is the traditional view of the loop invariant—it holds anywhere outside the body of the loop. In our case, however, the mere act of assessing the while-test may consume time and thus alter the value of a time-dependent expression in the invariant. In particular, there is always an overhead associated with evaluating the while-test for the final time, when it is false, and then branching out of the loop. This action, which does not change the program state, is normally unimportant, but when time is considered we must account for its effects. It means that a time-dependent expression in the invariant, which is true when the program counter is at the start of the loop, may no longer be true when the program counter is at the end of the loop, even when the while-test is false! To accommodate this, we adopt the view that the invariant is an expression that must hold *when we are about to evaluate* the while-test. However we do not necessarily assume that it holds *after* the while-test has been evaluated. Instead the invariant *plus* the overhead associated with exiting the loop must establish the post-condition of the original specification (see **final-condition**). Similarly, the bound function is always evaluated at the moment when the while-test *is about to be assessed* in **termination** and **progress**.

4 Example

This section presents a detailed example illustrating each of the proof obligations above. Again we emphasise that the rules are not normally meant to be used in this "raw" form, with the need to laboriously prove each obligation. Their ultimate purpose is to support later derived rules, in which many obligations have already been discharged, as part of a more user-friendly "real-time refinement calculus".

Only successful steps have been shown; our earlier paper illustrated a "timed refinement" that involved backtracking to correct errors [1]. Despite this the example is necessarily long in order to exercise all of the above proof obligations. It includes some rather intimidating expansions of the schemata; these are provided for readers intent on confirming the correctness of a particular obligation and may be safely skipped by readers merely seeking the overall flavour of the refinement.

4.1 Specification

The proposed program is intended to find the largest value in a non-empty integer array, of known maximum size, in a time proportional to the length of the array, with a constant bound between the minimum and maximum execution times.

$$
\begin{array}{|l}
\hline PSpace \underline{\hspace{3cm}} \\
s : 1 \mathinner{\ldotp\ldotp} n \to \mathbb{N} \\
r : \mathbb{N} \\
\hline
n \in 1 \mathinner{\ldotp\ldotp} 4 \\
\hline
\end{array}
$$

Variable s is the integer array, with a known constant size of n, and r is to hold the result.

$$
\begin{array}{|l}
\hline Max \underline{\hspace{3cm}} \\
\Delta PSpace \\
\Delta Time \\
\hline
now = 0 \\
s' = s \\
r' = max(\text{ran } s) \\
now' \in n * 35 \pm 35 \\
\hline
\end{array}
$$

The execution time has been specified absolutely, based on the array size, assuming that the program starts at time 0.

It is assumed that the target programming language will be Dijkstra's guarded command language, executing on a machine with timing characteristics as defined in appendix A and compiled with a compiler that obeys the laws in appendix B. In performing timing calculations it is always desirable to learn as much about the target environment as possible, so as to improve timing predictability. For the purposes of this example we assume that the compiler is known not to keep track of register usage for variables, and that all variable addresses are known at compile-time, thus allowing us to use the tighter time-bounds in appendix A. We also make the reasonable assumption that the compiler generates deterministic code for alternative constructs and we therefore use the timing formulae in section B.4.1.

To avoid a trivial solution we assume that the target language does not have a *"max"* function.

4.2 Refinement

This section presents a refinement of the above specification. Each of the sections 4.2.1 to 4.2.4 concentrates on one of the four rules defined in section 3. Similar "untimed" examples are common in the literature (*e.g.*, [8, §7.7.3]), so this presentation will focus on explaining the decisions relating to real time.

4.2.1 Introduce iteration

Obviously such a specification suggests an iterative solution, stepping through the array and setting r to be the maximum of its current value and the current array value at each iteration.

Firstly we introduce an index variable for accessing the array. Using Wordsworth's notation [8, p. 221],

$$
Max \sqsubseteq i : 1 \mathinner{\ldotp\ldotp} n \\
Max2
$$

where

$$
Max2 \mathrel{\widehat{=}} [\, Max; \; i, i' : 1 \mathinner{\ldotp\ldotp} n \,] \; .
$$

For convenience, assume the following definitions,

$$PSpace2 \cong [\, PSpace;\ i : 1 \mathinner{\ldotp\ldotp} n \,]$$

$$ChangeTime2 \cong [\, ChangeTime;\ i, i' : 1 \mathinner{\ldotp\ldotp} n \mid i' = i \,]$$

and a definition of the *age* function, as per section 3.1, but using *ChangeTime2* in place of *ChangeTime*.

Next we propose the initialisation code. An obvious initialisation program for the loop is as follows.

```
┌─ MaxInit ──────────────
│ Δ PSpace2
│ Δ Time
├────────────────────────
│ s' = s
│ i' = 1
│ r' = s(1)
│ now' − now ∈ 5 .. 12
```

Assign the first array element to r and set iteration counter i to 1.

The equivalent code is specified to take between 5 and 12 time units to execute. This requirement is proven in sections 4.2.2 and 4.2.3 below.

Prove init-safety. We can now discharge the first of the proof obligations for iteration, *i.e.*,

$$\text{pre } Max2 \vdash \text{pre } MaxInit\ .$$

An advantage of working with such "low-level" refinement rules is that proof obligations can usually be convincingly discharged merely by mechanically expanding the hypothesis and conclusion. The obligation above can be rewritten as

$$[\, PSpace2;\ Time \mid n \in 1 \mathinner{\ldotp\ldotp} 4 \wedge now = 0 \,] \vdash n \in 1 \mathinner{\ldotp\ldotp} 4$$

which follows immediately. (The RHS derives from the inclusion of *PSpace2* in *MaxInit*.)

More complex is our proposed loop invariant, a relation between the initial state and the state when the while-test is about to be evaluated.

```
┌─ MaxInv ───────────────
│ Δ PSpace2
│ Δ Time
├────────────────────────
│ s' = s
│ i' ⩽ n
│ r' = max(ran((1 .. i') ◁ s'))
│ now' ∈ ((i' − 1) * 31 + 5 ..
│         (i' − 1) * 51 + 12)
```

Ensure that r contains the maximum of the values in s from 1 up to i'.

The timing expression is explained as follows. Observing that the proposed initialisation program *MaxInit* uses much less than the time available for the first iteration, *i.e.*,

$$5 \mathinner{\ldotp\ldotp} 12 \subseteq 1 * 35 \pm 35\ ,$$

the programmer has used this "extra" time to give the subsequent iterations more "breathing space" than the 35 ± 35 time units specified for each. (To do this it is necessary to also allow for the time required to branch out of the loop when the while-test becomes false, i.e., $T(\text{do})$, which, as shown below, is $7 \mathrel{..} 10$.)

For instance, the maximum time value in *MaxInv* was calculated by re-expressing the requirement from *Max2* to separate out the first "iteration", i.e.,

$$i' * 35 + 35 = (i' - 1) * 35 + 70 \ .$$

Since *MaxInit* only takes up to 12 time units, however, and allowing for the worst-case time of 10 time units to exit the loop, the extra time that can be allocated to each of the remaining maximum of $n - 1$ iterations is

$$\left\lfloor \frac{70 - 12 - 10}{4 - 1} \right\rfloor = \left\lfloor \frac{48}{3} \right\rfloor = 16 \ .$$

Thus, replacing the maximum specified value for handling the first array element, i.e., 70, with its actual value, i.e., 12, and adding an extra 16 time units to the specified maximum of 35 for the subsequent iterations, yields a maximum time when the while-test is reached of

$$(i' - 1) * (35 + 16) + 12 = (i' - 1) * 51 + 12 \ .$$

Similar reasoning was used to establish the minimum invariant time.

Prove init-liveness. We can now show that *MaxInit* will establish *MaxInv*, i.e.,

$$\text{pre } Max2 \wedge (MaxInit \mathbin{\text{\textoninth}} age(T(;))) \vdash MaxInv \ .$$

In other words,

$$
\begin{aligned}
&[\,\Delta PSpace2;\ \Delta Time \mid \\
&\quad n \in 1 \mathrel{..} 4 \wedge now = 0 \wedge s' = s \wedge i' = 1 \wedge r' = s(1) \wedge \\
&\quad now' - now \in 5 \mathrel{..} 12 \dotplus \{0\}\,] \\
&\vdash n \in 1 \mathrel{..} 4 \wedge s' = s \wedge i' \leqslant n \wedge r' = max(\text{ran}((1 \mathrel{..} i') \lhd s')) \wedge \\
&\quad now' \in ((i' - 1) * 31 + 5 \mathrel{..} (i' - 1) * 51 + 12) \ ,
\end{aligned}
$$

which can be shown immediately by substituting hypothesis $i' = 1$ in the conclusion.

An obvious while-test for this example is represented by the following schema.

MaxGuard	Iteration counter has not yet
PSpace2	reached array length.
Time	
$i \neq n$	

Using the formula in section B.5 and the primitive times in appendix A we can now calculate the overhead required to reach the loop body, or exit the loop, as

$$
\begin{aligned}
T(\mathbf{do}) &= T(\mathrm{i} \neq \mathrm{n}) \dotplus T(\mathrm{cbr}) \\
&= (T(\mathrm{lvar}) \dotplus T(\mathrm{lcon}) \dotplus T(\mathrm{comp})) \dotplus T(\mathrm{cbr}) \\
&= (\{2,3\} \dotplus \{0,1,2\} \dotplus \{3\}) \dotplus \{2\} \\
&= 7\mathinner{.\,.}10 \;.
\end{aligned}
$$

We also assume, from section B.5 and appendix A, that

$$
T(\mathbf{od}) = \{1\} \;.
$$

Prove final-condition. We can now discharge the obligation for exiting the loop,

$$
\begin{aligned}
&(\mathrm{pre}\, \mathit{Max2}) \wedge (\mathit{MaxInv} \, \raise.5ex\hbox{$\scriptstyle\circ$}\kern-.1em\lower.5ex\hbox{$\scriptstyle\circ$}\, \mathit{age}(T(\mathbf{do}))) \wedge \neg\, \mathit{MaxGuard}' \\
&\vdash \mathit{Max2} \;.
\end{aligned}
$$

In other words,

$$
\begin{aligned}
&[\,\Delta \mathit{PSpace2};\ \Delta \mathit{Time}\ | \\
&\quad n \in 1\mathinner{.\,.}4 \wedge \mathit{now} = 0 \wedge s' = s \wedge i' = n \wedge \\
&\quad r' = \mathit{max}(\mathrm{ran}((1\mathinner{.\,.}i') \lhd s')) \wedge \\
&\quad \mathit{now}' \in ((i'-1)*31+5\mathinner{.\,.}(i'-1)*51+12) \dotplus 7\mathinner{.\,.}10\,] \\
&\vdash n \in 1\mathinner{.\,.}4 \wedge \mathit{now} = 0 \wedge s' = s \wedge r' = \mathit{max}(\mathrm{ran}\, s) \wedge \\
&\quad \mathit{now}' \in n*35 \pm 35 \;.
\end{aligned}
$$

The requirements for program variables s and r in the conclusion follow easily from the hypothesis that $i' = n$ (from the negation of $\mathit{MaxGuard}$). The timing requirement can be demonstrated on a case-by-case basis. For instance, if $n = 1$,

$$
\begin{aligned}
&((1-1)*31+5\mathinner{.\,.}(1-1)*51+12) \dotplus 7\mathinner{.\,.}10 \\
&= 12\mathinner{.\,.}22 \\
&\subseteq 1*35 \pm 35 \\
&= 0\mathinner{.\,.}70 \;,
\end{aligned}
$$

and similarly if $n = 4$,

$$
\begin{aligned}
&((4-1)*31+5\mathinner{.\,.}(4-1)*51+12) \dotplus 7\mathinner{.\,.}10 \\
&= 105\mathinner{.\,.}175 \\
&\subseteq 4*35 \pm 35 \\
&= 105\mathinner{.\,.}175 \;.
\end{aligned}
$$

Normally a while-test is devised so that when it is false it makes the invariant implement the specification [8, p. 219]. However, as noted in section 3.5, when time is considered we must account for the time required to evaluate the while-test the final time, when it is false, and branch out of the loop. Thus MaxInv, which is guaranteed to be true only when the while-test is *about to be* made, implements the specification only when a delay of $T(\mathbf{do})$ is added.

Next we need to propose a bound function. An obvious choice in this example is

$$n - i \; .$$

Prove termination. We can now show that

$$(\text{pre } Max2) \wedge MaxInv \wedge (age(T(\text{do})) \wedge MaxGuard')'$$
$$\vdash bf\theta X' > 0 \; ,$$

which can be written in full as

$$
\begin{aligned}
&[\Delta PSpace2; \; \Delta Time \;| \\
&\quad n \in 1..4 \wedge now = 0 \wedge s' = s \wedge i' \leqslant n \wedge \\
&\quad r' = max(\text{ran}((1..i') \lhd s')) \wedge \\
&\quad now' \in (i'-1)*31+5 .. (i'-1)*51+12 \wedge \\
&\quad i'' \neq n \wedge s'' = s' \wedge i'' = i' \wedge r'' = r' \wedge \\
&\quad now'' - now' \in 7..10] \\
&\vdash n - i' > 0 \; .
\end{aligned}
$$

The conclusion follows directly from the hypothesis conjuncts relating i'', i' and n.

Our proposed loop body is then specified as follows.

MaxBody
$\Delta PSpace2$
$\Delta Time$
$s' = s$
$i' = i + 1$
$r' = max\{r, s(i')\}$
$now' - now \in 23..40$

Increment iteration counter i and assign r the maximum of its current value and the next value in array s.

The allowable duration for the body was calculated from *MaxInv*, which tells us that each iteration may occupy between 31 and 51 time units. However this also includes the time required to evaluate the guard and perform branching operations, *i.e.*,

$$T(\text{do}) \dotplus T(MaxBody) \dotplus T(\text{od}) \subseteq 31..51 \; ,$$

which has solution

$$T(MaxBody) \subseteq 23..40 \; .$$

Prove progress. The requirement,

$$
\begin{aligned}
&(\text{pre } Max2) \wedge MaxInv \wedge (age(T(\text{do})) \wedge MaxGuard')' \wedge \\
&(MaxBody \, \mathbin{\raise1pt\hbox{$\scriptstyle\circ$}} \, age(T(\text{od})))'' \\
&\vdash bf\theta X''' < bf\theta X' \; ,
\end{aligned}
$$

can be expanded to

$$
\begin{aligned}
&[\,\Delta\,PSpace2;\ \Delta\,Time\mid\\
&\quad n \in 1 \mathinner{.\,.} 4 \wedge now = 0 \wedge s' = s \wedge i' \leqslant n \wedge\\
&\quad r' = max(ran((1 \mathinner{.\,.} i') \lhd s')) \wedge\\
&\quad now' \in (i' - 1) * 31 + 5 \mathinner{.\,.} (i' - 1) * 51 + 12 \wedge\\
&\quad i'' \neq n \wedge s'' = s' \wedge i'' = i' \wedge r'' = r' \wedge\\
&\quad now'' - now' \in 7 \mathinner{.\,.} 10 \wedge\\
&\quad i'' < n \wedge i''' = i'' + 1 \wedge s''' = s'' \wedge r''' = max\{r'', s''(i''')\} \wedge\\
&\quad now''' - now'' \in 23 \mathinner{.\,.} 40 \dotplus \{1\}\,]\\
&\vdash n - i''' < n - i'\,.
\end{aligned}
$$

The conclusion follows directly from the conjuncts in the hypothesis relating i''' to i'' and i'' to i'.

Prove body-safety. The obligation,

$$
\begin{aligned}
&(pre\,Max2) \wedge MaxInv \wedge (age(T(do)) \wedge MaxGuard')'\\
&\vdash (pre\,MaxBody)''\,,
\end{aligned}
$$

expands to

$$
\begin{aligned}
&[\,\Delta\,PSpace2;\ \Delta\,Time\mid\\
&\quad n \in 1 \mathinner{.\,.} 4 \wedge now = 0 \wedge s' = s \wedge i' \leqslant n \wedge\\
&\quad r' = max(ran((1 \mathinner{.\,.} i') \lhd s')) \wedge\\
&\quad now' \in (i' - 1) * 31 + 5 \mathinner{.\,.} (i' - 1) * 51 + 12 \wedge\\
&\quad i'' \neq n \wedge s'' = s' \wedge i'' = i' \wedge r'' = r' \wedge\\
&\quad now'' - now' \in 7 \mathinner{.\,.} 10\,]\\
&\vdash i'' < n
\end{aligned}
$$

(the pre-condition on $MaxBody$ is implicit). Again the conclusion follows easily from the hypothesis conjuncts involving i' and i''.

Prove body-liveness. The obligation

$$
\begin{aligned}
&(pre\,Max2) \wedge MaxInv \wedge (age(T(do)) \wedge MaxGuard')'\\
&(MaxBody \,\fatsemi\, age(T(od)))''\\
&\vdash MaxInv[\_'''/\_']\,,
\end{aligned}
$$

expands to

$$
\begin{aligned}
&[\,\Delta\,PSpace2;\ \Delta\,Time\mid\\
&\quad n \in 1 \mathinner{.\,.} 4 \wedge now = 0 \wedge s' = s \wedge i' \leqslant n \wedge\\
&\quad r' = max(ran((1 \mathinner{.\,.} i') \lhd s')) \wedge\\
&\quad now' \in (i' - 1) * 31 + 5 \mathinner{.\,.} (i' - 1) * 51 + 12 \wedge\\
&\quad i'' \neq n \wedge s'' = s' \wedge i'' = i' \wedge r'' = r' \wedge\\
&\quad now'' - now' \in 7 \mathinner{.\,.} 10 \wedge\\
&\quad i'' < n \wedge s''' = s'' \wedge i''' = i'' + 1 \wedge r''' = max\{r'', s''(i''')\} \wedge\\
&\quad now''' - now'' \in 23 \mathinner{.\,.} 40 \dotplus \{1\}\,]\\
&\vdash i''' \leqslant n \wedge s''' = s \wedge r''' = max(ran((1 \mathinner{.\,.} i''')) \lhd s''') \wedge\\
&\quad now''' \in (i''' - 1) * 31 + 5 \mathinner{.\,.} (i''' - 1) * 51 + 12\,.
\end{aligned}
$$

The conclusions for s and i are satisfied trivially. From $r' = max(\text{ran}((1 .. i') \lhd s'))$ and the conjuncts in the hypothesis equating the singly and doubly primed versions of s and i we can determine that $r'' = max(\text{ran}((1 .. i'') \lhd s''))$. From this, and the conjuncts in the hypothesis defining i''', s''' and r''' we can readily satisfy the conclusion for r'''.

The timing requirement is discharged as follows. From the hypothesis conjuncts for now', now'' and now''' we know that

$$now''' \in ((i' - 1) * 31 + 5 .. (i' - 1) * 51 + 12) \dotplus$$
$$(7 .. 10) \dotplus (23 .. 40 \dotplus \{1\})$$
$$\Rightarrow now''' \in ((i' - 1) * 31 + 5 .. (i' - 1) * 51 + 12) \dotplus 31 .. 51$$
$$\Rightarrow now''' \in i' * 31 + 5 .. i' * 51 + 12 .$$

The conclusion then follows from conjuncts $i'' = i'$ and $i''' = i'' + 1$.

4.2.2 Introduce sequence

To illustrate refinement into sequential code, this section begins refining the *MaxInit* schema introduced above.

Firstly we propose a sequence,

$$MaxInit \sqsubseteq Initr \,; Initi$$

where the two components are specified as follows.

Initr	*Initi*
$\Delta PSpace2$	$\Delta PSpace2$
$\Delta Time$	$\Delta Time$
$s' = s$	$s' = s$
$i' = i$	$r' = r$
$r' = s(1)$	$i' = 1$
$now' - now \in 4 .. 8$	$now' - now \in 1 .. 4$

Prove seq-safety1. We must show that

$$\text{pre } MaxInit \vdash \text{pre } Initr \,,$$

which, using the implicit pre-condition in *Initr*, becomes

$$[\Delta PSpace2; \Delta Time \mid n \in 1 .. 4]$$
$$\vdash 1 \in \text{dom } s \,.$$

The conclusion follows immediately from the hypothesis and the declaration of s.

Prove seq-safety2. The second safety requirement, *i.e.*,

$$(\text{pre } MaxInit) \wedge (Initr \,\fatsemi\, age(T(;))) \vdash (\text{pre } Initi)' \,,$$

can be expanded as

$$[\Delta PSpace2;\ \Delta\, Time\ |$$
$$n \in 1\mathinner{\ldotp\ldotp}4 \wedge s' = s \wedge r' = s(1) \wedge i' = i \wedge$$
$$now' - now \in 4\mathinner{\ldotp\ldotp}8 + \{0\}\,]$$
$$\vdash true$$

because *Initi* has no initial requirements, and follows without further proof.

Prove seq-liveness. Finally, the liveness condition for sequential composition, *i.e.*,

$$(\text{pre } MaxInit) \wedge (Initr \mathbin{\raise1pt\hbox{$_9^\circ$}} age(T(;))) \wedge Initi'$$
$$\vdash MaxInit[\_''/\_']\,,$$

can be expressed as

$$[\Delta PSpace2;\ \Delta\, Time\ |$$
$$n \in 1\mathinner{\ldotp\ldotp}4 \wedge s' = s \wedge r' = s(1) \wedge i' = i \wedge$$
$$now' - now \in 4\mathinner{\ldotp\ldotp}8 + \{0\} \wedge$$
$$s'' = s' \wedge r'' = r' \wedge i'' = 1 \wedge$$
$$now'' - now' \in 1\mathinner{\ldotp\ldotp}4\,]$$
$$\vdash s'' = s \wedge i'' = 1 \wedge r'' = s(1) \wedge now'' - now \in 5\mathinner{\ldotp\ldotp}12\,,$$

which is easily proven.

4.2.3 Introduce assignment

To illustrate refinement into assignment statements, this section completes the refinement of *MaxInit*.

Firstly we propose a refinement of *Initr* into an assignment,

$$Initr \sqsubseteq r := s[1]\,.$$

To show the validity of this we express the assignment statement as the following equivalent Z schema.

```
┌─ Assr ─────────────────────────────────
│ Δ PSpace2
│ Δ Time
├────────────────────────────────────────
│ s' = s
│ i' = i
│ r' = s(1)
│ now' - now ∈ T(gadd) + T(s[1]) + T(stor)
└────────────────────────────────────────
```

We must then show that *Assr* is a refinement of *Initr*.

Prove safety. The requirement

$$\text{pre } Initr \vdash \text{pre } Assr$$

follows trivially.

Prove liveness. The requirement

$$(\text{pre } \textit{Initr}) \wedge \textit{Assr} \vdash \textit{Initr}$$

can be expressed as

$$[\,\Delta \textit{PSpace2}; \ \Delta \textit{Time} \mid$$
$$s' = s \wedge r' = s(1) \wedge i' = i \wedge$$
$$now' - now \in \{0\} \dotplus (\{0,1,2\} \dotplus \{3,4\}) \dotplus \{1,2\}\,]$$
$$\vdash s' = s \wedge i' = i \wedge r' = s(1) \wedge now' - now \in 4\,..\,8\,,$$

which again follows immediately. In the hypothesis we have substituted primitive time values from appendix A, assuming that

$$T(\textsf{s}[1]) = T(\textsf{lcon}) \dotplus T(\textsf{larr})\,.$$

A similar procedure allows us to assert that

$$\textit{Initi} \sqsubseteq \textsf{i}:=1$$

where

$$T(\textsf{i}:=1) = \{0\} \dotplus \{0,1,2\} \dotplus \{1,2\} = 1\,..\,4\,.$$

4.2.4 Introduce alternation

To illustrate a refinement involving alternation we now refine the *MaxBody* schema introduced in section 4.2.1.

Firstly, however, we propose the following sequence

$$\textit{MaxBody} \sqsubseteq \textit{Incri}\,;\ \textit{FindMax}$$

where the components are as follows.

```
┌─ Incri ──────────────        ┌─ FindMax ──────────────
│ ΔPSpace2                      │ ΔPSpace2
│ ΔTime                         │ ΔTime
├──────────────                 ├──────────────
│ s' = s                        │ s' = s
│ r' = r                        │ i' = i
│ i' = i + 1                    │ r' = max{r, s(i')}
│ now' − now ∈ 4..8             │ now' − now ∈ 19..32
└──────────────                 └──────────────
```

This can be readily proven using the same approach as in section 4.2.2. It is also easy to show that

$$\textit{Incri} \sqsubseteq \textsf{i}:=\textsf{i}+1$$

as in section 4.2.3.

To refine *FindMax*, in the absence of a target language *max* function, we propose

$$FindMax \sqsubseteq \textbf{if}$$
$$s[i] > r \rightarrow Updater$$
$$[]$$
$$s[i] \leqslant r \rightarrow Skip$$
$$\textbf{fi} \ .$$

The boolean guards can be expressed in Z as follows.

─ *Guard1* ────────
PSpace2
Time
$s(i) > r$

─ *Guard2* ────────
PSpace2
Time
$s(i) \leqslant r$

The two alternative actions are defined via the following schemata.

─ *Updater* ────────
$\Delta PSpace2$
$\Delta Time$
$s' = s$
$i' = i$
$r' = s(i)$
$now' - now \in 6 \ .. \ 9$

─ *Skip* ────────
$\Xi PSpace2$
$\Xi Time$

At this point we can calculate the overheads associated with the proposed alternative construct, using the formulae in section B.4.1.

$$
\begin{aligned}
T(\textbf{if}_1) &= T(s[i] > r) \dotplus T(\text{cbr}) \\
&= (T(\text{lvar}) \dotplus T(\text{larr}) \dotplus T(\text{lvar}) \dotplus T(\text{comp})) \dotplus T(\text{cbr}) \\
&= (\{2,3\} \dotplus \{3,4\} \dotplus \{2,3\} \dotplus \{3\}) \dotplus \{2\} \\
&= 12 \ .. \ 15
\end{aligned}
$$

$$
\begin{aligned}
T(\textbf{if}_2) &= T(\textbf{if}_1) \dotplus T(s[i] \leqslant r) \dotplus T(\text{cbr}) \\
&= 12 \ .. \ 15 \dotplus (\{2,3\} \dotplus \{3,4\} \dotplus \{2,3\} \dotplus \{3\}) \dotplus \{2\} \\
&= 24 \ .. \ 30
\end{aligned}
$$

$$T(\textbf{fi}_1) = T(\text{br}) = \{1\}$$

$$T(\textbf{fi}_2) = \{0\}$$

The two guards are mutually exclusive in this instance. We have conservatively assumed that the compiler is not capable of recognising this. (In fact, for this particular example, the timing behaviour would be unchanged even if it could.)

Prove alt-safety. To show

$$\text{pre } FindMax \vdash (age(T(\text{if}_1)) \ ; \ Guard1) \ \vee$$
$$(age(T(\text{if}_2)) \ ; \ Guard2)$$

we expand it as follows, using a zero-subscript as a way of systematically renaming variables,

$$[\, PSpace2; \ Time \mid i \in \text{dom } s \,]$$
$$\vdash (\exists \, PSpace2_0; \ Time_0 \bullet$$
$$\quad s_0 = s \wedge r_0 = r \wedge i_0 = i \wedge now_0 - now \in 12 \dots 15 \wedge s_0(i_0) > r_0)$$
$$\vee$$
$$(\exists \, PSpace2_0; \ Time_0 \bullet$$
$$\quad s_0 = s \wedge r_0 = r \wedge i_0 = i \wedge now_0 - now \in 24 \dots 30 \wedge s_0(i_0) \leqslant r_0).$$

We then observe that the disjunction of the two guards must always be true and since they are not time-dependent, the updates to *now* do not alter this.

Prove alt-liveness. We must prove liveness for both alternatives. The obligation for the first alternative,

$$FindMax[\_''/\_'] \wedge (age(T(\text{if}_1)) \wedge Guard1')$$
$$\sqsubseteq (age(T(\text{if}_1)) \ ; \ Updater \ ; \ age(T(\text{fi}_1)))[\_''/\_']$$

can be expanded as

$$[\, PSpace2; \ Time; \ PSpace'; \ Time'; \ PSpace''; \ Time'' \mid$$
$$\quad n \in 1 \dots 4 \wedge s' = s \wedge i' = i \wedge r' = r \wedge$$
$$\quad now' - now \in 12 \dots 15 \wedge s'(i') > r' \wedge$$
$$\quad s'' = s' \wedge i'' = i' \wedge r'' = max\{r, s(i'')\} \wedge$$
$$\quad now'' - now \in 19 \dots 32 \,]$$
$$\sqsubseteq [\, PSpace2; \ Time; \ PSpace''; \ Time'' \mid$$
$$\quad n \in 1 \dots 4 \wedge s'' = s \wedge i'' = i \wedge r'' = s(i) \wedge$$
$$\quad now'' - now \in 19 \dots 25 \,],$$

which can be seen to be a valid refinement. On the LHS r'' will always be assigned $s(i'')$ (because $s'(i') > r'$) as on the RHS. The timing value on the RHS was calculated from the time specified for *Updater* plus the times calculated for $T(\text{if}_1)$ and $T(\text{fi}_1)$ above and is satisfactory because it is a subset of that on the LHS. (To be more thorough we could formally prove the safety and liveness obligations for this refinement [8, p. 208].)

A similar procedure allows us to demonstrate the correctness of the second alternative, *i.e.*, by expanding

$$FindMax[\_''/\_'] \wedge (age(T(\text{if}_2)) \wedge Guard2')$$
$$\sqsubseteq (age(T(\text{if}_2)) \ ; \ Skip \ ; \ age(T(\text{fi}_2)))[\_''/\_']$$

as

$$[\, PSpace2;\ Time;\ PSpace';\ Time';\ PSpace'';\ Time'' \mid$$
$$n \in 1\,..\,4 \wedge s' = s \wedge i' = i \wedge r' = r \wedge$$
$$now' - now \in 24\,..\,30 \wedge s'(i') \leqslant r' \wedge$$
$$s'' = s' \wedge i'' = i' \wedge r'' = max\{r, s(i'')\} \wedge$$
$$now'' - now \in 19\,..\,32\,]$$
$$\sqsubseteq [\, PSpace2;\ Time;\ PSpace'';\ Time'' \mid$$
$$n \in 1\,..\,4 \wedge s'' = s \wedge i'' = i \wedge r'' = r \wedge$$
$$now'' - now \in 24\,..\,30\,] \ .$$

These two alternatives show that our refinement of *FindMax* will have actual execution time bounds of $19\,..\,30$, rather than the specified $19\,..\,32$, but a refinement that has *tighter* time bounds than those specified is always acceptable, of course.

The example is then completed by showing that

$$Updater \sqsubseteq r := s[i]$$

and

$$Skip \sqsubseteq \textbf{skip} \ ,$$

both of which can be proven easily.

4.3   Final code

Putting all of these components together yields the final code, proven correct with respect to time.

```
var i : 1 .. n
[ i := 1;
  r := s[1];
  do i ≠ n →
       i := i+1;
       if
         s[i] > r → r := s[i]
       []
         s[i] ≤ r → skip
       fi
  od
]
```

Figure 1 shows the actual execution time for this program, calculated using the assumptions outlined in section 4.1, plotted against that originally specified. It can be seen that for an array longer than 4 this code could not have satisfied the specification because the execution time bounds become too broad. Iterative constructs typically exhibit this characteristic of cumulative unpredictability in their execution times, and it was for this reason that we were careful to specify a maximum array size in section 4.1. (Alternatively,

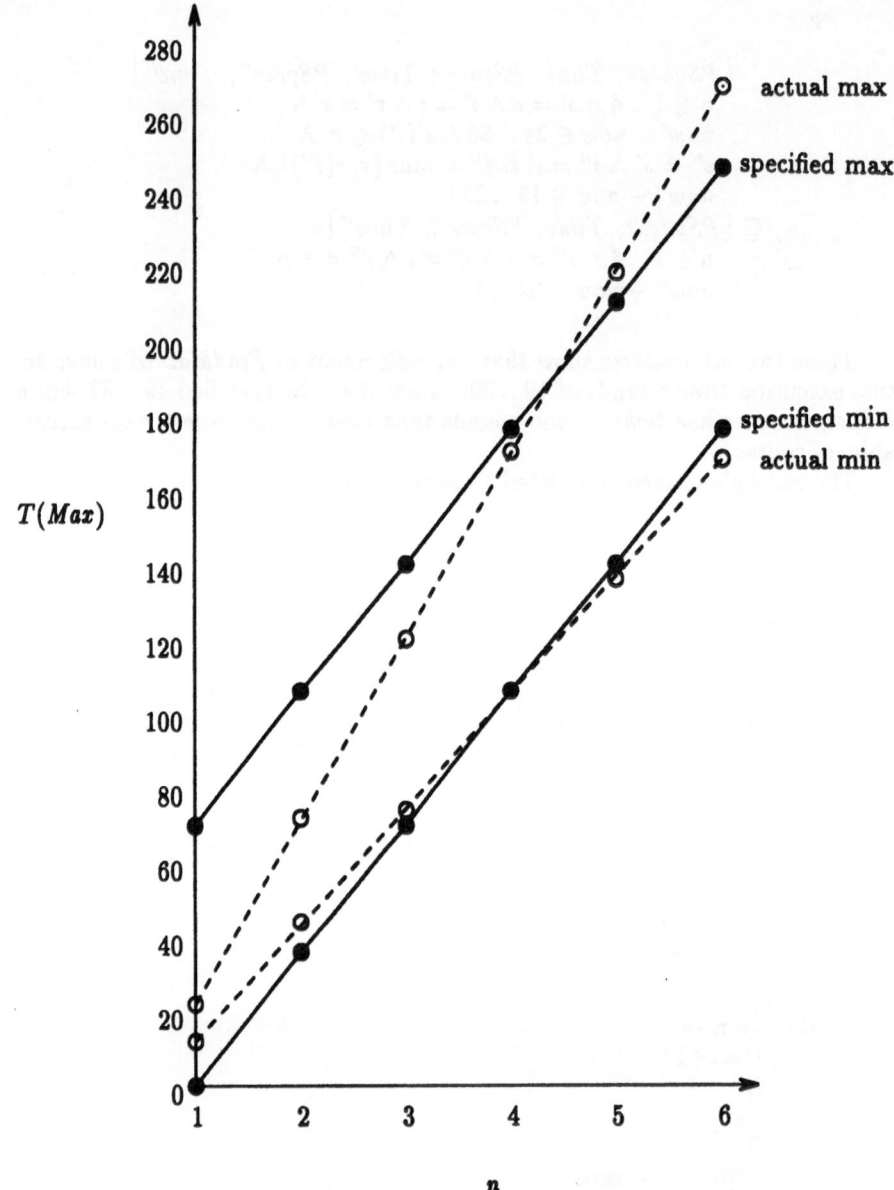

Figure 1: Specified versus actual timing behaviour for *Max*.

we could have found the range of array lengths for which a solution was possible, for this particular refinement.) The margin for error when n is 4 can be seen to be quite small—it would not have been possible to prove the correctness of this code if the programmer had not taken the "saving" in time due to the initialisation code into account when devising the loop invariant in section 4.2.1.

5   Discussion

Future work will see the development of "derived rules", in which the proof obligations have already been discharged, in order to make the method practical, in the same way that Wordsworth defines shortcut rules once his proof obligations have been defined [8, §7.5.3, 7.5.4, 7.6.4].

Apart from classical structured programming constructs, the requirements of embedded programming dictate that we must also develop rules for low-level input/output, time-dependent statements, interrupt handling, concurrency, *etc.*, none of which are usually treated by contemporary refinement methods.

Care was taken above to ensure that boolean expressions were known to be true at a well-defined point in time, to allow for the possibility that they are time sensitive. A planned future extension, suggested by Ian Hayes, is to treat expressions not as predicates but as relations (in fact we have already taken the liberty of using the alternative guards in this way in **alt-safety**). This will allow us to directly refer to the way that *now* changes while an expression is being evaluated and to model the possibility that memory-mapped i/o locations used in expressions may change their value, or even be in an indeterminate state, while the expression is being assessed. Indeed, the entire question of refining expressions, largely glossed over herein, needs to be considered in depth.

For the purposes of this paper we defined absolute time to be discrete and hence represented it by natural numbers, but the approach does not preclude other representations. In particular, continuous time could be modelled by using reals, or a distributed notion of time could be described via a partially ordered representation.

The timing prediction methods used for high-level language statements, based on previous work in the software engineering literature [7, 5, 6, 3], are a weak link in the methodology. Since they do not take the context of statements into account, and do not explicitly model run-time influences such as operating system behaviour, they frequently produce estimates that are unnecessarily pessimistic. Programs resulting from using such worst-case estimates will always satisfy their timing requirements, but working with poor timing values often causes the programmer to put unnecessary effort into optimising code performance when, in fact, the availability of more accurate timing values would reveal that the code has already met its specification. It would appear that the best place to perform timing calculations is in a suitably instrumented high-level language compiler because much of the information necessary for producing accurate timing estimates, *i.e.*, knowledge of the source program, object code and target architecture, is found there.

6   Conclusion

We have presented a set of fundamental proof obligations that refinement rules must satisfy in order to guarantee correct real-time behaviour, and have demonstrated their application via a detailed example. We have improved on previous work by generalising the form of timing specification allowed and presenting a general approach to iteration.

Acknowledgements

I wish to thank the anonymous referees for their helpful comments and the University of Queensland's refinement interest group for their many valuable suggestions, in particular Ian Hayes, David Carrington and Dan Johnston. Special thanks to Mark Utting for correcting a number of errors in this paper.

References

[1] C.J. Fidge. Real-time refinement. In J. Woodcock and P. Larsen, editors, *FME'93: Industrial-Strength Formal Methods*, volume 670 of *Lecture Notes in Computer Science*, pages 314–331. Springer-Verlag, 1993.

[2] INMOS Ltd. *Product Information - The transputer Family 1987*, April 1987.

[3] H. Kopetz, R. Zainlinger, G. Fohler, H. Kantz, P. Puschner, and W. Schütz. The design of real-time systems: From specification to implementation and verification. *Software Engineering Journal*, 6(3):72–82, May 1991.

[4] C. Morgan. *Programming from Specifications*. Prentice-Hall, 1990.

[5] C.Y. Park and A.C. Shaw. Experiments with a program timing tool based on source-level timing schema. In *Proc. IEEE Real-Time Systems Symposium*, pages 72–81, Florida, December 1990.

[6] P. Puschner and Ch. Koza. Calculating the maximum execution time of real-time programs. *Journal of Real-Time Systems*, 1(2):159–176, September 1989.

[7] A.C. Shaw. Reasoning about time in higher-level language software. *IEEE Transactions on Software Engineering*, 15(7):875–889, July 1989.

[8] J.B. Wordsworth. *Software Development with Z*. Addison-Wesley, 1992.

A Primitive timings

The following primitive timing values, expressed in machine cycles, were used for the example in section 4. They are loosely based on the (average) execution times provided for the T414 processor [2].

Notation	Times	Description
$T(\text{gadd})$	$\{0, 1, 2\}$	Get address of a variable.
$T(\text{lvar})$	$\{0, 2, 3\}$	Load value of an integer variable.
$T(\text{stor})$	$\{0, 1, 2\}$	Store value of an integer variable.
$T(\text{lcon})$	$\{0, 1, 2\}$	Load an integer constant.
$T(\text{comp})$	$\{3\}$	Perform an integer comparison.
$T(\text{plus})$	$\{1\}$	Perform an integer addition.
$T(\text{br})$	$\{1\}$	Unconditionally branch.
$T(\text{cbr})$	$\{2\}$	Conditionally branch.
$T(\text{noop})$	$\{0\}$	No-op.
$T(\text{larr})$	$\{0, 3, 4\}$	Load an element from an integer array (assuming index has already been calculated).

For example, the time required at run-time to load the value of an integer variable may be 0, if it is known at compile-time to already be in a register, 2, if it is in local memory, or 3, if it must be fetched from secondary storage. Some simplifying assumptions have been made here as well. For instance, we have assumed that the time to execute a conditional branch instruction is the same whether the branch is taken or not. Also the operating system has been assumed to be minimal, or nonexistent, so that any run-time influences on performance have already been factored into the above figures.

Given the knowledge that the compiler does not keep track of which variables are in registers, and thus *always* loads and stores variable values, and that all variable addresses are known at compile-time for our example, we can then make use of the following revised, tighter time bounds.

Notation	Times	Description
$T(\text{gadd})$	$\{0\}$	Get address of a variable.
$T(\text{lvar})$	$\{2, 3\}$	Load value of an integer variable.
$T(\text{stor})$	$\{1, 2\}$	Store value of an integer variable.
$T(\text{larr})$	$\{3, 4\}$	Load an element from an integer array.

These stronger bounds are used throughout section 4.

B Structured construct timings

This appendix gives the formulae used to calculate execution times of guarded command language components in terms of the primitive execution times given in appendix A.

These are not the only such formulae definable. They reflect implicit assumptions about the object code generated by the compiler and may need to be rewritten for different target systems. For instance, $T(\text{do})$ and $T(\text{od})$ in section B.5 would need to be redefined if the object code generated made the while-test at the *end* of the loop body.

304

B.1 Assignment

Assuming that we have accounted for the time required to get the target address and evaluate the expression, then

$$T(:=) = T(\text{stor}) \ .$$

B.2 Sequence

A reasonable assumption for contemporary programming languages and architectures is that sequential behaviour involves no overhead, *i.e.*,

$$T(;) = T(\text{noop}) \ .$$

B.3 Skip

By definition a "skip" operation involves no overhead, *i.e.*,

$$T(\textbf{skip}) = T(\text{noop}) \ .$$

B.4 Alternatives

Execution times for components of an alternative construct,

$$\textbf{if} \ (\mathbin{[\!]}_{i \in I} B_i \to A_i) \ \textbf{fi} \ ,$$

differ markedly depending on whether we assume a deterministic, or nondeterministic order for guard evaluation.

B.4.1 Deterministic alternatives

In the deterministic case, assumed in section 4, the overhead associated with reaching an alternative A_i consists of the time required to evaluate its own "true" guard B_i and conditionally branch, plus the time required to evaluate all preceding "false" guards and branch past each, *i.e.*,

$$\forall i \in I \bullet T(\textbf{if}_i) = \sum_{a \leqslant i} (T(B_a) \dotplus T(\text{cbr})) \ .$$

Also, for every alternative A_i except the last, it is necessary to branch around the code generated for all following alternatives when A_i is finished, *i.e.*,

$$\forall i \in I \bullet T(\textbf{fi}_i) = \begin{cases} T(\text{br}), & i < max \ I \\ T(\text{noop}), & i = max \ I \end{cases} \ .$$

B.4.2 Nondeterministic alternatives

In the nondeterministic case guards taken from any subset X of I may have been evaluated before a true guard B_i is found, thus

$$\forall i \in I \bullet T(\textbf{if}_i) = \bigcup_{\{X \subseteq I | i \in X\}} \left(\sum_{a \in X} (T(B_a) \dotplus T(\text{cbr})) \right) \ .$$

Again there will be a distinguished alternative A_x that involves no final branch, but in the nondeterministic case we do not know which one it will be, *i.e.*,

$$\exists_1 x \in I \bullet \forall i \in I \bullet T(\text{fi}_i) = \left\{ \begin{array}{ll} T(\text{br}), & i \neq x \\ T(\text{noop}), & i = x \end{array} \right. .$$

Obviously the execution time predictions are far worse in the nondeterministic case and a predictable order of guard evaluation should be assumed wherever possible.

B.5 Iteration

In a "one-armed" iterative statement,

do $B \rightarrow A$ od ,

the overhead involved in reaching the body (or exiting the loop) is the time required to evaluate the guard and conditionally branch, *i.e.*,

$$T(\text{do}) = T(B) \dotplus T(\text{cbr}) .$$

At the end of each iteration there is an unconditional branch back to the start of the loop, therefore

$$T(\text{od}) = T(\text{br}) .$$

Author Index

Published in 1990–92

AI and Cognitive Science '89, Dublin City
University, Eire, 14–15 September 1989
Alan F. Smeaton and Gabriel McDermott (Eds.)

**Specification and Verification of Concurrent
Systems,** University of Stirling, Scotland,
6–8 July 1988
C. Rattray (Ed.)

Semantics for Concurrency, Proceedings of the
International BCS-FACS Workshop, Sponsored
by Logic for IT (S.E.R.C.), University of
Leicester, UK, 23–25 July 1990
M. Z. Kwiatkowska, M. W. Shields and
R. M. Thomas (Eds.)

Functional Programming, Glasgow 1989
Proceedings of the 1989 Glasgow Workshop,
Fraserburgh, Scotland, 21–23 August 1989
Kei Davis and John Hughes (Eds.)

Persistent Object Systems, Proceedings of the
Third International Workshop, Newcastle,
Australia, 10–13 January 1989
John Rosenberg and David Koch (Eds.)

Z User Workshop, Oxford 1989, Proceedings of
the Fourth Annual Z User Meeting, Oxford,
15 December 1989
J. E. Nicholls (Ed.)

**Formal Methods for Trustworthy Computer
Systems (FM89),** Halifax, Canada,
23–27 July 1989
Dan Craigen (Editor) and Karen Summerskill
(Assistant Editor)

Security and Persistence, Proceedings of the
International Workshop on Computer
Architectures to Support Security and Persistence
of Information, Bremen, West Germany,
8–11 May 1990
John Rosenberg and J. Leslie Keedy (Eds.)

**Women into Computing: Selected Papers
1988–1990**
Gillian Lovegrove and Barbara Segal (Eds.)

3rd Refinement Workshop (organised by
BCS-FACS, and sponsored by IBM UK
Laboratories, Hursley Park and the Programming
Research Group, University of Oxford),
Hursley Park, 9–11 January 1990
Carroll Morgan and J. C. P. Woodcock (Eds.)

Designing Correct Circuits, Workshop jointly
organised by the Universities of Oxford and
Glasgow, Oxford, 26–28 September 1990
Geraint Jones and Mary Sheeran (Eds.)

Functional Programming, Glasgow 1990
Proceedings of the 1990 Glasgow Workshop on
Functional Programming, Ullapool, Scotland,
13–15 August 1990
Simon L. Peyton Jones, Graham Hutton and
Carsten Kehler Holst (Eds.)

4th Refinement Workshop, Proceedings of the
4th Refinement Workshop, organised by BCS-
FACS, Cambridge, 9–11 January 1991
Joseph M. Morris and Roger C. Shaw (Eds.)

AI and Cognitive Science '90, University of
Ulster at Jordanstown, 20–21 September 1990
Michael F. McTear and Norman Creaney (Eds.)

Software Re-use, Utrecht 1989, Proceedings of
the Software Re-use Workshop, Utrecht,
The Netherlands, 23–24 November 1989
Liesbeth Dusink and Patrick Hall (Eds.)

Z User Workshop, 1990, Proceedings of the Fifth
Annual Z User Meeting, Oxford,
17–18 December 1990
J.E. Nicholls (Ed.)

IV Higher Order Workshop, Banff 1990
Proceedings of the IV Higher Order Workshop,
Banff, Alberta, Canada, 10–14 September 1990
Graham Birtwistle (Ed.)

ALPUK91, Proceedings of the 3rd UK
Annual Conference on Logic Programming,
Edinburgh, 10–12 April 1991
Geraint A.Wiggins, Chris Mellish and
Tim Duncan (Eds.)

Specifications of Database Systems
International Workshop on Specifications of
Database Systems, Glasgow, 3–5 July 1991
David J. Harper and Moira C. Norrie (Eds.)

**7th UK Computer and Telecommunications
Performance Engineering Workshop**
Edinburgh, 22–23 July 1991
J. Hillston, P.J.B. King and R.J. Pooley (Eds.)

Logic Program Synthesis and Transformation
Proceedings of LOPSTR 91, International
Workshop on Logic Program Synthesis and
Transformation, University of Manchester,
4–5 July 1991
T.P. Clement and K.-K. Lau (Eds.)

Declarative Programming, Sasbachwalden 1991
PHOENIX Seminar and Workshop on Declarative
Programming, Sasbachwalden, Black Forest,
Germany, 18–22 November 1991
John Darlington and Roland Dietrich (Eds.)